The Funniest Thing You Never Said

For Milena

The Funniest Thing You Never Said

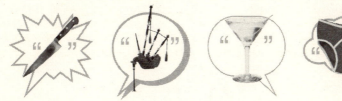

THE ULTIMATE COLLECTION OF
HUMOROUS
QUOTATIONS

ROSEMARIE JARSKI

EBURY
PRESS

23 25 27 29 30 28 26 24

First published 2004 by Ebury Press,
an imprint of Random House,
20 Vauxhall Bridge Road, London SW1V 2SA

The Random House Group Limited supports The Forest Stewardship Council (FSC®), the leading international forest certification organisation. Our books carrying the FSC label are printed on FSC® certified paper. FSC is the only forest certification scheme endorsed by the leading environmental organisations, including Greenpeace. Our paper procurement policy can be found at www.randomhouse.co.uk/environment

The Random House Group Limited Reg. No. 954009

www.randomhouse.co.uk

Printed andbound by CPI Group (UK) Ltd, Croydon, CR0 4YY

A CIP catalogue record for this book is available from the British Library.

Cover designed by Two Associates
Typeset by seagulls.net

ISBN 9780091897666

CONTENTS

SCIENCE & TECHNOLOGY

SOCIETY & POLITICS

NATIONS

INTRODUCTION

Backward, turn backward, O Time in thy flight,
Just thought of a comeback I needed last night.
Les Dawson

We've all been there. Desperate to impress, perhaps during a dinner party, a presentation or a date, but when opportunity knocks, instead of unleashing a sparkling gem of repartee, we're struck dumb or, worse still, make some cringe-worthy remark, and only later realise what we *should* have said. In 18th-century France, this syndrome was known as *l'esprit d'escalier* – 'staircase wit' – because that's where you tended to be when your brain belatedly kicked into gear with a great line. Modern equivalents include 'elevator wit', 'way-homer' and 'D'oh'. What it boils down to is the funniest thing you never said.

Sounds like a good title for a book. Imagine it. A book that delivers the perfect quip for every occasion. A book that ensures you'll never again find yourself in the ghastly position of looking verbally flat-footed in front of people you want to dazzle. The smart remark, the snappy comeback, the sharp one-liner would always be right there at your fingertips. It would be like having your own personal team of gag-writers on call 24/7. Like being Bob Hope.

Because you never know when you might be caught short comedically-speaking, this repository of wit would have to embrace a wide range of topics. You might be in a French restaurant ('I don't eat snails. I prefer fast food.' – Roger Von Oech); at the opera ('I went to watch Pavarotti once. He doesn't like it when you join in.' – Mick Miller); at a funeral ('They say such lovely things about people at their funerals, it's a shame I'm going to miss mine by just a few days.' – Bob Monkhouse); or in Mexico having to give a weather forecast ('Chilli today and hot tamale.' – Paul Rodriguez). And it wouldn't be enough to just cover the standard quoted subjects like God, politics, money, theatre, et cetera. Zingers would be needed on the latest obsessions such as dieting, mobile phones, parking spaces and bagpipes. (Each to his own obsession.)

Because you never know when you need to be funny fast, the quips would have to be organized into easily accessible categories. There is only ever a brief window of opportunity to make the world's funniest conversational slam-dunk so you can't be faffing around flicking through complicated indices. The moment will be lost and with it the guy, the gal, the job, or at the very least, your pride. A simple thematic arrangement would work best, together with an author index for those occasions when it simply *has* to be Oscar.

The heady scent of Mr Wilde's green carnation would doubtless pervade the pages, blending redolently with Groucho Marx's smouldering stogey, Mae West's pungent patchouli pomade and W.C. Fields' bourbon-sodden breath. But no fellow of infinite jest, however fragrant, however celebrated, would be a shoo-in at this laughfest. It would have to be a meritocracy of mirth. The aim would be to assemble a cast of the brightest and best wits on earth and, in the case of comedian Steven Wright, beyond: 'A friend sent me a postcard with a satellite picture of the entire planet taken from space. On the back it said, "Wish you were here".'

Since many of today's funniest lines are freshly minted in television sitcoms, old favourites like Mark Twain, P.G. Wodehouse, Dorothy Parker and Woody Allen would have to make room for quotable 'sitcomedians' like Frasier, Blackadder, Larry Sanders and Homer Simpson. Strange comic bedfellows some might say. Yeah, but imagine the pillow talk. Real or imaginary, living or dead, what does it matter, just so long at they make you laugh till milk shoots out of your nose?

Laughter must be the guiding principle (a radical notion for a humour book it has to be said). Which naturally rules out political correctness. This equal opportunities offender would hold nothing sacred – not women, not children, not fluffy lickle kittens, no, not even the Welsh. And whilst no particular viewpoint, whether political, religious, racial or moral, would be espoused, nor would it seek to be representative. If the majority of quotes about the Welsh, say, are anti-Welsh that'll be because the funniest quotes happen to take that stance and not because the Welsh actually are a race of barbaric, bigoted, belligerent, leek-waving sheepshaggers. And if the overall tone and tenor of the quotes is nastier than the love-child of Simon Cowell and Anne Robinson, that'll be because they happen to be funniest.

Given this formidable set of requirements, what sort of person would be up to the Herculean task of compiling the compendium of hilarity? Someone who knows good comedy and isn't afraid to share. A gag-groupie who's anyone's for a good one-liner – well, except Bernard Manning. Unless it's really really good. Someone whose proudest moment was getting suspended from convent school after being overheard telling a risqué joke in chapel.* Someone who's spent half a lifetime scouring books and newspapers and television and movies and comedy clubs and people's T-shirts and gravestones and car bumpers for the funniest thing you never said. Someone who's prepared to sit through an entire Jim Davidson routine without being bound, gagged and superglued to the seat. Someone who converted to Judaism just for the jokes.

Oy vey, sounds like a terrific book. Too bad it won't ever happen. Where would they find somebody who could endure the Jim Davidson torture?

---

* If you're wondering what the joke was that earned the suspension, here it is: A nun goes to her Mother Superior and asks her to hear her confession: 'Last night I enjoyed the pleasures of the flesh. Father Conner came to me and told me that I had the Gates of Heaven here between my legs. Then he said that he had the Key to Heaven, and he put it in the Gates.' *'Bastard!'* cries the Mother Superior, 'For years, he told me it was Gabriel's Trumpet and I've been blowing it.'

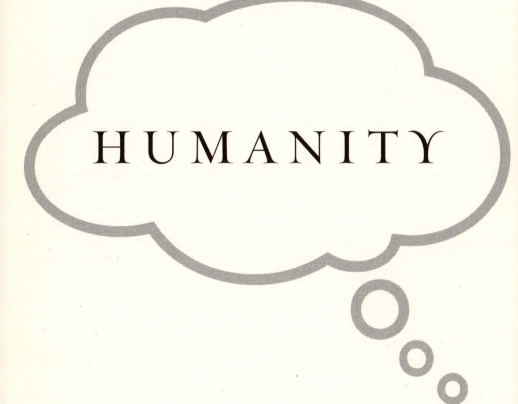

HUMANITY

PEOPLE

I love mankind; it's people I can't stand.

Charles M. Schulz

I think I'm a pretty good judge of people, which is why I hate most of them.

Roseanne

Other people? They are usually a mistake.

Quentin Crisp

I hate people. People make me pro-nuclear.

Margaret Smith

There are three kinds of people: those who can count, and those who cannot.

George Carlin

There are 10 types of people in the world – those who understand binary and those who don't.

Johnny Ball

There are two types of people in this world, good and bad. The good sleep better, but the bad seem to enjoy the waking hours more.

Woody Allen

It is absurd to divide people into good and bad. People are either charming or tedious.

Oscar Wilde

There are two classes of people in the world: those who divide people into two classes and those who don't.

Robert Benchley

People who should be phased out: people who wink when they're kidding; people who have memorized a lot of TV-show theme-songs and are really proud of it; people who always harmonize the last few notes of 'Happy Birthday'; people who give their house or car a name; blind people who don't want any help.

George Carlin

People shouldn't be treated like objects. They're not that valuable.

P.J. O'Rourke

The average person thinks he isn't.

Larry Lorenzoni

No man is an island but some of us are pretty long peninsulas.

Ashleigh Brilliant

MEN

My mom said the only reason men are alive is for lawn care and vehicle maintenance.

Tim Allen

The useless piece of flesh at the end of a penis is called a man.

Jo Brand

Men are those creatures with two legs and eight hands.

Jayne Mansfield

A man is two people, himself and his cock. A man always takes his friend to the party. Of the two, the friend is the nicer, being more able to show his feelings.

Beryl Bainbridge

Deep down inside, men are biological creatures, like jellyfish or trees, only less likely to clean the bathroom.

Dave Barry

Men are like linoleum floors. Lay 'em right and you can walk all over them for thirty years.

Betsy Salkind

One of the things that being in politics has taught me is that men are not a reasoned or a reasonable sex.

Margaret Thatcher

God gave men both a penis and a brain, but only enough blood supply to run one at a time.

Robin Williams

It's a pity more men are not bastards by birth instead of vocation.

Katharine Whitehorn

They act like God Almighty 'cos they've got a cock and they can mend a flex.

Victoria Wood

There are three types of men in the world. One type learns from books. One type learns from observations. And one type just has to urinate on the electric fence himself.

Carl Barney

Men think they're more important than women because their jackets have secret inside pockets.
Rita Rudner

The difference between a man and a battery is that a battery has a positive side.
Jo Brand

A woman's rule of thumb: if it has tyres or testicles, you're going to have trouble with it.
Ella Gough

Men talk to women so they can sleep with them, and women sleep with men so they can talk to them.
Jay McInerney

I finally figured out that being male is the same thing, more or less, as having a personality disorder.
Carol Shields

Men hate to lose. I once beat my husband at tennis. I asked him, 'Are we going to have sex again?' He said, 'Yes, but not with each other.'
Rita Rudner

I'd like somebody to breed a male, genus homo, who would go and fetch a 12-inch by 8-inch black suede purse lying in the middle of a white bedspread and not come back looking baffled and saying he couldn't find it.
Margaret Halsey

If they ever invent a vibrator that can open pickle jars, men have had it.
Jeff Green

Men do cry, but only when assembling furniture.
Rita Rudner

Men are like car alarms – they both make a lot of noise no one listens to.
Diane Jordan

When a woman tries on clothing from her closet that feels tight, she assumes she has gained weight. When a man tries on clothing from his closet that feels tight, he assumes the clothing has shrunk.
Rita Rudner

Can you imagine a world without men? No crime and lots of happy, fat women.
Nicole Hollander

A man is designed to walk three miles in the rain to phone for help when the car breaks down, and a woman is designed to say, 'You took your time' when he comes back dripping wet.
Victoria Wood

A hard man is good to find.
Mae West

How do I know so much about men? Baby, I went to night school.
Mae West

Where would men be today if it weren't for women? In the Garden of Eden eating watermelon and taking it easy.
C. Kennedy

If a man speaks in the forest, and there's no woman around to hear him, is he still wrong?
Rich Makin

You could lay your pussy on a table right in front of a man and still not know what he's thinking.
Samantha Jones, *Sex and the City*

The main difference between men and women is that men are lunatics and women are idiots.
Rebecca West

Men don't live well by themselves. They don't even live like people. They live like bears with furniture.
Rita Rudner

What are the three words guaranteed to humiliate men everywhere? 'Hold my purse.'
François Morency

The more I see of men, the more I admire dogs.
Marie de Rabutin-Chantal

It's not the men in your life that counts – it's the life in your men.
Mae West

A man without a woman is like a neck without a pain.
W.C. Fields

A man in the house is worth two in the street.
Mae West

Give a man a free hand and he'll run it all over you.

Mae West

You can tell a lot about a man by the way he handles lost luggage and tangled Christmas tree lights.

Rich Makin

No man who has wrestled with a self-adjusting card table can ever be quite the man he once was.

James Thurber

A woman's a woman until the day she dies, but a man's only a man as long as he can.

Moms Mabley

Macho? Moi?

John Prescott

Macho does not prove mucho.

Zsa Zsa Gabor

They claim to be he-men, but the hair from their combined chests wouldn't have made a wig for a grape.

Robert Benchley

He may have hair upon his chest but sister, so has Lassie...

Cole Porter, *I Hate Men*

My ancestors wandered lost in the wilderness for forty years because even in biblical times, men would not stop to ask for directions.

Elayne Boosler

Men read maps better than women because only a male mind could conceive of an inch equalling a hundred miles.

Roseanne

A man without a woman is like a moose without a hat-rack.

Arthur Marshall

WOMEN

What would men be without women? Scarce, sir, mighty scarce.

Mark Twain

Women, can't live with 'em, pass the beer nuts.

Norm Peterson, *Cheers*

Women are like elephants to me. I like to look at them, but I wouldn't want to own one.
W.C. Fields

I never panic when I get lost. I just change where it is I want to go.
Rita Rudner

We have a saying in Russia: 'Women are like buses.' That's it.
Yakov Smirnoff

I love women, though I couldn't eat a whole one. But I think I know where I'd start.
Jonathan Ross

God created women because sheep can't type.
Kenneth Armbrister

One of the great mysteries to me about women is the fact that they can pour hot wax on their legs, rip the hair out by the roots, and still be afraid of a spider.
Jerry Seinfeld

A woman is like a tea bag – you can't tell how strong she is until you put her in hot water.
Nancy Reagan

I went to the grocery store to buy a pint of Ben and Jerry's Super Fudge Chunk Ice Cream, and a box of tampons. Because if you're shopping for one you're shopping for the other.
Sabrina Matthews

You don't know a woman until you've met her in court.
Norman Mailer

Women complain about PMS, but I think of it as the only time of the month I can be myself.
Roseanne

Next Mood Swing: 6 minutes.
Slogan on T-shirt

Women might start a rumour, but not a war.
Marga Gomez

I thought I had PMS, but my doctor said, I've got good news and bad news. The good news is, you don't have PMS. The bad news is, you're a bitch.'

Rhonda Bates

If women ran the world, there would be not wars, just intense negotiations every twenty-eight days.

Robin Williams

Being a woman is of special interest only to aspiring male transsexuals. To actual women it is merely a good excuse not to play football.

Fran Lebowitz

The great and almost only comfort about being a woman is that one can always pretend to be more stupid than one is and no one is surprised.

Freya Stark

I'd rather be a woman than a man. Women can cry, wear cute clothes, and they're first to be rescued off sinking ships.

Gilda Radner

The only reason they say 'women and children first' is to test the strength of the lifeboats.

Jean Kerr

To judge from the covers of countless women's magazines, the two topics most interesting to women are 1) why men are all disgusting pigs and 2) how to attract men.

Dave Barry

If there had been three wise women instead of men, they'd have asked for directions, arrived on time, helped deliver the baby, and bought disposable diapers as gifts.

Jill Wood

Good women always think it is their fault when someone else is being offensive. Bad women never take the blame for anything.

Anita Brookner

All the reasons of a man cannot outweigh a single feeling of a woman.

Voltaire

Intuition is the strange instinct that tells a woman she is right, whether she is or not.

Oscar Wilde

Women, can't live with them, can't bury them in the back yard without
the neighbours seeing.   Sean Williams

Women want men, careers, money, children, luxury, friends, freedom,
love and three-dollar pantyhose that won't run.   Phyllis Diller

Women, can't live with 'em, can't have heterosexual sex without 'em.
                                                          Joel Mason

A woman is a person who can look in a drawer and find a man's socks
that aren't there.   Dan Bennett

Smart girls know how to play tennis, piano and dumb.
                                                          Lynn Redgrave

The most important things to a Southern girl are God, family, and hair,
almost never in that order.   Lucinda Ebersole

Anyone who says he can see through women is missing a lot.
                                                          Groucho Marx

Women, can't live with them, can't get them to dress up in a skimpy Nazi
costume and beat you with a warm squash.   Emo Philips

There is no bigger fan of the opposite sex than me, and I have the bills to
prove it.   Alan J. Lerner

Show me a woman who doesn't feel guilt and I'll show you a man.
                                                          Erica Jong

A wise woman puts a grain of sugar into everything she says to a man,
and takes a grain of salt with everything he says to her.   Helen Rowland

A woman could never be President. A candidate must be 35 or over, and
where are you going to find a woman who will admit she's over 35?
                                                          E.W. Howe

She was one of those women who go through life demanding to see the manager.
George Patrick

Now that women are jockeys, baseball umpires, atomic scientists, and business executives, maybe someday they can master parallel parking.
Bill Vaughan

My wife is one of the best women on this continent, although she isn't always as gentle as a lamb with mint sauce.
Charles Farrar Browne

Wild horses couldn't drag a secret out of most women; however, women seldom have lunch with wild horses.
Ivern Boyett

A woman needs only two tools in life: WD-40 and duct tape. If it doesn't move and it should, use WD-40. If it moves and shouldn't, use the tape.
Nicola Zweig

A woman's preaching is like a dog's walking on his hinder legs. It is not done well; but you are surprised to find it done at all.
Samuel Johnson

The trouble with women is that they never put the toilet seat back up.
Simon Nye

What a nasty mind you have, Bruce. Where did you learn to think like a woman?
Frank G. Slaughter

Women, can't live with 'em ... end of sentence. Jack McFarland, *Will and Grace*

BATTLE OF THE SEXES

I've been reading up on the differences between men and women. I read, *The Rules*, the Mars and Venus books, *Dating for Dummies*, and here's the real difference: women buy the books.
Daryl Hague

A woman without a man is like a fish without a bicycle. Florynce Kennedy

When women are depressed, they eat or go shopping. When men are depressed, they invade another country.   Elayne Boosler

Women want to be loved, to be listened to, to be desired, to be respected, to be needed, to be trusted, and sometimes, just to be held. Men just want tickets for the cup final.   Dave Barry

Women look in the mirror and always think they look worse than they are. Men look in the mirror and always think they look better than they are. They reckon they're three or four sit-ups away from being in a hot tub with Elle McPherson.   Richard Jeni

I'm not a breast man. I'm a breast person.   John Wilson

Women speak because they wish to speak, whereas a man speaks only when driven to speech by something outside himself – like, for instance, he can't find any clean socks.   Jean Kerr

Ask a woman how she feels and she'll tell you about every relationship she's ever been in. Ask a man what he feels and he'll tell you he feels like a pizza.   Diana Ford

A man at his desk in a room with a closed door is a man at work. A woman at a desk in any room is available.   Marya Mannes

A man has to be Adolf Hitler to be called ruthless. All a woman has to do is put you on hold.   Marlo Thomas

Feminism is a wonderful idea – until the car goes wrong.   Nicola Zweig

The main achievement of the Women's Movement was the right to go Dutch.   Gloria Steinem

Women now have the right to plant rolled-up dollar bills in the jockstraps of steroid-sodden male strippers.   Howard Ogden

No woman ever shot her husband while he was doing the dishes.   George Coote

People call me a feminist whenever I express sentiments that differentiate me from a doormat or a prostitute.   **Rebecca West**

I am all for women's rights – and for their lefts too.   **Groucho Marx**

—Name one job a man can handle that a woman can't.
—Female impersonator.   **Rhoda Morgenstern and Lou Grant, *Rhoda***

I don't call myself a feminist. I call myself a killer bitch.   **Roseanne**

When a woman says she wants to go out and get a job to express herself it usually means she's hopelessly behind in the ironing.   **Oliver Reed**

They say a woman's work is never done. All I'm saying is, maybe if you organized yourselves a bit better...   **Jimmy Carr**

I'm a male feminist. I'd never call a nasty sales clerk a bitch. I stick with gender-neutral terms like 'asshole'.   **Daniel Liebert**

The Women's Movement would be a lot more successful if men were running it.   **Alan Clark**

The best way to get a husband to do anything is to suggest that he is too old to do it.   **Felicity Parker**

Women now have choices. They can be married, not married, have a job, not have a job, be married with children, unmarried with children. Men have the same choice we've always had: work or prison.   **Tim Allen**

Whatever women do they must do twice as well as men to be thought half as good. Luckily, this is not difficult.   **Charlotte Whitton**

I've been married to a communist and a fascist, and neither of them would take out garbage.   **Zsa Zsa Gabor**

People ask me how many children I have and I say one boy and seven mistakes.   **Muhammad Ali**

Twenty years ago, there were all sorts of words you couldn't say in front of a girl. Nowadays, you can say all the words, but you mustn't say 'girl'.
Tom Lehrer

I did everything Fred Astaire did, except I did it backwards and in high heels.
Ginger Rogers

If you think women are the weaker sex, try pulling the blankets back to your side.
Stuart Turner

People say to me, 'You're not very feminine.' Well, they can just suck my dick.
Roseanne

When a woman behaves like a man, why can't she behave like a *nice* man?
Edith Evans

Women who complain of sexual harassment are, more often than not, revoltingly ugly.
Auberon Waugh

—How many feminists does it take to change a light bulb?
—That's not funny.
Anon

Men are superior to women. For one thing, men can urinate from a speeding car.
Will Durst

I suppose true sexual equality will come when a general called Anthea is found having an unwise lunch with a young, unreliable male model from Spain.
John Mortimer

It is noticeable that in all the discussion about the femininity of God, the masculinity of the Devil goes unchallenged. This is unfair and revealing.
Christopher Russell

Men are from earth. Women are from earth. Deal with it. **Slogan on T-shirt**

A boastful male once spoke to me of the beauties of the penis, saying it could even write a sentence in the snow; could a woman's organ do that? I told him: a woman could at least provide a full stop. **Djuna Barnes**

Women – we're our own worst enemies a lot of the time. But I still blame men.
Janeane Garofalo

I didn't fight to get women out from behind the vacuum cleaner to get them on to the board of Hoover.
Germaine Greer

I decided to get in touch with my feminine side. Now I find I've got a yeast infection.
Bob Delaney

All women become like their mothers. That is their tragedy. No man does. That is his.
Oscar Wilde

When they told me that by the year 2100 women would rule the world, my reply was, 'Still?'
Winston Churchill

GENDER

Coo-eee! Anyone homo?
Harry Enfield

It's just a phase I'm going through. Last year it was miniature golf.
Jeremy Arlen

Asking me if I'm homosexual is a little like asking a man crawling across the Sahara whether he would prefer Perrier or Malvern water.
Alan Bennett

I figured I must be gay because my parents gave me a chemistry set for my birthday and I used it to make my own line of skincare products.
Bob Smith

As a child, your favourite nursery rhyme was 'Rub-a-Dub-Dub, Three Men in a Tub'.
Ellen Truman, *Will and Grace*

You know you're gay if you bend over and see four balls.   Graham Norton

If Michelangelo had been heterosexual, the Sistine Chapel would have been painted basic white and with a roller.
Rita Mae Brown

You're as gay as a clutch purse on Tony night.   Will Truman, *Will and Grace*

To find out if a salesman at Gap is gay, ask him to name the colours of stuff in the store. If he says chestnut, sable, taupe and sandstone, he's gay. If he says brown, brown, brown, and brown, he's straight.   Jeff Fessler

Well, that's the pot calling the kettle beige.   Harvey Fierstein

In Newcastle-upon-Tyne, gay means 'owns a coat'.   Jimmy Carr

I remember when outing meant a family picnic.   Rodney Dangerfield

You may not be one but you certainly look like one, which is even worse.
Lord Queensberry

There are easier things in life than being a drag queen. But I ain't got no choice. Try as I may, I just can't walk in flats.   Harvey Fierstein

There are no straight men, only men that haven't met Jack.
Jack McFarland, *Will and Grace*

Straight! He's about as straight as the Yellow Brick Road.   Harvey Fierstein

Straight guys think the world's problems can be solved by nuking the bastards. Gay guys say the world would be a far better place if everyone was given a makeover.   Jeff Fessler

My brother is gay and my parents don't care, as long as he marries a doctor.   Elayne Boosler

I once had a large gay following, but I ducked into an alleyway and lost him.   Emo Philips

I didn't choose to be gay. I just got lucky.   Edward Taussig

I was born a heterosexual. It's not a choice. Who would choose this? The guilt, the shame. And do you think I'm happy having to hire a decorator?
Garry Shandling

I've been outed and I'm not even in.   **Jerry Seinfeld**

A study has found that gay men, on average, have substantially larger organs than straight men. You know what that means? Oh my God, I'm gay.
                                                        Jay Leno

The men in Hollywood are all either married, going through a divorce, or want to do your hair.   **Doris Day**

You're very soft for a Rock.   **Humphrey Bogart to Rock Hudson**

You can count on a gay guy to light scented candles at every party. Leave it to a straight guy to test the theory that you can light farts.
                                                        Karen Rauch

If homosexuality were normal, God would have created Adam and Bruce.
                                                        Anita Bryant

Homophobia is the irrational fear that three fags will break into your house and redecorate it against your will.   **Tom Ammiano**

The heterosexuals who hate us should just stop having us.
                                                        Lynda Montgomery

—My mother made me a homosexual.
—If I send her the wool, will she make me one?   **Anon**

Homosexuality in Russia is a crime and the punishment is seven years in prison, locked up with other men. There is a three-year waiting list.
                                                        Yakov Smirnoff

Looks like your new sweetie's turned his back on homosexuals. And not in a good way.   **Karen Walker,** *Will and Grace*

Dip me in chocolate and throw me to the lesbians!   **Slogan on T-shirt**

If it wasn't for gay men, fat women would have no one to dance with.
                                                        Roseanne

Some men think that they can convert gay women, and turn them straight. No way could I do that. But I could make a straight woman gay.

Jeff Tilson

I used to be a homosexual, but I had to give it up because it made my eyes water.

Michael Gambon

—Are you a lesbian?
—Are you my alternative?

Male heckler and Rhona Cameron

I don't think she's a lesbian. I think she just ran out of men.

Charlotte York, *Sex and the City*

I knew I must be a lesbian because when I was a kid I spent hours counting the freckles on Julie Andrews' face on the back album cover of *The Sound of Music*.

Cherry Jones

Heterosexuals are always asking me, 'What do you lesbians do in bed?' And I tell them, 'Well, it's a lot like heterosexual sex – only one of us doesn't have to fake an orgasm.'

Suzanne Westenhoefer

The first day I met my producer, she said, 'I'm a radical feminist lesbian.' I thought what would the Queen Mum do? So I just smiled and said, 'We shall have fog by tea-time.'

Victoria Wood

—So, what should we call you, gay or lesbian?
—How about Ellen?

Ellen DeGeneres

I have a bad feeling that whenever a lesbian looks at me they think, 'That's why I'm not a heterosexual.'

George Costanza, *Seinfeld*

It's interesting that when you play a lesbian, people ask you if you're a lesbian, but if you play a serial killer, nobody asks if you are a serial killer.

Nora Dunn

I Don't Mind Straight People as Long as They Act Gay in Public
Slogan on T-shirt

There's no such thing as bisexuality. It's just greediness. Linda La Hughes, *Gimme, Gimme, Gimme*

They say that lesbians hate men, but why on earth would a lesbian hate men? They don't have to fuck them.
Roseanne

Thank you for the lovely bracelet, but I still haven't changed my mind. I have no desire to touch you in places that I already own.
Gail Parent

—I'm a lesbian trapped in a man's body.
—A bit like Martina Navratilova.
Eddie Izzard and Frank Skinner

Like most men, I am consumed with desire whenever a lesbian gets within twenty feet.
Taki

Men love to watch two women make love. Is it because it turns them on or are they trying to figure out how to do it right?
Joy Behar

A friend of mine writes from Austria that she has been raped by six Cossacks. (Hard cheese as she is a lesbian.)
Nancy Mitford

I chased a woman for almost two years only to discover her tastes were exactly like mine – we were both crazy about girls.
Groucho Marx

If all gay people are going to hell, I'd like to see everyone in heaven get their hair done.
Judy Carter

Gay people should be allowed to marry. Just because somebody's gay doesn't mean they shouldn't suffer like the rest of us.
Jeff Shaw

Bisexuality immediately doubles your chances of a date on Saturday night.
Woody Allen

If there's one thing I hate, it's a bisexual homosexual – or is it the other way around? I guess it works either way.
Neil Simon

I'm a trisexual. I'll try anything once.
Samantha Jones, *Sex and the City*

All these different sexualities are so confusing. As I understand it, transvestites are the ones that grow down from the ceiling and transsexuals are the ones that grow up.
Pamela Yager

We had a lot of trouble with one man who wanted the full conversion job, pipes re-laid, all on-site rubbish removed. He came to the surgery several times, getting very unpleasant in a pinafore dress, complaining he still can't get to the top C on 'Midnight in the Oasis'.
Victoria Wood

One company has installed a third restroom for a transsexual employee. The employee leaves the toilet seat halfway up.
Craig Kilborn

Do men who like to dress up as women find they can no longer parallel park?
Roseanne

It's better to be black than gay because when you're black you don't have to tell your mother.
Charles Pierce

We had gay burglars the other night. They broke in and rearranged the furniture.
Robin Williams

Even though most gays blame Margaret Thatcher for Section 28, they still admire her as a drag idol.
Ivan Massow

The Bible is my least favourite book. It is to gays what *Mein Kampf* is to Jews.
Peter Tatchell

My wife had half a dozen sex change operations, but couldn't find anything she liked.
Woody Allen

ATTRACTION

If you're given a choice between money and sex appeal, take the money. As you get older, the money will become your sex appeal.

Katharine Hepburn

—Will you look at her! Oh my God. If I wasn't married, you know what I'd do?
—Wear the same underwear every day?

Bernie Stein and Ray Barone, *Everybody Loves Raymond*

So, Debbie McGee, what first attracted you to the millionaire Paul Daniels?

Mrs Merton

Most women are attracted to the simple things in life. Like men.

Henny Youngman

Friend of mine wrote a book called *How to Attract Men*. Her main advice is to be naked and have a bar by your bed.

John Waters

Choosing a woman is like choosing a car – we all want a Ferrari, sometimes want a pickup truck, and end up with a station wagon.

Tim Allen

Men always say the most important thing in a woman is a sense of humour. You want to know what that means? He's looking for someone to laugh at *his* jokes.

Sheila Wenz

To attract men, I wear a perfume called 'New Car Interior'.

Rita Rudner

I have so little sex appeal my gynaecologist calls me 'sir'.

Joan Rivers

You wouldn't have to be drunk to bed Catherine Deneuve, I don't care what your sexual history to that point had been.

Susan Sarandon

Scientists now believe that the primary biological function of breasts is to make males stupid.

Dave Barry

He was formed for the ruin of our sex.   Tobias Smollett

Her breasts filled out the front of her blouse like the humps of a small camel. Not the kind you smoke, but the kind you ride.   Kinky Friedman

A lot of guys think the larger a woman's breasts are, the less intelligent she is. I think it's the opposite. I think the larger a woman's breasts are, the less intelligent the men become.   Anita Wise

Working with Sophia Loren was like being bombed with watermelons.
Alan Ladd

Elizabeth Taylor looks like two small boys fighting underneath a mink blanket.   Mr Blackwell

No man has ever tried to look up a woman's nostril. You don't unhook anything to get to a nose.   Jerry Seinfeld

I was so flat I used to put Xs on my chest and write, 'You are here.'
I wore angora sweaters just so the guys would have *something* to pet.
Joan Rivers

It's called a Wonderbra because when you take it off, the guy is thinking, 'I wonder where her boobs went?'   Rebecca Nell

I look like the girl next door – if you happen to live next to an amusement park.   Dolly Parton

I'll sing to you, bring spring to you,
And worship the trousers that cling to you,
Bewitched, bothered and bewildered am I.   Lorenz Hart

Sex appeal is fifty per cent what you've got and fifty per cent what people think you've got.   Sophia Loren

According to a recent survey, men say the first thing they notice about women is their eyes. And women say the first thing they notice about men is they're a bunch of liars.   Jay Leno

When she raises her eyelids, it's as if she were taking off all her clothes.

Colette

Those aren't come-to-bed eyes – who needs a bed?   William McIlvanney

She would serve after a long voyage at sea.   William Shakespeare

Men of every age flocked around Diana Cooper like gulls round a council tip.   John Carey

Men seldom make passes at girls who wear glasses.   Dorothy Parker

See the mothers in the park,
Ugly creatures chiefly;
Someone must have loved them once —
in the dark and briefly.   Anon

I don't have a type. It took me this long to narrow it down to a gender.   Ellen DeGeneres

A girl who is bespectacled,
She may not get her nectacled.   Ogden Nash

Men aren't attracted to me by my mind. They're attracted to me by what I don't mind.   Gypsy Rose Lee

I have no sex appeal. I have to blindfold my vibrator.   Joan Rivers

Ah, sweet pity. Where would my love life have been without it?   Homer Simpson

Wouldn't it be great if we lived in a world where insecurity and desperation made us more attractive?   Albert Brookes

Is that a gun in your pocket, or are you just glad to see me?   Mae West

SEX

—Wanna fuck?
—Looks like you talked me into it, you sweet-talking bastard.

Australian joke

Sex between a man and a woman can be wonderful – provided you get between the right man and woman. **Woody Allen**

I believe that sex is the most beautiful, natural and wholesome thing that money can buy. **Steve Martin**

Sex without love is an empty experience, but as empty experiences go, it's one of the best. **Woody Allen**

Had God consulted me in the matter, I should have advised him to continue the generation of the species by fashioning them out of clay.

Martin Luther

The pleasure is momentary, the position is ridiculous, and the expense damnable. **Lord Chesterfield**

Sex is like money; only too much is enough. **John Updike**

My wife and I have Olympic sex. Once every four years.

Rodney Dangerfield

Until I was fifteen I was more familiar with Africa than my own body.

Joe Orton

I don't know if my first experience was heterosexual or homosexual because I was too polite to ask. **Gore Vidal**

I remember the first time I had sex because I kept the receipt. **Bill Brandis**

As a child of eight, he had once kissed a girl of six under the mistletoe at a Christmas party, but there his sex life had come to an abrupt halt.

P.G. Wodehouse

I'm a great lover – I'll bet.

Emo Philips

Don't have sex. It leads to kissing and pretty soon you have to start talking to them.

Steve Martin

Meet me in the bedroom in five minutes and bring a cattle prod.

Woody Allen

He made love faster than the time it takes to get a vaccination.

Roz Doyle, *Frasier*

Remember, if you smoke after sex, you're doing it too fast.

Woody Allen

Men are like firemen. To us, sex is an emergency, and no matter what we're doing we can be ready in two minutes. Women, on the other hand, are like fire. They're very exciting, but the conditions have to be exactly right for it to occur.

Jerry Seinfeld

If you run out of KY Jelly, a fine emergency substitute is something called 'foreplay'.

Jeff Green

Foreplay is like beefburgers – three minutes on each side.

Victoria Wood

It wasn't that he was bad in bed. He knew where all the parts were. Unfortunately, most of them were his own.

Roz Doyle, *Frasier*

I once dated a waitress. In the middle of sex she'd say, 'How is everything? Is everything okay over here?'

David Corrado

I once made love to a female clown. She twisted my penis into a poodle.

Dan Whitney

Of course size matters. Whoever says it doesn't matter is just a liar with a small dick.

Pamela Anderson

An Australian guy's idea of foreplay is, 'Are you awake?'   Paul Hogan

I had phone sex and got an ear infection.   Richard Lewis

The perfect lover is one who turns into a pizza at 4.00 am.   Charles Pierce

The three words you don't want to hear, while you're making love are, 'Honey, I'm home.'   Ken Hammond

My girlfriend said to me in bed the other night, 'You're a pervert.' I said to her, 'That's a big word for a girl of nine.'   Emo Philips

—Back to my place?
—Can two people fit under a rock?   Rita Rudner

Conventional sexual intercourse is like squirting jam into a doughnut.   Germaine Greer

I could have sex with a Cheerio without breaking it.   Richard Jeni

If you want sex, have an affair. If you want a relationship, buy a dog.   Julie Burchill

Why do Mike Tyson's eyes water when he has sex? Mace.   John Camponera

I tried phone sex once. Got my penis stuck in the nine.   Kevin Meaney

One night I made love from one o'clock to five past two. It was when they put the clocks forward.   Garry Shandling

Two's company. Three's fifty bucks.   Joan Rivers

Sex is one of the nine reasons for reincarnation. The other eight are unimportant.   Henry Miller

A psychiatrist told me and my wife that we should have sex every night. Now we never see each other.   Rodney Dangerfield

I did not suspect it was an orgy until three days later. S.J. Perelman

All human beings connect sex and love – except for men. Roseanne

—Have you ever paid for sex?
—Only emotionally. Lee Hurst

Love is the answer, but while you're waiting for the answer, sex raises some pretty interesting questions. Woody Allen

You know that look women get when they want sex? Me neither. Drew Carey

I'm not against half-naked girls. Not as often as I'd like to be. Woody Allen

My wife and I keep fighting about sex and money. I think she charges me too much. Rodney Dangerfield

Two minutes of gooey near-satisfaction followed by weeks of haunting guilt is so much more easily attained at Häagen-Dazs. Florence Campbell

—But isn't sex better when you're with one person you love?
—Maybe. In a poem. Ross Geller and Joey Tribbiani, *Friends*

People think I hate sex. I don't. I just don't like things that stop you seeing the television properly. Victoria Wood

I practise safe sex. I use an airbag. It's a little startling at first when it flies out. Then the woman realizes it's safer than being thrown clear. Garry Shandling

The only way to have really safe sex is to abstain. From drinking. Wendy Liebman

Popular music artist Sting is always boasting about his eight hours a night sex sessions with his wife Trudi. Imagine how long he could last if she was a looker. Jimmy Carr

I thank God I was raised Catholic, so sex will always be dirty.

John Waters

She tore her clothes off like a nun forsaking her vows.   Peter de Vries

They made love as though they were an endangered species.   Peter de Vries

I think I mentioned to Bob Geldof I could make love for eight hours. What I didn't say was that this included four hours of begging, then dinner and a movie.

Sting

The only difference between sex and death is, with death, you do it alone and nobody's going to make fun of you.

Woody Allen

What do I know about sex? I'm a married man.

Tom Clancy

My husband and I had our best sex during the divorce. It was like cheating on our lawyers.

Priscilla Lopez

I can count all the lovers I've ever had on one hand – if I'm holding a calculator.

Tom Cotter

When David Copperfield gets an erection, he passes a hoop over it to show there are no wires attached.

Garry Shandling

I hear your favourite sexual position is man on top, woman in magazine.

Caitlin Moore

My wife's favourite position is back to back.   Rodney Dangerfield

I'm never through with a girl until I've had her three ways.

John F. Kennedy

I've tried several varieties of sex. The conventional position makes me claustrophobic, and the others give me a stiff neck or lockjaw.

Tallulah Bankhead

A survey asked married women when they most want to have sex. 84 per cent of them said right after their husband is finished. Jay Leno

I like kinky sex with chocolate. I call it S&M&M. Roseanne

When my wife has sex with me, there's always a reason. One night she used me to time an egg. Rodney Dangerfield

The big difference between sex for money and sex for free is that sex for money usually costs a lot less. Brendan Francis

An empty aluminium cigar tube filled with angry wasps makes an inexpensive vibrator. Top tip, *Viz*

My wife told me she wanted to have sex in the back seat of the car. She wanted me to drive. Rodney Dangerfield

Listen carefully, or a sexual perversion (5,2,4,4).
Crossword clue in *Financial Times* (Answer: Prick up your ears)

A chicken and an egg are lying in bed. The chicken is smoking a cigarette with a satisfied smile on its face, and the egg is frowning and looking put out. The egg mutters to no one in particular, 'I guess we answered *that* question.' Woody Allen

Let's forget about the six feet and talk about the seven inches. Mae West

Any impotent men in here tonight? Oh, I see, you can't get your hands up either. Roseanne

There are a number of mechanical devices which increase sexual arousal, particularly in women. Chief among these is the Mercedes 380SL convertible. P.J. O'Rourke

Nothing was happening in the bedroom. I nicknamed our waterbed the Dead Sea.
                                                                    Phyllis Diller

It's been so long since I made love, I can't remember who gets tied up.
                                                                    Joan Rivers

My love life is so bad I'm taking part in the world celibacy championships. I meet the Pope in the semi-finals.   **Guy Bellamy**

I know nothing about sex because I was always married.   **Zsa Zsa Gabor**

When a man talks dirty to a woman, it's sexual harassment. When a woman talks dirty to a man, it's five dollars a minute.   **Steven Wright**

I feel like a million tonight – but one at a time.   **Mae West**

For a man, sex is a hunger. If he can't get to a fancy French restaurant, he'll go to a hot dog stand.   **Joan Fontaine**

Why fuck the girl in the skirt, when you can fuck the girl in the ad for the skirt?   **Candace Bushnell**

My mother is sixty, and her whole life she only ever slept with one guy. She won't tell me who.   **Wendy Liebman**

I only take Viagra when I'm with more than one woman.   **Jack Nicholson**

They're working on Viagra for women. Are they crazy? That's been around for hundreds of years – it's called cash.   **Alonzo Boden**

Sex is the most fun I've ever had without laughing.   **Woody Allen**

It's okay to laugh in the bedroom so long as you don't point.   **Will Durst**

My girlfriend always laughs during sex – no matter what she's reading.   **Steve Jobs**

Orgies: participate once, you're a philosopher; twice, a pervert.   **Voltaire**

A woman reading *Playboy* feels a little like a Jew reading a Nazi manual.
Gloria Steinem

A man has missed something if he has never left a brothel at dawn feeling like throwing himself into the river out of sheer disgust with life.
Gustave Flaubert

It doesn't matter what you do in the bedroom as long as you don't do it in the street and frighten the horses. Mrs Patrick Campbell

I don't remember having a sexual peak when I was nineteen. I just remember apologizing a lot. Jeff Stilson

We learned sexual technique from our dog. He taught me how to beg, and he taught my wife how to roll over and play dead. Rodney Dangerfield

The difference between seduction and rape is salesmanship. Roy Herbert

Women are like banks. Breaking and entering is a serious business.
Joe Orton

Sex and golf are the only things you can enjoy without being any good at them. Jimmy Demarest

I have so much cybersex, my baby's first words will probably be, 'You've got mail.' Paulara Hawkins

After we made love, I said to my girlfriend, 'Was it good for you, too?' And she said, 'I don't think that was good for anybody.' Garry Shandling

The woman I broke up with is going round telling all her friends that I gave her an anticlimax. Richard Lewis

I wonder if she actually had an orgasm in the two years we were married, or did she fake it that night? Woody Allen

He wanted to have his cake and eat me. Ally McBeal

Some women take so long to come that you have to be willing to lay aside, say, the month of June, with sandwiches having to be brought in.
Bruce Jay Friedman

A multiple orgasm is like a good music system – something you see in magazines and which other people have.
Jeremy Hardy

I have heard that women can have multiple orgasms, but I'll believe it when I see it.
Larry Sanders

The only time my wife and I had a simultaneous orgasm was when the judge signed the divorce papers.
Woody Allen

Who is this Greek chap Clitoris they're talking about?
Lord Albermarle

I could never understand what he saw in her until I saw her at the Caprice eating corn-on-the-cob.
Coral Browne

You know the worst thing about oral sex? The view.
Maureen Lipman

Can you shave or something? Blowing you is like getting my teeth flossed.

Samantha Jones, *Sex and the City*

—Do you remember the minuet?
—Dahling, I can't even remember the men I *slept* with!
Tallulah Bankhead

If we could perpetually do blowjobs to every guy on earth, we would own the world. And at the same time have our hands free.
Samantha Jones, *Sex and the City*

My wife gives good headache.
Rodney Dangerfield

I went to a meeting for premature ejaculators. I left early.
Red Buttons

Lulabelle, it's you! I didn't recognize you standing up.
Groucho Marx

Do I talk to my wife while having sex? Sure, if I happen to be near the phone.
                                                                    Marty Aldman

Sex with Nicholas Soames was like having a large wardrobe fall on top of you with the key still in the lock.
                                                                    Anon

I married a German. Every night I dress up as Poland and he invades me.
                                                                    Bette Midler

The mirror above my bed reads: objects appear larger than they are.
                                                                    Garry Shandling

A sexagenarian? At his age? That's disgusting.   Gracie Allen

The only thing I miss about sex is the cigarette afterwards.   Florence King

There goes the good time that was had by all.   Bette Davis

Is your vagina listed in the New York City guidebooks? Because it should be. Hottest spot in town. Always open!   Charlotte York, *Sex and the City*

Easy is an adjective used to describe a woman who has the sexual morals of a man.
                                                                    Nancy Linn-Desmond

Nobody in their right mind would call me a nymphomaniac. I only sleep with good-looking men.
                                                                    Fiona Pitt-Kethley

You were born with your legs apart. They'll send you to the grave in a Y-shaped coffin.
                                                                    Oscar Wilde

A Jewish nymphomaniac is a woman who will make love with a man the same day she has her hair done.
                                                                    Maureen Lipman

Dear Lord, give me chastity, but not yet.   Saint Augustine

If all the girls at the Yale Prom were laid end to end, I wouldn't be a bit surprised.   Dorothy Parker

I had ambitions to be a sex maniac but I failed the practical.   Les Dawson

You wanna hear my personal opinion on prostitution? If men knew how to do it, they wouldn't have to pay for it.   Roseanne

Women need a reason to have sex. Men just need a place.   Billy Crystal

When a guy goes to a hooker, he's not paying her for sex; he's paying her to leave.   Anon

Husbands are chiefly good lovers when they are betraying their wives.
                                                                        Marilyn Monroe

I blame my father for telling me about the birds and the bees. I was going steady with a woodpecker for two years.   Bob Hope

All my mother told me about sex was that the man goes on top, and the woman goes on the bottom. For three years my husband and I slept in bunk beds.   Joan Rivers

Sex education will encourage kids to have sex? No way. I had four years of algebra and I never do math.   Elayne Boosler

Make love to every woman you meet; it you get five per cent of your outlay, it's a good investment.   Arnold Bennett

A woman's most erogenous zone is her mind.   Raquel Welch

The thing women like most in bed is breakfast.   Robin Williams

My wife is a sex object. Every time I ask for sex, she objects.   Les Dawson

A woman for duty, a boy for pleasure, a goat for ecstasy.   Greek proverb

A woman is only a woman, but a good cigar is a smoke.   Rudyard Kipling

My classmates would make out with anything that moved, but I never saw any reason to limit myself.

Emo Philips

I think that sex is a beautiful thing between two people. Between five it's fantastic.

Woody Allen

The trouble with group sex is that you never know where to put your elbows.

Martin Cruz Smith

A threesome was never a fantasy of mine. What, wake up with *two* disappointed ladies in the morning?

Bobcat Goldthwait

All this fuss about sleeping together. For physical pleasure, I'd sooner go to the dentist any day.

Evelyn Waugh

My sex life is now reduced to fan letters from an elderly lesbian who wants to borrow $800.

Groucho Marx

My own belief is that there is hardly anyone whose sex life, if it were broadcast, would not fill the world at large with surprise and horror.

Somerset Maugham

Erotic is when you use a feather. Kinky is when you use the whole chicken.

Anon

I'm not kinky, but occasionally I like to put on a robe and stand in front of a tennis ball machine.

Garry Shandling

The difference between pornography and erotica is lighting.

Gloria Leonard

My boyfriend used to say, 'I read *Playboy* for the articles.' Right, and I go to shopping malls for the music.

Rita Rudner

If sex is such a natural phenomenon, how come there are so many books on how to?

Bette Midler

Is sex dirty? It is if you're doing it right.

Woody Allen

I'm going to write a sex manual called, *Ouch! You're on my Hair!*

Richard Lewis

I've been on more laps than a napkin.

Mae West

I like to wake up every morning feeling a new man.

Jean Harlow

I am always looking for meaningful one-night stands.

Dudley Moore

For flavour, instant sex will never supersede the stuff you have to peel and cook.

Quentin Crisp

—Guess who Sue spent the night with?
—Come on, Mary, I've got to be home in an hour.

Mary Richards and Murray Slaughter, *Rhoda*

A promiscuous person is someone who is getting more sex than you are.

Victor Lownes

If I'd had as many women as I've been given credit for, I'd be in a jar in the Harvard Medical School.

Frank Sinatra

I don't think sex has much to do with morals. It's more a compulsion – like murder.

Alice Thomas Ellis

An erection at will is the moral equivalent of a valid credit card.

Alex Comfort

Sex is a powerful aphrodisiac.

Keith Waterhouse

It is conduct unbecoming to a lady or gentleman when being treated at the VD clinic to names as contacts those who spurned your advances.

George Moore

Oh, yes, I've tried my hand at sex.

Emo Philips

Ninety per cent of men masturbate and the other ten per cent have no arms. Sixty per cent of women masturbate and the other forty per cent expect you to believe it takes them that long to take a bath.   Richard Jeni

I'll come to your room at eight o'clock. If I'm late start without me.
Tallulah Bankhead

The good thing about masturbation is that you don't have to dress up for it.   Truman Capote

Don't knock masturbation. It's sex with someone I love. Woody Allen

—There is no word in the Irish language for what you were doing.
—In Lapland, they have no word for snow.   Joe Orton

If God had meant us not to masturbate, he would have made our arms shorter.   George Carlin

Masturbation: the amazing availability of it!   James Joyce

I was the best I ever had.   Richard Jeni

Masturbation is the thinking man's television.   Christopher Hampton

—Stop that, son, you'll go blind!
—I'm over here, Dad!   Anon

I'm such a good lover because I practise a lot on my own.   Woody Allen

How does a lazy Californian guy masturbate? Digs a hole, put his penis in, and waits for an earthquake.   Anon

Pass me my teeth, and I'll bite you.   George Burns

Your place or back to the sheltered accommodation?   Barry Cryer

I had a wank in the car the other day. I won't be doing that again. The cab driver was furious.

Clyde West

It's a fallacy that males stop masturbating after seventeen. Most usually stop after one.

Jeff Green

The last time I was inside a woman was when I visited the Statue of Liberty.

Woody Allen

If it weren't for speed bumps, pickpockets and frisking at airports, I'd have no sex life at all.

Rodney Dangerfield

Nowadays I reserve my sexual activities for special occasions such as the installation of a new Pope.

Dave Barry

I can still enjoy sex at 75. I live at 76, so it's no distance.   Bob Monkhouse

Now that I'm 78, I do tantric sex because it's very slow. My favourite position is called the plumber. You stay in all day but nobody comes.

John Mortimer

—Your fly-buttons are undone.
—No matter. The dead bird does not leave the nest.   Winston Churchill

At my age, getting a little action means your prune juice is working.

George Burns

Sex at 93 is like playing billiards with a rope.   George Burns

Like being unchained from a lunatic.   Sophocles on his declining sexual powers

On my 85th birthday, I felt like a 20-year-old. But there wasn't one around.

Milton Berle

KISS

I've tried everything but coprophagia and necrophilia, and I like kissing best.

John Waters

A kiss is an application on the top floor for a job in the basement.

Brian Johnson

I kissed my first woman and smoked my first cigarette on the same day; I have never had time for tobacco since.

Arturo Toscanini

I feel great and I kiss even better.

Emo Philips

I haven't seen a kiss that uncomfortable since Richard Gere and Jodie Foster in *Sommersby*.

Will Truman, *Will and Grace*

It takes a lot of experience for a girl to kiss like a beginner.

Joan Rivers

Oh, innocent victims of Cupid,
Remember this terse little verse,
To let a fool kiss you is stupid,
To let a kiss fool you is worse.

E.Y. Harburg

Kissing Marilyn Monroe was like kissing Hitler.

Tony Curtis

With lips like those, Mick Jagger could French-kiss a moose.

Joan Rivers

Buy me a Mercedes and I'll make your neck look like a relief map of the Andes.

Roz Doyle, *Frasier*

Kissing Edwina Currie was like kissing a can opener.

Godfrey Barker

When women kiss, it always reminds me of prize-fighters shaking hands.

H.L. Mencken

He kissed her once by the pigsty when she wasn't looking and never kissed her again although she was looking all the time.

Dylan Thomas

How about a Spanish kiss under the mistletoe? It's like a French kiss only a little further south.

Lorna Adler

People who throw kisses are mighty hopelessly lazy.

Bob Hope

I wasn't kissing her. I was just whispering in her mouth.

Chico Marx

DATING

—Where? – When? – How much?
—Your place – Tonight – Free.

Prince de Jounville and Great Rachel

What is a date really, but a job interview that lasts all night? The only difference is that in not many job interviews is there a chance you'll wind up naked at the end of it.

Jerry Seinfeld

Have the florist send some roses to Mrs Upjohn and write 'Emily, I love you,' on the back of the bill.

Groucho Marx

—My idea of a perfect date would be a man who takes me for a romantic dinner, and then we walk along the beach barefoot discussing books and music.
—No wonder you're still a virgin.

Cheryl Frasier and Karen Krantz, *Miss Congeniality*

I went out on a first date, but I don't think I'll be seeing her again. She got mad when I didn't open the car door. I just swam to the surface.

Emo Philips

A man on a date wonders if he'll get lucky. The woman knows.

Monica Piper

A woman waits motionless until she is wooed. That is how the spider waits for the fly.

George Bernard Shaw

In time, you'll meet someone very special. Someone who won't press charges.

Gomez Addams, *The Addams Family*

Everyone says that looks don't matter, age doesn't matter, money doesn't matter. But I never met a girl yet who has fallen in love with an old ugly man who's broke.

Rodney Dangerfield

One woman's *Titanic* is another woman's *Love Boat.*

Carrie Bradshaw, *Sex and the City*

Employees make the best dates. You don't have to pick them up and they're always tax-deductible.

Andy Warhol

I'll meet you tonight under the moon. Oh, I can see you now, you and the moon. You wear a necktie so I'll know you.

Groucho Marx

It's nights like this that drive men like me to women like you for nights like this.

Bob Hope

So, do you live around here often?

Steven Wright

Sometimes I'd rather stay home and watch the new movie of the week on TV than go out to a bar and see reruns of guys I've dated.

Pamela Yager

I asked my date what she wanted to drink. She said, 'Oh, I guess I'll have champagne.' I said, 'Guess again.'

Slappy White

I'm dating a homeless woman. It was easier talking her into staying over.

Gary Shandling

I was on a date with this really hot model. Well, it wasn't really a date date. We just ate dinner and saw a movie. Then the plane landed.

Dave Attell

I prefer young girls. Their stories are shorter.

Thomas McGuane

A good place to meet a man is the dry cleaner's. These men usually have jobs and bathe.

Rita Rudner

I was with this girl the other night and from the way she was responding to my skilful caresses, you would have sworn that she was conscious from the top of her head to the tag on her toes.
Emo Philips

I could sit in your lap all day if you don't stand up.
Groucho Marx

The worst is when a guy lies to you about being married. He tells you he is when he isn't.
Rhoda Morgenstern, *Rhoda*

—You wanna go see a movie?
—No, thanks, I've already seen one.
Phoebe Buffay, *Friends*

A woman says to a man, 'I haven't seen you around here.' 'Yes,' he says, 'I just got out of jail for killing my wife.' 'So you're single...'
Bernard Manning

I have no self-confidence. When girls say yes, I tell them to think it over.
Rodney Dangerfield

—What's your new boyfriend like?
—Did you ever see *An Officer and a Gentleman*? Well, he's kinda like the guy I went to see that with.
Phoebe Buffay, *Friends*

I asked this girl out and she said, 'You got a friend?' I said yes, she said, 'Then go out with him.'
Dom Irrera

I was dating a guy for a while because he told me he had an incurable disease. I didn't realize it was stupidity.
Gracie Hart

I had a great time tonight. Really. It was like the Nuremberg Trials.
Woody Allen

I was dating a transvestite. My mother said, 'Marry him. You'll double your wardrobe.'
Joan Rivers

The advantages of dating younger men is that on them everything, like hair and teeth, is in the right place as opposed to being on the bedside table or bathroom floor.
Candace Bushnell

When going away for the weekend with a man, the woman has her hair cut, her bikini waxed, borrows a skirt from her best friend, buys a new top, dyes her eyelashes, diets, fills fifteen small plastic containers with lotion, tries on all her clothes, irons them, packs something 'sexy'. The man wonders if his wellies are in the car. **Deborah McKinlay**

There is no fury like an ex-wife searching for a new lover. **Cyril Connolly**

I was dating a younger man. I asked him where he was when Elvis died. He said he was in amniotic fluid. **Robin Roberts**

The older he gets, the younger his girlfriends get. Soon, he'll be dating sperm. **Billy Crystal**

I once had three dates on a single Saturday and still had time to defrost my refrigerator and rotate my tyres. **Roz Doyle, *Frasier***

I've been chased by women before but never while I was awake. **Bob Hope**

The nice thing about a stalker – they're always there for you. **Jenny Abrams**

Natural childbirth classes are a great place to meet chicks, if you're into the fuller figure. And you can be reasonably sure these girls put out. **Jonathan Katz**

People are going on dates now to coffee bars. This is a bad idea. Four cappuccinos later, your date does not look any better. **Margot Black**

I have such poor vision, I can date anybody. **Garry Shandling**

I don't have a girlfriend. But I do know a woman who'd be mad at me for saying that. **Mitch Hedberg**

Oh, those June nights on the Riviera … we were young, gay, and reckless! I drank champagne from your slipper – two quarts. It would have been more but you were wearing inner soles. **Groucho Marx**

Do you like Piña Colonics and getting caught in the rain?   **Homer Simpson**

—It was so romantic, Mr Rigsby – champagne, soft lights,
Tchaikovsky in the background...
—Oh, was he there too?   **Miss Jones and Rigsby,** *Rising Damp*

Your idea of romance is popping the can away from my face.   **Roseanne**

Romance is dead. It was acquired in a hostile takeover by Hallmark and
Disney, homogenized, and sold off piece by piece.   **Lisa Simpson**

I want a man who is kind and understanding. Is that too much to ask of a millionaire?   Zsa Zsa Gabor

Women might be able to fake orgasms, but men can fake whole
relationships.   **Jimmy Shubert**

When I date a guy, I think, is this the man I want my children to spend
their weekends with?   **Rita Rudner**

Men date thin girls because they're too weak to argue and they only
eat salads.   **Jennifer Fairbanks**

A lot of girls date me just to further their careers. Damn anthropologists.   **Emo Philips**

—How many women have you slept with?
—Roughly...
—I don't care *how* you did it ... just the number.
James Herbert and Stuart Bondek, *Spin City*

Odds on meeting a single man: 1 in 23; a cute, single man: 1 in 529;
a cute, single, smart man, 1 in 3,245,873; when you look your best,
1 in a billion.   **Lorna Adler**

I'm married now, so I do most of my dating on the Internet.

Buddy Parkes

I'm all for computer dating but I wouldn't want my sister to marry one.

Emo Philips

The difference between Charles Manson and every woman I've dated is that Manson had the decency to look like a nut the first time you meet him.

Richard Jeni

Why is it so difficult to find men who are sensitive, caring and good-looking? They all already have boyfriends.

Jane Caron

I have no problem with British men. I think there is something endearing about desperation and hopelessness.

Melinda Messenger

I like only two types of men – domestic and foreign.

Mae West

—What are you doing in the closet?
—Nothing. Come on in.

Groucho Marx

Many men like to pursue an elusive woman, like a cake of wet soap in a bathtub.

Gelett Burgess

—I'm a southern belle. Flirting is part of my heritage.
—What she means is, her mother was a slut too.

Blanche Deveraux and Dorothy Zbornak, *The Golden Girls*

She plucked from my lapel the invisible strand of lint – the universal act of women to proclaim worship.

O. Henry

Using a complex, sophisticated technique to get a man excited is like preparing a gourmet French meal for a Labrador retriever.

Dave Barry

I'm not into that one-night thing. I think a person should get to know someone and even be in love with them before you use them and degrade them.

Steve Martin

One woman I was dating called and said, 'Come on over, there's nobody home.' I went over. Nobody was home.   **Rodney Dangerfield**

Valerie fondles men like a mousetrap fondles mice.   **Roger McGough**

Oh, why can't we break away from all this, just you and I, and lodge with my fleas in the hills – I mean, flee to my lodge in the hills.
                    Groucho Marx

Last night she was banging on my door for forty-five minutes – but I wouldn't let her out.   **Dean Martin**

I go from stool to stool in singles bars hoping to get lucky, but there's never any gum under any of them.   **Emo Philips**

I took up a collection for a man in our office but I didn't get enough money to buy one.   **Ruth Buzzi**

Another one of your 'till dawn do us part' relationships?
                    Frasier Crane, *Frasier*

I'm a one-man woman. One man at a time.   **Mae West**

I can't get a relationship to last longer than it takes to copy their CDs.
                    Margaret Smith

When I'm not in a relationship, I shave one leg. That way, when I sleep, it feels like I'm with a woman.   **Garry Shandling**

I am going to cancel my date and spend the evening eating doughnuts in a cardigan with egg on it.   **Helen Fielding**

Young man, if she asks you if you like her hair that way, beware; the woman has already committed matrimony in her heart.   **Don Marquis**

When I finally met Mr Right, I had no idea his first name was 'Always'.
                    Rita Rudner

Few things in life are more embarrassing than the necessity of having to inform an old friend that you have just got engaged to his fiancée.

W.C. Fields

Don't think of him as a date, think of him as a dinner.   Lucille Ball

My girlfriend told me she was seeing another man. I told her to rub her eyes.   Emo Philips

I've been on so many blind dates, I should get a free dog.   Wendy Liebman

I was on a date recently, and the guy took me horseback riding. That was fun until we ran out of quarters.   Susie Louks

Every man I meet wants to protect me. I can't figure out from what.

Mae West

Two out of five Irish women prefer alcohol to sex and it's just my luck to have gone out with both of them.   Joseph O'Connor

The only place men want depth in a woman is in her décolletage.

Zsa Zsa Gabor

A woman, especially if she has the misfortune of knowing anything, should conceal it as well as she can.   Jane Austen

I think … therefore I'm single.   Liz Winston

No man ever stuck his hand up your dress looking for a library ticket.

Joan Rivers

A woman who has a head full of Greek or carries on fundamental controversies about mechanics, might as well have a beard. Immanuel Kant

Boys don't make passes at female smart-asses.   Letty Cottin Pogrebin

Brains are never a handicap to a girl if she hides them under a see-through blouse.   Bobby Vinton

Most beautiful but dumb girls think they are smart and get away with it, because other people, on the whole, aren't much smarter. **Louise Brooks**

I don't know what went wrong between me and my girlfriend – or Tubby as I called her. **Stewart France**

The fastest way to a man's heart is through his chest. **Roseanne**

To keep a man you must be a maid in the living room, a cook in the kitchen and a whore in the bedroom. I hire the other two and take care of the bedroom bit myself. **Jerry Hall**

—What do *you* do when the romance starts to go out of a relationship?
—I get dressed and go home. **Frasier Crane and Roz Doyle, *Frasier***

I don't use the word 'relationship'. Unless you're screwing your cousin, that's a 'relationship'. **Lewis Grizzard**

I was dating this girl for two years, and then the nagging starts, 'I wanna know your name.'

Mike Binder

If you never want to see a man again say, 'I love you, I want to marry you, I want to have your children.' Sometimes they leave skid marks. **Rita Rudner**

I broke up with my girlfriend. She moved in with another guy, and I draw the line at that. **Garry Shandling**

I'd be equally as willing for a dentist to be drilling than to ever let a woman in my life. **Henry Higgins, *My Fair Lady***

I'm single by choice. Not my choice. **Orny Adams**

If you can't live without me, why aren't you dead yet? **Anon**

I'm still going on bad dates when by now I should be in a bad marriage.

Laura Kightlinger

—I saw her giving me the once over.
—Yes, she looked once and it was all over.   Frasier Crane and Roz Doyle, *Frasier*

Once a woman has given her heart you can never get rid of the rest
of her.   John Vanbrugh

Take me or leave me. Or as most people do – both.   Dorothy Parker

—What do you say when you break up with a woman?
—I usually say, 'I'll call you tomorrow.'   Rebecca Howe and Sam Malone, *Cheers*

My boyfriend and I broke up. He wanted to get married and I didn't
want him to.   Rita Rudner

Breaking up is like knocking over a Coke machine. You can't do it in one
push. You have to rock it back and forth a few times until it goes over.

Jerry Seinfeld

If you leave me, can I come too?   Anon

This guy dumped me because he said I have low self-esteem. I said,
'No kidding. I slept with you didn't I?'   Tracey Macdonald

Get your tongue out of my mouth, I'm kissing you goodbye. Cynthia Heimel

When someone asks, 'Why do you think he's not calling me?' there's
always one answer – 'He's not interested.' There's not ever any other
answer.   Fran Lebowitz

If he hasn't called you in about three weeks and you have no idea where
he is, the chances are he's not in an emergency room moaning your name.

Diane Conway

I waited for the phone to ring, and when at last it didn't, I knew it
was you.   Karen Muir

If you love someone, set them free. If they come back, they're probably broke.
Rhonda Dickson

If you love someone, let them go. If they come back, great. If they don't, they're probably having dinner with someone more attractive than you.
Bill Greiser

When it's over, it's over. And I should know. I would get into bed and she would mentally dress me.
Richard Lewis

You can always tell when the relationship is over. Little things start grating on your nerves, 'Would you please stop that! That breathing in and out, it's so repetitious.'
Ellen DeGeneres

Sensitive break-up letters are my speciality: Dear Baby, Welcome to Dumpsville. Population: you. P.S. I'm gay.
Homer Simpson

Only time can heal a broken heart, just as only time can heal his broken arms and legs.
Miss Piggy

The day he moved out was terrible – that evening she went through hell. His absence wasn't a problem but the corkscrew had gone as well.
Wendy Cope

LOVE

Love is that feeling you get in your guts when you see a girl across a crowded room and think, 'Wow. One day I'm going to make you the unhappiest woman alive.'
Jeff Green

My wife and I thought we were in love but it turned out to be benign.
Woody Allen

A lot of people wonder how you can tell if you're really in love. Just ask yourself this question: 'Would I mind being financially destroyed by this person?'
Ronnie Shakes

You know you're in love when you're willing to share your cash-machine number.
Elayne Boosler

Love conquers all things – except poverty and toothache.
Mae West

Love is just a system for getting someone to call you darling after sex.
Julian Barnes

Love can leave you reeling faster than a one-eyed cat in a fish market.
Felicia R. Lee

Love is a temporary insanity curable by marriage.
Ambrose Bierce

I would worship the ground you walk on, if you only lived in a better neighbourhood.
Billy Wilder

Love, like poetry, is a kind of homesickness, the kind which made medieval monks sleep in their coffins.
Jennifer Stone

You know it's love when you dream of slitting his throat.
Wendy Cope

A guy knows he's in love when he loses interest in his car for a couple of days.
Tim Allen

I fall in love real quick, which can scare guys away. I'm like, 'I love you, I want to marry you, I want to move in with you.' And they're like, 'Ma'am, just give me the ten bucks for the pizza and I'll be out of here.'
Penny Wiggins

Adam invented love at first sight, one of the greatest labour-saving devices the world ever saw.
Josh Billings

If I gave my heart to you … I'd have none and you'd have two.
Paul Hogan

Love is much nicer to be in than an automobile accident, a tight girdle, a higher tax bracket or a holding pattern over Philadelphia.
Judith Viorst

If love is the answer, could you rephrase the question.   **Lily Tomlin**

When you're in love, it's the most glorious two and a half days of your life.   **Richard Lewis**

Better to have loved a short man than never to have loved a tall.   David Chambless

Everything was going great until I said, 'I love you,' then he got this look on his face like he'd taken a wrong turn in a really bad neighbourhood.

Roz Doyle, *Frasier*

Ill-conceived love is like a Christmas cracker – one massively disappointing bang and the novelty soon wears off.

Edmund Blackadder, *Blackadder's Christmas Carol*

There's a fine line between true love and a conviction for stalking.

Buzz Nutley

Some guys are afraid of commitment. I was playing tennis with a man and he couldn't say, 'Thirty-love.' He kept saying, 'Thirty, I really like you but I still have to see other people.'   **Rita Rudner**

Only one kind of love lasts – unrequited.   **Somerset Maugham**

Nothing takes the taste out of peanut butter quite like unrequited love.

Charlie Brown

People would never fall in love if they had not heard love talked about.

La Rochefoucauld

Love is loving someone no matter what their faults in a blind and unconditional way. Like the love Tony Blair has for George Bush.

Hugh Grant

The main purpose of love is to provide a theme for novels.   **Piers Paul Read**

Love is the delightful interval between meeting a beautiful girl and discovering that she looks like a haddock.   John Barrymore

I've been in love with the same woman for forty years. If my wife ever finds out, she'll kill me.   Henny Youngman

I judge how much a man cares for a woman by the space he allots her under a jointly shared umbrella.   Jimmy Cannon

Love is the delusion that one woman differs from another.   H.L. Mencken

The fickleness of the women I love is only equalled by the infernal constancy of the women who love me.   George Bernard Shaw

No woman is worth more than a fiver unless you're in love with her. Then she's worth all she costs you.   Somerset Maugham

Many a man has fallen in love with a girl in a light so dim he would not have chosen a suit by it.   Maurice Chevalier

I've learned that you can't make someone love you. All you can do is stalk them and hope they'll panic and give in.   Emo Philips

Oh, life is a glorious cycle of song,
A medley of extemporanea;
And love is a thing that can never go wrong;
And I am Marie of Roumania.   Dorothy Parker

When we want to read the deeds that are done for love, whither do we turn? To the murder columns.   George Bernard Shaw

Love is just a chocolate substitute.   Miranda Ingram

Love is a great glue, but there's no cement like mutual hate.   Loise Wyse

—Everyone knows that hate is not the opposite of love. Indifference is.
—Well, whatever. I don't really care.

Diane Chambers and Sam Malone, *Cheers*

The world's tragedy is that men love women, women love children, and children love hamsters.

Joanna Trollope

In Ireland, you're allowed to say you love God and babies and horses that win, but anything else is a softness in the head.

Frank McCourt

Love, the quest; marriage, the conquest; divorce, the inquest.

Helen Rowland

Love and murder will out.

William Congreve

When love congeals, it soon reveals, the faint aroma of performing seals, the double-crossing of a pair of heels. I wish I were in love again!

Lorenz Hart

MARRIAGE

Will you marry me? Did he leave you any money? Answer the second question first.

Groucho Marx

There's a way of transferring funds that's even faster than electronic banking. It's called marriage.

Ronnie Shakes

Never marry for money. Divorce for money.

Wendy Liebman

Marriage is based on the theory that when a man discovers a brand of beer exactly to his taste, he should at once throw up his job and go to work in the brewery.

George Jean Nathan

I think marriage is a marvellous thing for other people, like going to the stake.

Philip Larkin

Marriage is just the first step towards divorce.

Zsa Zsa Gabor

It is a truth universally acknowledged that a single man in possession of a good fortune must be in want of a wife.

Jane Austen

I wouldn't want any woman who'd have me as a husband.

Mark Lamarr

Marriage is like the Middle East. There is no solution.

Willy Russell

Marriage is a punishment for shoplifting in some countries.

Wayne Campbell, *Wayne's World*

Marriage is forever. It's like cement.

Peter O'Toole

Marriage is like a 5,000-piece jigsaw of the sky.

Cathy Ladman

Marry me and you'll be farting through silk for the rest of your life.

Robert Mitchum

This afternoon he asked me to be his wife, and I turned him down like a bedspread.

P.G. Wodehouse

Bachelorhood, like being alive, is more depressing than anything but the known alternative.

P.J. O'Rourke

Somehow a bachelor never quite gets over the idea that he is thing of beauty and boy forever.

Helen Rowland

Damn it, sir, it is your duty to get married. You can't be always living for pleasure.

Oscar Wilde

Marriage isn't that big a deal any more 'cause it's so easy to get divorced. You want commitment? Buy a house. Nothing says love like thirty years of debt together.

Tom Pecora

You're 40 and he's 22. Do you have to marry him? Couldn't you just adopt him?

Ann Stanley, *Forty Carats*

Yes, my husband is younger than me, but it's not a problem. If he dies, he dies.

Joan Collins

Before a marriage, a man declares that he would lay down his life to serve you. After marriage, he won't even lay down his newspaper to talk to you.
                                                                    Helen Rowland

I wouldn't be caught dead marrying a woman old enough to be my wife.
                                                                    Tony Curtis

Marriage is the alliance of two people, one of whom never remembers birthdays and the other who never forgets them.
                                                                    Ogden Nash

My wife and I were happy for 20 years. Then we met.
                                                            Rodney Dangerfield

—What do think of my fiancée?
—She's a lovely girl. She deserves a good husband. Marry her before she finds one.
                                                Harpo Marx and Robert Benchley

I met my wife during the war. She blew in through the drawing room window with a bit of shrapnel, became embedded in the sofa, and one thing led to her mother and we were married within the hour.   **Peter Cook**

The trouble with some women is that they get all excited about nothing – and then marry him.
                                                                    Cher

Trust your husband, adore your husband, and get as much as you can in your own name.
                                                                    Joan Rivers

It's a sad fact that 50 per cent of marriages end in divorce. But the other half end in death. You could be one of the lucky ones.   **Richard Jeni**

Getting married for sex is like buying a 747 for the free peanuts.
                                                                    Jeff Foxworthy

Take care of him. And make him feel important. And if you can do that, you'll have a happy and wonderful marriage. Like two out of every ten couples.
                                        Ethel Banks, *Barefoot in the Park*

In Hollywood, marriage is a success if it outlasts milk.　　Rita Rudner

Nowadays, only the gay people get married in LA. Straight people don't bother any more.　　Craig Chester

A woman with fair opportunities and without a positive hump may marry whom she likes.　　William Makepeace Thackeray

A wedding is a funeral where you smell your own flowers.　　Eddie Cantor

I wanted to look good for my wedding pictures. You might be looking at those things for four or five years.　　Tom Arnold

Marriage is the result of the longing for the deep, deep peace of the double bed after the hurly-burly of the chaise longue.　　Mrs Patrick Campbell

Marriage is a great institution, but I'm not ready for an institution yet.　　Mae West

It should be a very happy marriage – they're both so in love with him. Irene Thomas

Always get married early in the morning. That way, if it doesn't work out, you haven't wasted a whole day.　　Mickey Rooney, married eight times

In perhaps the single most money-saving word in the English language he cried, 'Elope.'　　Peter de Vries

My mum promised me I could have the wedding I want, as soon as I have a daughter who gets engaged.　　Daphne Moon, *Frasier*

I told a friend I was getting married, and he said, 'Have you picked a date yet?' I said, 'Wow, you can bring a date to your own wedding? What a country!"　　Yakov Smirnoff

No man should marry until he has studied anatomy and dissected at least one woman.
Honoré de Balzac

Having a wedding without mentioning divorce is like sending someone to war without mentioning that people are going to get killed.
Richard Curtis

Why buy a book when you can join the library?
Lily Savage

My husband and I didn't sign a prenuptial agreement. We signed a mutual suicide pact.
Roseanne

When we got married, we had our wedding list at Bloomingdale's, because you can exchange everything for cash. Each place-setting kept me in beer money for three months.
Gary Barkin

In olden times, sacrifices were made at the altar – a practice which is still continued.
Helen Rowland

The longest sentence you can form with two words is 'I do.'
H.L. Mencken

I should have known it was the wrong church when they started wheeling the coffin down the aisle.
Rigsby, *Rising Damp*

The first part of our marriage was very happy. Then, on the way back from the ceremony...
Henny Youngman

No matter what kind of music you ask them to play, your wedding band will play it in such a way that it sounds like 'New York, New York'.
Dave Barry

Next to hot chicken soup, a tattoo of an anchor on your chest, and penicillin, I consider a honeymoon one of the most overrated events in the world.
Erma Bombeck

We went to Mexico on our honeymoon, and spent the entire two weeks in bed. I had dysentery.
Woody Allen

Marrying a man is like buying something you've been admiring for a long time in a shop window. You may love it when you get it home, but it doesn't always go with everything else in the house.　　Jean Kerr

No matter who you marry, you wake up married to someone else.

Marlon Brando

Being married to Marge is like being married to my best friend – and he lets me feel his boobs.　　Homer Simpson

You may marry the man of your dreams, but fourteen years later, you're married to a couch that burps.　　Roseanne

It was a mixed marriage. I'm human, he was a Klingon.　　Carol Leifer

I love being married. It's so great to find that one special person you want to annoy for the rest of your life.　　Rita Rudner

My wife told me I'll drive her to her grave. I had the car out in two minutes.　　Tommy Cooper

My wife gets so jealous. She came home from work and was mad at me because there was a pretty girl on the bus she thought I would have liked.

Ray Romano

You know what I did before I married? Anything I wanted to.

Henny Youngman

Married life is like being banged up in prison but with fewer screws.

Anon

—Sybil, do you remember when we were first manacled together, we used to laugh quite a lot?
—Yes, Basil, but not at the same time.　　Basil and Sybil Fawlty

On quiet nights, when I'm alone, I like to run our wedding video backwards, just to watch myself walk out of the church a free man.

Jim Davidson

It was a perfect marriage – she didn't want to and he couldn't.

Spike Milligan

I've known for years our marriage has been a mockery. My body lying there night after night in the wasted moonlight. I know now how the Taj Mahal must feel.

Alan Bennett

—Homer, is this the way you pictured married life?
—Yeah, pretty much. Except we drove around in a van solving mysteries.

Homer and Marge Simpson

The only thing that keeps me from being happily married is my husband.

Andra Douglas

Marriage is the most advanced form of warfare in the modern world.

Malcolm Bradbury

—I'm afraid that after we've been married a while a beautiful girl will come along and you'll forget all about me.
—Don't be silly. I'll write you twice a week.

Groucho Marx

The pain of death is nothing compared to the pain of sharing a coffeepot with a peevish woman.

John Cheever

My husband said he needed more space. So I locked him outside. Roseanne

Never feel remorse for what you have thought about your wife. She has thought much worse things about you.

Jean Rostand

She was a freelance castrator.

James Thurber

The comfortable estate of widowhood is the only hope that keeps up a wife's spirits.

John Gay

Nagging is the repetition of unpalatable truths.

Edith Summerskill

Basically my wife was immature. I'd be at home taking a bath and she'd come in and sink my boats.

Woody Allen

My wife's nagging is like living near the airport. After a while you don't notice it any more.

Tom Arnold

That married couples can live together day after day is one miracle the Vatican has overlooked.

Bill Cosby

After seven years of marriage, I'm sure of two things: first, never wallpaper together; and second, you'll need two bathrooms, both for her.

Dennis Miller

I have often wanted to drown my troubles, but I can't get my wife to go swimming.

Roy Chubby Brown

Marriage is the roughest thing you ever gonna get into. Nelson Mandela, he endured 27 years in prison in South Africa. But once he was out, it only took two years before his marriage busted his ass.

Chris Rock

I was married for two years, which is a long time if you break it down into half-hour segments.

Charisse Savarin

My parents stayed together for 40 years but that was out of spite.

Woody Allen

The best way to remember your wife's birthday is to forget it once. Joseph Cossman

Take my wife – please.

Henny Youngman

At whatever stage you apologize to your wife, the answer is always the same: 'It's too late now.'

Denys Parsons

You can tell a marriage is on the rocks when a couple talk to each other rationally.

Rod Cohen

My wife said, 'Can my mother come down for the weekend?' So I said, 'Why?' And she said, 'Well, she's been up on the roof two weeks already.'

Bob Monkhouse

Some people ask what is the secret of our long marriage. Two times a week, we take time to go to a nice restaurant, candlelight, a little wine, soft music. She goes Tuesdays. I go Fridays.

Henny Youngman

I married beneath me. All women do.

Nancy Astor

When a man brings his wife a gift for no reason, there's a reason.

Molly McGee

Marriage is a wonderful invention; but, then again, so is a bicycle repair kit.

Billy Connolly

For the first year of marriage, I had a bad attitude. I tended to place my wife under a pedestal.

Woody Allen

We sleep in separate rooms, we have dinner apart, we take separate vacations – we're doing everything we can to keep our marriage together.

Rodney Dangerfield

In a marriage, it takes just one to make a quarrel.

Ogden Nash

Never go to bed mad. Stay up and fight.

Phyllis Diller

My wife and I had words – but I never got to use mine.

Carl Gilligan

I screamed a lot, but it was that or firearms.

Roseanne

You can't go by what a girl says when she's giving you hell. It's like Shakespeare. Sounds well but doesn't mean anything.

P.G. Wodehouse

My parents had only one argument in 45 years. It lasted 43 years.

Cathy Ladman

The most difficult year of marriage is the one you're in.

Minnie Peal

When you see a married couple coming down the street, the one who is two or three steps ahead is the one that's mad.

Helen Rowland

The full potentialities of human fury cannot be reached until a friend of both parties tactfully intervenes.

G.K. Chesterton

It was our son that kept our marriage together. Neither of us wanted custody of him.

Roy Chubby Brown

I can't for the life of me understand why people keep insisting that marriage is doomed. All five of mine worked out.

Peter de Vries

What ought to be done to the man who invented the celebrating of anniversaries? Mere killing would be too light.

Mark Twain

Wives are people who think it's against the law not to answer the phone when it rings.

Ring Lardner

This wife-swapping business wasn't such a bad idea. I only hope our wives are hitting it off as well as we are.

Frank Reid

He had married young and kept on marrying, springing from blonde to blonde like the chamois of the Alps leaping from crag to crag.

P.G. Wodehouse

I don't think I'll marry again. I'll just find a woman I hate and give her a house.

Lewis Grizzard

I always say a girl must get married for love – and just keep on getting married until she finds it.

Zsa Zsa Gabor

I remember my brother once saying, 'I'd like to marry Elizabeth Taylor,' and my father said, 'Don't worry, son, your turn will come.'

Spike Milligan

The first time you buy a house you see how pretty the paint is and buy it. The second time you look to see if the basement has termites. It's the same with men.

Lupe Velez

Taking advice about marriage from Elizabeth Taylor is like taking sailing lessons from the captain of the *Titanic*.

Joan Rivers

I had bad luck with both my wives. The first one left me and the second one didn't.

Bob Monkhouse

I got married again last year because my first wife died in a wishing well.

Tony Gerrard

I'd only marry again if I found a man who had 15 million dollars, would sign over half of it to me before marriage, and guarantee he'd be dead within a year.

Bette Davis

I've been married eight times. My marriage licence reads, 'To Whom it May Concern.'

Mickey Rooney

I think every woman's entitled to a middle husband she can forget.

Adela Rogers St Johns

When a divorced man marries a divorced woman, four get into bed.

The Talmud

I married a few people I shouldn't have, but haven't we all?

Mamie Van Doren

FAMILY PLANNING

Somewhere on this globe, every ten seconds, there is a woman giving birth to a child. She must be found and stopped.

Sam Levenson

Let me tell you a terrific story about oral contraception. I asked a girl to sleep with me and she said, 'No.'

Woody Allen

—I have thirteen children. It's not a burden. I love my husband.
—Lady, I love my cigar, but I take it out of my mouth once in a while.

Groucho Marx

Contraceptives should be used on every conceivable occasion.

Spike Milligan

I'm Catholic. When my mother found my diaphragm, I had to tell her it was a bathing cap for my cat.

Lizz Winstead

New coil inserted. Recall Edward II disembowelled at Berkeley Castle.

Sue Limb

Condoms aren't completely safe. A friend of mine was wearing one and got hit by a bus.

Bob Rubin

Why do they make condom packets so hard to open? Is it to give the woman a chance to change her mind?

Jerry Seinfeld

I practise birth control, which is being around my brother's children.

Brett Butler

If men could get pregnant, abortion would be a sacrament.

Florynce Kennedy

When it's us, it's an abortion; when it's a chicken, it's an omelette.

George Carlin

The Jewish position on abortion is that a foetus is a foetus until it gets out of medical school.

Chaim Pflaum

The most common reason for contraceptives being ineffective in developing countries is that men wear condoms on their finger. The most common pitfall with the pill is that men take it instead of women.

United Nations report

There should be a birth control pill for men. It makes more sense to take the bullets out of the gun than to wear a bulletproof vest.

Greg Travis

A friend of mine confused her Valium with her birth control pills. She had 14 kids but didn't give a shit.

Joan Rivers

Even the best birth control method is only effective 99 out of 100 times.
I can't beat those odds! Roz Doyle, *Frasier*

For birth control, I rely on my personality. Milt Able

CHILDREN AND FAMILY

My husband and I are either going to buy a dog or have a child. We can't
decide whether to ruin our carpet or ruin our lives. Rita Rudner

—Imagine a child with my beauty and your brains.
—Yes, but what if the child inherits my beauty and your brains?
Isadora Duncan and George Bernard Shaw

My friends are like, oh, you should have a baby. You'll learn all sorts of
stuff, like how to survive on two hours' sleep. If I want to learn that, I'll
just become a political prisoner. Cathryn Michon

I was asking a friend who has children, 'What if I have a baby and
I dedicate my life to it and it grows up to hate me, and it blames
everything wrong with its life on me.' And she said, 'What do you
mean, if?' Rita Rudner

Pregnancy is incredible. I can't believe you can create a human being
just from the things you have around the house. Shang

Parenthood is a lot easier to get into than out of. Bruce Lansky

I can't have children because I have white couches. Carrie Snow

I do get broody occasionally – like when I'm lying on the couch and
can't reach the remote I think, a kid would be nice right now.
Kathleen Madigan

I'll never have a baby because I'm scared I'll leave it on top of my car.
Lizz Winstead

Humans are the only animals that have children on purpose with the exception of guppies who like to eat theirs.   P.J. O'Rourke

My husband and I have decided to start a family while my parents are still young enough to look after them.   Rita Rudner

Giving away baby clothes and nursery furniture is a major cause of pregnancy.   Esther Selsdon

Oh, what a tangled web we weave when first we practise to conceive.
                Don Herold

I envy kangaroos. The baby crawls out of the womb when it is about two inches long, gets into the pouch, and starts to grow. I'd have a baby if it would mature in my handbag.   Rita Rudner

To enter life by way of the vagina is as good a way as any.   Henry Miller

My sister's expecting a baby, and I don't know if I'm going to be an uncle or an aunt.   Gracie Allen

—What are you hoping it is?
—My husband's.   Roy Chubby Brown

I'm hoping my baby boy is a homosexual because they're so good to their mothers.   Ruth Sansom

By far the most common craving of pregnant women is not to be pregnant.   Phyllis Diller

It's kind of ironic that they caution pregnant women not to drink alcohol in case it harms the baby. If it wasn't for alcohol most women wouldn't be that way.   Rita Rudner

Good work, Mary. We all knew you had it in you.   Dorothy Parker

My wife, God bless her, was in labour for 32 hours, and I was faithful to her the entire time.   Jonathan Katz

I got married and we had a baby nine months and ten seconds later.

Jayne Mansfield

I told my wife I don't want to be there at the birth. I don't see why my evening should be ruined too.

Dennis Wolfberg

For a father, a home birth is preferable. That way you're not missing anything on television.

Jeremy Hardy

I felt like a man trapped in a woman's body. Then I was born.

Chris Bliss

I remember the very first time I ever held my son in my arms as a newborn. Everything else in the universe melted away. There was just a father, a son, and the distant sound of my wife saying, 'If you ever come near me again, I'll drop you with a deer rifle.'

Frasier Crane, *Frasier*

When they first brought the baby in to me I stared inert, and thought, *this* is the author of my pain.

Bessie Breuer

One of my friends told me she was in labour for 36 hours. I don't even want to do anything that feels good for 36 hours.

Rita Rudner

You have this myth, as the father, that if you're there at the birth, you're sharing the birthing experience. Unless you're opening an umbrella up your ass, I don't think so.

Robin Williams

Giving birth is like taking your lower lip and forcing it over your head.

Carol Burnett

To simulate the birth experience, take one car jack, insert into rectum, pump to maximum height and replace with a jack-hammer. And that would be a good birth.

Kathy Lette

If pregnancy were a book, they would cut the last two chapters.

Nora Ephron

I love children – if they're properly cooked.

W.C. Fields

I was a caesarean birth, but you can't really tell, except that every time
I leave the house I go out by the window.
                                                    Steven Wright

My friends keep wanting to show me films of their baby's birth.
No, thanks, but I'll look at the video of the conception, if you have one.
                                                    Garry Shandling

Having a baby is like suddenly getting the world's worst roommate, like
having Janis Joplin with a bad hangover and PMS come to stay with you.
                                                    Anne Lariott

When I got my foster son, he was the cutest little guy I'd ever seen,
but there was always that little voice at the back of my mind going,
'Remember, the saxophone was in the closet after a month.'
                                                    Paula Poundstone

A baby is nothing more than a loud noise at one end and no sense of
responsibility at the other.   Ronald Knox

When I was born I was so surprised that I didn't talk for a year and
a half.   Gracie Allen

I was never my mother's favourite – and I was an only child. Thomas Berger

My mother had morning sickness after I was born.   Rodney Dangerfield

I knew I was an unwanted baby when I saw my that my bath toys were a
toaster and a radio. My parents gave me a rattle that was still attached to
the snake.   Joan Rivers

My father thought I was so ugly he carried around the picture of the kid
who came with his wallet.   Rodney Dangerfield

If your baby is beautiful and perfect, never cries or fusses, sleeps on
schedule and burps on time – you're the grandma.   Theresa Bloomingdale

Becoming a grandmother is great fun because you can use the kid to get
back at your daughter.   Roseanne

Adam and Eve had many advantages, but the principal one was that they escaped teething.
                                                                    Mark Twain

I love children, especially when they cry, because then somebody takes them away.
                                                                    Nancy Mitford

Having children gives your life a purpose. Right now, my purpose is to get some sleep.
                                                                    Reno Goodale

The only thing you have to remember about babies is not to stick your thumb in that soft bit on their heads.
                                                                    Linda Smith

They fuck you up, your mum and dad.
They may not mean to, but they do.
And fill you with the faults they had
And add some extra, just for you.
                                                                    Philip Larkin

My unhealthy affection for my second daughter has waned. I now despise all of my seven children equally.
                                                                    Evelyn Waugh

—Yeah, sure, for you, a baby's all fun and games. For me, it's diaper changes and midnight feedings.
—Doesn't Mom do all that stuff?
—Yeah, but I have to hear about it.
                                                    Homer and Lisa Simpson

I love to go down to the playground and watch all the kiddies jumping and shouting. They don't know I'm firing blanks.
                                                                    Emo Philips

The thing that best defines a child is the total inability to absorb information from anything not plugged in.
                                                                    Bill Cosby

I had dinner with my father last night, and made a classic Freudian slip. I meant to say, 'Please pass the salt,' but it came out, 'You prick, you ruined my childhood.'
                                                                    Jonathan Katz

A successful parent is one who raises a child who grows up and is able to pay for their own psychoanalysis.   Nora Ephron

You know you're a mother when you use your own saliva to clean your child's face, and when your child throws up, you catch it.   Erma Bombeck

A woman knows everything about her children. She knows about dental appointments and football games and best friends and favourite foods and romances and secret fears and hopes and dreams. A man is vaguely aware of some short people living in the house.   Dave Barry

All a child can expect is that its father be present at the conception.
                                                                    Joe Orton

Fatherhood is pretending the present you love most is soap-on-a-rope.
                                                                    Bill Cosby

I come from a typical American family. You know, me, my mother, her third husband, his daughter from a second marriage, my stepsister, her illegitimate son.   Carol Henry

I believe in large families. Everyone should have at least three husbands.

Zsa Zsa Gabor

A family is a unit composed of a man, a woman, children, an occasional animal, and the common cold.   Ogden Nash

—Are you the oldest in the family?
—No, no, my mother and father are much older.   Gracie Allen

Remember, as far as anyone knows, we're a nice normal family.
                                                              Homer Simpson

I never saw my granddad as I was growing up, because he was excellent at hiding.   Harry Hill

My father was a relentlessly self-improving boulangerie owner from Belgium with low-grade narcolepsy and a penchant for buggers. My mother was a fifteen-year-old French prostitute named Chloe with webbed feet. My childhood was typical: summers in Rangoon; luge lessons. In the spring, we'd make meat helmets. **Austin Powers**

When I was a baby, my father used to throw me up in the air and then go and answer the phone. **Rita Rudner**

When I was little, my father used to make me stand in a closet for five minutes without moving. He said it was elevator practice. **Steven Wright**

We used to have fire drill practice in my house. Everyone had their own special duty. My dad had to get the pets, my mom took the jewellery, my brother ran to get help. They told me to save the washer and dryer. **Ellen DeGeneres**

When I was a kid my parents moved a lot. But I always found them. **Rodney Dangerfield**

Everyone had an uncle who tried to steal their nose. **Peter Kay**

My dad was a joker. Whenever I misbehaved, he would bury me in the backyard. Only up to the waist, but you can get real dizzy when all the blood rushes to your head. **Emo Philips**

If murder had been allowed when Dad was in his prime, our home would have been like the last act of *Othello* almost daily. **Nancy Mitford**

Coming from my family, having a happy childhood was as likely as Jeffrey Dahmer being the food critic of the *New York Times*. **Gloria Brinkworth**

The black dog was the only intelligent member of the family. He died a few years later. He was poisoned, and no one will convince me it wasn't suicide. **Hugh Leonard**

If I ever had twins, I'd use one for parts. **Steven Wright**

My mother loved children. She would have given anything if I had been one.

Groucho Marx

Most children threaten at times to run away from home. This is the only thing that keeps many parents going.

Phyllis Diller

I played with my grandfather a lot when I was a kid. He was dead, but my parents had him cremated and put his ashes in my Etch-a-Sketch.

Alan Havey

My family is so dysfunctional that when I looked up the word 'dysfunctional' in the dictionary there was a picture of my mother.

Paulara Hawkins

I like flipping through our family photo albums. It's fun to see what I looked like as a baby, and what my apartment furniture looked like new.

Jeff Shaw

My mother bores everyone with our photo albums. There's even one called 'Pictures We Took Just To Use Up The Rest Of The Film'.

Penelope Lombard

It was on my fifth birthday, my dad put his hand on my shoulder and said, 'Remember, son, if you ever need a helping hand, you'll find one on the end of your arm.'

Sam Levenson

I love my kids. Of course, I'd trade any one of them for a dishwasher.

Roseanne

The quickest way for a parent to get a child's attention is to sit down and look comfortable.

Lane Olinghouse

An advantage of having only one child is that you always know who did it.

Erma Bombeck

If you desire to drain to the dregs the fullest cup of scorn and hatred that a fellow human being can pour out for you, let a young mother hear you call her baby 'it'.

Jerome K. Jerome

I've got two wonderful children – and two out of five ain't bad.

Henny Youngman

I have three children – one of each.

Rodney Dangerfield

Never change diapers in mid-stream.

Don Marquis

When your first baby drops its dummy, you sterilize it. When your second baby drops its dummy, you tell the dog to 'Fetch!'

Bruce Lansky

All babies are supposed to look like me – at both ends.

Winston Churchill

When I was born, my mother looked at me and looked at the afterbirth and screamed, 'Twins!'

Joan Rivers

I was so ugly when I was born, the doctor slapped my mother.

Henny Youngman

Like so many infants of tender years, he presented to the eye the aspect of a mass murderer suffering from an ingrowing toenail.

P.G. Wodehouse

I was so ugly as a kid, when I played in the sand pit, the cat kept covering me up.

Rodney Dangerfield

I have good-looking kids. Thank goodness my wife cheats on me.

Rodney Dangerfield

I can't get past the fact that milk is coming out of my wife's breasts. What once was an entertainment centre has turned into a juice bar.

Paul Reiser

My mother didn't breastfeed me. She said she just liked me as a friend.

Rodney Dangerfield

Kids are great. You can teach them to hate the things you hate and they practically raise themselves nowadays, you know, with the Internet and all.

Homer Simpson

I hate to see women breastfeeding in public. The baby's head obscures your view.

Sean Meo

Out of the mouths of babes – usually when you've got your best suit on.

Geraldine Baxter

Men who have fought in the world's bloodiest of wars are apt to faint at the sight of a truly foul diaper.

Gary Christenson

Warning: remove child before folding.

Instructions on pushchair

Notoriously insensitive to subtle shifts in mood, children will persist in discussing the colour of a recently sighted cement-mixer long after one's own interest in the topic has waned.

Fran Lebowitz

It is not advisable to put your head around your child's door to see if it is asleep. It was.

Faith Hines

Don't buy one of those baby monitors. Babies pretend to be dead. They're bastards and they do it on purpose.

Billy Connolly

What is a home without children? Quiet.

Henny Youngman

Children and zip fasteners do not respond to force. Except occasionally.

Katharine Whitehorn

The child was a keen bed-wetter.

Noël Coward

When I was a kid, I played doctors and nurses with the boy next door and got sued for malpractice.

Phyllis Diller

I didn't get a toy train set like other kids. I got a toy subway instead. You couldn't see anything, but every so often, you'd hear this rumbling noise go by.

Steven Wright

Big sisters are the crabgrass on the lawn of life.

Charlie Brown

Until I was thirteen, I thought my name was 'shut up'. Joe Namath

Most men are secretly still mad at their mothers for throwing out their comic books, which would be very valuable now. Rita Rudner

When I was a kid, we had a quicksand pit in our backyard. I was an only child ... eventually. Steven Wright

Fortunately, my parents were intelligent, enlightened people who accepted me for what I was – a punishment from God. David Steinburg

My mother hated me. Once she took me to an orphanage and told me to mingle. Joan Rivers

My very first day of school, my parents dropped me off at the wrong nursery. I didn't know anyone. And there were lots of trees. Brian Kiley

I told my mom I was gonna run away from home. She said, 'On your marks...' Rodney Dangerfield

My mother never saw the irony in calling me a son of a bitch. Richard Jeni

Ask your child what he wants for dinner only if he's buying. Fran Lebowitz

Kids will eat anything – snot, scabs, soil, earwax, toenail clippings. But not sprouts. Tony Burgess

Toddlers are more likely to eat healthy food if they find it on the floor. Jan Blaustone

In general, my children refuse to eat anything that hasn't danced on television. Erma Bombeck

Little kids in supermarkets buy cereal the way men buy lingerie. They get stuff they have no interest in just to get the prize inside. Jeff Foxworthy

The trouble with children is that they are not returnable. Quentin Crisp

The main purpose of children's parties is to remind you that there are children worse than your own.

Katharine Whitehorn

One time I had to go out, so I asked Woody Allen to watch the children. When I returned less than an hour later, he was throwing his hats and gloves into the fire. The kids were ecstatic. Woody just shrugged and said, 'I ran out of things to do.'

Mia Farrow

The worst sensation I know of is getting up at night and stepping on a toy train.

Kin Hubbard

Children can be horrible – manipulative, aggressive, rude and unfeeling to a point where I often think that, if armed, they would make up the most terrifying fighting force the world has ever seen.

Jill Tweedie

I was there at the first night of J.M. Barrie's play, *Peter Pan*. Oh, for an hour of Herod!

Anthony Hope

My mother was like a sister to me, only we didn't have sex quite so often.

Emo Philips

The real menace in dealing with a five-year-old is that in no time at all you start to sound like a five-year-old.

Jean Kerr

When my kids become wild and unruly, I use a nice safe playpen. When they're finished, I climb out.

Erma Bombeck

Patience and restraint are what parents have when there are witnesses.

Franklin P. Jones

If a child shows himself to be incorrigible, he should be decently and quietly beheaded at the age of twelve lest he grow to maturity, marry and perpetuate his kind.

Don Marquis

Kids are like husbands – they're fine as long as they're someone else's.

Marsha Warfield

Any kid will run any errand for you, if you ask at bedtime.

Red Skelton

Oh, honey, you're not the world's worst mother. What about the freezer lady in Georgia?

Homer Simpson

I remember the time I was kidnapped and they sent a piece of my finger to my father. He asked for more proof.

Rodney Dangerfield

My parents finally realize that I've been kidnapped and they snap into action immediately: they rent out my room.

Woody Allen

You can tell the kids are growing up: their bite marks are higher.

Phyllis Diller

I am fond of all children except boys.

Lewis Carroll

My eight-year-old bought a bicycle with the money he saved by not smoking.

Phyllis Diller

Don't bother discussing sex with small children. They rarely have anything to add.

Fran Lebowitz

I'd say half of all our Lego has been through this kid.

Reese, *Malcolm in the Middle*

I'd like to smack smug parents who say, 'Our three-year-old's reading *Harry Potter*.' Well, my three-year-old's smearing his shit on the fridge door.

Jack Dee

Even when freshly washed and relieved of all obvious confections, children tend to be sticky.

Fran Lebowitz

There are three ways to get something done: do it yourself, hire someone, or forbid your kids to do it.

Mona Crane

If a kid asks where rain comes from, I think a cute thing to tell them is, 'God is crying.' And if they ask why God is crying, another cute thing to tell them is, 'Probably because of something you did.'

Jack Handey

When I was a young child, I had an imaginary friend, and I thought that he went everywhere with me, and that I could talk to him, and he could talk to me, and he could grant me wishes and stuff. And then I grew up – and I stopped going to church.

Jimmy Carr

Any child who is anxious to mow the lawn is too young to do it.

Bob Phillips

Everyone wants to save the earth. No one wants to help Mom dry the dishes.

P.J. O'Rourke

I had a happy childhood. We were poor, but we were shoplifters. Lily Savage

When I was a kid, I had no friends. If I wanted to play on the seesaw, I had to keep running from one end to the other.

Rodney Dangerfield

When I was a girl I had only two friends, and they were imaginary. And they would only play with each other.

Rita Rudner

I was the kid next door's imaginary friend.

Emo Philips

Any man who hates dogs and babies can't be all bad.

Leo Rosten on W.C. Fields

There are only two things that a child will share willingly – communicable diseases and its mother's age.

Benjamin Spock

Money isn't everything, but it sure keeps you in touch with your children.

John Paul Getty

I'm against corporal punishment. Mental torture is much more effective.

Lily Savage

The best way to keep children home is to make the home atmosphere pleasant – and let the air out of their tyres.

Dorothy Parker

One thing they never tell you about child-raising is that for the rest of your life, at the drop of a hat, you are expected to know your child's name and how old he or she is.   Erma Bombeck

Parents are not interested in justice, they are interested in quiet. Bill Cosby

If thine enemy offend thee, give his child a drum.   Fran Lebowitz

I take my children everywhere but they always find their way back home.
Robert Orben

If your parents never had children, chances are you won't either.
Dick Cavett

Yes, I did take money from the kids' piggy banks, but I always left an IOU.   W.C. Fields

My kids always perceived the bathroom as a place where you wait it out until all the groceries are unloaded from the car.   Erma Bombeck

When I was a boy of 14, my father was so ignorant I could hardly stand to have the old man around. But when I got to be 21, I was astonished at how much he had learned in seven years.   Mark Twain

My teenage son is half-man, half-mattress.   Val Valentine

Always be nice to your children because they are the ones who will choose your rest home.   Phyllis Diller

One thing about parents is that no matter what stage your child is in, the parents who have older children always tell you the next stage is worse.
Dave Barry

Adolescence is the stage between puberty and adultery.   Denis Norden

So, you're my daughter's date. Let me warn you – anything happens to my daughter, I've got a .45 and a shovel. I doubt anybody would miss you.   Mel Horowitz, *Clueless*

Teenagers are God's punishment for having sex.

Patrick Murray

If Abraham's son had been a teenager it wouldn't have been a sacrifice.

Scott Spendlove

If you've never seen a real, fully developed look of disgust, tell your son how you conducted yourself when you were a boy.

Elbert Hubbard

My daughter thinks I'm nosy – at least, that's what she wrote in her diary.

Jenny Abrams

Watching your daughter being collected by her date feels like handing over a million-dollar Stradivarius to a gorilla.

Jim Bishop

The worst eternal triangle known is teenager, parent and telephone.

Lavonne Mathison

The only thing I ever said to my parents when I was a teenager was 'Hang up, I got it!'

Carol Leifer

Remember that as a teenager you are in the last stage of your life when you will be happy to hear that the phone is for you.

Fran Lebowitz

I am absolutely certain there is no life on Mars. It's not listed on my teenage daughter's phone bills.

Larry Matthews

—Jack's up in his room planning his future.
—The only thing he's planning is his next wank. Whether he's going to use his left hand or his right.

Ozzy and Sharon Osbourne

You know your kids are growing up when they start asking questions to which there are answers.

John Plomp

There's nothing wrong with teenagers that reasoning with them won't aggravate.

Jean Kerr

Adults are obsolete children.

Doctor Seuss

Never lend your car to anyone to whom you have given birth.

Nora Ephron

No need to worry about teenagers when they're not at home. A national survey revealed that they all go to the same place – 'out' – and they all do the same thing – 'nothing'.

Bruce Lansky

Telling a teenager the facts of life is like giving a fish a bath.

Arnold Glasgow

Saw my mom today. It was all right, she didn't see me.

Margaret Smith

There are few things more satisfying than seeing your children have teenagers of their own.

Doug Larson

The only advantage to being an adult is that you can eat your dessert without having eaten your vegetables.

Lisa Alther

To lose one parent may be regarded as a misfortune; to lose both looks like carelessness.

Oscar Wilde

If I turn into my parents, I'll either be an alcoholic blonde chasing 21-year-old boys, or I'll wind up like my mother.

Chandler Bing, *Friends*

When I looked up my family tree I found out I was the sap.

Rodney Dangerfield

I don't visit my parents often because Delta Airlines won't wait in the yard while I run in.

Margaret Smith

Many people would rather tour a sewer than visit their relatives.

Jane Howard

I took the wife's family out for tea and biscuits. They weren't too happy about having to give blood though.

Les Dawson

You'll have to excuse my mother. She suffered a slight stroke a few years ago which rendered her totally annoying.

Dorothy Zbornak, *The Golden Girls*

When I was a teenager, every Saturday night I'd ask my dad for the car keys and he'd always say the same thing: 'All right, son, but don't lose them, because some day we may get a car.' Yakov Smirnoff

I get along great with my parents. I still talk to them at least once a week. It's the least I can do. I still live in their house. David Corrado

I took my parents back to the airport today. They leave tomorrow.

Margaret Smith

HOME

Home is the place where, when you have to go there, they have to take you in. Robert Frost

Home is where the mortgage is. Billy Connolly

Home is the place where you can scratch any place you itch. David Brenner

What's with the people who put carpeting on the lid of their toilet seat? What are they thinking: 'Gosh, if we have a party, there may not be enough standing room; I'd better carpet the toilet too.' Jerry Seinfeld

All I need is room enough to lay my hat and a few friends. Dorothy Parker

There comes a time in every man's life when he needs his own toilet.

Patrick Süskind

I'm being shown round this house and the realtor says, 'It's got a great view.' And I'm thinking, for the money they're asking, I'd better open up the curtains and see breasts against the window. Garry Shandling

Does that screwdriver really belong to Philip? George Carlin

A friend of mine bought a castle in Scotland. When his daughter had a birthday party, he hired a bouncy council estate.

Harry Hill

The person who owns their own home is always just coming out of a hardware store.

Kin Hubbard

I went to the hardware store and bought some used paint. It was in the shape of a house.

Steven Wright

Our terraced house was so small the mice walked about on their back legs.

Les Dawson

Joe Beamish was knitting a sock in the tiny living-room which smelled in equal proportions of mice, ex-burglars and shag tobacco.

P.G. Wodehouse

I know the room looks small. That's the heavy wallpaper.

Rigsby, *Rising Damp*

An attic is where you store all the junk you'd throw away if you didn't have one.

Herbert Prochnow

I woke up the other morning and found that everything in my room had been replaced by an exact replica.

Steven Wright

I'm a wonderful housekeeper. Every time I get a divorce, I keep the house.

Zsa Zsa Gabor

There are two things we can all live without – haemorrhoids and neighbours.

Spike Milligan

A neighbour is someone who has just run out of something.

Robert Benchley

I went to the store and bought some blank CDs. When I got home, I put one in my CD player and turned it up full blast. I was walking around my house, when I heard a knock at my door. It was my neighbour complaining about the noise. He's a mime.

Steven Wright

The Bible tells us to love our neighbours, and also to love our enemies; probably because they are generally the same people.   G.K. Chesterton

The walls of my apartment are so thin that when my neighbours have sex, I have an orgasm.   Linda Herskovic

Love your neighbour, but don't pull down your hedge.   Benjamin Franklin

Housework is what a woman does that nobody notices unless she hasn't done it.   Evan Esar

Excuse the mess, but we live here.   Roseanne

If your house is really a mess and a stranger comes to the door, greet them with, 'Who could have done this? We have no enemies.'   Phyllis Diller

I hate housework. You make the beds, you do the dishes, and six months later, you have to start all over again.
Joan Rivers

The way I figure it, when my husband comes home from work, if the kids are still alive, I've done my job.   Roseanne

Cleaning your house while the kids are still growing is like shovelling the walk before it stops snowing.   Phyllis Diller

Housework can kill you if done right.   Erma Bombeck

I do clean up sometimes. If I'm expecting company, I'll wipe the lipstick off the milk container.   Elayne Boosler

Three roommates, and still nobody washes a dish in my apartment. Last week I was thirsty and I had to get out my Yahtzee game for a clean cup.
Dobie Maxwell

Have you ever taken anything out of the laundry basket because it
has become, relatively, the cleaner thing?   Katharine Whitehorn

My mother from time to time puts on her wedding dress. Not because
she's sentimental. She just gets really far behind with her laundry.
                                                             Brian Kiley

You know it's time to do the laundry when you dry off with a sneaker.
                                                             Zach Galifianakis

I washed a sock. Then I put it in the dryer. When I took it out, it
was gone.   Ron Schmidt

I'm eighteen years behind on my ironing. There's no use doing it now, it
doesn't fit anyone I know.   Phyllis Diller

My second favourite household chore is ironing, my first being
hitting my head on the top bunk bed until I faint.   Erma Bombeck

I buried a lot of my ironing in the back yard.   Phyllis Diller

Don't spend two dollars to dry-clean a shirt. Donate it to the
Salvation Army instead. They will clean it and put it on a hanger.
Then you can buy it back for seventy-five cents.   Billiam Coronel

As far as I know, a single man has never vacuumed behind a couch.
                                                             Rita Rudner

I would rather lie on a sofa than sweep beneath it.   Shirley Conran

Don't cook. Don't clean. No man will ever make love to a woman
because she waxed the linoleum. 'My God, the floor's immaculate.
Lie down, you hot bitch.'   Joan Rivers

Blood is thicker than water and much more difficult to get out of
the carpet.   Woody Allen

Cleanliness is next to impossible.   Audrey Austin

My mother wrapped the living room furniture in plastic. We practised safe sitting in our household.
                                                            Adam Ferrara

She's incredibly organized. She folds her underwear like origami.
                                                            Linda Barnes

She's not organized. She's insane. She's got a shoebox labelled, 'Pieces of String Too Small to Use.'   Frank Barone, *Everybody Loves Raymond*

Have a place for everything and keep the thing somewhere else. This is not a piece of advice, it is merely a custom.   Mark Twain

I would like to marry a nice, domesticated homosexual guy who has a fetish for wiping down Formica and different vacuum-cleaner attachments.   Jenny Eclair

A guy gets married and the morning after his wedding night, goes into the bathroom and finds a dead horse in the bathtub. He runs out and says, 'Darling, there's a dead horse in the bathtub.' And his wife replies, 'Well, I never said I was neat.'   Walter Matthau

I will clean the house when Sears comes out with a riding vacuum cleaner.   Roseanne

A man with a vacuum cleaner just has to discover exactly what the machine will suck up. Full ashtrays are fun. A gentleman of my acquaintance burned the guts out of three consecutive vacuum cleaners by cleaning out the grate with them. All the same, when vacuuming, one should resist the goldfish bowl.   Joe Bennett

The only thing I've ever been able to figure out about stove cleaning is to move house every couple of years.   P.J. O'Rourke

There is no need to do any housework at all. After the first four years, the dust doesn't get any worse.   Quentin Crisp

If your children write their names in the dust on the furniture, don't let them put the year.   Phyllis Diller

How often does a house need to be cleaned anyway? Just once every girlfriend. After that she can get to know the real you.   P.J. O'Rourke

It was a swell house, with all the modern inconveniences.   Mark Twain

I used to live in a house that ran on static electricity. If you wanted to cook, you had to pull off a sweater real quick.   Steven Wright

My husband and I save pounds each year on household wear and tear by living in a tent in our garden.   Ivy Stokes

You can tell a man isn't handy when he asks the man next door how to get blood off a saw.   Milton Berle

The most popular labour-saving device today is still money.   Joey Adams

The house was full of dry rot. The only reason the building still stood was that the woodworm obligingly held hands.   Daphne Du Maurier

It takes only four men to wallpaper a house, but you have to slice them thinly.   Jo Brand

In painting a ceiling, a good rule of thumb is that there should be at least as much paint on the ceiling as on your hair.   P.J. O'Rourke

If it wasn't for Venetian blinds, it would be curtains for all of us.   Eric Morecambe

I'm moving to Mars next week, so if you have any boxes...   Steven Wright

CHEATING

I can't believe this – both my boyfriends are cheating on me!   Lucy Wilde

They kept mistresses of such dowdiness they might almost have been mistaken for wives.   Robertson Davies

The only way to keep your dick under control is to cut it off. Unfortunately I don't have my nail scissors with me.

Tanya Laslett, *Footballers' Wives*

Husbands are like fires. They go out when unattended.   **Zsa Zsa Gabor**

I wouldn't trust my husband with a young woman for five minutes, and he's been dead for twenty-five years.   **Kathleen Behan**

The worst thing about having a mistress is those two dinners you have to eat.

Oscar Levant

—I've spent enough on you to buy a battleship.
—And you've spent enough *in* me to float one.

King Edward VII and Lillie Langtry

Eighty per cent of married men cheat in America. The rest cheat in Europe.   **Jackie Mason**

I discovered my wife in bed with another man and I was crushed. So I said, 'Get off me, you two.'   **Emo Philips**

I think my husband is having an affair with his secretary, because I would find lipstick on his shirt, covered with white-out.   **Wendy Liebman**

I'm sure Mick Jagger will find someone else to be unfaithful to soon.

Jerry Hall

One husband said he could always tell when his wife was having an affair because the poetry books were suddenly at the horizontal on top of the shelves.   **Jilly Cooper**

The man who marries his mistress creates a vacancy in that position.

James Goldsmith

The world is full of people who are ready to think the worst when they
see a man sneaking out of the wrong bedroom in the middle of the night.

Slappy White

My wife met me at the door wearing a see-through negligée.
Unfortunately, she was just coming home.

Rodney Dangerfield

—How many husbands have you had?
—You mean apart from my own?

Zsa Zsa Gabor

It's easier to shoot your wife than to have to shoot a different man
every week.

Pete Grahame

I've respected your husband for many years, and what's good enough
for him is good enough for me.

Groucho Marx

Robert Benchley and I shared an office that was so tiny, if it were
an inch smaller it would have been adultery.

Dorothy Parker

My mother-in-law broke up my marriage. My wife came home from
work one day and found us in bed together.

Lenny Bruce

I would never be unfaithful to my wife for the simple reason that
I love my house too much.

Bob Monkhouse

I don't believe in extra-marital relationships. I think people should
mate for life, like pigeons and Catholics.

Woody Allen

You know, of course, that the Tasmanians, who never committed
adultery, are now extinct.

Somerset Maugham

Adultery is the application of democracy to love.

H.L. Mencken

There is one thing I would break up over, and that is if she caught me
with another woman. I wouldn't stand for that.

Steve Martin

When a man steals your wife, there is no better revenge than to let him
keep her.

Sacha Guitry

'Why go out for a hamburger when you've got steak at home,' says
Paul Newman about his lovely wife Nanette, and he should know.

Mrs Merton

Gay men look at fidelity differently. It's not called cheating unless
you're actually playing cards.

Scott Thompson

DIVORCE

When I won the golf challenge in South Africa, I asked my wife if she'd
like a designer dress or diamonds as a present, but she said, 'No, I want
a divorce.' I said I wasn't planning on spending that much.

Nick Faldo

Divorce comes from the Latin word *divorcerum* meaning 'to have
your genitals torn out through your wallet'.

Robin Williams

I never even believed in divorce until after I got married.

Diane Ford

It was a very messy divorce because there was a baby involved. Him.

Wendy Liebman

My wife and I pondered whether to take a vacation or get a divorce.
We decided that a trip to Bermuda is over in two weeks, but a divorce
is something you always have.

Woody Allen

Divorce is the sacrament of adultery.

Jean Guichard

Divorce can be seen as the legal alternative to murder.

Jeff Foxworthy

It's tough. After five years of marriage, it's difficult to lose the one with
the good credit rating.

Rich Voss

Honey, I'm going to miss you so much. And it's not just the sex.
It's also the food preparation.

Homer Simpson

I still miss my ex, but my aim is improving.

Woody Woodbury

I'm not upset about my divorce. I'm only upset I'm not a widow.   **Roseanne**

Roseanne went on *Saturday Night Live* and said I had a 3-inch penis. Well, even a 747 looks small if it's landing in the Grand Canyon.
                                                                    Tom Arnold

I never speak about my ex-husbands except under hypnosis.   **Joan Collins**

If you made a list of the reasons why any couple got married, and another list of the reasons for their divorce, you'd have a hell of a lot of overlapping.   **Mignon McLaughlin**

Why do Hollywood divorces cost so much? Because they're worth it.
                                                                 Johnny Carson

Being a divorcee in a small town is a little like playing Monopoly; eventually you land on all the properties.   **John Updike**

When I got divorced, I went through the various stages of grieving – anger, denial, and dancing around my settlement cheque.   **Maura Kennedy**

Saddam Hussein went from living in a palace to a one-bedroom hovel with next to no possessions. Where I come from, we call that divorce.
                                                                Johnnie Casson

Getting divorced just because you don't love a man is almost as silly as getting married just because you do.   **Zsa Zsa Gabor**

My husband and I divorced over religious differences. He thought he was God, and I didn't.   **Vera Foster**

I know what 'custody of the children' means. It means 'get even'.
                                                                  Lenny Bruce

The happiest time of anyone's life is just after the first divorce.
                                                                J.K. Galbraith

Alimony is the screwing you get for the screwing you got.   **Jim Davidson**

When you live by yourself again, it's like, as if by magic, all your annoying habits are gone.

Merrill Markoe

I come from a wealthy divorced family. My mom's wealthy. My dad's divorced.

Pauley Shore

The difference between divorce and legal separation is that a legal separation gives a husband time to hide his money.

Johnny Carson

Conrad Hilton was very generous to me in the divorce settlement. He gave me 5,000 Gideon Bibles.

Zsa Zsa Gabor

A lawyer is never entirely comfortable with a friendly divorce, any more than a good mortician wants to finish his job and then have the patient sit up on the slab.

Jean Kerr

Marriage is but for a little while. It is alimony that is for ever.

Quentin Crisp

My wife got the house, the car, the bank account, and if I marry again and have children, she gets them too.

Woody Allen

Divorce is like being hit by a Mack truck. If you live through it, you start looking very carefully to the right and to the left.

Jean Kerr

I've never been married, but I tell people I'm divorced so they won't think something's wrong with me.

Elayne Boosler

Divorce? Never. Murder? Often!

Sybil Thorndike

My wife and I are getting remarried. Our divorce didn't work out.

Rodney Dangerfield

I never hated a man enough to give his diamonds back.

Zsa Zsa Gabor

FRIENDSHIP

Of all the friends I've ever had, you're the first.   **Bender, *Futurama***

She's my best friend. She thinks I'm too thin, and I think she's a natural blonde.   **Carrie Snow**

Friends are people who borrow books and set wet glasses on them.   **E.A. Robinson**

A friend is someone who will hide you.   **Philip Roth**

Friends help you move. Real friends help you move bodies.   **Milton Berle**

A friend is someone you don't have to talk to any more once the food is on the table.   **Sabrina Matthews**

My mother used to say, there are no strangers, only friends you haven't met yet. She's now in a maximum-security twilight home in Australia.   **Dame Edna Everage**

A true friend is one who stabs you in the front.   **Oscar Wilde**

My true friends have always given me that supreme proof of devotion – a spontaneous aversion to the man I loved.   **Colette**

A friend is someone who will tell you she saw your old boyfriend – and he's a priest.   **Erma Bombeck**

My best friend ran away with my wife, and let me tell you, I miss him.   **Henny Youngman**

Harry Truman said, 'If you want a friend in Washington, get a dog,' but I don't need one because I have Barbara.   **George Bush Sr**

The great thing about befriending recovering alcoholics is that you're never short of a ride home.   **Billy Connolly**

The draft board examiner asked me if I thought I was capable of killing. I told him I wasn't sure about strangers, but friends, certainly.

Oscar Levant

Doc Daneeka was his friend and would do just about nothing in his power to help him.

Joseph Heller

Baldrick, does it have to be this way? Our valued friendship ending with me cutting you into long strips and telling the Prince you walked over a very sharp cattle grid in an extremely heavy hat?

Blackadder III

The lion and the calf shall lie down together, but the calf won't get much sleep.

Woody Allen

If your friend is already dead, and being eaten by vultures, I think it's okay to feed some bits of your friend to one of the vultures, to teach him to do some tricks. But *only* if you are serious about adopting the vulture.

Jack Handey

One sure way to lose another woman's friendship is to try to improve her flower arrangements.

Marcelene Cox

Save, save, oh, save me from the Candid Friend.

George Canning

I prefer acquaintances to friends. They don't expect you to call or go to their children's weddings.

A.A. Gill

Love your enemies, just in case your friends turn out to be a bunch of bastards.

R.A. Dickson

Money can't buy you friends but you get a better class of enemy.

Spike Milligan

A man cannot be too careful in the choice of his enemies.

Oscar Wilde

It is always painful to part from people whom one has known for a very brief space of time. The absence of old friends one can endure with equanimity.

Oscar Wilde

The Bible tells us to forgive our enemies; not our friends.   **Margot Asquith**

There is no spectacle more agreeable than to observe an old friend
fall from a rooftop.   **Confucius**

Whenever a friend succeeds, a little something dies in me.   **Gore Vidal**

Greater love hath no man than this, that he lay down his friends
for his life.   **Jeremy Thorpe**

The proper office of a friend is to side with you when you are in the
wrong. Nearly everybody will side with you when you are in the right.
Mark Twain

He has not an enemy in the world, and none of his friends like him.
Oscar Wilde

I once had a dog who actually believed he was man's best friend. He kept
trying to borrow money from me.   **Gene Perret**

Outside of a dog, a book is a man's best friend. Inside of a dog,
it's too dark to read.   **Groucho Marx**

CHARACTER

He's a self-made man, the living proof of the horrors of unskilled labour.
Ed Wynn

Few great men could pass Personnel.   **Paul Goodman**

I like her from a distance. You know, the way you like the sun.
Maris is like the sun – except without the warmth.   **Frasier Crane**, *Frasier*

As a source of entertainment, conviviality and good fun, she ranks
somewhere between a sprig of parsley and a single ice-skate.
Dorothy Parker

If you don't like my opinion of you, you can always improve.

Ashleigh Brilliant

I am a doormat in a world of boots.

Jean Rhys

If you think you're too small to make an impact, try going to bed with a mosquito in the room.

Betty Reese

Lady Constance looks on me as a sort of cross between a leper and a nosegay of deadly nightshade.

P.G. Wodehouse

One of the worst things in life is not how nasty the nasty people are. You know that already. It is how nasty the nice people can be.

Anthony Powell

W.C. Fields never wanted to hurt anyone. He just felt an obligation.

Gregory LaCava

The Texan turned out to be good-natured, generous and likeable. In three days, no one could stand him.

Joseph Heller

I admire his work, but I couldn't warm to him if I was cremated next to him.

Keith Richards

Not everybody hates me.
Only the people who've met me. Emo Philips

I've had death threats before – well, okay, a petition.

Jack Dee

If you think nobody cares if you're alive or dead, try missing a couple of car payments.

Flip Wilson

Know him? I know him so well that I haven't spoken to him for ten years.

Anon

There's just something I don't like about him. I can't put my finger on it, but if I did, I'd have to wash it.

Dorothy Zbornak, *The Golden Girls*

He's as slippery as an eel that's been rubbed all over with axle-grease.

P.G. Wodehouse

Always acknowledge a fault frankly. This will throw those in authority off their guard and give you opportunity to commit more.   Mark Twain

I could never learn to like her – except on a raft at sea with no other provisions in sight.   Mark Twain

My idea of an agreeable person is a person who agrees with me.

Benjamin Disraeli

Don't say you agree with me. Whenever people agree with me, I always feel I must be wrong.   Oscar Wilde

I could see that, if not actually disgruntled, he was far from gruntled.

P.G. Wodehouse

My veins are filled once a week with a Neapolitan carpet cleaner distilled from the Adriatic and I am bald as an egg. However, I still get around and am mean to cats.   John Cheever

The English instinctively admire any man who has no talent and is modest about it.   James Agate

You have to admire Madonna. She hides her lack of talent so well.

Manolo Blahnik

The only flair is in her nostrils.   Pauline Kael

Do you know how helpless you feel if you have a cupful of coffee in your hand and you start to sneeze?   Jean Kerr

Before they made S.J. Perelman they broke the mould.   Groucho Marx

We are all worms, but I do believe I am a glow-worm.   Winston Churchill

I was going to buy a book called *The Power of Positive Thinking* and then I thought, what the hell good would that do?   Ronnie Shakes

I thought I wasn't gonna make it. Then I started to think positive. Now I'm positive I'm not gonna make it.   Sammy Shaw

Experience is a comb life gives you after you lose your hair.   Judith Stern

Check your neck. You may be a redneck if … you own a home with wheels on it and several cars without; you've worn a tube top to a wedding; your family tree doesn't fork; in tough situations you ask yourself, 'What would Curly do?'   Jeff Foxworthy

Dean Martin could make a plate of cooked spaghetti seem tense.
          Frank Sinatra

I'm as comfortable as a lame turkey sat on a pile of Paxo listening to Christmas carols.   Les Dawson

You're the only man in the world with clenched hair.
          Oscar Madison, *The Odd Couple*

I've tried listening to a relaxation tape. The rain is supposed to calm me down but I keep worrying that I left my car windows down.
          Rose Martin, *The Golden Girls*

My mom is so cautious. I broke a glass on the kitchen floor in 1954, my parents sold the house in 1985, and my mom warns the new owners, 'I think we got all the big pieces, but watch out for slivers.'   Elayne Boosler

—Sir, you try my patience.
—I don't mind if I do. You must come over and try mine some time.
          Groucho Marx

You know you're trailer trash when you allow your 12-year-old daughter to smoke at the dinner table in front of all her kids.   Greta Garbage

I have my standards. They may be low, but I have them.   Bette Midler

Mom said she learned to swim when someone rowed her out in the lake and threw her off the boat. I said, 'Mom, they weren't trying to teach you how to swim.'
Paula Poundstone

I have a really nice step ladder but, sadly, I never knew my real ladder.
Harry Hill

Experience is the name everyone gives to their mistakes.
Oscar Wilde

Patience is the willingness to listen to the other person tell you his troubles before you tell him yours.
Herbert Prochnow

When a person tells you, 'I'll think it over and let you know' – you know.
Olin Miller

If you can keep your head when all about you are losing theirs, it is possible you haven't grasped the gravity of the situation.
Jean Kerr

If there is one thing hypocrites hate, it's hypocrisy.
Jack Rosenthal

If I were two-faced, would I be wearing this one?
Abraham Lincoln

Men are never so serious, thoughtful, and intent, as when they are at stool.
Jonathan Swift

I was so embarrassed I could feel my nerves curling like bacon over a hot fire.
Margaret Halsey

Self-respect is the secure feeling that no one, as yet, is suspicious.
H.L. Mencken

To be positive is to be mistaken at the top of one's voice.
Ambrose Bierce

Few things are harder to put up with than the annoyance of a good example.
Mark Twain

I have the heart of a small boy. I keep it in a jar on my desk.   **Stephen King**

I'm afraid of sharks, but only in a water situation.   **Demetri Martin**

Mothers, food, love and career are the four major guilt groups.
Cathy Guisewite

She's the sort of person who goes through life holding on to the sides.
Alice Thomas Ellis

I discovered I scream the same way whether I'm about to be devoured by a Great White or if a piece of seaweed touches my foot.   **Kevin James**

You don't have to swim faster than the shark, just faster than the guy next to you.   **Peter Benchley**

I'm not afraid of heights but I'm afraid of widths.   **Steven Wright**

I don't think I've ever been to an appointment in my life where I wanted the other guy to show up.   **George Costanza, *Seinfeld***

I used to be indecisive, but now I'm not so sure.   Boscoe Pertwee

A coward dies a hundred deaths, a brave man only once. But then once is enough isn't it?   **Harry Stone**

The most dangerous thing in the world is to leap a chasm in two jumps.
David Lloyd George

He has a heart like a twelve-minute egg.   **Jay McInerney**

I may be middle class, but I'm hard. *Al dente*, you might say.   **Jimmy Carr**

No man in the world has more courage than the man who can stop after eating one peanut.   **Channing Pollock**

He's a very weak-minded fellow and, like the feather pillow, bears the marks of the last person who has sat on him.   Earl Haig

I wish I was as cocksure of anything as Tom Macaulay is of everything.
                                                        Lord Melbourne

It ain't the things you don't know that get you into trouble; it's the things you know for sure which ain't so.   Josh Billings

Confidence is simply that quiet, assured feeling you have before you fall flat on your face.   L. Binder

Nobody knows anything, but I, knowing I know nothing, am the smartest man in the world.   Socrates

He has as much backbone as a chocolate éclair.   Theodore Roosevelt

Ask him the time and he'll tell you how the watch was made.
                                                        Jane Wyman

People in a temper often say a lot of silly things that they really mean.
                                                        Penelope Gilliat

She was heaving gently like a Welsh rarebit about to come to the height of its fever.   P.G. Wodehouse

He never let the sun go down on his wrath, though there were some colourful sunsets while it lasted.   A.A. Thomson

The worst-tempered people I've ever met were people who knew they were wrong.   Wilson Mizner

Infamy, infamy, they've all got it in for me!   Kenneth Williams

His neck looks as if it could dent an axe.   Richard Brautigan

It's innocence when it charms us, ignorance when it doesn't.
                                                        Mignon McLaughlin

She looked as if butter wouldn't melt in her mouth. Or anywhere else.

Elsa Lanchester

My grandmother was a very tough woman. She buried three husbands and two of them were just napping.

Rita Rudner

The meek shall inherit the earth, but not the mineral rights.

John Paul Getty

The meek shall inherit the earth. Serves them right.

Denis Leary

He is a very hard guy, indeed. In fact, the softest thing about him is his front teeth.

Damon Runyon

Aunt Agatha, who eats broken bottles and wears barbed wire next to the skin.

P.G. Wodehouse

I don't have ulcers. I give them.

Harry Cohn

Remember, you're fighting for this woman's honour – which is probably more than she ever did.

Groucho Marx

The louder he talked of his honour, the faster we counted our spoons.

Ralph Waldo Emerson

I don't fit in. I'm like the only one in a nudist colony with a duffel coat.

Victoria Wood

I'm an electric eel in a pond full of flatfish.

Edith Sitwell

He was dull in a new way, and that made many people *think* him great.

Samuel Johnson

VOICE

She had a slow, pleasant voice, like clotted cream made audible.

P.G. Wodehouse

Truman Capote had a voice so high is could be detected only by a bat.

Tennessee Williams

My voice is like playing a trombone underwater.   Al Jolson

He could say the word 'succulent' in such a way that when you
heard it you thought you were biting into a ripe peach.

Georg Christoph Lichtenberg

If Rice Krispies could talk, they would sound like Barbra Streisand.

John Simon

That voice! She sounds as if she thinks a crèche is something that
happens on the M1.   Jeananne Crowley

Ruby Wax talks like a cement mixer from Brooklyn.   David Naughton

Barry Manilow's singing sounds like a bluebottle caught in the curtains.

Jean Rook

Have you heard Brian Sewell, the art critic? I bet even the Queen laughs
at his accent.   Paul Merton

My voice sounds like a mafioso pallbearer.   Sylvester Stallone

He had a voice like water going out of the bath.   Geoffrey Madan

Her voice is quintessentially Radio 4, like someone talking down a
would-be suicide from a high window-ledge.   Anon

She was giving the impression of a hyena which had just heard a good
one from another hyena.   P.G. Wodehouse

I cannot bring myself to vote for Margaret Thatcher, a woman who has been voice-trained to speak to me as though my dog has just died.

Keith Waterhouse

Phyllis Diller has a laugh like an old Chevrolet starting up on a below-freezing morning.

Bob Hope

His voice faded off into a sort of sad whisper, like a mortician asking for a down payment.

Raymond Chandler

She has a voice like ground-up heaven sieved through silk underwear.

Pete Stanton

UPPER CLASS

Gentility is what's left over from rich ancestors after the money is gone.

John Ciardi

When I want a peerage, I shall buy one like any honest man.

Lord Northcliffe

On being told that one of his three pastry chefs would have to be let go because of enforced cost savings, Lord Marmsbury implored, 'May not a man have a biscuit?

Auberon Waugh

How shall we ever know if it's morning if there's no servant to pull up the blinds?

J.M. Barrie

The difference between a man and his valet: they both smoke the same cigars, but only one pays for them.

Robert Frost

The English country gentleman galloping after a fox – the unspeakable in full pursuit of the uneatable.

Oscar Wilde

Fox hunting would be a fine sport, if only the fox had a gun. **W.S. Gilbert**

The butler entered the room, a solemn procession of one. **P.G. Wodehouse**

When I take a gun in hand, the safest place for a pheasant is just opposite the muzzle.   Sydney Smith

Rich kids and poor kids are alike. They both go round huge estates with guns out of their minds on drugs.   Jeremy Hardy

SNOBBERY

I'm not a snob. Ask anybody. Well, anybody who matters.   Simon LeBon

The only thing that sustains one through life is the consciousness of the immense inferiority of everybody else and this is a feeling I have always cultivated.   Oscar Wilde

It's my sister, Violet. She's the one with the Mercedes, swimming pool, and room for a pony.   Hyacinth Bucket, *Keeping Up Appearances*

Never try to keep up with the Joneses. It's much cheaper to drag them down to your level.   Quentin Crisp

—This store is not open to the public.
—I am not the public.   Shopkeeper and Lauren Bacall

The trouble with Michael Heseltine is that he has had to buy all his furniture.   Alan Clark

She deserves a doctor or a lawyer – someone for whom a T-shirt is an undergarment.   Niles Crane, *Frasier*

—When I see a spade, I call it a spade.
—I am glad to say that I have never seen a spade.   Oscar Wilde

The man who would call a spade a spade should be compelled to use one. It is the only thing he is fit for.   Oscar Wilde

You'd eat a worm if I gave it a French name.   Daphne Moon, *Frasier*

I have no concern for the common man except that he should not
be so common.
Angus Wilson

When I agreed to drive you, you didn't say it was on Staten Island.
How the hell am I ever gonna get the stench of landfill and working-class
families out of tropical lightweight wool?
Karen Walker, *Will and Grace*

To Venice for a few days, for a bracing glimpse of the poor.
Auberon Waugh

I hate the poor and look forward eagerly to their extermination.
George Bernard Shaw

—You posted a letter that's only going as far as next door? Why didn't
you just push it through their letterbox?
—Because I like people to know that I use first-class stamps.
Postman and Hyacinth Bucket, *Keeping Up Appearances*

Turn first right after the Picasso.
Jeffrey Archer directing someone to the bathroom, in his London penthouse

People who try to pretend they're superior make it so much harder for
those of us who really are.
Hyacinth Bucket, *Keeping Up Appearances*

You can be in the Horseguards and still be common, dear. Terrence Rattigan

I've just had my TV mended. I say mended – a shifty young man in
plimsolls waggled my aerial and wolfed my Gipsy Creams, but that's
the comprehensive system for you.
Victoria Wood

People who know nothing about cheeses reel away from Camembert,
Roquefort and Stilton because the plebeian proboscis is not equipped
to differentiate between the sordid and the sublime.
Harvey Day

Things taste better in small houses.
Queen Victoria

Among top Africans today, the true status symbol is having a white
chauffeur.
Lord Deedes

EGO

There are two types of people: those who walk into a room and
say, 'Well, here I am,' and those who walk into a room and say,
'Ah, there you are.'   Frederick Collins

—Is your husband religious?
—Oh, yes, he thinks he's God Almighty.   Mrs David Frost

He was a cock who thought the sun had come up to hear him crow.
                                                    George Eliot

In one year, I travelled 450,000 miles by air. That's about twenty times
around the world or once around Howard Consell's head.   Jackie Stewart

In my case, self-absorption is completely justified.   Clifton Webb

Every time I'm wrong, the world makes a little less sense.
                                                    Frasier Crane, *Frasier*

If I only had a little humility, I'd be perfect.   Ted Turner

I've given up reading books. I find it takes my mind off myself.
                                                    H.L. Mencken

She had a blind and uncritical admiration of her own genius in the
blaze of which her sense of humour evaporated like a dewdrop on
a million-watt arc lamp.   Rodney Ackland

Sometimes I just stare at a photograph of me and miss myself.   Larry Sanders

But enough about me, let's talk about you. What do you think of me?
                                                    Bette Midler

There, but for the grace of God, goes God.   Winston Churchill

Mr Whistler always spelt art with a capital 'I'.   Oscar Wilde

—I simply cannot find the words to tell you how superb you were.
—Try.   Claire Trevor and Judith Anderson

Niles, I've got news for you. Copernicus called and you're *not* the centre
of the universe.   Frasier Crane, *Frasier*

I have my faults, but being wrong isn't one of them.

Jimmy Hoffa

My father wanted to be the baby at every christening, the bride at every
wedding, and the corpse at every funeral.   Alice Roosevelt Longworth

He had a genius for backing into the limelight.   Lord Berners

Sherard Blaw arrived, the dramatist who had discovered himself, and
who had given so ungrudgingly of his discovery to the world.   Saki

He has love bites on his mirror.   Kathy Lette

—I only know of two painters in the world – yourself and Velasquez.
—Why drag in Velasquez?   Art-lover and James McNeill Whistler

She's always nice to her inferiors, whenever she can find them.
Dorothy Parker

—Do you think you've learned from your mistakes?
—What mistakes?   Leslie Caron

I like to be introduced as America's foremost actor. It saves the
necessity of further effort.   John Barrymore

An inferiority complex would be a blessing if only the right people had it.
Alan Reed

I question everything I do in the light of what Jesus Christ would
have done.   Jane Fonda

Some of the greatest love affairs I have known involved one actor, unassisted.
                                                                    Wilson Mizner

My chief regret in the theatre is that I could never sit in the audience and watch me.
                                                                    John Barrymore

Pavarotti is not vain, but conscious of being unique.
                                                                    Peter Ustinov

She has an ego like a raging tooth.
                                                                    W.B. Yeats

An egotist is a person of low taste, more interested in himself than in me.
                                                                    Ambrose Bierce

He's a self-made man who worships his creator.
                                                                    William Cowper

If you had to do it all over would you fall in love with yourself again?
                                                    Oscar Levant to George Gershwin

His great dream is to die in his own arms.
                                                                    Irving Rudd

Winston Churchill would make a drum out of the skin of his mother the louder to sing his own praises.
                                                                    David Lloyd George

I'm ready to meet my Maker. Whether my Maker is ready for the ordeal of meeting me is another matter.
                                                                    Winston Churchill

To love oneself is the beginning of a lifelong romance.
                                                                    Oscar Wilde

Modesty is the hope that other people will discover by themselves how wonderful we really are.
                                                                    Aldo Cammarota

Don't be so humble. You're not that great.
                                                                    Golda Meir

The nice thing about egoists is that they don't talk about other people.

                                                                    Lucille S. Harper

MANNERS AND ETIQUETTE

I don't stand on protocol. Just call me Your Excellency.   **Henry Kissinger**

—Oh, Your Excellency.
—You're not so bad yourself.   **Groucho Marx**

Curtsey while you're thinking what to say. It saves time.   **Lewis Carroll**

—Pass the salt.
—And what's the magic word?
—NOW!   **Wednesday and Morticia Addams,** *The Addams Family*

Good breeding consists in concealing how much we think of ourselves and how little we think of the other person.   **Mark Twain**

Etiquette is knowing how to yawn with your mouth closed.
         Herbert Prochnow

Manners are especially the need of the plain. The pretty can get away with anything.   **Evelyn Waugh**

You probably wouldn't worry about what people think of you if you could know how seldom they do.   **Olin Miller**

If your lips are extended beyond your nose then you are about to do something rude.   **Scott Adams**

More people will get out of your way if you say, 'I'm about to puke!' than if you say, 'Excuse me.'   **Sally Berger**

I'm so turned on, I'm even holding in my gas.   **Howard Stern**

The trouble nowadays is that no one stares, however outrageous one's behaviour.   **Quentin Crisp**

Every man likes the smell of his own farts.   **Icelandic proverb**

I had to stop farting because I was losing friends. I don't mean they
didn't want to be my friends any more – I mean I almost killed two
of my friends with my gas.   **John Pinette**

When you have to kill a man, it costs nothing to be polite.
                                                  Winston Churchill

What always staggers me is that when people blow their noses, they
always look into their hankies to see what came out. What do they
expect to find? A silver sixpence?   **Billy Connolly**

Never pick your nose when you're working with superglue.   **Emo Philips**

Vulgarity is simply the conduct of other people.   **Oscar Wilde**

Travelling in non-British ships is preferable as there is none of that
nonsense about women and children first.   **Somerset Maugham**

The English are polite by telling lies. The Americans are polite by telling
the truth.   **Malcolm Bradbury**

To Americans, English manners are far more frightening than none at all.
                                                  Randall Jarrell

The English never speak to anyone unless they have been properly
introduced (except in case of shipwreck).   **Pierre Daninos**

I have always carried a black tie in my bag since I was stranded in
Khartoum in 1945 at the death of Queen Mary.   **Philip Hope-Wallace**

The Japanese have perfected good manners and made them
indistinguishable from rudeness.   **Paul Theroux**

There is no way of making vomiting courteous. You have to do the
next best thing, which is to vomit in such a way that the story you
tell about it later will be amusing.   **P.J. O'Rourke**

'We must do lunch sometime' is the polite euphemism for, 'I don't care
if I never see you again.'

Marcus Hunt

Comedies of manners swiftly become obsolete when there are no
longer any manners.

Noël Coward

Say you're sorry. No one says you have to mean it.

Jeff Green

I made a terrible social gaffe. I went to a Ken and Barbie party dressed
as Klaus Barbie.

Arthur Smith

'Yes, but not in the South,' with slight adjustments will do for any
argument about any place, if not about any person.

Stephen Potter

Beware the conversationalist who adds 'in conclusion'. He is
merely starting afresh.

Robert Morley

If the hostess feels the need to move on, she should say to her guest,
'If you will excuse me, I have to see the housekeeper about some
jellies for the Almshouse.'

Mary Dunn

Take a first right and go along the corridor. You'll see a door marked
Gentlemen, but don't let that deter you.

F.E. Smith

A gentleman never heard the story before.

Austin O'Malley

Gentlemen prefer blondes. Anita Loos

Taboo areas of conversation: the toupees worn by our friends; not
having any credit cards; a fear of ladybirds; being unable to admit that
you have gone right off what everyone thinks is your favourite dish;
never having tried marijuana; the admission that one does not have a
satisfactory sex life; the admission that one does not even particularly
want a satisfactory sex life.

Miles Kington

He was a gentleman who was generally spoken of as having nothing
a-year, paid quarterly.

R.S. Surtees

The etiquette question that troubles so many fastidious people on
New Year's Day is: How am I ever going to face those people again?

Judith Martin

Immigration is the sincerest form of flattery.

Jack Paar

The only infallible rule we know is, that the man who is always
talking about being a gentleman never is one.

R.S. Surtees

When a man opens a car door for his wife, it's either a new car
or a new wife.

Prince Philip

The final test of a gentleman is his respect for those who can be
of no possible service to him.

William Lyon Phelps

A lady is a woman who never shows her underwear unintentionally.

Lilian Day

The difference between tact and politeness: if a man surprises a
naked lady in the bathroom, politeness is to say 'Sorry,' tact is to
say, 'Sorry, *sir*.'

Hermione Bute

Tact is the ability to describe others as they see themselves.

Abraham Lincoln

Being complimented always embarrasses me. I always feel that they
have not said enough.

Mark Twain

Some people pay a compliment as if they expected a receipt.

Kin Hubbard

The truly free man is the one who will turn down an invitation to
dinner without giving an excuse.

Jules Renard

Women are never disarmed by compliments. Men always are.
That is the difference between the two sexes.

Oscar Wilde

Flattery hurts no one – so long as you don't inhale.

Adlai Stevenson

I can live for two months on a good compliment.

Mark Twain

The art of hospitality is to make guests feel at home when you wish they were.

Violet Smart

'Easy come, easy go,' does not apply to houseguests.

Leo Rosten

It was a delightful visit; perfect, in being much too short.

Jane Austen

I said to my mother-in-law, 'My house is your house.' She said, 'Get the hell off my property.'

Joan Rivers

If guests outstay their welcome, try treating them like the rest of the family. If they don't leave then, they never will.

Martin Ragway

Santa Claus has the right idea. Visit people once a year.

Victor Borge

Thank you, Sister. May you be the mother of a Bishop.

Brendan Behan to a nun nursing him on his deathbed

As the cow said to the farmer, 'Thank you for a warm hand on a cold morning.'

John F. Kennedy

Blessed is he who expects no gratitude, for he shall not be disappointed.

W.C. Bennett

Copulation was Marilyn Monroe's uncomplicated way of saying thank you.

Nunnally Johnson

Gratitude is merely a secret hope of further favours.

La Rochefoucauld

ADVICE

No vice is so bad as advice.

Marie Dressler

I always advise people never to give advice.

P.G. Wodehouse

The best advice I was ever given was on my twenty-first birthday when my father said, 'Son, here's a million dollars. Don't lose it.'   **Larry Niven**

When a man comes to me for advice, I find out the kind of advice he wants, and I give it to him.   **Josh Billings**

Advice is what we ask for when we already know the answer but wish we didn't.   **Erica Jong**

Remember: it takes 42 muscles to frown and only 4 to pull the trigger of a decent sniper rifle.   Mitch Henderson

I always pass on good advice. It is the only thing to do with it. It is never of any use to oneself.   **Oscar Wilde**

For sincere advice and the correct time, call any number at random at 3.00 am.   **Steve Martin**

Start off every day with a smile and get it over with.   **W.C. Fields**

Let a smile be your umbrella, and you'll end up with a faceful of rain.   **George Carlin**

Always buy a good pair of shoes and a good bed, because if you're not in one, you're in the other.   **Joan Collins**

Never put off until tomorrow what can be put off until the day after tomorrow.   **Mark Twain**

The good thing about procrastination is that you always have something planned for tomorrow.   **Anon**

Build a man a fire and he'll be warm for a day. Set a man on fire and he'll be warm for the rest of his life.   **Terry Pratchett**

If you can't take the heat, don't tickle the dragon. **Scott Fahlman**

Pissing in his shoe keeps no man warm for long. **Icelandic proverb**

Never do anything in bed that you can't pronounce.
Mitch Murray

Always be wary of any helpful item that weighs less than its operating manual. **Terry Pratchett**

Never be afraid to try something new. Noah was an amateur; the *Titanic* was built by professionals. **James Prentice**

A red port-wine stain on the face can be removed with white wine or lemon. **Vic Reeves**

Always say Benjamin Franklin said it first and people will accept your idea much more readily. **David Comins**

Just remember: it's lonely at the top, when there's no one on the bottom. **Rodney Dangerfield**

'You haven't got the guts to pull that trigger' is almost always a bad thing to say. **Russell Bell**

Never accept a drink from a urologist. **Erma Bombeck**

To be sure of hitting the target, shoot first and call whatever you hit the target. **Ashleigh Brilliant**

Always burn correspondence. Disregard everybody. Faint gracefully. Howsoever interpret John Keats. Learn macramé. Nibble only. Untangle vines. **Edward Gorey**

If you just try long enough and hard enough, you can always manage to boot yourself in the posterior. **A.J. Liebling**

'If you want something done right, you have to do it yourself,' as
O.J. Simpson once told me.   **Anon**

If you can't beat them, arrange to have them beaten.   **George Carlin**

If you've got them by the balls, their hearts and minds will follow.
                                        Military motto, the Green Berets

Two heads are better than one – unless they're on the same body.
                                               Harry Hershfield

I'm reading *Hints From Heloise* and she says that if you put an angora
sweater in the freezer for an hour, it won't shed for the rest of the day.
And I'm thinking, my cat sheds an awful lot.   **Ellen DeGeneres**

Of all the thirty-six alternatives, running away is best.   **Chinese proverb**

Never buy a portable television set in the street from a man who is
out of breath.   **Arnold Glasgow**

Everything is in the hands of man. Therefore wash them often.
                                               Stanislaw J. Lec

If you're going through hell, keep going.   **Winston Churchill**

It's easier to put on slippers than to carpet the whole world.   **Al Franken**

You will always find some Eskimo ready to instruct the Congolese on how to cope with heatwaves. Stanislaw J. Lec

If you want to get rid of somebody, just tell them something for their
own good.   **Kin Hubbard**

When you come to a fork in the road, take it.   **Yogi Berra**

When I asked my accountant if
anything could get me out of the
mess I am in now, he thought for a
long time ... 'Yes,' he said.
'Death would help.'

Robert Morley

There are few problems that cannot be solved through a suitable
application of high explosive.

Merv Price

I am an old man and have known a great many troubles, but most
of them never happened.

Mark Twain

People who live in glass houses might as well answer the door.

Morey Amsterdam

If you cannot get rid of the family skeleton, you may as well
make it dance.

George Bernard Shaw

The eleventh commandment: thou shalt not be found out.

George Whyte-Melville

'Be yourself!' is about the worst advice you can give to some people.

Tom Masson

Always look out for number one and be careful not to step in
number two.

Rodney Dangerfield

Distrust any enterprise that requires new clothes.

Henry David Thoreau

It is useless to hold a person to anything he says while he's in
love, drunk, or running for office.

Shirley MacLaine

If you're going to do something tonight that you'll be sorry for
tomorrow morning ... sleep late.

Henny Youngman

Treat a whore like a lady and a lady like a whore.   Wilson Mizner

It is better to give than to lend, and it costs about the same.   Philip Gibbs

No problem is insoluble given a big enough plastic bag.   Tom Stoppard

Keep cool. It will be all one a hundred years hence.   Ralph Waldo Emerson

It is a mistake to think you can solve any major problem just with potatoes.   Douglas Adams

Solutions are not the answer.   Dan Quayle

There are ways out of everything, apart from Birmingham's one-way system.   Jasper Carrott

I have had more trouble with D.L. Moody than with any other man I ever met.   D.L. Moody

I have problems flown in fresh daily wherever I am.   Richard Lewis

You'll find as you go through life that great depth and smouldering sexuality don't always win, I'm sorry to say.   Woody Allen

Do not take life too seriously. You'll never get out of it alive.   Elbert Hubbard

If you want people to think you're wise, just agree with them.   Leo Rosten

PROFESSION

I am glad to hear you smoke. A man should always have an occupation of some kind.   Oscar Wilde

At the unemployment exchange, my father gave his occupation as an astronaut but not prepared to travel.   Roy Chubby Brown

If the garbage man calls, tell him we don't want any.

Groucho Marx

One of my first office jobs was cleaning the windows on the brown envelopes.

Rita Rudner

My mother is a travel agent for guilt trips.

Ruby Wax

For a long time, I wanted to become a nun. Then I realized that what I really wanted to be was a lesbian.

Mabel Maney

My mother wanted me to become a nun. It's steady work, they supply the uniform, and you're married to God – at least he's home every night.

Dorothy Zbornak, *The Golden Girls*

The easiest job in the world has to be a coroner. Surgery on dead people – what's the worst thing that could happen? Maybe you'd get a pulse.

Dennis Miller

Being an astronomer is a very noble profession, but it does leave you at rather a loose end during the day.

Patrick Moore

I called a temp agency for work and they asked me if I had any phone skills. I said, 'I called you, didn't I?'

Zach Galifianakis

The easiest job I ever had was store detective in a piano shop.

Rainer Hersch

What is it about people who repair shoes that makes them so good at cutting keys?

Harry Hill

With all due respect, it ain't rocket surgery.

Yogi Berra

I had a job selling hearing aids door to door. It wasn't easy, because your best prospects never answered.

Bob Monkhouse

If you really want to hurt your parents and you are not brave enough to become a homosexual, go into the arts.

Kurt Vonnegut

Help wanted: Telepath. You know where to apply. Steven Wright

I don't have a job. I'm still waiting for Bill Gates to reply to my business plan for him to invest in my new pencil sharpening company. Harry Hill

I got a job at an amusement park. I liked to make the rides more terrifying by throwing a couple of screws onto the seats. Emo Philips

Always suspect any job men willingly vacate for women. Jill Tweedie

Let me put it this way, I have an extensive collection of nametags and hairnets. Wayne Campbell, *Wayne's World*

I work for a company that makes deceptively shallow dishes for Chinese restaurants. Woody Allen

People make a living donating to sperm banks. Last year I let $500 slip through my fingers. Robert Schimmel

After I finished school, I took one of those aptitude tests, and based on my verbal score, they suggested I become a mime. Tim Cavanagh

I used to be translator for bad mimes. Steven Wright

At a job interview, tell them you're willing to give 110 per cent – unless the job is statistician. Adam Gropman

I had a secretarial job but I called in sick a lot. I would say I had 'female troubles'. My boss didn't know I meant her. Wendy Liebman

Of course prostitutes have babies. Where do you think traffic wardens come from?

Dave Dutton

Did you ever hear of a kid, while playing, pretend to be an accountant, even if he wanted to be one?

Jackie Mason

Actuaries are about as interesting as the footnotes on a pension plan.

George Pitcher

I used to be the bartender at the Betty Ford Clinic.

Steven Wright

My dad used to say, 'Always fight fire with fire,' which is probably why he was thrown out of the fire brigade.

Harry Hill

A vocation is any badly paid job that someone has taken out of choice.

Mike Barfield

I had a job as an airline pilot. I was fired because I kept locking the keys in the plane. They caught me on an 80-foot stepladder with a coat hanger.

Steven Wright

I've never fired anyone in my life. I had a cleaning lady once I couldn't fire, so I had to move.

Mary Richards, *Rhoda*

Looking for a career in television is like looking for love in the eyes of a Bangkok bargirl. It can only end in tears.

Tony Parsons

I worked on a suicide hotline for a while. Every time I tried to call in sick, my boss would talk me out of it.

Wally Wang

I was ashamed of being a lawyer, so now I manually masturbate caged animals for artificial insemination.

Virginia Smith

Estate agents are people who didn't make it as second-hand car dealers.

Bob Newhart

I would prefer to be a judge than a coal miner because of the absence
of falling coal.   Peter Cook

I used to be a proofreader for a skywriting company.   Steven Wright

I like being President. The pay is good and I can walk to work.
                                                         John F. Kennedy

I used to work at the unemployment office. I really hated that job
because when they fired me, I still had to show up at work the next day.
                                                              Wally Wang

As the mentally unstable become psychiatrists, and the impotent
become pornographers, so writers of thrillers tend to gravitate to
the Secret Service.   Malcolm Muggeridge

Normally when I'm on holiday and I'm asked what I do, I say
that I'm a traffic warden. That makes me much more popular.
                                                      Steve Pound, MP

Wanted: curate for country parish, slow left-arm bowler preferred.
                                                     Advert in *The Times*

I should be working in a job that I have some kind of aptitude for
– like donating sperm to an artificial insemination lab.   Woody Allen

If you can keep your head while those about you are losing theirs, have
you considered becoming a guillotine operator?   Don Geddis

When you go for a job interview, I think a good thing to ask is if they ever press charges.

Jack Handey

The only difference between a pigeon and a farmer today is that a pigeon
can still make a deposit on a tractor.   Mervyn Evans

I remember how me and my family would huddle around the fire
on cold winter evenings, my father fretting about the coming harvest,
my mother consoling him because he was a chartered accountant.

Harry Hill

A secretary is not a toy.

Frank Loesser

A good rule of thumb is if you've made it to 35 and your job still
requires you to wear a nametag, you've probably made a serious
vocational error.

Dennis Miller

Diamonds is my career.

Mae West

A man was mugged and lay bleeding to death by the side of the road.
A social worker passed by and said, 'Tell me the name of the person
who did this to you. He needs help immediately.'

Murray Watts

Interviewing a tree surgeon on his television quiz show *You Bet Your
Life*, Groucho Marx asked: 'Tell me, doctor, did you ever fall out of
a patient?'

Bill Jenks

The longer the title, the less important the job.

George McGovern

Don't tell my mother I work in an advertising agency. She thinks
I play the piano in a whorehouse.

Jacques Seguela

As repressed sadists are supposed to become policemen or butchers,
so those with an irrational fear of life become publishers.   **Cyril Connolly**

I used to sell furniture for a living. The trouble was, it was my own.

Les Dawson

WORK

Every morning I get up and look through the Forbes list of the richest people in America. If I'm not there, I go to work.   **Robert Orben**

Work is the refuge of those who have nothing better to do.   **Oscar Wilde**

Work is the curse of the drinking classes.   **Oscar Wilde**

I don't like work even when someone else does it.   **Mark Twain**

They were a people so primitive they did not know how to get money except by working for it. Joseph Addison

I'm so against working, I won't even take a blow job.   **Gretchen Cole**

Never work before breakfast. If you have to work before breakfast, eat your breakfast first.   **Josh Billings**

If you really want something in this life, you have to work for it. Now, quiet! They're about to announce the lottery numbers...   **Homer Simpson**

All I ever wanted was an honest week's pay for an honest day's work.   **Sergeant Bilko**

I'm as busy as a one-armed taxi-driver with crabs.   **Sir Les Patterson**

I'm busier than a whore working two beds.   **Lily Savage**

In the days when I went to work, I never once knew what I was doing. These days, I never work. Work does age one so.   **Quentin Crisp**

A job is death without the dignity.   **Brendan Behan**

There's not a single job in this town. There's nothin', nada, zip. Unless you wanna work forty hours a week.

Jeff Daniels

I used to work at the International House of Pancakes. It was a dream, and I made it happen.

Paula Poundstone

A foolproof plan for not getting a job – show up for your interview wearing flip-flops.

Alan Davies

Sexual harassment at work: is it a problem for the self-employed? Victoria Wood

When you go to work, if your name is on the building, you're rich. If your name is on your desk, you're middle class. And if your name is on your shirt, you're poor.

Rich Hall

Not everyone works in an office, including those who work in an office.

Jim Davidson

People don't think of their office as a workplace any more. They think of it as a stationery store with Danish. You want to get your pastry, your envelopes, your supplies, your toilet paper, six cups of coffee, and you go home.

Jerry Seinfeld

A survey has shown that two out of three women have had sex with someone in their office. I can't even get the toner cartridge to go in the copier.

Jay Leno

Accomplishing the impossible means only that the boss will add it to your regular duties.

Doug Larson

I wish my son would learn a trade. At least we'd know what kind of work he's out of.

Henny Youngman

After you get a job and before you have to do it. Nothing beats that.

Jerry Seinfeld

You don't have to be mad to work here – but it helps.   **Anon**

Excuse me for not turning up to work today, I'll be stalking my previous boss, who fired me for not showing up for work, okay?   **Anon**

I work for myself, which is fun. Except when I call in sick, I know I'm lying.   **Rita Rudner**

I only use my sick days for hangovers and soap opera weddings.
                    Kate O'Brien

He did nothing in particular, and did it very well.   **W.S. Gilbert**

—Bubble, what do you do?
—I don't know. Get paid.   **Edina Monsoon and Bubble, *Absolutely Fabulous***

My son has taken up meditation. At least it's better than sitting and doing nothing.   **Max Kauffmann**

Anyone can do any amount of work provided it isn't the work he is supposed to be doing at the moment.   **Robert Benchley**

Most people like hard work, particularly when they're paying for it.
                    Elbert Hubbard

I like work; it fascinates me; I can sit and look at it for hours.
                    Jerome K. Jerome

Hard work never killed anybody, but I figure why take the chance?   **Edgar Bergen**

I have long been of the opinion that if work were such a splendid thing the rich would have kept more of it for themselves.   **Bruce Grocott**

Set me anything to do as a task, and it is inconceivable the desire I have to do something else.   **George Bernard Shaw**

I do most of my work sitting down; that's where I shine.   **Robert Benchley**

Nothing makes a person more productive than the last minute.   **Anon**

Working for Warner Bros is like fucking a porcupine – it's a hundred pricks against one.   **Wilson Mizner**

By working faithfully eight hours a day, you may eventually get to be a boss and work twelve hours a day.   **Robert Frost**

The only way to enjoy life is to work. Work is much more fun than fun.   **Noël Coward**

Nobody works as hard for their money as the person who marries it.   **Elbert Hubbard**

Nothing is really work unless you would rather be doing something else.   **J.M. Barrie**

So much of what we call management consists in making it difficult for people to work.   **Peter Drucker**

The trouble with the rat-race is that even if you win, you're still a rat.   **Lily Tomlin**

—What a day I've had! I've been at work ever since I left here this morning.
—You want some lunch?   **Edina and Saffy Monsoon,** *Absolutely Fabulous*

The trouble with unemployment is that the minute you wake up in the morning, you're on the job.   Slappy White

SUCCESS AND FAILURE

My formula for success is rise early, work late, and strike oil. **Paul Getty**

The secret of success is sincerity. If you can fake that, you've got it made.
George Burns

Success is the reward of anyone who looks for trouble. **Walter Winchell**

I have been a success: for sixty years I have eaten, and have avoided being eaten. **Logan Pearsall Smith**

Success to me is having ten honeydew melons, and eating only the top half of each one. **Barbra Streisand**

My formula for success is dress British, look Irish, think Jewish.
Murray Koffler

Success is the one unpardonable sin against our fellows. **Ambrose Bierce**

Behind every successful man stands a woman. And behind her stands his wife. **Fay Weldon**

It doesn't matter whether you win or lose. What matters is whether *I* win or lose. **Darrin Weinburg**

I couldn't wait for success, so I went ahead without it. **Jonathan Winters**

Success means having to worry about every damn thing in the world, except money. **Johnny Cash**

If at first you don't succeed, don't take up skydiving. **Anon**

Coulda, shoulda, woulda – didn't. **Fran Drescher**

Be nice to people on your way up, because you'll meet them on your way down. **Wilson Mizner**

Dear Randolph, utterly unspoiled by failure.   Noël Coward

If we don't succeed, we run the risk of failure.   Dan Quayle

I haven't failed. I've just found ten thousand ways that don't work.
                                                              Thomas Edison

Failure is the only thing I've ever been a success at.   Bob Hope

If at first you don't succeed, find out if the loser gets anything.   Bill Lyon

No matter how great your triumphs or how tragic your defeats remember that approximately one billion Chinese people couldn't care less.

Abraham Lazlo

He was as successful as a celluloid dog chasing an asbestos cat
through hell.   Elbert Hubbard

Winning is only important in war and surgery.   Al McGuire

The sooner we get rid of losing, the happier everyone will be.
                                                              Philip Roth

Nothing is impossible for the man who doesn't have to do it himself.
                                                              A.H. Weiler

Eighty per cent of success is showing up.   Woody Allen

If at first you don't succeed, try, try again. Then quit. No use being a
damn fool about it.   W.C. Fields

Success didn't spoil me; I've always been insufferable.   Fran Lebowitz

You write a hit the same way you write a flop.   Alan J. Lerner

It is not enough to succeed. Others must fail.   Gore Vidal

I'm such a failure. I became a kamikaze pilot, but I kept landing.
                                                                  Jenny Abrams

If at first you don't succeed – you're fired.   Jean Graman

I never climbed any ladder: I have achieved eminence by sheer
gravitation.   George Bernard Shaw

He rose without trace.   Kitty Muggeridge

If at first you don't succeed, failure might be your style.   Quentin Crisp

Trying is the first step to failure.   Homer Simpson

If at first you don't succeed, you're not the only son.   Stephen Fry

If at first you don't succeed, cheat.   Red Buttons

If at first you don't succeed, reload and try again.   Scott Adams

When all else fails, there's always self-delusion.   Conan O'Brien

We didn't lose the game. We just ran out of time.   Vince Lombardi

AWARDS

The Oscars are two hours of sparkling entertainment packed into
a four-hour show.   Johnny Carson

I'm going to Iowa to collect an award. Then I'm appearing at Carnegie
Hall, it's sold out. Then I'm sailing to France to pick up an honour from
the French government. I'd give it all up for one erection.   Groucho Marx

I can't see the sense in making me a Commander of the British Empire. They might as well make me a Commander of Milton Keynes – at least that exists.

Spike Milligan

Oscar night at my house is known as Passover.

Bob Hope

The only great acting we see nowadays is from the losing nominees on Oscar Night.

Will Rogers

I thought I might win the Oscar for *The Apartment* but then Elizabeth Taylor had her tracheotomy.

Shirley MacLaine

I don't deserve this award, but I have arthritis, and I don't deserve that either.

Jack Benny

I didn't show up at the awards ceremony to collect any of my first three Oscars. One time, I went fishing; another time, there was a war on; and on the last occasion, I remember, I was suddenly taken drunk.

John Ford

The good thing about winning an Oscar is that if you forget to rewind, Blockbuster generally look the other way.

David Letterman

Two Americans have been awarded the Nobel Prize for Economics. They are the first to figure out all the charges on their phone bill.

Jay Leno

At the Grammy Awards, Keith Richards became the first performer ever to accept a posthumous award in person.

Jay Leno

If I'd known I was going to win a BAFTA, I would have bleached my moustache.

Eileen McCallum

Who needs awards? Best Fascist Dictator: Adolf Hitler.

Woody Allen

The prize I value most I won sixty years ago. I was named the girl
with the cleanest fingernails.   Beryl Bainbridge

I never accepted a knighthood because to be me is honour enough.
                                        George Bernard Shaw

The winner of the Westminster Dog Show gets to drink champagne –
out of the toilet.   David Letterman

Not only should you never accept a prize, you should try not to
deserve one either.   Jean Cocteau

To refuse awards is another way of accepting them with more noise
than is normal.   Peter Ustinov

Awards are like haemorrhoids; sooner or later, every asshole gets one.
                                        Frederic Raphael

I'd kill for a Nobel Peace Prize.   Steven Wright

SPORT AND LEISURE

SPORT

Sports are dangerous and tiring activities performed by people with whom I share nothing in common except the right to trial by jury.

Fran Lebowitz

I hate all sports as rabidly as a person who likes sports hates common sense.

H.L. Mencken

Games are the last resort of those who do not know how to idle.

Robert Lynd

Serious sport is war minus the shooting.

George Orwell

Son, when you participate in sporting events, it's not whether you win or lose, it's how drunk you get.

Homer Simpson

Football is not a matter of life and death. It's far more serious than that.

Bill Shankly

The English football team – brilliant on paper, shit on grass.

Arthur Smith

Come on you blue two-tone hoops with red and white trim and a little emblem on the sleeve and the manufacturer's logo and the sponsor's name across the chest.

Mike Ticher

Premier League football is a multi-million-pound industry with the aroma of a blocked toilet and the principles of a knocking shop.

Michael Parkinson

Well, either side could win, or it could be a draw.

Ron Atkinson

I never make predictions, and I never will.

Paul Gascoigne

The manager still has a fresh pair of legs up his sleeve.

John Greig

Steve McCahill has limped off with a badly cut forehead.

Tom Ferrie

Luke Chadwick is proving he's a good footballer. He's no David
Beckham, but then again, not many players are.   **Tim Flowers**

If that had gone in it would have been a goal.   **David Coleman**

I think the action replay showed it to be worse than it actually was.
                                                        Ron Atkinson

The sending off? Well, Jason McAteer would annoy anyone.   **Dave Jones**

In 1971, I was sent off the football field for arguing with one of my
own team-mates.   **George Best**

On the Richter scale, this defeat was a force eight gale.   **John Lyall**

I never comment on referees and I'm not going to break the habit of a
lifetime for that prat.   **Ron Atkinson**

There are only two types of manager. Those who've just been sacked and
those who are going to be sacked.   **Ben Philip**

The entire contents of the Manchester City trophy room have been
stolen. Police are looking for a man carrying a light blue carpet.
                                                        Bernard Manning

In 1978, in between Manchester City winning one game and their next
win, there had been three Popes.   **Frank Skinner**

You'd think if any team could put up a decent wall, it would be China.
                                                        Terry Venables

If Everton were playing down at the bottom of my garden, I'd draw
the curtains.   **Bill Shankly**

The first time I went skiing I wasn't very good, and broke a leg.
Luckily, it wasn't one of mine.   **Michael Green**

Luge strategy? Lie flat and try not to die.   **Tim Steeves**

Skiing? I do not participate in any sport that has ambulances at the
bottom of the hill.   Erma Bombeck

When middle-class people and women started going to matches,
I thought it's a shame that hooliganism has stopped because that
used to keep them out.   Frank Skinner

Footballers are miry gladiators whose sole purpose in life is to position
a surrogate human head between two poles.   Elizabeth Hogg

I resigned as coach because of illness and fatigue. The fans were sick
and tired of me.   John Ralston

Skiing combines outdoor fun with knocking down trees with your face.
                                                        Dave Barry

Stretch pants – the garment that made skiing a spectator sport.   Anon

The only interesting part of skiing is seeing someone crash. Violently.
                                                        Denis Leary

If you ever see any blacks or Mexicans on top of a snow-capped
mountain, call 911. There's been a plane accident.   Paul Rodriguez

Snowboarding is an activity that is very popular with people who
do not feel that regular skiing is lethal enough.   Dave Barry

The luge is what I would call the ultimate laxative. Otto Jelinek

My favourite sport in the Olympics is the one in which you make
your way through the snow, you stop, you shoot a gun, and then
you continue on. In most of the world it is known as the biathlon,
except in New York City, where it is known as winter. Michael Ventre

It is impossible to look cool in a go-kart.   Conan O'Brien

I don't think the discus will ever attract any interest until they let them
start throwing them at each other.   Al Oerter

Beer and rugby are more or less synonymous.   Chris Laidlaw

Once rugby players have succeeded in getting their boots on the right
feet, the mental challenge of the game is largely over.   Derek Robinson

If you think squash is a competitive activity, try flower arrangement.
                                                             Alan Bennett

I went to a fight the other night and an ice hockey game broke out.
                                                       Rodney Dangerfield

Red ice sells hockey tickets.   Bob Stewart

Our team lives hockey, it dreams hockey, it eats hockey. Now if it could only play hockey.   Milton Berle

—I could have been a pretty good ice hockey player. I was big, tough,
and I had good hand-eye co-ordination.
—Yeah, but eventually you would've had to let go of the side.
                            Robert and Ray Barone, *Everybody Loves Raymond*

Jews aren't athletes. I love hockey, but if you see a Jew on ice,
he's in the morgue.   Brad Garrett

American football combines the two worst features of American life.
It is violence punctuated by committee meetings.   George F. Will

If a man watches three American football games in a row, he should
be declared legally dead.   Erma Bombeck

90 per cent of this game is half mental.   Yogi Berra

No one is more serious about his game than a weekend tennis player.
                                                           Jimmy Cannon

An otherwise happily married couple may turn a mixed doubles game into a scene from *Who's Afraid of Virginia Woolf*. Rod Laver

'What about apologizing?' my tennis partner said. 'Shall we do it after every stroke, or at the end of each game, or never? I get so tired of saying, "Sorry".' A.A. Milne

I don't want to sound paranoid, but that electronic line judge knows who I am. John McEnroe

Golf balls are attracted to water as unerringly as the eye of a middle-aged man to a female bosom. Michael Green

The worst thing I ever said to a tennis umpire was: 'Are you sure?' Rod Laver

—I can't play tennis. My plastic surgeon doesn't want me doing any activity where balls fly at my nose.
—Well, there goes your social life. Amber Mariens and Dionne Davenport, *Clueless*

I play Cinderella tennis, that is, I don't quite get to the ball. Larry Adler

The depressing thing about tennis is that no matter how good I get, I'll never be as good as a wall. Mitch Hedberg

Torvill and Dean were very good on the ice, but you get them out on the street – they're all over the place. Harry Hill

I was thrown out of the ice skating rink today. Apparently they don't allow ice fishing. Kevin Nealon

If you watch a game, it's fun. If you play at it, it's recreation. If you work at it, it's golf. Bob Hope

Anybody can win, unless there happens to be a second entry.   George Ade

Triple jump is only jumping into a sandpit.   Jonathan Edwards

Playing golf is like going to a strip joint. Eighteen holes later, you're
tired and frustrated, and most of your balls are missing.   Tim Allen

For me, the worst part of playing golf has always been hitting the ball.
                                                               Dave Barry

I've got a feeling for the game of golf. I did very well on the course in
Skegness, until I got stuck in one of the little wooden windmills.
                                                      Rigsby, *Rising Damp*

A caddie is someone who accompanies a golfer and didn't seen the
ball either.   Anon

When I play golf, I don't rent a cart. I don't need one. When I hit
the ball, I need public transport.   Gene Perret

Watching Sam Snead practise hitting a golf ball is like watching a
fish practise swimming.   John Schlee

Anyone who would pass up an opportunity to see Sam Snead swing a
golf club at a golf ball would pull down the shades when driving past
the Taj Mahal.   Jim Murray

Be funny on the golf course? Do I kid my best friend's mother about
her heart condition?   Phil Silvers

The secret of missing a tree is to aim straight at it.   Michael Green

Is my friend in the bunker or is the bastard on the green?   David Feherty

A hole-in-one is an occurrence in which a ball is hit directly from the
tee into the hole on a single shot by a golfer playing alone.   Roy McKie

Golf is a good walk spoiled.   Mark Twain

The least thing upsets him in the links. He missed short putts because of the uproar of the butterflies in the adjoining meadows.   P.G. Wodehouse

When you are putting well, you are a good putter; when your opponent is putting well, he has a good putter.   John D. Sheridan

While playing golf today, I hit two good balls. I stepped on a rake.
     Henny Youngman

My golf practice is coming on. I can put seven into the downstairs lav from the landing.   Rigsby, *Rising Damp*

—I have this extraordinary golf ball. If it goes into the rough, it sends out a radio bleep. If it falls into the water, it rises to the surface, and it glows in the dark.
—Amazing. Where did you get it?
—I found it.   Anon

If I had to choose between my wife and my putter – I'd miss her.
     Gary Player

Anyone can be a golf commentator. You just have to use that voice you put on when you call in sick at work. 'I won't be coming in to work today, I've got to give a golf commentary.'   Mike Rowe

You can make a lot of money out of golf. Ask any of my ex-wives.
     Lee Trevino

Golf is the loneliest of all games, not excluding postal chess.
     Peter Dobereiner

Golf is an expensive way of playing marbles.   G.K. Chesterton

To me, golf is something you did with your hands while you talked. Unless you smoked. Then you never had to leave the clubhouse.
     Erma Bombeck

Golf is not a sport; it's a career move.   Rachel Bradley, *Cold Feet*

—What's your handicap?
—I'm a coloured, one-eyed Jew – do I need anything else?

Sammy Davis Jnr

Golf is an ineffectual attempt to direct an uncontrollable sphere into an inaccessible hole with instruments ill-adapted to the purpose.

Winston Churchill

I refuse to play golf with Errol Flynn. If I want to play with a prick, I'll play with my own.

W.C. Fields

Give me my golf clubs, fresh air and a beautiful partner, and you can keep my golf clubs and the fresh air.

Jack Benny

If you think it's difficult to meet new people, try picking up the wrong golf ball.

Jack Lemmon

Show me a man who is a good loser, and I'll show you a man who is playing golf with his boss. Jim Murray

It's good sportsmanship not to pick up lost balls while they are still rolling.

Mark Twain

The difference between golf and government is that in golf you can't improve your lie.

George Deukmajian

Seve Ballesteros hits the ball further than I go on my holidays. **Lee Trevino**

He enjoys that perfect peace, that peace that beyond all understanding, which comes at its maximum only to the man who has given up golf.

P.G. Wodehouse

Playing polo is like trying to play golf during an earthquake.

Sylvester Stallone

You never see a fish on the wall with its mouth shut.   Sally Berger

My mom has been nagging my father to take up a sport, so he took
up bird-watching. He's very serious about it. He bought binoculars.
And a bird.   Rita Rudner

Give a man a fish and he eats for a day. Teach him to fish and you
get rid of him for the entire weekend.   Zenna Schaffer

Fishing is something between a sport and a religion.
Josephine Tey

There's a fine line between fishing and just standing on the shore looking
like an idiot.   Steven Wright

Good fishing is just a matter of timing. You have to get there yesterday.
Milton Berle

Fishing is a jerk on one end of the line waiting for a jerk on the
other end of the line.   Michael Palin

Dr Strabismus of Utrecht is carrying out research work with a view
to crossing salmon with mosquitoes. He says it will mean a bite
every time for fishermen.   J.C. Morton

Losing the Super Bowl is worse than death. With death, you don't
have to get up next morning.   George Allen

Practically every game played internationally today was invented in
Britain, and when foreigners became good enough to match or even
defeat the British, the British quickly invented a new game.
Peter Ustinov

Karate is a form of martial arts in which people who have had years
and years of training can, using only their hands and feet, make some
of the worst movies in the history of the world.   Dave Barry

Show me a good sport and I'll show you a player I'm looking to trade.

Leo Durocher

Auto racing is boring except when a car is going at least 172 miles per hour upside down.

Dave Barry

Cornering is like bringing a woman to a climax.

Jackie Stewart

The racing car in front is absolutely unique, except for the racing car behind which is absolutely identical.

Murray Walker

The biggest mistake I ever made at the Monte Carlo Rally was to let my wife go shopping by herself.

Mario Andretti

Never bet on the white guy – that's all I know when it comes to boxing.

Lt Frank Drebin, *Naked Gun*

To me, boxing is like ballet, except there's no music, no choreography, and the dancers hit each other.

Jack Handey

Boxing is a lot of white men watching two black men beat each other up.

Muhammad Ali

I got into the ring with Muhammad Ali once and I had him worried for a while. He thought he'd killed me.

Tommy Cooper

My toughest fight was with my first wife.

Muhammad Ali

I'd like to borrow Muhammad Ali's body for just 48 hours. There are three guys I'd like to beat up and four women I'd like to make love to.

Jim Murray

Mike Tyson brought the evening to a premature close by snacking on the ears of Evander Holyfield. The rules of boxing are quite clear on this: fighters are not allowed to eat each other.

Giles Smith

When Mike Tyson gets mad, you don't need a referee, you need a priest.

Jim Murray

Ocean racing is like standing under a cold shower in a howling gale
tearing up twenty-pound notes.

Edward Heath

To own a racehorse is the equivalent of burning a yacht on the front
lawn every year.

Adam Nicholson

John McCririck looks like a hedge dragged through a man backwards.

Clive James

My horse was in the lead, coming down the home stretch, but the
caddie fell off.

Sam Goldwyn

Bill Shoemaker didn't ride a horse, he joined them. Most riders beat
horses as if they were guards in slave-labour camps. Shoe treated them
as if he were asking them to dance.

Jim Murray

If horse racing is the sport of kings, then drag racing must be the
sport of queens.

Bert R. Sugar

Snooker is just chess with balls.

Clive James

The miss on the red will go straight out of my head as soon as I collect
my pension book.

John Parrott

I took an American friend to watch her first ever game of cricket.
She took one look at the umpires and said, 'What are the butchers for?'

Alan Henderson

I watched a cricket match for three hours waiting for it to start.

Groucho Marx

Cricket is basically baseball on Valium.

Robin Williams

Personally, I have always looked on cricket as organized loafing.

William Temple

My definition of a foreigner is someone who doesn't understand cricket.
Anthony Couch

If the French noblesse had been capable of playing cricket with their peasants, their chateaux would never have been burnt. **George Trevelyan**

I am to cricket what Dame Sybil Thorndike is to non-ferrous welding.
Frank Muir

England is not ruined because sinewy brown men from a distant colony sometimes hit a ball further and oftener than we do. **J.B. Priestley**

Facing a fast bowler is like standing in the outside lane of the M1, and when a car is 22 yards away, try to get out of the way. **Alec Stewart**

A loving wife is better than making 50 at cricket or even 99; beyond that I will not go. **James Barrie**

The last positive thing England did for cricket was invent it. **Ian Chappell**

Baseball is like watching grass – no, Astroturf, grow. **Jeff Jarvis**

You know what I love best about baseball? The pine tar, the resin, the grass, the dirt – and that's just in the hot-dogs. **David Letterman**

Hating the New York Yankees is as American as apple pie, unwed mothers and cheating on your income tax. **Mike Royko**

A friend got me seats to the World Series. From where I sat, the game was just a rumour. **Henny Youngman**

I was watching what I thought was sumo wrestling on the television for two hours before I realized it was darts. **Hattie Hayridge**

I failed to make the chess team because of my height. **Woody Allen**

I had lunch with a chess champion the other day. I knew he was a chess champion because it took him 20 minutes to pass the salt.　　Eric Sykes

Chess is as elaborate a waste of human intelligence as you could find outside an advertising agency.　　Raymond Chandler

When I was four years old, I played chess against ten people all at once – blindfolded. I lost every game.　　Robert Benchley

Chess is seldom found above the upper-middle class. It's too hard.
　　Paul Fussell

The hardest thing about climbing Mount Everest was pissing through six inches of clothing with a three-inch penis.　　Unnamed climber

I climbed Mount Everest – from the inside.　　Spike Milligan

Climb every mountain, ford every burn,
Suffer a thrombosis, end up in an urn.　　Arthur Marshall

I'm afraid I play no outdoor games at all, except dominoes. I have sometimes played dominoes outside a French café.　　Oscar Wilde

I used to think the only use for sport was to give small boys something to kick besides me.　　Katharine Whitehorn

I know that you learned how to play bridge only yesterday, but what *time* yesterday?　　George S. Kaufman

You don't run 26 miles at five minutes a mile on good looks and a secret recipe.　　Frank Shorter

To describe the agony of a marathon to somebody who's never run it is like trying to explain colour to a person who was born blind.
　　Jerome Drayton

If you want to know what you'll look like in ten years, look in the mirror after you've run a marathon.　　Jeff Scaff

I am still looking for a pair of training shoes that will make running on streets seem like running barefoot across the bosoms of maidens.

Dave Brosnan

Cross-country skiing is great if you live in a small country. **Steven Wright**

In the steeplechase, Amos Biwott leaped the water jump as if he thought crocodiles were swimming in it. **Joe Henderson**

If you've got one day to live, come see the Toronto Maple Leafs play. It'll seem like forever. **Pat Foley**

Since I've retired, I eat less, weigh less, train less and care less.

Ray Mancini

HOBBIES AND PLEASURE

I have a large seashell collection, which I keep scattered on beaches all over the world. Maybe you've seen it? **Steven Wright**

I once built a ship in a bottle. They had to break the bottle to let me out. **Steven Wright**

—I wish I had time for a hobby.
—Norm, you've got time to make your own coal.
Norm Peterson and Cliff Clavin, *Cheers*

I love blinking, I do. **Helen Adams, *Big Brother 2***

He called me a fatalist, but I'd never collected a postage stamp in my life.

Yogi Berra

There is a very fine line between 'hobby' and 'mental illness'.   **Dave Barry**

Recreations: Gardening without bending.   **James Ferris, *Who's Who* entry**

Children are the most desirable opponents at Scrabble as they are both easy to beat and fun to cheat.   Fran Lebowitz

Who needs a hobby like tennis or philately?
I've got a hobby – re-reading *Lady Chatterley*.   **Tom Lehrer**

My only hobby is laziness, which naturally rules out all the others.
Granni Nazzano

The greatest pleasure in life is doing what people say you cannot do.
Walter Bagehot

Being ill is one of the greatest pleasures of life, provided one is not too ill and is not obliged to work until one is better.   **Samuel Butler**

Lying in bed would be an altogether perfect and supreme experience if only one had a coloured pencil long enough to draw on the ceiling.
G.K. Chesterton

People seem to enjoy things more when they know a lot of other people have been left out of the pleasure.   **Russell Baker**

A cigarette is the perfect type of a perfect pleasure. It is exquisite and leaves one quite unsatisfied. What more can one want?   **Oscar Wilde**

I've got a big scab on my knee. I'll save it for tonight when I'm in bed.
Victoria Wood

Hatred is by far the longest pleasure; men love in haste, but they detest at leisure.   **Lord Byron**

A good rousing sneeze, one that tears open your collar and throws your hair into your eyes is really one of life's sensational pleasures.

Robert Benchley

My kitchen linoleum is so black and shiny that I waltz while I wait for the kettle to boil. This pleasure is for the old who live alone.

Florida Scott-Maxwell

There is no greater bliss in life than when the plumber eventually comes to unblock your drains. No writer can give that sort of pleasure.

Victoria Glendinning

To knock a thing down, especially if it is cocked at an arrogant angle, is a deep delight of the blood.

George Santayana

Scratching an itch is one of nature's sweet pleasures, and so handy.

Michel de Montaigne

The greatest pleasure I know is to do a good action by stealth and have it found out by accident.

Charles Lamb

Waiting for the German verb is surely the ultimate thrill.

Flann O'Brien

Perhaps the most lasting pleasure in life is the pleasure of not going to church.

Dean Inge

Drinking the best tea in the world in an empty cricket ground – that, I think, is the final pleasure left to man.

C.P. Snow

All the things I really like to do are either illegal, immoral, or fattening.

Alexander Woollcott

No pleasure is worth giving up for the sake of two more years in a geriatric home in Weston-super-Mare.

Kingsley Amis

I am so busy doing nothing that the idea of doing anything – which, as you know, always leads to something – cuts into the nothing and then forces me to have to drop everything.

Jerry Seinfeld

She looks as if her idea of a good time would be knitting – preferably under the guillotine.   William McIlvanney

There is not enough time to do all the nothing we want to do.
                                                      Bill Watterson

There's no such thing as fun for the whole family – there are no massage parlours with ice cream and free jewellery.   Jerry Seinfeld

Incest – a game the whole family can play.   Anon

What is wrong with a little incest? It is both handy and cheap. James Agate

The trouble with incest is that it gets you involved with relatives.
                                                 George S. Kaufman

My idea of a good night out is a good night in.   Jack Rosenthal

Good friends, good books and a sleepy conscience: that is the ideal life.
                                                      Mark Twain

There are three things I've yet to do: opera, rodeo, and porno.   Bea Arthur

It is impossible to enjoy idling thoroughly unless one has plenty of work to do.   Jerome K. Jerome

How beautiful it is to do nothing and then to rest afterwards.
                                                  Spanish proverb

Why pay the earth for expensive jigsaws? Just take a bag of frozen chips from the freezer and try piecing together potatoes.   Top tip, *Viz*

It is better to have loafed and lost than never to have loafed at all.
                                                     James Thurber

There is no cure for birth or death save to enjoy the interval.
                                                   Samuel Johnson

SHOPPING

The only time a woman has a true orgasm is when she is shopping.

Joan Rivers

Shopping is better than sex. If you're not satisfied after shopping you can make an exchange for something you really like. **Adrienne Gusoff**

Shopping is like sex for men too. They can only manage it for five minutes and then they get tired. **Jeff Green**

If men liked shopping, they'd call it research. **Cynthia Nelms**

I bought some batteries, but they weren't included, so I had to buy them again. **Steven Wright**

I love to shop after a bad relationship. I buy a new outfit and it makes me feel better. Sometimes when I see a really great outfit, I'll break up with someone on purpose. **Rita Rudner**

Have you seen her among discounted cashmere? It's like the first twenty minutes of *Saving Private Ryan*. **Will Truman, *Will and Grace***

The ad in the paper said, 'Big Sale. Last week.' Why advertise? I already missed it. They're just rubbing it in. **Yakov Smirnoff**

Extravagance is anything you buy that is of no earthly use to your wife. **Franklin Adams**

My son is always buying me things, but I never let him buy me furniture. **Sheila, mother of Elton John**

I went to the butcher's the other day and I bet him fifty quid that he couldn't reach the meat off the top shelf. He said, 'No, the steaks are too high.' **Tommy Cooper**

If you can afford it, then there is no pleasure in buying it. **Wallis Simpson**

I bought a seven-dollar pen because I always lose pens and I got sick of not caring.

Mitch Hedberg

People who say money can't buy you happiness just don't know where to shop.

Tara Palmer-Tomkinson

You know when you go to the supermarket you step on that rubber part and the door opens? For years I thought that was a coincidence.

Richard Jeni

Is there anything more humiliating than shopping in a store you feel is beneath you and one of the customers mistakes you for an employee?

Dennis Miller

Sunday is the day God took off from creating the world to take Mrs God around IKEA.

Jeff Green

You can't have everything. I mean where would you put it?

Steven Wright

I found a great pair of shoes but they only had size nine, so I lied to the sales guy.

Jonathan Katz

Here is a useful shopping tip: you can get a pair of shoes for one pound at bowling alleys.

Al Clethen

My husband refuses to try anything on. Even shoes. He just holds the box up to the light and says, 'Yeah, these fit fine.'

Rita Rudner

Like all antique shops it was dingy outside and dark and smelly within. I don't know why it is, but the proprietors of these establishments always seem to be cooking some sort of stew in the back room.

P.G. Wodehouse

The post office is the last bargain left on earth. For 27 pence you can send a letter anywhere in the country. People moan when the price of a stamp goes up by a penny. I think the Post Office should turn around and say, 'Well, you fucking take it. See how far you get with your 27 pence train ticket.'

Jack Dee

I hate when they call up to check if your credit card is good. I always feel like they're talking about me. 'You won't believe what he's buying now. It's some kind of yellow thing. I don't even know what it is. Never sold one before.'

Jerry Seinfeld

Confectioners caught on that customers would happily buy a hole if it had a bit of mint around it.

Frank Muir

Last week, I went to a furniture store to look for a decaffeinated coffee table.

Steven Wright

Everything at IKEA is self-assembly. I bought a pillow, and they gave me a duck.

Todd Glass

One in ten Europeans is now conceived on an IKEA bed.   BBC news website

No, I Don't Want the Fucking Extended Warranty.   Slogan on T-shirt

HOLIDAYS AND CHRISTMAS

Don't forget Mother's Day. Or as they call it in Beverly Hills, Dad's Third Wife Day.

Jay Leno

I hate Father's Day. I can never find the right card. They're all too nice.

Margaret Smith

Guy Fawkes Day: October to February.   Tim Brooke-Taylor

Last Halloween I ran out of candy and had to give the kids nicotine gum.

David Letterman

They started Christmas early this year. You shouldn't oughta see a Santa with a pumpkin head.

Clinton Jackson

Christmas begins about December 1st with an office party and ends when you finally realize what you spent, around April 15th of the next year.

P.J. O'Rourke

Mail your packages early so the post office can lose them in time for Christmas.

Johnny Carson

Hey, Winona, only 153 shoplifting days till Christmas.

Anon

I bought my kids a set of batteries for Christmas with a note attached saying, 'Toys not included.'

Bernard Manning

Christmas, or as Sky TV calls it, When Relatives Attack.

Jenny Abrams

Xmas makes it sound like a skin complaint.

Audrey fforbes-Hamilton, *To The Manor Born*

What I hate about office Christmas parties is looking for a job the next day.

Phyllis Diller

I know nobody likes me. Why do we have to have a holiday season to emphasize it?

Charlie Brown

It will be a traditional Christmas, with presents, crackers, door slamming and people bursting into tears, but without the dead thing in the middle. We're vegetarians.

Victoria Wood

Every Christmas, I feel like a little child. But we always have turkey.

Joey Bishop

We were so poor that we couldn't afford a turkey. We gave the budgie chest expanders. It was five aside to a cracker.

Les Dawson

Clever food is not appreciated at Christmas. It makes the little ones cry and the old ones nervous.

Oliver Wendell Holmes

Don't invite drug addicts round for a meal on Boxing Day. They may find the offer of cold turkey embarrassing or offensive.

Top tip, *Viz*

You know you've had too much to eat for Christmas dinner when you slump down onto a beanbag and realize … there is no beanbag.

David Letterman

Christmas is a dangerous time. Seven people die each year believing Christmas decorations are chocolate.

Adam Marks

I gave my wife a brand new watch for Christmas – waterproof, shockproof, unbreakable, and antimagnetic. Absolutely nothing could happen to it. She lost it.

Milton Berle

I never know what to give my father for Christmas. I gave him $100 and said, 'Buy yourself something that will make your life easier.' So he went out and bought a present for my mother.

Rita Rudner

Last Christmas, in my stocking there was an Odour-Eater.

Rodney Dangerfield

—We're going to have a baby. That's my Christmas present to you.
—All I needed was a tie.

Woody Allen

What does one give to the man who has everything? A shot of penicillin.

Richard Pryor

On the twelfth day of Christmas
My true love sent to me:
Twelve nymphos mating,
Eleven virgins waiting,
Ten colonels spanking,
Nine schoolboys cranking,
Eight nuns assenting,
Seven monks repenting,
Six queers consenting,
Five dutch caps;
Four birth pills,
Three condoms,
Two IUDs,
And a call girl calling on me.

Anon

The nicest present I ever got was an exploding suppository.   **Emo Philips**

—I never get what I want at Christmas. I always get lots of stupid toys
or a bicycle or clothes or something like that.
—What is it you really want?
—Real estate.   **Lucy Van Pelt and Charlie Brown**

Women do not considered the following to be gifts: diet books,
cooking utensils, cleaning products, petrol for the car, anything
from the Pound Shop.   **Jeff Green**

Nothing compares to the paperweight as a bad gift. And where are
these people working that their papers are just blowing off their desks?
Are they typing up in the crow's nest of a clipper ship?   **Jerry Seinfeld**

One Christmas, my grandfather gave me a box of broken glass.
He gave my brother a box of Band Aids. Then he said, 'Now,
you two share.'   **Steven Wright**

What do you give the man who's had everyone?   **Alana Stewart**

Aren't we forgetting the true meaning of Christmas – the birth of Santa?
                                                          Bart Simpson

Christmas at my house is always more pleasant than anywhere else.
We start drinking early. And while everyone is seeing only one
Santa Claus, we're seeing six or seven.   **W.C. Fields**

Christmas was awful when I was a kid, because I believed in
Santa Claus. Unfortunately, so did my parents.   **Charlie Viracola**

I never believed in Santa Claus because I knew no white dude would
come into my neighbourhood after dark.   **Dick Gregory**

I stopped believing in Santa Claus when I was six. Mother took me to see
him in a department store and he asked for my autograph.   **Shirley Temple**

Meretricious and a Happy New Year.   **Gore Vidal**

My mother-in-law has come round to our house at Christmas seven years running. This year we're having a change. We're going to let her in.

Les Dawson

My worst Christmas? One Christmas morning, I woke up, I ran into the living room and my mother said, 'I just forgot.'

Rob Burton

In the school nativity play, I was always picked to play Bethlehem.

Jo Brand

I feel sorry for Jesus. It's always tough when your birthday's Christmas Day.

David Corrado

Do we have to keep talking about religion? It's Christmas!

Danielle Chase, *My So-Called Life*

—Where is the true spirit of Christmas?
—Bloomingdales, Ladies Apparel, third floor.

Dorothy Zbornak and Sophia Petrillo, *The Golden Girls*

What do a Christmas tree and a priest have in common? Their balls are just for decoration.

Graham Norton

Forgive us our Christmases, as we forgive those that Christmas against us.

Samuel Butler

A Merry Christmas to all my friends except two.

W.C. Fields, a display ad in *Variety*

If I sent a Christmas card to Gilbert Harding, he would add to the words 'from Hubert Gregg' the words 'and Gilbert Harding', and send it to someone else.

Hubert Gregg

Next to a circus there ain't nothing that packs up and tears out of town any quicker than the Christmas spirit.

Kin Hubbard

I return your seasonal greeting card with contempt. May your hypocritical words choke you and may they choke you early in the New Year, rather than later.   **Kennedy Lindsay**

Every idiot who goes about with Merry Christmas on his lips should be boiled with his own pudding, and buried with a stake of holly through his heart.   **Charles Dickens**

New Year's Eve, when auld acquaintance be forgot – unless, of course, those tests come back positive.   **Jay Leno**

PARTY

Nice party. I see a lot of familiar face-lifts.   **Lt Frank Drebin**, *Naked Gun 2½*

At every party, there are two kinds of people – those who want to go home and those who don't. The trouble is, they are usually married to each other.   **Ann Landers**

The best thing about a cocktail party is being asked to it.
                                        Gerald Nachman

Nothing is more irritating than not being invited to a party you wouldn't be caught dead at.   **Bill Vaughan**

No matter how many chairs you provide, guests always sit on the edge of a little table and knock sherry on the carpet.   **Paul Jennings**

At the end of every party there is always a girl crying.   **Peter Kay**

Did you ever go to a party, go in the bathroom, flush the toilet, and the water starts coming up? That is the most frightening moment in the life of a human being.   **Jerry Seinfeld**

You're the only person I know who called the police to complain about their own party.   **Karen Marsden**, *Cold Feet*

A hedgehog tamed to scuttle up and down the table from guest to guest makes an unusual mobile-cheese-and-pineapple-cube-nibble-dispenser at parties.

Top tip, *Viz*

You moon the wrong person at an office party and suddenly you're not 'professional' any more.

Jeff Foxworthy

It was one of those bachelor parties where all the married men had to meet at the end of the night and go, 'All right, here's what we say we did.'

Ray Romano

Celebrity party: it's eleven o'clock at night and you're watching Larry King play Twister.

David Letterman

I know the dying process begins the minute we are born, but sometimes it accelerates during dinner parties.

Carol Matthau

Dinner parties are given mostly in the middle classes by way of revenge.

William Thackeray

My wife spends dinner parties in the bedroom asleep under the guests' coats. She exhausts easily under the pressure to be interesting.

Niles Crane, *Frasier*

Politeness is not speaking evil of people with whom you have just dined until you are at least a hundred yards from their house. **André Maurois**

Dear Hostess, I apologize for my behaviour at your dinner party. I should never be allowed out in private. **Randolph Churchill**

The best number for a dinner party is two: myself and a damn good headwaiter.

Nubar Gulbenkian

THE
NATURAL
WORLD

THE ANIMAL KINGDOM

Animals may be our friends, but they won't pick you up at the airport.

Bobcat Goldthwait

When I was growing up, we had a petting zoo, and a heavy petting zoo – for people who really liked the animals a lot. Ellen DeGeneres

I like animals as much as the next guy, but if I'm hungry, I'll eat a panda sandwich. Howard Stern

There's only one thing that separates us from animals: we aren't afraid of vacuum cleaners. Jeff Stilson

—Where are you going with that elephant?
—What elephant? Jimmy Durante

I take my pet lion to church every Sunday. He has to eat. Marty Pollio

—You've got a spider on your nose.
—I know. I trained it to be there. *Just William*

I keep bees. Not for the honey. For the fur. Little bee pelts make excellent pea-cosies. Harry Hill

I got an ant farm. Them fellas don't grow shit. Mitch Hedberg

I don't kill flies. I like to mess with their minds. I hold them above globes. They freak out and yell, 'Whoa, I'm *way* too high.' Bruce Baum

When insects take over the world, we hope they will remember with gratitude how we took them along on all our picnics. Jim Koser

Ants are tiny creatures with a primitive brain no larger than that of a psychic-hotline caller. Dave Barry

A camel is a horse designed by a committee. Alec Issigonis

It's only when you look at an ant through a magnifying glass on a sunny day that you realize how often they burst into flames.   **Harry Hill**

Scientists say there are over 3,000 spiders for every human being on earth. Does anybody want mine? I certainly don't.   **Chuck Bonner**

You can't smell mothballs because it's hard to get their tiny legs apart.
                                                                  Rich Hall

It makes all the difference whether you hear an insect in the bedroom or in the garden.   **Robert Lynd**

Biologically speaking, if something bites you, it is more likely to be female.   **Desmond Morris**

The platypus: do you think God gets stoned once in a while?
                                                              Robin Williams

Animals have two functions in today's society: to be delicious and to fit well.

Greg Proops

A horse, like Cary Grant, lends romance to any venture.   **Roberta Smoodin**

The horse is dangerous at both ends and uncomfortable in the middle.
                                                               Ian Fleming

Horses are what glue is made from, which is a bit odd because if you touch a horse, they're not that sticky, are they?   **Harry Hill**

A racehorse is the only animal that can take thousands of people for a ride at the same time.   **Herbert Prochnow**

The camel: did you ever see anything that reminded you so much of a dowager duchess studying hoi polloi through a gold-rimmed lorgnette?
                                                              Fyfe Robinson

I planted some birdseed. A bird came up. Now I don't know what to feed it.
Steven Wright

Somewhere in the woods beyond the river a nightingale had begun to sing with all the full-throated zest of a bird conscious of having had a rave notice from the poet Keats.
P.G. Wodehouse

I took a walk in Central Park and got all excited when I thought I saw a robin redbreast. Turned out to be a pigeon with a knife wound.
David Letterman

Imagine if birds were tickled by feathers. You'd see a flock of birds fly by laughing hysterically.
Steven Wright

—What do you do if a bird craps on your windscreen?
—Don't ask her out again.
Anon

Anyone who says he's been eaten by a wolf is a liar.
J.B. Theberge

No one can feel as helpless as the owner of a sick goldfish.
Kin Hubbard

I can never remember if Moby Dick is the man or the whale.
James Thurber

Penguins mate for life. Which doesn't exactly surprise me that much 'cause they all look alike – it's not like they're gonna meet a better-looking penguin someday.
Ellen DeGeneres

The monkey is an organized sarcasm upon the human race.
Henry Ward Beecher

My favourite animal is steak.
Fran Lebowitz

My hamster died yesterday. Fell asleep at the wheel.
Frank Carson

Monkeys and apes have the ability to speak but keep silent to
avoid being put to work.

René Descartes

What is it with chimpanzees and that middle parting? It's so 1920s.

Harry Hill

Yesterday I saw a chicken crossing the road. I asked it why. It said
it was none of my business.

Steven Wright

The only sure guide to the sex of a pelican is another pelican.

David Eccles

Two little sardines swimming in the sea, came across a submarine.
'What's that?' said one, peering in. 'Only people in a tin.'

Spike Milligan

The rhinoceros is an animal with a hide two feet thick, and no
apparent interest in politics. What a waste.

James Wright

A zebra cannot change its spots.

Dan Quayle

Stuffed deer heads on walls are bad enough, but it's worse when
they are wearing dark glasses, and have streamers in their antlers
because then you know they were enjoying themselves at a party
when they were shot.

Ellen DeGeneres

If called by a panther
Don't anther.

Ogden Nash

I believe that lobsters are the result of a terrible genetic accident
involving nuclear radiation and cockroaches.

Dave Barry

Have you ever pondered on the similarity between a pelican and
British Gas? They can both stick their bills up their arses.

Stephen Fry

I was into animal husbandry – until they caught me at it.

Tom Lehrer

The only way to get rid of cockroaches is to tell them you want
a long-term relationship.

Jasmine Birtles

God in His wisdom made the fly, and then forgot to tell us why.

Ogden Nash

I don't dislike animals but eyeliner is important in my life. If ten chickens
have to die to make one drag queen happy, so be it. John Waters

I think animal testing is a terrible idea. They get all nervous and
give the wrong answers. Hugh Laurie

Cats have got nine lives which makes them ideal for experimentation.

Jimmy Carr

All Our Pets Are Flushable. Sign above Springfield pet shop

Kids, if you want a kitten, start out asking your parents for a horse.

Marty Allen

To his dog, every man is Napoleon; hence the constant popularity
of dogs. Aldous Huxley

I have a great dog. She's half Lab, half pit bull. Sure, she might
bite off my leg, but she'll bring it back to me. Wanda Lane

I loathe people who keep dogs. They are cowards who haven't
got the guts to bite people themselves. August Strindberg

The dog was licking its private parts with the gusto of an alderman
drinking soup. Graham Greene

I have a dog that's half pit bull, half poodle. Not much of a
guard dog, but a vicious gossip. Craig Shoemaker

Chihuahua, what a waste of dog food. Looks like a dog that is
still far away. Billiam Coronel

Why do dogs have no money? No pockets. Jerry Seinfeld

The dachshund is a German draught-excluder. Billy Connolly

I've got a paranoid retriever. When I throw things, he doesn't know whether he should fetch them or not.

Rodney Dangerfield

Dogs have a nice life. You never see a dog with a wristwatch.

George Carlin

I wonder if other dogs think poodles are members of a weird religious cult.

Rita Rudner

A man takes his Rottweiler to the vet. 'My dog's cross-eyed, is there anything you can do for him?' 'Let's have a look at him,' says the vet. So he picks him up and examines his eyes. Finally he says, 'I'm going to have to put him down.' 'Why?' says the man. 'Because he's cross-eyed? 'No, because he's really heavy.'

Tommy Cooper

A boy can learn a lot from a dog – obedience, loyalty, and the importance of turning around three times before lying down.

Robert Benchley

I bought a pedigree dog for £300. My friend said, 'Give me £300 and I'll shit on your carpet.'

Joan Rivers

My friend's dog has a sweater, but he wears it just wrapped around his shoulders.

Ellen DeGeneres

If you are a dog and your owner suggests that you wear a sweater, suggest that he wear a tail.

Fran Lebowitz

Is sex with poodles *always* wrong?

Jim Trott, *The Vicar of Dibley*

Do you recollect the Allington poodle – exactly like a typhoid germ magnified.

George Lyttleton

A psychologist is selling a video that teaches you how to test your dog's IQ. Here's how it works: if you spend $12.99 on the video, your dog is smarter than you.

Jay Leno

Did you ever walk in a room and forget why you walked in?
I think that's how dogs spend their lives.   Sue Murphy

My dog is so lazy. He doesn't chase cars, he just sits on the kerb,
taking down licence plate numbers.   Rodney Dangerfield

A man loses his dog, so he puts an ad in the paper. And the ad says,
'Here, boy!'   Spike Milligan

Your dog died? My dear, how awful. Never mind you could
always adopt.   Dorothy Parker

Don't accept your dog's admiration as conclusive proof that you
are wonderful.   Ann Landers

Maris is unable to have pets. She distrusts anything that loves her
unconditionally.   Niles Crane, *Frasier*

They say that dog is a man's best friend. I don't believe that.
How many of your friends have you had neutered?   Larry Reeb

I bought a book by a woman who claims her dog is immortal.
I couldn't put it down.   Frank Skinner

Dogs come when they are called. Cats take a message and get back to you.

Mary Bly

You don't need to hire a dog therapist, you just need to wake up
at 7.00 am and open the fucking door.   Ozzy Osbourne

A dog is not intelligent. Never trust an animal that is surprised by
its own farts.   Frank Skinner

I had a cat once. That was the roughest night of sex I ever had.

Matt Vance

—What are those two dogs doing?
—The dog in front is blind, and the other one has kindly offered to
push him all the way to St Dustan's.   **Noël Coward on two dogs copulating**

The dog is the one species I wouldn't mind seeing vanish from the face
of the earth. I wish they were like the White Rhino – six of them
left in the Serengeti National Park, and all males.   **Alan Bennett**

Cats are smarter than dogs. You can't get eight cats to pull a
sled through the snow.   **Jeff Valdez**

The simple rule about pet cats is this: like exclamation marks,
more than two signifies a complete nutcase.   **Jeff Green**

I had been told that the training procedure with cats was difficult.
It's not. Mine had me trained in two days.   **Bill Dana**

No amount of time can ever erase the memory of a pet cat you loved,
and no amount of masking tape can ever remove its fur from your couch.
Leo Dworken

I am fond of pigs. Dogs look up to us. Cats looks down on us.
Pigs treat us as equal.   **Winston Churchill**

I kept a pet goat that followed me like an unpaid bill.   **Myrtle Reed**

Here's a verse about rabbits
That doesn't mention their habits.   **Ogden Nash**

I find that ducks' opinion of me is greatly influenced by whether
or not I have bread.   **Mitch Hedberg**

Organizational structures can be found throughout nature. Monkeys
form troops, birds form flocks, fish form schools, intestinal parasites
form law firms.   **Dave Barry**

The most blatant example of cruelty to animals has to be the
rotisserie. It's just a morbid Ferris wheel for chickens.   **Mitch Hedberg**

Erratum. In my article on the price of milk, 'Horses' should have
read 'Cows' throughout.   J.C. Morton

I wouldn't really call it a cushion, Pekingese is a more common
name for them. No, well never mind, he was very old.   Stephen Fry

NATURE

I have no relish for the country; it is a kind of healthy grave.   Sydney Smith

I am not the type who wants to go back to the land. I am the type
who wants to go back to the hotel.   Fran Lebowitz

—I'm going ice-fishing. I've always thought of myself as a man of the
great *al fresco*.
—Niles, you get a runny nose watching ice-skating on TV.
                                        Niles and Frasier Crane, *Frasier*

I am at two with nature.   Woody Allen

That's the trouble with nature. Something's always stinging you or
oozing mucous on you. Let's go in and watch television.   Bill Watterson

The Great Outdoors is what you must pass through in order to
get from your apartment to a taxicab.   Fran Lebowitz

The English countryside is scoops of mint ice cream with chips of
chocolate cows.   Jim Bishop

Of all the wonders of nature, a tree in summer is perhaps the most
remarkable; with the possible exception of a moose singing,
'Embraceable You' in spats.   Woody Allen

As a gardener, your first job is to prepare the soil. The best tool for
this is your neighbour's motorized garden tiller. If your neighbour
does not own a garden tiller, suggest that he buy one.   Dave Barry

Won't you come into the garden? I would like my roses to see you.
Richard Brinsley Sheridan

Please Leave Heather For All to Enjoy   Sign in Scottish Highlands

A developer is someone who wants to build a house in the woods.
An environmentalist is someone who already owns a house in
the woods.   Dennis Miller

I'm an environmentalist. Most of my jokes are recycled.   David Letterman

My friend is so into recycling she insists on marrying a man who's
been married before.   Rita Rudner

Our oceans are getting so polluted, the other day I caught a tuna fish
that was already packed in oil.   Charlie Vircola

The best thing about rain forests is that they never suffer from drought.
Dan Quayle

It's so quiet out here in the wilds you can hear a mouse get a hard-on.
John Belushi

Anybody can be good in the country.   Oscar Wilde

The best time to take cuttings is when no one is looking.   Bob Flowerdew

Lord Illingworth told me this morning that there is an orchid in the
conservatory as beautiful as the seven deadly sins.   Oscar Wilde

Flowers are simply tarts – prostitutes for the bees.   Bruce Robinson

I was flattered to have a rose named after me until I read the description
in the catalogue: no good in a bed, but perfect up against a wall.
Eleanor Roosevelt

My main ambition as a gardener is to water my orange trees with
gin, then all I have to do is squeeze the juice into a glass.   W.C. Fields

My neighbour asked if he could borrow my lawnmower and I told him of course so long as he didn't take it out of my garden.   Eric Morecambe

Americans would rather live next to a pervert heroin addict communist pornographer than a person with an unkempt lawn.   Dave Barry

I've killed so many plants. I walked into a nursery once and my face was on a wanted poster.   Rita Rudner

I have a suspicion that the pictures on seed packets are posed by professional flowers.   Denis Norden

I like to tease my plants. I water them with ice cubes.   Steven Wright

Keep away from the wheelbarrow – what the hell do you know about machinery?   Elbert Hubbard

The best way to get real enjoyment out of the garden is to put on a wide straw hat, dress in thin loose-fitting clothes, hold a little trowel in one hand and a cool drink in the other, and tell the man where to dig.   Charles Barr

WEATHER

—Did you notice the heavy fog last night?
—No, nothing wakes me.   Morecambe and Wise

What a beautiful day! It's the kind of day that starts with a hearty breakfast and ends with a newsreader saying, '...before turning the gun on himself'.   Dan Conner, *Roseanne*

It was such a lovely day that it seemed a pity to get up.   Somerset Maugham

It was one of those perfect summer days – the sun was shining, a gentle breeze was blowing, the birds were singing and the lawnmower was broken.   James Dent

Hooray, hooray, the first of May,
Outdoor fucking begins today.   **American folk rhyme**

What men call gallantry, and gods adultery,
is much more common where the climate's sultry.   **Lord Byron**

A few summers like this and we'll all be behaving like Italians.
                                                 John Mortimer

One can always tell it's summer when one sees teachers hanging idly
about the streets, looking like cannibals during a shortage of
missionaries.   **Robertson Davies**

Fall in New York is so pretty – watching the trash change colours.
                                                 Billiam Coronel

It's spring in England. I missed it last year. I was in the bathroom.
                                                 Michael Flanders

It is easy to understand why the most beautiful poems about
England in the spring were written by poets living in Italy at the time.
                                                 Philip Dunne

Rain is one thing the British do better than anybody else.   **Marilyn French**

It always rains on tents. Rainstorms will travel thousands of miles against
the prevailing winds, for the opportunity to rain on a tent.   **Dave Barry**

Save a boyfriend for a rainy day and another in case it doesn't.   **Mae West**

Bad weather always looks worse through a window.   **John Kieran**

March is the month that shows people who don't drink exactly
how a hangover feels.   **Garrison Keillor**

Mexican weather report: Chilli today and hot tamale.   **Paul Rodriguez**

Weather forecast for tonight: dark.   **George Carlin**

I don't like all this fresh air. I'm from Los Angeles. I don't trust any air I can't see.
Bob Hope

Thank heavens, the sun has gone in, and I don't have to go out and enjoy it.
Logan Pearsall Smith

A barometer is an ingenious instrument that indicates what kind of weather we are having.
Ambrose Bierce

The English winter – ending in July, to recommence in August.   **Lord Byron**

The afternoon was cold as blue eyes that didn't love you any more.
Kinky Friedman

It's so cold I saw a politician with his hands in his own pockets.
Bob Hope

It's so cold in New York City. Today in Central Park, I saw a squirrel salting his nuts.
David Letterman

I was so cold when I was in England, I almost got married.
Shelley Winters

It's so cold in New York City that flashers are just describing themselves.
David Letterman

Our crack snow removal team has been removing snow around the clock. And now that the area around the clock is clear, they can start work on the streets.
Adam Cochran

How do the men who drive the snowplough get to work in the morning?
Steven Wright

Better the chill blast of winter than the hot breath of a pursuing elephant.
Chinese proverb

Today has been eighty degrees in the shade. I was clever. I stayed in the sun.
Tommy Cooper

In India, 'cold weather' is merely a phrase to distinguish between
weather which will melt a brass doorknob and weather which
only makes it mushy.
                                                          Mark Twain

—Is it always sunny in Jamaica?
—Never at night.
                                                          Noël Coward

One way to help the weather make up its mind is to hang out washing.
                                                          Marcelene Cox

I'm just scared there's going to be a major earthquake at the time
I'm getting a vasectomy.
                                                          Bob Saget

It was so hot today I went to a cash point machine just to enjoy
the feel of a cold gun against the back of my neck.
                                                          David Letterman

—Ninety-two this morning, Colonel Lawrence! Ninety-two.
What do you say to that?
—Many happy returns of the day!
                                                          T.E. Lawrence

Heat! It was so dreadful that I found there was nothing for it
but to take off my flesh and sit in my bones.
                                                          Sydney Smith

Whenever people talk to me about the weather, I always feel
certain that they mean something else.
                                                          Oscar Wilde

We shall never be content until each man makes his own weather
and keeps it to himself.
                                                          Jerome K. Jerome

ARTS AND ENTERTAINMENT

ART

How Botticellian! How Fra Angelican!   W.S. Gilbert

I couldn't have that painting hanging in my home. It would be
like living with a gas leak.   Dame Edith Evans

They couldn't find the artist so they hung the picture.   Frank Zappa

A picture is worth a thousand words – particularly if you can't read.
                                                          Harry Hershfield

Bring my umbrella – I am going to see John Constable's pictures.
                                                          Henry Fuseli

Michaelangelo's *David*? Now there's a guy who works out.   Graham Norton

When their backsides look good enough to slap, there's nothing
more to do.   Peter Paul Rubens

I would never have taken up painting if women did not have breasts.
                                                      Pierre Auguste Renoir

Graham Sutherland's portrait of me makes me look as if I was
having a difficult stool.   Winston Churchill

When having my portrait painted I don't want justice, I want mercy.
                                                          Billy Hughes

A portrait is a picture in which there is something wrong with the mouth.
                                                          Eugene Speicher

There are only two styles of portrait painting; the serious and the smirk.
                                                          Charles Dickens

Oh, I wish I could draw. I'd give my right arm to be able to draw.
                                                          Alan Ayckbourn

In a good portrait, the eyes follow you around the room.   Peter Cook

I do not paint a portrait to look like the subject, rather does
the person grow to look like his portrait.   Salvador Dali

—I like Chagall. It feels like how being in love should be –
floating through a dark blue sky.
—With a goat playing the violin.
          Anna Scott and William Thacker, *Notting Hill*

Van Gogh would have sold more than one painting if he'd put tigers
in them.   Tom Hobbes

There is something wrong with a work of art if it can be understood by a policeman.
          Patrick Kavanagh

Did you hear about the ship that ran aground carrying a cargo of red
and black paints? The entire crew was marooned.   William Bishop

The day is coming when a single carrot, freshly observed, will
spark off a revolution.   Paul Cezanne

There is no more sombre enemy of art than the pram in the hall.
          Cyril Connolly

Art is anything you can get away with.   Marshall McLuhan

Art, like morality, consists in drawing the line somewhere.   G.K. Chesterton

Dada wouldn't buy me a Bauhaus.   Joan Sloan

There are three kinds of people in the world: those who can't stand
Picasso, those who can't stand Raphael, and those who have never
heard of either.   John White

Every time I paint a portrait, I lose a friend.

John Singer Sargent

I simply refuse to countenance paintings that do not have at least
a horse, gladioli or a canal in them.

Dylan Moran

I hate flowers. I paint them because they're cheaper than models
and they don't move.

Georgia O'Keefe

Whistler, with all his faults, was never guilty of writing a line of poetry.

Oscar Wilde

If the old masters had labelled their fruit, one wouldn't be so
likely to mistake pears for turnips.

Mark Twain

I doubt that art needed Ruskin any more than a moving train
needs one of its passengers to shove it.

Tom Stoppard

The naked truth about me is to the naked truth about Salvador Dali
as an old ukulele in the attic is to a piano in a tree, and I mean a
piano with breasts.

James Thurber

Turner's painting *The Slave Ship* looks like a tortoiseshell cat
having a fit in a plate of tomatoes.

Mark Twain

—For two days' labour, you ask two hundred guineas?
—No, I ask it for the knowledge of a lifetime.

James McNeill Whistler

The more you look at modern art exhibits, the more everything
begins to look like an exhibit, including the attendant's chair and
the fire extinguisher.

Brian Sewell

Jeff Koon's work is the last bit of methane left in the intestine of
the dead cow that is post-modernism.

Robert Hughes

This is either a forgery or a damn clever original.

Frank Sullivan

Who among us has not gazed at a painting of Jackson Pollock's and thought, 'What a piece of crap'?
                                                                    Rob Long

He was our greatest living painter, until he died.
                                                                    Mark Twain

It's amazing that you can win the Turner Prize with an E in A-Level art, a twisted imagination and a chainsaw.
                                                                    Damien Hirst

Modern art is what happens when painters stop looking at girls and persuade themselves they have a better idea.
                                                                    John Ciardi

I inherited a painting and a violin, which turned out to be a Rembrandt and a Stradivarius. Unfortunately, Rembrandt made awful violins and Stradivarius was a terrible painter.
                                                                    Tommy Cooper

Rembrandt painted 700 pictures. Of these 3,000 are in existence.
                                                                    Wilhelm Bode

If a painting can be forged well enough to fool experts, why is the original so valuable?
                                                                    George Carlin

Any fool can paint a picture, but it takes a wise man to be able to sell it.
                                                                    Samuel Butler

How often my soul visits the National Gallery, and how seldom I go there myself.
                                                                    Logan Pearsall Smith

Visiting museums bastardizes the personality, just as hobnobbing with priests makes you lose your faith.
                                                                    Maurice Vlaminck

I went to a museum where they have all the heads and arms from the statues that are in all the other museums.
                                                                    Steven Wright

The only way I'd find a waxwork museum interesting is if it was set on fire.
                                                                    Daniel Liebert

Henry Moore's sculpture in Hyde Park looks like something that's fallen off a jumbo jet.
                                                                    Laura Milligan

One should either be a work of art, or wear a work of art.　　Oscar Wilde

Sculpture: mud pies which endure.　　Cyril Connolly

A sculpture is just a drawing you fall over in the dark.　　Al Hirschfield

Multi-images of Marilyn Monroe are now as dated as hula-hoops.
Where does that leave Warhol's art? On the wall, is the
unfortunate answer.　　Kenneth McLeish

He had the great traditional stimulant to the industry of an artist –
laziness and debt.　　John Mortimer

What is an artist? For every thousand people there's nine hundred
doing the work, ninety doing well, nine doing good, and one lucky
bastard who's the artist.　　Tom Stoppard

An amateur is an artist who supports himself with outside jobs which
enable him to paint. A professional is someone whose wife works to
enable him to paint.　　Ben Shahn

The true artist will let his wife starve, his children go barefoot,
his mother drudge for his living at seventy, sooner than work at
anything but his art.　　George Bernard Shaw

If you have a burning restless urge to paint, simply eat something
sweet and the feeling will pass.　　Fran Lebowitz

Art is art, isn't it? And water is water and east is east and west is
west and if you take cranberries and stew them like apple-sauce
they taste much more like prunes than rhubarb does.　　Groucho Marx

ARCHITECTURE

What a magnificent mansion! It's just what God would have
done if he had had the money.　　Alexander Woollcott

Times Square, New York: neon-classical.   Nicola Zweig

An architect is someone who forgets to put in the staircase.
                                                    Gustave Flaubert

A physician can bury his mistakes, but the architect can only advise
his client to plant vines.   Frank Lloyd Wright

In my experience, if you have to keep the lavatory door shut by
extending your left leg, it's modern architecture.   Nancy Banks Smith

Personally, I think all modern architects should be pulled down and
redeveloped as car parks.   Spike Milligan

I have a theory about architecture in Los Angeles. I think all the houses
came to a costume party and they all came as other countries.
                                                    Michael O'Donoghue

The Sydney Opera House looks as if it is something that has crawled
out of the sea and is up to no good.   Beverley Nichols

The Pyramids of Egypt will not last a moment compared to the daisy.
                                                    D.H. Lawrence

The higher the buildings, the lower the morals.   Noël Coward

Those comfortably padded lunatic asylums which are known,
euphemistically, as the stately homes of England.   Virginia Woolf

All architecture is great architecture after sunset.   G.K. Chesterton

MUSIC

The bagpipes are an instrument of torture consisting of a leaky bag
and punctured pipes, played by blowing up the bag and placing
the fingers over the wrong holes.   Dick Diabolus

Music hath charms to soothe the savage beast – but I'd try a
revolver first.

Josh Billings

I hate music – especially when it is played.

Jimmy Durante

You have delighted us long enough.

Jane Austen

A music teacher came twice each week to bridge the awful gap
between Dorothy and Chopin.

George Ade

Playing the bagpipes for the first time is like having sex with an octopus.

Andrew McDonald

Second violins can play a concerto perfectly if they're in their
own home and nobody's there.

Garrison Keillor

When Phyllis Diller started to play, Steinway came down personally
and rubbed his name off the piano.

Bob Hope

—Can you play the violin?
—I don't know. I've never tried.

George Burns

When is the Last Night at the Proms going to mean it?

Danny Bhoy

I know two kinds of audiences only – one coughing, and one not
coughing.

Artur Schnabel

If Beethoven had been killed in a plane crash at the age of 22, it would
have changed the history of music ... and of aviation.

Tom Stoppard

Too many pieces of music finish too long after the end.

Igor Stravinsky

If I play Tchaikovsky I play his melodies and skip his spiritual
struggles. If there's any time left over I fill in with a lot of runs up
and down the keyboard.

Liberace

What is too silly to be spoken can be sung. Pierre de Beaumarchais

The acoustics in King's College Chapel would make a fart sound
like a sevenfold Amen. David Willcocks

Muzak in pubs and hotel foyers seeps round us like nerve gas.
William McIlvanney

I worry that the person who thought up muzak may be thinking up
something else. Lily Tomlin

The secret of my piano playing is that I always make sure that the
lid over the keyboard is open before I start to play. Artur Schnabel

There are three kinds of pianists: Jewish pianists, homosexual
pianists and bad pianists. Vladimir Horowitz

When a piece gets difficult, make faces. Vladimir Horowitz

Richard Clayderman reminds us how cheap potent music can be.
Richard Williams

A violin is the revenge exacted by the intestines of a dead cat.
Ambrose Bierce

The difference between a violin and a viola is that a viola burns longer.
Victor Borge

The cello is not one of my favourite instruments. It has such a
lugubrious sound, like someone reading a will. Irene Thomas

The inventor of the bagpipes was inspired when he saw a man
carrying an indignant asthmatic pig under his arm. Alfred Hitchcock

Bagpipes are the missing link between music and noise. E.K. Kruger

The Irish gave the bagpipes to the Scots as a joke, but the Scots
haven't seen the joke yet. Oliver Herford

If there is music in hell, it will be bagpipes. Joe Tomelty

I find that distance lends enchantment to bagpipes. William Blezard

The bagpipes sound exactly the same when you have finished learning them as when you start. Thomas Beecham

Others, when the bagpipe sings in the nose, cannot contain their urine. William Shakespeare

It's an odd thing but a thousand bagpipers are no worse – if I may put it like that – than one. The noise does not seem to get any louder, only more edgy and irritable like live tinned bees. As the Duke of Wellington said: 'I don't know what they do to the enemy but I think I'll go and lie down for a bit.' Nancy Banks-Smith

Bring not a bagpipe to a man in trouble. Jonathan Swift

What's the difference between a bagpipe and an onion? Nobody cries when you chop up a bagpipe. Anon

Definition of a gentleman: someone who knows how to play the bagpipes, but doesn't. Al Cohn

The best that can be said for bagpipes is that they don't smell, too. Brendan Behan

I once saw an ad in the *Glasgow Herald* that went: 'Bagpipes for sale, used only once, owing to bereavement.' Billy Connolly

A harpsichord sounds like two skeletons copulating on a corrugated tin roof. Thomas Beecham

Madam, you have between your legs an instrument capable of giving pleasure to thousands – and all you can do is scratch it. Thomas Beecham to a cellist

When you have nothing to say, sing it. David Ogilvy

I do not like the saxophone, it sounds like the word,
'Reckankreuzungsklankwekzeuge.'
Robert Wagner

Anyone who has heard certain kinds of performances on the concertina
will admit that even suicide has its brighter aspects.
Stephen Leacock

The tuba is certainly the most intestinal of instruments – the very
lower bowel of music.
Peter de Vries

The upright piano is a musical growth found adhering to the walls
of most semi-detached houses in the provinces.
Thomas Beecham

A trombone is a quaint and antique drainage system applied to the face.
Thomas Beecham

Brass bands are all very well in their place – outdoors and several
miles away.
Thomas Beecham

I know only two tunes. One of them is 'Yankee Doodle', and the
other isn't.
Ulysees S. Grant

Listening to the 5th symphony of Ralph Vaughan Williams is like
staring at a cow for forty-five minutes.
Aaron Copeland

Brahms's German Requiem made me wish I was dead.
George Bernard Shaw

Fauré's music sounds like the kind of music a pederast might hum
when raping a choirboy.
Marcel Proust

Swans sing before they die. It would be no bad thing should certain
persons die before they sing.
Samuel Taylor Coleridge

His singing was something between that of a rat drowning, a lavatory
flushing and a hyena devouring her after-birth in the Appalachian
Mountains under a full moon.
Auberon Waugh

His vibrato sounded like he was driving a tractor over ploughed
fields with weights tied to his scrotum. Spike Milligan

People who have heard me sing say I don't. Mark Twain

I sing only to punish my children. Phyllis Diller

When she sings, deaf people refuse to watch her lips move. Jed Larson

If white bread could sing it would sound like Olivia Newton John. Anon

Bing Crosby sings like all people think they sing in the shower.
Dinah Shore

You sound like someone who should be singing on a cruise ship.
Halfway through your song, I wished the ship was sinking. Simon Cowell

The last telegram sent from the *Titanic* has been sold at auction. It said,
HELP. THEY WON'T STOP PLAYING CELINE DION'S TITANIC
SONG. And then everyone killed themselves. Conan O'Brien

Cole Porter sang like a hinge. Ethel Merman

Karaoke bars combine two of the nation's greatest evils: people
who shouldn't drink with people who shouldn't sing. Tom Dreesen

Talking about music is like dancing about architecture. Steve Martin

Music helps not the toothache. George Herbert

In order to compose, all you need to do is remember a tune that
nobody else has thought of. Robert Schumann

All the good music has already been written by people with wigs
and stuff. Frank Zappa

I write music as a sow piddles.   Wolfgang Amadeus Mozart

Give me a laundry list and I'll set it to music.   Gioacchino Rossini

Classical music is the kind you keep thinking will turn into a tune.
                                                              Kin Hubbard

Leonard Bernstein uses music merely as an accompaniment to his
conducting.   Oscar Levant

There is no doubt that the first requirement for a composer is to be dead.
                                                          Arthur Honegger

Berlioz says nothing in his music, but he says it magnificently. Victor Hugo

Baroque music: muzak for intelligentsia.   Edmund Wright

I can't listen to too much Wagner. I start getting the urge to
conquer Poland.   Woody Allen

Wagner's music is better than it sounds.

Mark Twain

Wagner has some wonderful moments but awful quarter-hours.
                                                        Gioacchino Rossini

The music of Wagner imposes mental tortures that only algebra
has a right to inflict.   Paul de Saint-Victor

My favourite two composers are the Bachs – Johann Sebastian and
Jacques Offen.   Victor Borge

Modern music is three farts and a raspberry, orchestrated.   John Barbirolli

I have never heard any Stockhausen, but I do believe I have
stepped in some.   Thomas Beecham

One good thing about playing a piece of modern music is that if you make a mistake, no one notices.

Gordon Brown

—How do you play so well when you're loaded?
—I practise when I'm loaded.

Zoot Sims

Jazz will endure just as long as people hear it through their feet instead of their brains.

John Philip Sousa

All rock 'n' roll singers sound like a nudist backing into a cold-nosed dog – set to music.

Robert Orben

In Kafka's book, *Metamorphosis*, the protagonist wakes one day believing himself to be a beetle. Do you think Noel Gallagher's read that book?

Jimmy Carr

We live in a country where John Lennon takes six bullets to the chest and Yoko Ono is standing next to him – no fucking bullet. Explain that to me.

Denis Leary

If Yoko Ono's voice was a fight, they'd stop it in the first round.

Anon

If Jimi Hendrix could see the current state of pop music he'd roll over in his own vomit.

David Corrado

Peter André's got two million fans. Imagine the draught if he turned them all on at once.

Ally Ross

The other day I was sitting around the house listening to some Alanis Morissette, and the doorbell rang, so I slipped the gun out of my mouth.

Vernon Chatman

—What's the difference between Madonna and a Rottweiler?
—Lipstick.

Anon

The rock music business is a cruel and shallow trench, a long plastic hallway where thieves and pimps run free, and good men lie like dogs. There is also a negative side.

Hunter S. Thompson

When the batteries run down on my Walkman, Bob Dylan still
sounds the same.   **Lance Crowther**

Keith Richards doesn't strike me as a morning person.   **Tom Ryan**

Ozzy Osbourne was invited to the White House to meet President
Bush. Just goes show that if you do a lot of controlled substances
and talk like a three-year-old you can go really far in America.
And Ozzy's doing okay, too.   **Greg Proops**

I occasionally play works by contemporary composers to remind
myself how much I appreciate Beethoven.   **Jascha Heifetz**

If you're in jazz and more than ten people like you, you're labelled
commercial.   **Herbie Mann**

I'm not proud of some of the things I've done in my life. I'm not
proud of having a poor education. I'm not proud of being an alcoholic.
I'm not proud of being a drug addict. I'm not proud of biting the
head off a bat. But it could be worse. I could be Sting.   **Ozzy Osbourne**

Sting – where is thy death?   **Joe Queenan**

Mick Jagger could French-kiss a moose. He has child-bearing lips.
                                                            Joan Rivers

The Rolling Stones have announced a new tour. Fans will be able
to recognize their tour bus as the one doing forty in the fast lane
with its indicator on.   **Kevin Nealon**

A homeless musician is one without a girlfriend.
                                                             Dave Barry

I bought an audio cleaning tape. I'm a big fan of theirs.   **Kevin Gildea**

Punk was just a way to sell trousers.   **Malcolm McLaren**

Michael Jackson, also known as 'the carrier bag' – white, plastic
and best kept away from kids.
Angus Deayton

Rap music sounds like someone feeding a rhyming dictionary to a
popcorn popper.
Tom Robbins

It's called rap music because the 'c' fell off the printer.
Allan Bease

I like both kinds of music – country and western.
John Belushi

I don't like country music, but I don't mean to denigrate those who do.
And for those who like country music, denigrate means 'put down'.
Bob Newhart

I wanted to be a country singer but I took the test and I had too
much self-esteem.
Brett Butler

The hardest thing about writing country music must be thinking
up clean words to rhyme with 'truck'.
Brian Kaufman

OPERA

Going to the opera, like getting drunk, is a sin that carries its own
punishment with it.
Hannah More

Opera is when a guy gets stabbed in the back and instead of bleeding
he sings.
Ed Gardner

No opera plot can be sensible for in sensible situations people do
not sing.
W.H. Auden

I do not mind which language an opera is sung in so long as it is
a language I don't understand.
Edward Appleton

I'm sitting at the opera, and I'm thinking, 'Look how much work
it takes to bore me.'
Dave Attell

No matter how late one gets to *Siegfried*, there seems always to be one more act.   Avery Hopwood

'Aria' is Italian for 'a song that will not end in your lifetime'.   Dave Barry

I went to watch Pavarotti once. He doesn't like it when you join in.
Mick Miller

Bed is the poor man's opera.   Italian proverb

No operatic tenor has yet died soon enough for me.   Thomas Beecham

I sometimes wonder, which would be nicer – an opera without an interval, or an interval without an opera.   Ernest Newman

My favourite opera is *La Bohème* because it is the shortest I know.
King George V

I go to the opera whether I need the sleep or not.   Henny Youngman

I love the opera. You can't sleep at home like that.   Janice Morden

DANCE

Dance? She looks at you as if you have just suggested instrumental rape.
Jay McInerney

My wife doesn't dance. She dislikes public displays of rhythm.
Niles Crane, *Frasier*

Dancing is a perpendicular expression of a horizontal desire.
George Bernard Shaw

She does a dance suggesting the life of a fern; I saw one of the rehearsals, and to me it could have equally well suggested the life of John Wesley.
Saki

—Start with your left foot.
—Which one?

Daphne Moon and Niles Crane, *Frasier*

I would believe only in a God that knows how to dance.

Friedrich Nietzsche

You should try everything once, except incest and folk-dancing.

Arnold Bax

When I dance, people think I'm looking for my keys.

Ray Barone, *Everybody Loves Raymond*

He was a man who never let his left hip know what his right hip
was doing.

P.G. Wodehouse

I wish I could shimmy like my sister Kate, she shivers like the
jelly on a plate.

Armand J. Piron

I could dance with you till the cows come home. On second thoughts,
I'd rather dance with the cows till you come home.

Groucho Marx

Dancing with her was like moving a piano.

Ring Lardner

British women dance as though they were riding on donkeys.

Heinrich Heine

For God's sake, go and tell that young dancer to take the Rockingham
tea service out of his tights.

Noël Coward

Have you seen the price of ballet tickets? That's a lot to see buggers
jump.

Nigel Bruce

Ballet is a bunch of men wearing pants so tight that you can tell
what religion they are.

Robin Williams

Disco dancing is really dancing for people who hate dancing, since
the beat is so monotonous. There is no syncopation, just the steady
thump of a giant moron knocking in an endless nail.

Clive James

I don't understand anything about the ballet. All I know is that during the intervals the ballerinas stink like horses.   **Anton Chekhov**

I was a ballerina, but I had to quit after I injured a groin muscle. It wasn't mine.   **Rita Rudner**

The trouble with nude dancing is that not everything stops when the music stops.   **Robert Helpmann**

In 'Electric Boogaloo' the dancers move as if they had an electric current going through them. If only.   **Julie Burchill**

Riverdance: you would get the same thrill if sixteen people were to brush their teeth in perfect unison to the beat of a jaunty reel.   **Thomas Sutcliffe**

He intensified the silent passion of his dancing, trying to convey the impression of being something South American, which ought to be chained up and muzzled in the interest of pure womanhood.
          P.G. Wodehouse

HOLLYWOOD AND FILM

Hollywood is a place where they shoot too many pictures and not enough actors.   **Walter Winchell**

Hollywood is a place where people from Iowa mistake each other for stars.   **Fred Allen**

Hollywood is a trip through a sewer in a glass-bottomed boat.
          Wilson Mizner

You can take all the sincerity in Hollywood, place it in the navel of a fruit fly and still have room for three caraway seeds and a producer's heart.   **Fred Allen**

Film is a collaborative art: bend over.   **David Mamet**

Half the people in Hollywood are dying to be discovered and the other half are afraid they will be.
Ethel Barrymore

—You know who runs Hollywood?
—The Jews?
—No, the gay Jews.
Hollywood joke

Strip away the phoney tinsel of Hollywood and you find the real tinsel underneath.
Oscar Levant

I've spent several years in Hollywood, and I still think the movie heroes are in the audience.
Wilson Mizner

They shoot too many pictures and not enough actors.
Walter Winchell

Hollywood must be the only place on earth where you can get fired by someone wearing a Hawaiian shirt and a baseball cap.
Steve Martin

An associate producer is the only guy in Hollywood who will associate with the producer.
Fred Allen

Movie directors are people too short to become actors.
Josh Greenfield

Most movie moguls couldn't produce a urine sample.
Kathy Lette

I've told my wife, if I ever need cardiac surgery, get me the heart of a movie mogul. It's never been used.
Jack Columbo

The British Film Industry is just a bunch of people in London who can't get green cards.
Alan Parker

The most important part in filmmaking is played by the writers. We must do everything in our power to keep them from finding out.
Irving Thalberg

American films usually involve a car chase whereas European films usually involve a small boy and a bicycle. **Boyd Farrow**

What could be better than to star in a porn film? It's sex and a pay cheque. **Linda LaHughes**, *Gimme, Gimme, Gimme*

I'm making a Jewish porno movie, it's 10 per cent sex, 90 per cent guilt. **Henny Youngman**

After the first ten minutes watching a porn film, I want to go home and screw. After the first twenty minutes, I never want to screw again as long as I live. **Erica Jong**

I don't like magic, because I try to figure out how it's done, and I get frustrated. Just like porn videos. **Garry Shandling**

My films are more appreciated in France than they are back home in America. The subtitles must be incredibly good. **Woody Allen**

Life in the movie business is like the beginning of a new love affair – it's full of surprises and you're constantly getting fucked. **David Mamet**

My agent said to me, 'In Hollywood, there is a yes list and a no list, and you aren't even on the no list.' **Alan Rudolph**

Tell me, how did you love my picture? **Samuel Goldwyn**

Did you hear about the starlet so dumb that she slept with the writer? **Producer's joke**

If my books had been any worse, I should not have been invited to Hollywood, and if they had been any better, I should not have come. **Raymond Chandler**

I was once sent a script combining *Wuthering Heights* and *Jane Eyre*, cunningly titled, 'Jane Heights'. **Cameron Mackintosh**

What do I look for in a good script? Days off. **Robert Mitchum**

I handed in a script last year and the studio didn't change one word.
The word they didn't change was on page 87.   **Steve Martin**

I do not fuck the star. That's a primary rule of mine on a picture.
The stand-in, maybe.   **Billy Wilder**

Shakespeare wrote, 'Kill all the lawyers.' That was before agents.
                                                            Robin Williams

My agent gets ten per cent of everything I get, except my blinding
headaches.   **Fred Allen**

In Hollywood, children don't wear masks on Halloween. Instead,
they usually dress up as agents, valet parkers, or second-unit directors.
                                                          Ellen DeGeneres

Popcorn is the last area of movie business where good taste is
still a concern.   **Mike Barfield**

Schmoozing is important in Hollywood. It's harder for someone
to screw you if they've had dinner at your house.   **Sue Mengers**

Show business is dog-eat-dog. It's worse than that. It's dog-doesn't-
return-other-dog's-phone-calls.   **Woody Allen**

My favourite conspiracy theory is 'Oliver Stone's *Titanic*'.
It shows a second iceberg.   **James Cameron**

They say the movies should be more like life. I think life should
be more like the movies.   **Myrna Loy**

Heaven's Gate is the most scandalous cinematic waste I have ever seen,
and remember, I've seen *Paint Your Wagon*.   **Roger Ebert**

I never go to movies where the hero's bust is bigger than the heroine's.
                                                             Groucho Marx

Most horror films are certainly that.   **Brendan Francis**

My boyfriend won't see anything he calls a 'chick flick'. That's any film where the woman talks.
Maura Kennedy

It was a cute picture. They used the basic story of *Wuthering Heights* and worked in surf riders.
Neil Simon

What do you have when you've got an agent buried up to his neck in the sand? Not enough sand.
Pat Williams

Good movies rarely contain a hot-air balloon.
John Snell

In any war movie, never share a foxhole with a character who carries a photo of his sweetheart.
Del Close

All movie bartenders, when first seen, are wiping the inside of a glass with a rag.
David W. Smith

Night watchmen in horror movies have a life expectancy of twelve seconds.
Sam Waas

I wouldn't say when you've seen one Western you've seen the lot. But when you've seen the lot you get the feeling you've seen one.
Katharine Whitehorn

Critics get hate mail from people when they reveal too much about the endings of thrillers. Here is the ending of *all* thrillers: the bad guy gets killed.
Rich Elias

A film so dire it would have difficulty in winning a prize at the Berlin Film Festival.
Jed Larson

The only problem I have with film festivals are the films.
Duane Byrge

Mary Poppins is unsupercalifragilisticexpialidocious.
Gilbert Adair

Wanna know what the summer's blockbuster is going to be?
See who McDonald's does the marketing tie-in with. Wanna know
what blockbuster will do disappointing business? See who Burger King
ties in with.

Dawson E. Rambo

To criticize *Hurry Sundown* would be like tripping a dwarf.

Wilfred Sheed

Transported to a surreal landscape, a young girl kills the first woman
she meets and then teams up with three strangers to kill again.

Review of *The Wizard of Oz* for Christian website

Charlton Heston's performance as a doctor made me want to call out,
'Is there an apple in the house?'

C.A. Lejeune

I'm a big fan of the movie *Das Boot*, or as we call it in English,
The Boot.

Mike Myers

There's a scene in *Thunderball* when I'm in the shower and James Bond
walks in. I say, 'Pass me something to slip on.' And he passes me my
slippers.

Luciana Paluzzi

Table for Five would be an ideal movie to watch on a plane; at least they
provide free sick bags.

Simon Rose

A gorilla in boxing gloves wielding a pair of garden shears could have
done a better job of editing *The Boyfriend*.

Ken Russell

They only got two things right in *Lawrence of Arabia*: the camels and
the sand.

Lowell Thomas

Jean Cocteau's *The Seashell and the Clergyman* is apparently
meaningless, but if it has any meaning it is doubtless objectionable.

British Board Film Censor

Picador and leave.

Christopher Tookey on *Matador*

What did I think of *Titanic*? I'd rather have been on it.

Miles Kruger

—No, Dougal, you can't stay up and watch the scary film. The last time you stayed up and watched a scary film you ended up having to sleep in my bed. I wouldn't mind, but it wasn't even a scary film.
—Come on, Ted. A Volkswagen with a mind of its own. If that's not scary, I don't know what is.   **Father Ted and Father Dougal,** *Father Ted*

The two most important words in *Last Tango in Paris* are 'tango' and 'Paris', both of which are regarded as sophisticated and adult. *Last Hokey-Cokey in Macclesfield* wouldn't be the same at all.   **Mark Steyn**

This is one of those films that should never have been released – not even on parole.   **Christopher Tookey**

Another Woman is a feel-good movie only in the sense that you feel much better when you stop watching it.   **Simon Rose**

Any film, even the worst, is better than real life.   **Quentin Crisp**

MUSICAL

It seems that the moment anyone gets hold of an exclamation mark these days, he promptly sits down and writes a musical around it.
                                                      George Jean Nathan

Writing a musical is like doing your own root canal work.   **Don Black**

Godspell is back in London at the Young Vic. For those who missed it the first time, this is your golden opportunity: you can miss it again.
                                                      Michael Billington

I could eat alphabet soup and *shit* better lyrics.   **Johnny Mercer**

'Rod Stewart Songs to Become Musical'   **Headline, BT News website**

If Hitler's still alive, I hope he's on the road with a musical.
                                                      John Schlesinger

Maris was devastated to be kicked out of the music society production of *Cats*. She kept forgetting the words to the song 'Memory'.

Niles Crane, *Frasier*

Andrew Lloyd Webber's music is everywhere – but so is AIDS.

Malcolm Williamson

—Who do I have to screw to get out of this show?
—The same person you screwed to get in.　　**Stephen Sondheim and Larry Kert**

THEATRE

I go to the theatre to be entertained. I don't want to see plays about rape, sodomy and drug addiction. I can get all that at home.　　**Peter Cook**

Very few people go to the doctor when they have a cold. They go to the theatre instead.　　**James Agate**

I saw the play under adverse conditions. The curtain was up.　　**Robert Benchley**

Apart from that, Mrs Lincoln, how did you enjoy the play?　　**Anon**

You people in the cheaper seats clap your hands, and the rest of you just rattle your jewellery.　　**John Lennon, at the Royal Variety Performance, 1963**

The play was a great success but the audience was a total failure.

Oscar Wilde

What is my play about? It's about to make me very rich.　　**Tom Stoppard**

I daren't tell my mother I'm starring in *The Vagina Monologues*. I've told her it's called *The Geneva Monologues*, and it's about women in banking.　　**Maureen Lipman**

Comedy is love and a bit with a dog. That's what people want.

Tom Stoppard

In the theatre I'm playing, there's a hole in the wall between the
ladies' dressing room and mine. I've been meaning to plug it up,
but what the hell – let them enjoy themselves.   **George Burns**

He directed rehearsals with all the airy deftness of a rheumatic
deacon producing *Macbeth* for a church social.   **Noël Coward**

Nudity on stage is disgusting. But if I were 22 with a great body,
it would be artistic, tasteful, patriotic and a progressive religious
experience.   **Shelley Winters**

In every play by Ibsen a stranger comes into the room, opens a window
to let in fresh air and everyone dies of pneumonia.   **Somerset Maugham**

What is *Uncle Vanya* about? I'd say it is about as much as I can take.
                                                            Roger Garland

I thought I'd begin by reciting a sonnet by Shakespeare but then
I thought why should I? He never reads any of mine.   **Spike Milligan**

He didn't believe the works of Shakespeare were written by
Shakespeare but by someone else of the same name.   **Mark Twain**

I don't know whether or not Bacon wrote Shakespeare's plays.
But if he didn't he missed the chance of a lifetime.   **Mark Twain**

If you had a million Shakespeares, would they write like a monkey?
                                                            Steven Wright

Shakespeare is fantastic. And to think he wrote it all with a feather!
                                                            Sam Goldwyn

Acting in Shakespeare's plays, you never get a chance to sit down
unless you're a king.   **Josephine Hull**

George Bernard Shaw writes like a Pakistani who has learned
English when he was twelve years old in order to become a
chartered accountant.   **John Osborne**

Creston Clark played the King as though under premonition that
someone else was about to play the ace.   Eugene Field

Said Hamlet to Ophelia, 'I'll draw a sketch of thee; what kind of pencil
shall I use? To be or not to be?'   Spike Milligan

Omlet, Omlet, dies is dien Feyder's spooke.   *Hamlet*, Dutch

Hamlet is a terrific play, but there are way too many quotations in it.
                                                    Hugh Leonard

Are the commentators on *Hamlet* really mad, or only pretending to be?
                                                    Oscar Wilde

If she says your behaviour is heinous,
Kick her right in the Coriolanus.   Cole Porter, *Brush up Your Shakespeare*

A bad experience of Shakespeare is like a bad oyster – it puts you off
for life.   Judi Dench

The only thing I didn't like about *The Barretts of Wimpole Street*
was the play.   Dorothy Parker

Opening night: the night before the play is ready to open.
                                                George Jean Nathan

—How long do you think the play will last?
—What's the time now?   Terry-Thomas

The opening night audience is mostly friends of the cast and backers
of the show, and they've come to applaud their money.   Al Hirschfield

I find writing about the Canadian theatre of drama depressingly like
discussing the art of dinghy-sailing among Bedouins.   Merrill Denison

There are three rules for a playwright. The first rule is not to write like
Henry Arthur Jones. The second and third rules are the same.
                                                    Oscar Wilde

Last time I acted my name was so low on the programme I was getting orders for the printing.
                                                              Frank Carson

A woman on hearing Macbeth say, 'Tomorrow and tomorrow and tomorrow,' remarked to her companion, 'So that'll be Monday then.'
                                                              Sheridan Morley

ACTORS AND ACTING

I always knew that if all else failed I could become an actor – and all else failed.
                                                              David Niven

I come from a long line of actors. It's called the dole queue.   Alan Davies

The actor and the streetwalker. The two oldest professions in the world, ruined by amateurs.
                                                              Alexander Woollcott

There are five stages in the life of an actor: Who's Mary Astor? Get me Mary Astor. Get me a Mary Astor type. Get me a young Mary Astor. Who's Mary Astor?
                                                              Mary Astor

She goes, 'I'm an actress.' I go, 'Sure, which restaurant?'   Sarah Bernhard

Mummy, what is that lady *for*?   Child watching Hermione Gingold on stage

—Acting is a rough business. Only 10 per cent is talent, 20 per cent is looks, and 70 per cent is luck of the draw.
—That's so depressing. I mean, you wanna believe that sexual favours play *some* part.   Bobby Adler and Jack McFarland, *Will and Grace*

An actor is not quite a human being – but then, who is?   George Sanders

It is no accident that an anagram of 'actors' is 'scrota'.   Alfred Hitchcock

—How many actors does it take to change a light bulb?
—One hundred. One to change the bulb, and ninety-nine to say, 'I could have done that.'
                                                              Anon

Herbert Ross told me that I couldn't act. I said, 'Well, that's no news to me. If you're any kind of a director, you'll make it look like I'm acting.'

Dolly Parton

A starlet is any girl under thirty in Hollywood who is not regularly employed in a brothel.

Ben Hecht

Acting is merely the art of keeping a large group of people from coughing.

Ralph Richardson

My acting range? Left eyebrow raised, right eyebrow raised.

Roger Moore

One critic complained that I had only two gestures – left hand up, and right hand down. What did he expect me to do? Bring out my prick?

John Gielgud

As a young actress, I always had a rule: if I didn't understand anything I always said it as if it were improper.

Edith Evans

Edith Evans took her curtain calls as though she had just been un-nailed from the cross.

Noël Coward

Just know your lines and don't bump into the furniture.

Noël Coward

Meryl Streep can act Polish or English or Australian but she sure as hell can't act blonde.

Joan Bennett

That actress couldn't get a laugh if she pulled a kipper out of her cunt.

Noël Coward

You can pick out actors by the glazed look that comes into their eyes when the conversation wanders away from themselves.

Michael Wilding

Fans are people who let an actor know he's not alone in the way he feels about himself.

Jack Carson

An actor's success has the life expectancy of a small boy about to look into a gas tank with a lighted match.

Fred Allen

An actor can remember his briefest notice well into senescence and long after he has forgotten his phone number and where he lives.

Jean Kerr

He brought to every one of his roles the quality of needing the money.

Stephen Fry

I knew Doris Day before she was a virgin.

Groucho Marx

Doris Day is as wholesome as a bowl of cornflakes and at least as sexy.

Dwight MacDonald

I was pretty – so pretty that actresses didn't want to work with me.

Roger Moore

Peter O'Toole has a face not so much lived-in as infested.

Paul Taylor

One casting director said to me, 'This role calls for a guy-next-door type. You don't look as if you've ever lived next door to anybody.

Donald Sutherland

What's the difference between a short actor and a short star? The short actor stands on an orange box, and the short star has them dig ditches for everyone else.

Michael J. Fox

Julie Andrews has that wonderful British strength that makes you wonder why they lost India.

Moss Hart

Steve McQueen had that look people get when they ride in elevators.

Anatole Broyard

Howard Hughes said one time: 'My God, Mitch, you're just like a pay toilet – you don't give a shit for nothin'.'

Robert Mitchum

Everyone wants to be Cary Grant. Even I want to be Cary Grant.

Cary Grant

Ingrid Bergman had a superabundance of all the virtues of the Swedes –
innocence, romanticism and emotional recklessness, and all their faults –
innocence, romanticism and emotional recklessness.   **Sam White**

Arnold Schwarzenegger's body is like a condom full of walnuts.
Clive James

Cary Grant made men seem like a good idea.   **Graham McCann**

You always knew exactly where you were with Errol Flynn because
he *always* let you down.   **David Niven**

What when drunk one sees in other women, one sees in Garbo sober.
Kenneth Tynan

Greta Garbo made you eat a mile of her shit, just to get a whiff
of her asshole.   **John Gilbert**

Dear Ingrid Bergman – speaks five languages and can't act in any
of them.   **John Gielgud**

Katharine Hepburn runs the gamut of emotions from A to B.
Dorothy Parker

Michael Caine can out-act any, well nearly any, telephone kiosk
you care to mention.   **Hugh Leonard**

Clint Eastwood is looking increasingly like an Easter Island statue.   **Anon**

Sarah Brightman couldn't act scared on the New York subway at
four o'clock in the morning.   **Joel Segal**

Edith Evans looks like something that would eat its young. **Dorothy Parker**

The acting career of Sylvester Stallone is more of a mystery than
cot death.   **Rex Reed**

Life is difficult enough without Meryl Streep movies.   **Truman Capote**

Marilyn Monroe was good at playing abstract confusion in the
same way that a midget is good at being short.   **Clive James**

I was the only director who ever made two pictures with Marilyn
Monroe. Forget the Oscar, I deserve the Purple Heart.   **Billy Wilder**

FAME AND CELEBRITY

—Are you Groucho Marx?
—No, are you?   **Groucho Marx**

—Are you Robert Mitchum?
—Well, somebody has to be.   **Robert Mitchum**

—Are you Woody Allen?
—Yes.
—Are you *sure* you're Woody Allen?   **Woody Allen**

—Are you Peter Sellers?
—Not today.   **Peter Sellers**

—Are you Tallulah Bankhead?
—What's left of her.   **Tallulah Bankhead**

—You're Michael Caine.
—I know.   **Michael Caine**

I was in New Hampshire with my family at a pizza place. The kid
working there goes, 'Hey, you look like Adam Sandler.' I said, 'Yeah,
I know.' He goes, 'What's your name?' I go, 'Adam Sandler.'
And he goes, 'Whoa, that's a coincidence!'   **Adam Sandler**

Ava Gardner, complaining that the maître d' at Ciro's had not
shown her and Frank Sinatra immediately to the best table, grumbled,
'We had to tell him who we were.' Sammy Davis Jr, interested,
enquired, 'And who were you?'   **Lisa Marchant**

A man only has to murder a series of wives in a new way to
become known to millions of people who have never heard of Homer.

Robert Lynd

—Name?
—Cary Grant.
—You don't look like Cary Grant.
—Nobody does.

Studio security guard and Cary Grant

I had one guy at a gas station in New York say to me, 'Hey, you
look like that Hugh Grant. No offence.'

Hugh Grant

People come up to me and say, 'Emo, do people really come up to you?'

Emo Philips

I always wanted to be somebody, but I should have been more specific.

Lily Tomlin

I'm never going to be famous. I don't do anything, not one single
thing. I used to bite my nails, but I don't even do that any more.

Dorothy Parker

In the future, everyone will be famous for fifteen minutes.

Andy Warhol

Appreciate me now, and avoid the rush.

Ashleigh Brilliant

To be popular one must be a mediocrity.

Oscar Wilde

I pretended to be somebody I wanted to be until I finally became that
person. Or he became me.

Cary Grant

There are pluses and minuses to fame. The plus is that I am known by
everybody. The minus is that I am known by everybody.

Jerry Springer

You know what I hate most about being a public figure? The public.

Howard Stern

Celebrity opens doors and lowers drawers.

Eddie Izzard

If you're famous over twenty minutes, you get your own cologne.

Kim Castle

If O.J. wasn't famous, he'd be in jail right now. If O.J. drove a bus, he wouldn't even be O.J. He'd be Orenthal, the bus-driving murderer.

Chris Rock

Don't confuse fame with success. One is Madonna; the other is Helen Keller.

Erma Bombeck

A celebrity is any well-known TV or movie star who looks like he spends more than two hours working on his hair.

Steve Martin

The nice thing about being a celebrity is that if you bore people they think it's their fault.

Henry Kissinger

They say I slept with seven Miss Worlds. I didn't – it was only four. I didn't turn up for the other three.

George Best

Stardom: some pigs have it, some pigs don't.

Miss Piggy

Once, I walked out of a bathroom stall at O'Hare Airport, and three women applauded. That's when I knew: I am famous. **Oprah Winfrey**

You're not famous until my mother has heard of you.

Jay Leno

Dahling, I have enemies I've never met. That's fame! **Tallulah Bankhead**

My new line is, 'In fifteen minutes, everybody will be famous.' **Andy Warhol**

He is remembered chiefly as the man about whom all is forgotten.

Nicholas Bentley

I turned down *This is Your Life*. I couldn't bear to think of all those cross wives.

Roger Moore

I was afraid of losing my obscurity. Genius only thrives in the dark. Like celery.

Aldous Huxley

You can't get spoiled if you do your own ironing.   Meryl Streep

Some movie stars wear their sunglasses even in church. They're afraid
God might recognize them and ask for autographs.   Fred Allen

—What do you think China should do about Tibet?
—Who cares what I think China should do? I'm a fucking actor.
I'm a grown man who puts on make-up.   Interviewer and Brad Pitt

Does success turn you into a monster? Most of them were monsters
before they ever became successful.   Bette Davis

I'm not interested in throwing TVs out of windows. Besides, plasma
screens are really heavy and most windows are double-glazed these days.
                    Ronan Keating

The crowds cheered me as I passed by, but they would be just as
noisy if they were going to see me hanged.   Oliver Cromwell

We can't all be heroes. Someone has to sit on the kerb and clap as
they go by.   Will Rogers

When everyone is somebody, then no one's anybody.   W.S. Gilbert

The best fame is a writer's fame. It's enough to get a table at a good
restaurant, but not enough that you get interrupted when you eat.
                    Fran Lebowitz

My reputation is terrible, which comforts me a lot.   Noël Coward

The only time you realize you have a reputation is when you're not
living up to it.   Jose Iturbi

Stardom? I never touch the stuff.   John Lithgow

In order to keep a sense of perspective, pin a picture of a supermodel on
your kitchen wall and write above it, 'Today, someone, somewhere, is
taking her shit.'   Tom Lowe

GOSSIP AND PUBLICITY

If you haven't got anything good to say about anyone come sit by me.
Alice Roosevelt Longworth

'Conversation' is when three women stand on the corner talking.
'Gossip' is when one of them leaves.
Herb Shriner

It is perfectly monstrous the way people go about nowadays, saying things against one, behind one's back, that are absolutely and entirely true.
Oscar Wilde

Live that you wouldn't be ashamed to sell the family parrot to the town gossip.
Will Rogers

Three may keep a secret, if two of them are dead.
Benjamin Franklin

Don't forget to tell everyone it's a secret.
Gerald Lieberman

Joan Collins is a commodity who would sell her own bowel movement.
Anthony Newley

When a woman says, 'I don't wish to mention any names,' it's not necessary to mention any names.
Kin Hubbard

There is only one thing in the world worse than being talked about, and that is not being talked about.
Oscar Wilde

Some are born great, some achieve greatness, and some hire public relations officers.
Daniel J. Boorstin

Dead? With the newspaper strike on, I wouldn't even consider it.
Bette Davis

All publicity is good, except your own obituary notice.
Brendan Behan

I improve on misquotation.
Cary Grant

TELEVISION AND MEDIA

Television is a weapon of mass distraction.   **Larry Gelbart**

Television has proved that people will look at anything rather than
each other.   **Ann Landers**

It's not easy to juggle a pregnant wife and a troubled child, but somehow
I managed to squeeze in eight hours of TV a day.   **Homer Simpson**

The other day a woman came up to me and said, 'Didn't I see you on
television?' I said, 'I don't know. You can't see out the other way.'
                                                              Emo Philips

Television is an invention that permits you to be entertained in your
living room by people you wouldn't have in your home.   **David Frost**

Men don't care what's on TV. They only care what else is on TV.
                                                            Jerry Seinfeld

If anyone is in the grip of some habit of which they are greatly ashamed,
I implore you not to give way to it in secret, but to do it on television.
                                                             Quentin Crisp

You have to be pretty special to be able to cheapen TV any further.
I can't take credit for that. It's like finding a way of making the sun
hotter.   **Jerry Springer**

There's all this talk about violence on TV causing violence on the
street. Well, there's so much comedy on television. Does that cause
comedy on the street?   **George Carlin**

Don't you wish there was a knob on the TV to turn up the intelligence?
There's one marked 'brightness' but it doesn't work.   **Gallagher**

I watch about six hours of TV a day. Seven if there's something good on.
                                                             Bart Simpson

Television is for appearing on, not for looking at.   Noël Coward

Never miss a chance to have sex or appear on television.   Gore Vidal

With high definition TV, everything looks bigger and wider. Kind of
like going to your 25th high school reunion.   Jay Leno

I prefer television to movies. It's not so far to the bathroom.   Fred Allen

The cable TV sex channels don't expand our horizons, don't make
us better people, and don't come in clearly enough.   Bill Maher

You don't own a TV? What's all your furniture pointed at?
                                                    Joey Tribbiani, *Friends*

In Los Angeles, they don't throw their garbage away. They make it
into television shows.   Woody Allen

Americans call it the *Tonight Show* so they can remember when it's on.
                                                                    Jo Brand

As an American, I classify *I'm a Celebrity, Get me out of Here* in the
category of Impenetrable British Mysteries – like beans on toast.
                                                                  Molly Ivins

Ideas for television shows: Knowing M.E. Knowing You; Inner City
Sumo; Cooking in Prison; Youth Hostelling With Chris Eubank;
Monkey Tennis.   Alan Partridge

Fine art and pizza delivery – being a talk-show host falls neatly in
between.   David Letterman

I have a problem with the strip that runs along the bottom of
programmes. Do you want me to watch the show, or do you want me
to read the strip? Don't these idiots who run the networks know we
don't want to read? That's why we're watching TV.   Jerry Seinfeld

I keep Radio Three on all the time, just to deter burglars.   Joan O'Hara

If you read a lot of books, you're said to be well-read, but if you watch a lot of television you're not said to be 'well-viewed'.   **Lily Tomlin**

Television is very educational. Every time it comes on, I go into another room and read a book.   **Groucho Marx**

On television you can say you've pricked your finger but not the other way around.   **George Carlin**

In Russia, we had only two TV channels. Channel One was propaganda. Channel Two consisted of a KGB officer telling you, 'Turn back immediately to Channel One.'   **Yakov Smirnoff**

The American people love the Home Shopping Network because it's commercial-free.   **Will Durst**

Norwegian television gives you the sensation of a coma without the worry and inconvenience.   **Bill Bryson**

I don't watch television. I think it destroys the art of talking about oneself.   **Stephen Fry**

Need a hug? Then call now for tickets to a taping of *The Daily Show with Jon Stewart*! And good luck with that hug.   **Jon Stewart**

The media. It sounds like a convention of spiritualists.   **Tom Stoppard**

COMEDY

The producer said, 'How are you feeling?' I said, 'I'm feeling a bit funny.' He said, 'Well, get out there before it wears off.'   **Tommy Cooper**

I'm naturally funny. Sometimes I walk down the street and people just burst out laughing.   **Linda LaHughes, *Gimme, Gimme, Gimme***

A rich man's joke is always funny.   **Heywood Broun**

In Chicago, a clown was arrested for exposing himself. It was the first time anyone ever laughed at him.

Jon Stewart

Everybody laughed when I first told them I wanted to be a comedian – well, they're not laughing now.

Bob Monkhouse

I've seen him entertain fifty times and I've always enjoyed his joke.

Johnny Carson

Stand-up comedy is still the last refuge of the bitter alcoholic.

Bob Odenkirk

The first rule of comedy is never to perform in a town where they still point at aeroplanes.

Bobby Mills

I don't make jokes; I just watch the government and report the facts.

Will Rogers

If you tell a joke in the forest but nobody laughs, is it still a joke?

Steven Wright

Practically anything you say will seem amusing if you're on all fours.

P.J. O'Rourke

Tragedy is when I have a hangnail. Comedy is when I accidentally walk into an open sewer and die.

Mel Brooks

California? You can't write comedy in California. It's not depressing enough.

Alan Swann

The difference between English and American humour is $150 a minute.

Eric Idle

The first thing a comedian does on getting an unscheduled laugh is to verify the state of his buttons.

Alva Johnson

He's not laughing at you. He's laughing with me, who is laughing at you.

Grace Adler, *Will and Grace*

The person who knows how to laugh at himself will never cease
to be amused.   **Russ Dudley**

—Groucho Marx, do you have any special memories of your brother,
Chico, you'd like to share with us?
—Chico brought gonorrhoea to the Vaudeville circuit.
                                        Interviewer and Groucho Marx

You wouldn't get away with that
if my scriptwriter was here. **Bob Hope**

For what do we live, but to make sport for our neighbours, and
laugh at them in our turn?   **Jane Austen**

When people ask me where I get my ideas from I say, 'A little man in
Swindon. But I don't know where *he* gets them from.'   **John Cleese**

The reason angels can fly is that they take themselves lightly.
                                                    G.K. Chesterton

Bob Hope was a slave-driver with his gag writers. You'd be in the
bathroom and he'd shout through, 'Hope you're using the paper in there.
You gotta pen?'   **Bob Monkhouse**

Everything is funny as long as it is happening to someone else. **Will Rogers**

If Racine knew any jokes, he kept them to himself.   **Arthur Marshall**

The secret of all comedy writing is: write Jewish and cast Gentile.
                                                    Robert Kaufman

Analysing humour is like dissecting a frog. Few people are interested, and
the frog dies.   **E.B. White**

Gimme, Gimme, Gimme puts the 'h' into sitcom.   **Anon**

Irony! We haven't had any irony here since about 1983, when I was
the only practitioner of it, and I stopped because I was tired of
being stared at.
Steve Martin

Chevy Chase couldn't ad-lib a fart after a baked bean dinner.
Johnny Carson

Only dull people are brilliant at breakfast.
Oscar Wilde

—How I wish I had said that.
—You will, Oscar, you will.
Oscar Wilde and James McNeill Whistler

Everything I've ever said will be credited to Dorothy Parker.
George S. Kaufman

I often quote myself. It adds spice to my conversation.
George Bernard Shaw

CRITICS

—You know, Homer, it's very easy to criticize.
—Fun, too.
Marge and Homer Simpson

Critic is a six-letter word for a four-letter concept.
Piers Anthony

Anyone who can fill out a laundry slip thinks of himself as a writer.
Those who can't fill out a laundry slip think of themselves as critics.
George Seaton

A critic is a louse in the locks of literature.
Alfred, Lord Tennyson

A critic is a person who will slit the throat of a skylark to see what
makes it sing.
J.M. Synge

Before you criticize someone, walk a mile in their shoes. That way
when you criticize them, you'll be a mile away and have their shoes.
Frieda Norris

Believe a woman or an epitaph before you trust in critics.   **Lord Byron**

A drama critic is a person who surprises a playwright by informing him what he meant.   **Wilson Mizner**

Drama critics are there to show gay actors what it's like to have a wife.
Hugh Leonard

The function of the film critic is precisely to interpret the audio-visual electronic image and fragmentize individual coercive response against a background of selective subjectivity. He can do this either standing up or sitting.   **Woody Allen**

See that critic? He used to hate every movie. Then he married a young, big-bosomed woman, and now he loves every movie.   Woody Allen

Critics are like eunuchs in a harem; they know how it's done, they've seen it done every day, but they're unable to do it themselves.
Brendan Behan

Honest criticism is always hard to take particularly from a relative, a friend, an acquaintance or a stranger.   **Franklin P. Jones**

I like the kind of critics who just put people's names down.   **Andy Warhol**

Asking a working writer what he thinks about critics is like asking a lamppost how it feels about dogs.   **Christopher Hampton**

A bad review is wonderful when it isn't you.   **John Gielgud**

I've sold too many books to get good reviews any more.   **John Grisham**

I never read bad reviews about myself because my best friends
invariably tell me about them.
                                                          Oscar Levant

I approach reading reviews the way some people anticipate anal warts.
                                                          Roseanne

A bad review may spoil your breakfast but you shouldn't allow it
to spoil your lunch.   Kingsley Amis

I am sitting in the smallest room of my house. Your review is before
me. In a moment, it will be behind me.   Noël Coward

Don't pay any attention to the critics; don't even ignore them.
                                                          Sam Goldwyn

A bad review is even less important than whether it is raining in
Patagonia.   Iris Murdoch

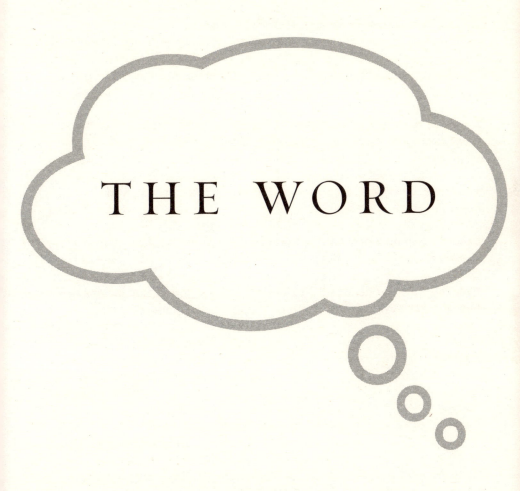

THE WORD

LANGUAGE

My wife is teaching me Cuban. It's like Spanish but with fewer words for luxury goods.
Emo Philips

I would love to speak Italian but I can't, so I grew underarm hair instead.
Sue Kolinsky

You don't have to have a language in common with someone for a sexual rapport. But it helps if the language you don't understand is Italian.
Madonna

What have you got when an Italian has one arm shorter than the other? A speech impediment.
Jackie Martling

Is there anything worse than speaking a foreign language to someone who turns out to be English?
Michael Frayn

Aside from a few odd words in Hebrew, I take it completely for granted that God has never spoken anything but the most dignified English.
Clarence Day

Learning English was like moving from one darkened house to another on a starless night during a strike of candlemakers and torchbearers.
Vladimir Nabokov

The interpreter was the harder to understand of the two.
Richard Brinsley Sheridan

There are over thirty words in the Irish language which are equivalent to the Spanish 'mañana'. But, somehow, none of them conveys the same sense of urgency.
Patrick Kavanagh

Boy, those French, they have a different word for everything. **Steve Martin**

There's a store in New York called Bonjour Croissant. It makes me want to go to Paris and open a store called Hello Toast. **Fran Lebowitz**

I don't speak French. But I do kiss that way.   **Lt Frank Drebin, *Naked Gun 2½***

I asked the barmaid for a quickie. The man next to me said,
'It's pronounced quiche.'   **Luigi Amaduzzi, Italian Ambassador**

Afrikaans sounds like Welsh with attitude and emphysema.   **A.A. Gill**

They did a survey of Scots to find out if they speak Gaelic. 90 per cent
said yes, six per cent said yes, and four per cent said they didn't know.
Tom Shields

German is the most extravagantly ugly language. It sounds like
someone using a sick bag on a 747.   **Willie Rushton**

Before we got engaged, he never farted. Now it's a second language.
Caroline Rhea

She speaks eighteen languages, and can't say 'No' in any of them.
Dorothy Parker

Dutch is not so much a language as a disease of the throat.   **Mark Twain**

Japanese has fewer sounds than any other language and therefore has to
ascribe a lot of meanings to the few it does have. 'Seikan' can mean a
sexual feeling, naval construction, can manufacturing, or serene
contemplation.   **Robert Christopher**

The Norwegian language is merely German spoken underwater.
Jed Larson

The one phrase it is imperative to know in every foreign language is,
'My friend will pay.'   **Alan Whicker**

I am sorry that I cannot address the people of Latin America in their
own language – Latin.   **Dan Quayle**

England and America are two countries separated by a common
language.   **George Bernard Shaw**

Statements to curdle the blood: 'One moment, please, while I check your account details'; 'I know all the Python scripts by heart'; 'Did I tell you, we did all our own conveyancing.'

Jenny Abrams

Victoria Beckham speaks two languages – English and Gucci.

Nicola Zweig

I speak Esperanto like a native.

Spike Milligan

The most beautiful words in the English language are, 'Cheque enclosed.'

Dorothy Parker

The most beautiful words in the English language are, 'It's benign.'

Woody Allen

The most beautiful words in the English language are, 'Have one on the house.'

Wilson Mizner

The most beautiful words in any language are, 'Not guilty.' Maxim Gorky

The sweetest words in the English language are, 'I told you so.' Gore Vidal

The most awful words in the English language are, 'Just coffee.'

Robert Morley

The most dreaded words in the English language are, 'Some assembly required.'

Bill Cosby

The saddest words in the English language are, 'Partick Thistle, nil.'

Billy Connolly

The most terrifying words in the English language are, 'I'm from the government and I'm here to help.'

Ronald Reagan

The worst words in the English language are, 'We have to talk.' Either
that or, 'Whose bra is this?'
Jerry Seinfeld

In England, an elevator is called a lift, a mile is called a kilometre,
and botulism is called a steak and kidney pie.
Greg Daniels

If anyone corrects your pronunciation of a word in a public place,
you have every right to punch him in the nose.
Heywood Broun

Slang is language that takes off its coat, rolls up its sleeves, spits
on its hands, and goes to work.
Carl Sandburg

I know only two words of American slang: 'swell' and 'lousy'.
I think 'swell' is lousy, but 'lousy' is swell.
J.B. Priestley

Children who have difficulty with 'cat' and 'mat' have no difficulty
with four letter words.
Pam Brown

All Englishmen talk as if they've got a bushel of plums stuck in their
throats, and then after swallowing them get constipated from the pits.
W.C. Fields

Sean Connery's amazing array of accents includes Russian-Scottish,
Irish-Scottish, Spanish-Scottish, Arabian-Scottish, and English-Scottish.
Simon Rose

WORDS AND GRAMMAR

The trouble with words is that you never know whose mouths
they've been in.
Dennis Potter

Whom is a word invented to make everyone sound like a butler.
Calvin Trillin

If you have a big enough dictionary, just about everything is a word.
Dave Barry

Whom is just womb with a breeze.   George S. Kaufman

Why is 'abbreviated' such a long word?   Michael Davis

It should be a law that if you use the word 'paradigm' without
knowing what it means, you go to jail. No exceptions.   Dave Jones

Ms is a syllable which sounds like a bumblebee breaking wind.
                                                        Hortense Calisher

'Fragile' is usually interpreted by postal workers as 'please
throw underarm'.   Harry Hershfield

Priceless like a mother's love, or the good kind of priceless?   Bart Simpson

The difference between light and hard is that you can sleep with a light on.

                                                                   Anon

The word 'duck' is 75 per cent obscene.   Lenny Bruce

Et cetera – the expression that makes people think you know
more than you do.   Herbert Prochnow

The word 'good' has many meanings. For example, if a man were
to shoot his grandmother at a range of 500 yards, I should call him
a good shot, but not necessarily a good man.   G.K. Chesterton

When she saw the sign 'Members only' she thought of him.   Spike Milligan

The difference between the right word and the almost right word
is the difference between lightning and lightning-bug.   Mark Twain

I have always wanted to write a book that ended with the word
'mayonnaise'.   Richard Brautigan

This sentence has three erors.   **Anon**

The difference between a misfortune and a calamity is this: if Gladstone
fell into the Thames, it would be a misfortune, and if someone hauled
him out again, that would be a calamity.   **Benjamin Disraeli**

You know the phrase, 'to take care of something' – well, I realize now
that you meant it in a sort of Al Pacino way. Whereas I was thinking
more along the lines of Julie Andrews.   **Father Ted to Tom, *Father Ted***

Paragraphing is one of the lower forms of cunning, like a way with
women.   **Harry Wade**

The art of newspaper paragraphing is to stroke a platitude until
it purrs like an epigram.   **Don Marquis**

Metaphors be with you.   **Harvey Mindess**

The cure for mixed metaphors is for the patient to be obliged to
draw a picture of the result.   **Bernard Levin**

We didn't have metaphors in my day. We didn't beat about the bush.
                                                         Fred Truman

I think the expression, 'It's a small world' is really a euphemism for,
'I keep running into people I can't stand.'   **Brock Cohen**

Collective nouns: a chapter of authors; a Parthenon of columnists; a
percentage of agents; a remainder of publishers; a rumour of diarists,
a shortage of jockeys.   **Anon**

She was the only person I ever met who used semicolons in her
love letters.   **John Sullivan**

I adore adverbs; they are the only qualifications I really much respect.
                                                         Henry James

Is 'tired old cliché' one?   **Steven Wright**

A preposition is something you should never end a sentence with.

Jill Etherington

Why did you bring that book that I didn't want to be read to out of up for?

H.L. Mencken

A footnote is like running downstairs to answer the doorbell on your wedding night.

John Barrymore

An exclamation point is like laughing at your own joke. F. Scott Fitzgerald

Why is the alphabet in that order? Is it because of the song? Steven Wright

He respects Owl, because you can't help respecting anybody who can spell TWESDAY, even if he doesn't spell it right.

A.A. Milne

When I was at school I learned to spell the word 'myrrh'. I have never had cause to write the word again.

Tony Hawks

A synonym is a word you use when you can't spell the word you first thought of.

Burt Bacharach

For Pheasant *read* Peasant throughout.

W.C. Sellar and R.J. Yeatman

If you take hyphens seriously, you will surely go mad.

John Benbow

Read over your compositions and wherever you meet with a passage that you think particularly fine, strike it out.

Samuel Johnson

Even if you learn to speak correct English, to whom are you going to speak it?

Clarence Darrow

WRITER

Times are bad. Children no longer obey their parents and everyone is writing a book.

Cicero, circa 43 BC

The writer's way is rough and lonely, and who would choose it
while there are vacancies in more gracious professions, such as,
say, cleaning out ferryboats? **Dorothy Parker**

There was a time when I thought my only connection with the
literary world would be that I had once delivered meat to T.S. Eliot's
mother-in-law. **Alan Bennett**

Writing is not a profession, but a vocation of unhappiness.

Georges Simenon

Writing is like the world's oldest profession. First you do it for your
own enjoyment. Then you do it for a few friends. Eventually, you
figure, what the hell, I might as well get paid for it. **Irma Kalish**

You, a writer? Listen, dear, you couldn't write 'fuck' on a dusty
Venetian blind. **Coral Browne**

Everybody can write. Writers can't do anything else. **Mignon McLaughlin**

Writing is one-tenth perspiration and nine-tenths masturbation.

Alan Bennett

Writing is the hardest way to earn a living, with the possible
exception of wrestling alligators. **William Saroyan**

When I was a teenager, I wanted to write The Great American Novel. But
then I realized that I didn't even want to read The Great American Novel.
Ray Barone, *Everybody Loves Raymond*

Advice to writers: sometimes you just have to stop writing.
Even before you begin. **Stanislaw J. Lec**

Let us reflect whether there be any living writer whose silence
we would consider to be a literary disaster. **Cyril Connolly**

Your life story would not make a good book. Don't even try.

Fran Lebowitz

Frankly, my dear, I should bury your script in a drawer and put
a lily on top.
Noël Coward

Having been unpopular in high school is not just cause for book
publication.
Fran Lebowitz

Your manuscript is both good and original; but the part that is good
is not original, and the part that is original is not good. Samuel Johnson

—Should I put more fire in my stories?
—No. Vice versa.
Aspiring author and Somerset Maugham

Write something, even if it's just a suicide note.
Gore Vidal

In a profession like publishing where simple accountancy is preferable to
a degree in English, illiteracy is not considered to be a great drawback.
Dominic Behan

My advice to aspiring writers: marry money.
Max Shulman

One editor said to me, 'You could be the next Dorothy Parker.' I thought,
'What? Keep slashing my wrists and drinking shoe polish?' Lynne Truss

Writers should be read and not seen. Rarely are they a winsome sight.
Edna Ferber

I hate authors. I wouldn't mind them so much if they didn't write books.
Elizabeth Von Arnim

I can't understand why a person will take a year to write a novel
when he can easily buy one for a few dollars.
Fred Allen

It took me fifteen years to discover I had no talent for writing, but I
couldn't give it up because by that time I was too famous.
Robert Benchley

Anybody who can write home for money can write for magazines.
Wilson Mizner

The way British publishing works is that you go from not being published no matter how good you are, to being published no matter how bad you are.

Tibor Fischer

Gentlemen, I agree with you that Napoleon is a tyrant, a monster, the sworn foe of our nation, and if you will, of the whole human race. But, gentlemen, we must not forget that he once shot a publisher.

Thomas Campbell

I'm writing a book. I've got the page numbers done.

Steven Wright

Every time you think you've been screwed by publishers in every possible way, you meet one who has read the Kama Sutra.

Anon

I always start writing with a clean piece of paper and a dirty mind.

Patrick Dennis

Don't ask a writer what he's working on. It's like asking someone with cancer about the progress of his disease.

Luke Angel

When our friend is delivered of a couplet, with infinite labour and pain, he takes to his bed, has straw laid down, the knocker tied up, and expects his friends to call and make enquiries.

Sydney Smith

—I have writer's block. It's the worst feeling in the world.
—Try ten days without a bowel movement sometime.

Blanche Deveraux and Sophia Petrillo, *The Golden Girls*

This writing business. Pencils and whatnot. Overrated, if you ask me.

Winnie the Pooh

This book is dedicated to my brilliant and beautiful wife without whom I would be nothing. She always comforts and consoles, never complains or interferes, asks nothing and endures all. She also writes my dedications.

Albert Malvino

Anyone could write a novel given six weeks, pen, paper, and no telephone or wife.
Evelyn Waugh

Nothing I have written is factual except the bits that sound like fiction.
Clive James

The hardest thing is writing a recommendation for someone you know.
Kin Hubbard

An author who talks about his own books is almost as bad as a mother who talks about her own children.
Benjamin Disraeli

In America, only the successful writer is important, in France, all writers are important, in England, no writer is important, and in Australia, you have to explain what a writer is.
Geoffrey Cottrell

Everywhere I go I am asked if university stifles writers. My opinion is that it doesn't stifle enough of them.
Flannery O'Connor

The secret of writing great literature is to be under house arrest.
Georg Lukacs

If you steal from one author, it's plagiarism; if you steal from many, it's research.
Wilson Mizner

I do borrow from other writers. I can only say in my defence, like the woman brought before the judge on a charge of kleptomania, 'I do steal; but, Your Honour, only from the very best stores.'
Thornton Wilder

There are just three rules for writing but nobody knows what they are.
Somerset Maugham

I dedicate this book to my daughter Leonora without whose never-failing sympathy and encouragement it would have been finished in half the time.
P.G. Wodehouse

This book is dedicated to the one woman Fate created just for me. So far I've managed to avoid her.
Jon Winokur

If you want to get rich from writing, write the sort of thing that's read by persons who move their lips when reading to themselves.   **Don Marquis**

The first thing a writer has to do is find another source of income.
Ellen Gilchrist

A professional writer is an amateur who didn't quit.   **Richard Bach**

Whenever I am asked what kind of writing is the most lucrative,
I have to say, a ransom note.   **H.N. Swanson**

I called my first book *The Collected Works of Max Beerbohm,
Volume One*.   **Max Beerbohm**

My Opus Number One cost me an unconscionable quantity of paper, and was called, with merciless fitness, 'Immaturity'. Part of it was devoured by mice, though even they had not been able to finish it.
George Bernard Shaw

On the day when a young writer corrects his first proof sheets,
he is as proud as a schoolboy who has just got his first dose of pox.
Charles Baudelaire

In every first novel, the hero is the author as Christ or Faust.   **Oscar Wilde**

I never can understand how two people can write a book together; to me that's like three people getting together to have a baby. One of them is superfluous.   **Evelyn Waugh**

I am writing a book about the Crusades so *dull* that I can scarcely write it.   **Hilaire Belloc**

Writing is easy. All you have to do is stare at a blank piece of paper until drops of blood form on your forehead.   **Gene Fowler**

A good many young writers make the mistake of enclosing a stamped self-addressed envelope, big enough to send the manuscript back in. This is too much of a temptation for the editor.   **Ring Lardner**

I love deadlines. I like the whooshing sound they make as they fly by.

Douglas Adams

He had long held one of the most fundamental of all literary convictions, that the world owed him a living.

G.K. Chesterton

Most writers are vain, so I try to ensure than any author who comes to stay will find at least one of their books in their room.

Duke of Devonshire

I asked my publisher what would happen if he sold all the copies of my book he had printed. He said, 'I'll just print another ten.'

Eric Sykes

A magnum opus is a book which when dropped from a three-storey building is big enough to kill a man.

Edward Wilson

The greatest masterpiece in literature is only a dictionary out of order.

Jean Cocteau

The principle of procrastinated rape is said to be the ruling one in all the great best-sellers.

V.S. Pritchett

There is many a best-seller that could have been prevented by a good teacher.

Flannery O'Connor

The pen is mightier than the sword, and considerably easier to write with.

Marty Feldman

George Bernard Shaw's handwriting was exquisite – like a fly which had been trained at the Russian ballet.

James Agate

Most people enjoy the sight of their own handwriting as they enjoy the smell of their own farts.

W.H. Auden

A signature always reveals a man's character – and sometimes even his name.

Evan Essar

It's all very well to be able to write books, but can you waggle your ears?

J.M. Barrie to H.G. Wells

If you can't annoy somebody, there's little point in writing.   **Kingsley Amis**

When I get sent manuscripts from aspiring poets, I do one of two
things: if there is no stamped self-addressed envelope, I throw it
into the bin. If there is, I write and tell them to fuck off.   **Philip Larkin**

BOOKS

People say that life is the thing, but I prefer reading.   **Logan Pearsall Smith**

'I have 20,000 books,' Jeremy Beadle boasted, which is rather like
learning that Stephen Hawking has 20,000 pairs of trainers.
Victor Lewis-Smith

No furniture is so charming as books, even if you never open
them or read a single word.   **Sydney Smith**

—Homer, are you coming with us to the book fair?
—If it doesn't have Siamese twins in a jar, it's not a fair.
Marge and Homer Simpson

I like a thin book because it will steady a table; a leather volume because
it will strop a razor; and a heavy book because it can be thrown at a cat.
Mark Twain

I have a bit of a problem with reading. I read slowly, and get my words
jumbled up. I had some tests done and apparently it's not dyslexia
– I'm just thick. At least now I have a name for it.   **Jack Dee**

It's not easy having dyslexia. Last week I went to a toga party as a goat.
Arthur Smith

A book reads the better which is your own, and has been so long known
to us, that we know the topography of its blots, and dog's ears, and can
trace the dirt in it to having read it at tea with buttered muffins.
Charles Lamb

I'm dyslexic. There was a sign outside my school that said, 'Slow Children' which didn't do much for our self-esteem. Then again, we couldn't read it.

Jimmy Carr

Magazines all too frequently lead to books and should be regarded as the heavy petting of literature.

Fran Lebowitz

Literature is mostly about having sex and not much about having children. Life is the other way round.

David Lodge

All literature is a footnote to Faust. I have no idea what I mean by that.

Woody Allen

A man came to my door and said, 'I'd like to read your gas meter.' I said, 'Whatever happened to the classics?'

Emo Philips

A classic is a book that everybody wants to have read and nobody wants to read.

Mark Twain

A classic is a book that everybody is assumed to have read and often think they have.

Alan Bennett

Paradise Lost is a book that, once put down, is very hard to pick up again.

Samuel Johnson

A man who has not read Homer is like a man who has not seen the ocean. There is a great object of which he has no idea.

Walter Bagehot

There are seventy million books in American libraries, but the one you want to read is always out.

Tom Masson

I have hundreds of books, but no bookcase. Nobody would lend me a bookcase.

Henny Youngman

Rare volume: a returned book. *Harry Herschelovitzer*

There is no tribe of human beings more pestiferous than the people who insist on lending you books whether you wish to borrow them or not. *Robert Lynd*

I do a lot of reading about serial killers, mostly *How To* books. *Roseanne*

I gave my young nephew a book for Christmas. He's spent six months looking for where to put the batteries. *Milton Berle*

The big advantage of a book is it's very easy to rewind. Close it and you're right back at the beginning. *Jerry Seinfeld*

I always read the last page of a book first so that if I die before I finish, I will know how it turned out. *Nora Ephron*

First time I read the dictionary, I thought it was a poem about everything. *Steven Wright*

I know a guy who reads mystery novels backwards. He knows who did it, but he doesn't know what he did. *Sandy Sherwood*

I've just been reading the dictionary. Turns out the zebra did it. *Steven Wright*

Never judge a book by its movie. *J.W. Eagan*

Join the book club! As an introductory offer we'll send you the following books absolutely free: *Eat, Run, Stay Fit and Die Anyway; What to Wear on the Toilet; 124 Simple Exercises for the Teeth; Apartment Hunting for Devil-Worshippers; How to Get a Tan With a Flashlight; The Lives of Six Extremely Short Saints; How to Organize a Tupperware Gangbang; How to Turn Unbearable Pain Into Extra Income; 64 Good Reasons for Giving up Hope.* *George Carlin*

A good title is the title of a successful book. *Raymond Chandler*

I'm bringing out a book for the building trade called
The Dictionary of Ludicrous Quotations.

Barry Cryer

My favourite quotation is eight pounds ten for a second-hand suit.

Spike Milligan

An encyclopaedia is a system for collecting dust in alphabetical order.

Mike Barfield

What's another word for thesaurus?

Steven Wright

There is a new dictionary for masochists. It lists all the words but
not in alphabetical order.

Frank Tyger

I'm writing an unauthorized autobiography.

Steven Wright

Next to the writer of real estate advertisements, the autobiographer
is the most suspect of prose artists.

Donal Henahan

Even when Micheál MacLiammoir took in later life to autobiographies,
they were about as reliable as his hairpieces.

Sheridan Morley

I'm a minor player in my *own* life story.

Tony Wilson

Every great man nowadays has his disciples, and it is always Judas who
writes the biography.

Oscar Wilde

I never read the life of an important person without discovering that
he knew more and could do more than I could ever hope to know
or to do in half a dozen lifetimes.

J.B. Priestley

I have decided to keep a full journal, in the hope that my life will
perhaps seem more interesting when it is written down.

Adrian Mole

I remember my first diary entry: '1st January 1937. Hung about.'

John Julius Norwich

My favourite book, movie and food is *Fried Green Tomatoes*. **Jane Radcliffe**

Once I read her diary. I was twenty pages in before I realized it wasn't a Sidney Sheldon novel.
Sophia Petrillo, *The Golden Girls*

I never travel without my diary. One should always have something sensational to read on the train.
Oscar Wilde

Keep a diary and someday it'll keep you.
Mae West

It's the good girls keep diaries. The bad girls never have the time.
Tallulah Bankhead

To write a diary every day is like returning to one's own vomit.
Enoch Powell

I took a speed-reading course, and read *War and Peace* in 20 minutes. It's about Russia.
Woody Allen

I just got out of hospital. I was in a speed-reading accident. I hit a bookmark.
Steven Wright

The first porn book I wrote, I called, *House of Leather.* I published it under the name of the headmaster who threw me out of prep school.
Fran Lebowitz

I am the kind of writer that people think other people are reading.
V.S. Naipaul

There are only two kinds of P.G. Wodehouse readers: those who adore him, and those who have never read him.
Richard Usborne

Oh fuck! Not another elf.   **Hugo Dyson, editor, on a J.R.R. Tolkien manuscript**

Lord of the Rings is simply unreadable, and for me that always sort of spoils a book.
Will Cuppy

Hitler's original title for *Mein Kampf* was *Four and a Half Years of Struggle Against Lies, Stupidity and Cowardice*. Everyone needs an editor.

Tim Foote

Agatha Christie has given more pleasure in bed than any other woman.

Nancy Banks-Smith

From the moment I picked up your book until the moment I put it down I could not stop laughing. Someday I hope to read it.

Mark Twain

Last time I went to Portugal I got through six Jeffrey Archer novels. I must remember to take enough toilet paper next time.

Bob Monkhouse

Have you ever struggled through one of Salman Rushdie's books to the end? Neither have I and neither, I bet, did the Ayatollah.

Boris Johnson

Why pay a dollar for a bookmark? Use the dollar as a bookmark.

Fred Stoller

Henry Kissinger may be a great writer, but anyone who finishes his book is definitely a great reader.

Walter Isaacson

Most jazz books possess all the charm and wit of manuals on the construction of gas-cooled nuclear generators.

Clive Davis

There is nothing so rare as a Woollcott first edition except perhaps a Woollcott second edition.

Franklin P. Adams

Jane Austen's books are absent from this library. Just that one omission alone would make a fairly good library out of a library that hadn't a book in it.

Mark Twain

Some editors are failed writers, but so are most writers.

T.S. Eliot

I never read a book before reviewing it; it prejudices a man so.

Sydney Smith

I have only read one book in my life, and that is *White Fang*. It's so frightfully good that I've never bothered to read another.　Nancy Mitford

Jack Kerouac? That's not writing, that's typing.　Truman Capote

Watership Down? I would rather read a novel about civil servants written by a rabbit.

Craig Brown

My Canapé Hell: if I were ever going to read a book, it would be this one.

Caroline Aherne

The Far Pavilions is one of those big, fat paperbacks, intended to while away a monsoon or two, which, if thrown with a good overarm action, will bring a water buffalo to its knees.　Nancy Banks-Smith

Despite being a best-seller in the United States, *The Corrections* is really a wonderful novel.

Ramona Koval

And it is that word 'hummy', my darlings, that marks the first place in *The House at Pooh Corner* at which Tonstant Weader fwowed up.

Dorothy Parker

This is not a book to be tossed aside lightly. It should be thrown with great force.

Dorothy Parker

I read part of it all the way through.　Sam Goldwyn

Many thanks for your book. I shall waste no time in reading it.　Benjamin Franklin

POETRY

Poetry is sissy stuff that rhymes. Weedy people say la and fie and swoon when they see a bunch of daffodils.
Geoffrey Willans

Rodney Spelvin was the sort of man who would produce a slim volume of verse bound in squashy mauve leather at the drop of a hat, mostly on the subject of sunsets and pixies.
P.G. Wodehouse

Poetry books are handy implements for killing persistent irritating flies.
Geoffrey Grigson

Writing a poem is a bit like throwing up. It's quick and efficient and you always feel better after.
Sara-Jane Lovett

If you are of the opinion that the contemplation of suicide is sufficient evidence of a poetic nature, do not forget that actions speak louder than words.
Fran Lebowitz

A publisher would rather see a burglar in his office than a poet.
Don Marquis

Publishing a volume of verse is like dropping a rose petal down the Grand Canyon and waiting for the echo.
Don Marquis

If Galileo had said in verse that the world moved, the inquisition might have left him alone.
Thomas Hardy

It occurred to me that I would like to be a poet. The chief qualification, I understand, is that you must be born. Well, I hunted up my birth certificate, and found that I was all right on that score.
Saki

I was working on the proof of one of my poems all the morning and took out a comma. In the afternoon, I put it back in.
Oscar Wilde

My favourite poem is the one that starts 'Thirty days hath September' because it actually tells you something.
Groucho Marx

I can't pretend to be a judge of poetry. I'm an English teacher not a
homosexual.
Hugh Baxter

Baldrick, I would rather French-kiss a skunk than listen to your poetry.
Captain Blackadder, *Blackadder Goes Forth*

We're just waiting for the moment his poetic licence expires.
Noël Coward

The poetry of Seth will be remembered long after that of Homer
and Virgil is forgotten – but not until then.
Richard Porson

Perhaps the saddest lot that can befall mortal man is to be the
husband of a lady poet.
George Jean Nathan

If you imagine a Scotch commercial traveller in a Scotch commercial
hotel leaning on the bar and calling the barmaid Dearie, then you
will know the keynote of Burns' verse.
A.E. Housman

A new firm of publishers has written to me proposing to publish
'the successor' of *A Shropshire Lad*. But as they don't also offer
to write it, I have to put them off.
A.E. Housman

John Donne's poems are like the peace of God; they pass all
understanding.
King James I

On the day that God made Carl Sandburg, he didn't do anything
else that day but feel good.
Edward Steichen

T.S. Eliot's face had deep lines. I cannot say the same for his poetry.
Melville Cane

For twenty years, I've stared my level best to see if evening –
any evening – would suggest a patient etherized upon a table;
in vain. I simply wasn't able.
C.S. Lewis

There was a young man from Peru
Whose limericks stopped at line two.
Anon

Immature poets imitate; mature poets steal.

T.S. Eliot

To see Stephen Spender fumbling with our rich and delicate language is to experience all the horror of seeing a Sèvres vase in the hands of a chimpanzee.

Evelyn Waugh

Poets have been mysteriously silent on the subject of cheese.

G.K. Chesterton

I used to think all poets were Byronic – mad, bad and dangerous to know. And then I met a few. They're mostly wicked as ginless tonic and wild as pension plans.

Wendy Cope

Today, the main difference between poetry and prose is that, dreadful though it is, poetry doesn't go on for nearly so long.

Richard Ingrams

The reason modern poetry is difficult is so that the poet's wife cannot understand it.

Wendy Cope

JOURNALISM AND NEWS

—What's large and hard and pink in the morning?
—The *Financial Times* crossword.

Anon

Journalism consists in buying paper at two cents a pound and selling it for ten cents a pound.

Cyril Connolly

People everywhere confuse what they read in newspapers with news.

A.J. Liebling

Journalism largely consists in saying 'Lord Jones Dead' to people who never knew Lord Jones was alive.

G.K. Chesterton

What makes me qualified to be a reporter? Well, I'm willing to violate anyone's privacy for my personal gain and then claim with a straight face that the public has a right to know.

Dogbert

There are four sexes: men, women, clergymen and journalists.

Somerset Maugham

A journalist is somebody who possesses himself of a fantasy and lures the truth towards it.

Arnold Wesker

The only qualities essential for real success in journalism are rat-like cunning, a plausible manner, and a little literary ability.

Nicholas Tomalin

He's a fastidious journalist. He once telephoned a semicolon from Moscow.

James Bone

A reporter is someone who has renounced everything in life except the world, the flesh, and the devil.

David Murray

No news is good news; no journalists is even better.

Nicholas Bentley

A foreign correspondent is someone who flies around from hotel to hotel and thinks the most interesting thing about any story is the fact that he has arrived to cover it.

Tom Stoppard

A reporter for *Time* magazine was spending two weeks on an aircraft carrier, but sent back an expenses claim which included a sum for 'taxis'. His editor asked him to justify the item. He cabled back, 'Big ship.'

Craig Cardman

There is much to be said in favour of modern journalism. By giving us the opinions of the uneducated, it keeps us in touch with the ignorance of the community.

Oscar Wilde

Modern journalism is survival of the vulgarest.

Oscar Wilde

It's amazing that the amount of news that happens in the world every day always just exactly fits the newspaper.

Jerry Seinfeld

I like *The Times*. It's not too rough on the buttocks.

Owen Newitt, *The Vicar of Dibley*

No self-respecting fish would be wrapped in a Murdoch newspaper.

Mike Royko

Never criticize a man who buys ink by the barrel.   **Mark Twain**

Here's the weird thing about the Murdoch family – they believe
what they read in the papers.   **Matthew Freud**

You should always believe all you read in the newspapers, as
this makes them more interesting.   **Rose Macaulay**

Everything you read in the newspapers is absolutely true, except
for that rare story of which you happen to have first-hand knowledge,
which is absolutely false.   **Erwin Knoll**

Except for the Flood, nothing was ever as bad as reported.

Edward Howe

Most of what you read in the papers is lies. I should know.
A lot of the lies are mine.   **Max Clifford, PR guru**

Exclusives aren't what they used to be. We tend to put 'exclusive'
on everything just to annoy other papers. I once put 'exclusive'
on the weather by mistake.   **Piers Morgan**

Freedom of the press in Britain means freedom to print such of the
proprietor's prejudices as the advertisers don't object to.   **Hannen Swaffer**

Whenever I write for the *Times Literary Supplement*, I feel I ought
to be wearing a knitted tie.   **David Sexton**

Politicians who complain about the media are like ships' captains
who complain about the sea.   **Enoch Powell**

I thought about becoming a political cartoonist because they only
have to come up with one idea a day, but then I thought I'd become
a sportswriter because they don't have to come up with any. It's the
toy department.   **Sam Snead**

Rock journalism is people who can't write interviewing people who can't talk for people who can't read.

Frank Zappa

An editor is a person employed on a newspaper, whose business it is to separate the wheat from the chaff, and to see that the chaff is printed.

Elbert Hubbard

Half of the American people never read a newspaper. Half never vote for President. One hopes it is the same half.

Gore Vidal

If you can't plug it into the mains or fuck it, the editor's not interested.

Unidentified journalist about Andrew Neil

The conscience of an editor is purely decorative.

Oscar Wilde

An editor should have a pimp for a brother so he'd have someone to look up to.

Gene Fowler

Only editors, presidents and people with tapeworms have the right to use the editorial 'we'.

H.L. Mencken

If you are Editor of *The Times*, you can never get away for an evening. It's worse than a herd of dairy cows.

Alan Clark

Although most magazines pay so much a word, virtually none of them will be words submitted individually.

Edward Morris

No passion in the world, no love or hate, is equal to the passion to alter someone else's copy.

H.G. Wells

Give someone half a page in a newspaper and they think they own the world.

Jeffrey Bernard

Sorry the article's late. Someone was using the pencil.   Dorothy Parker

The article is long yet vigorous, like the penis of a jackass.   Sydney Smith

I get up in the morning with an idea for a three-volume novel
and by nightfall, it's a paragraph in my column.   Don Marquis

A daily column is a grave two inches wide and twenty inches deep.
                                                          Don Marquis

I daren't take a holiday. If I stop writing my column for a month it might
affect the circulation of the newspaper – or it might not.   Arthur Brisbane

As a humour columnist, I don't do witty off the cuff remarks; it's
like throwing five-pound notes into the gutter.   Keith Waterhouse

Every good journalist has a novel in him – which is an excellent
place for it.   Russell Lynes

Reading someone else's newspaper is like sleeping with someone
else's wife. Nothing seems to be precisely in the right place, and
when you find what you are looking for, it is not clear then how
to respond to it.   Malcolm Bradbury

I was on the subway sitting on a newspaper, and a guy comes up and
says, 'Are you reading that?' I didn't know what to say, so I just said,
'Yes,' stood up, turned the page and sat down again.   David Brenner

The one function TV news performs very well is that when there is no
news we give it to you with the same emphasis as if there were.
                                                          David Brinkley

Radio news is bearable. This is due to the fact that while the news is
being broadcast the disc jockey is not allowed to talk.   Fran Lebowitz

The dumbest question I was ever asked by a sports reporter was
whether I hit harder with red or white gloves. As a matter of fact,
I hit harder with red.   Frank Crawford

Facing the press is more difficult than bathing a leper.   Mother Teresa

Tell me what you want to ask me about before I open my mouth
and let you shit down my throat.   Jonathan Miller to a reporter

If you don't like the news, buy a gun and go out and make your own.
          W.C. Fields

WORDPLAY

A pun is the lowest form of humour – when you don't think of it first.
          Oscar Levant

Hanging is too good for a man who makes puns. He should be
drawn and quoted.   Fred Allen

Aardvark never killed anyone.   Spike Milligan

If it's not baroque, don't fix it.   Anon

Too many cooks spoil the brothel.   Polly Adler

Absinthe makes the tart grow fonder.   Hugh Drummond

Castration is a eunuch experience.   Paul Jennings

It is better to copulate than never.   Robert Heinlein

With friends like you, who needs enemas?   Anon

An ill-favoured thing, but Minoan.   Anon

Coincide – what you do when it starts raining.   Anon

You can lead a horse to water, but a pencil must be lead.   Stan Laurel

On the other hand, you have different fingers.   Emo Philips

Old professors never die, they merely lose their faculties.   Stephen Fry

You can lead a whore to culture but you can't make her think.

Dorothy Parker

I'm too fucking busy, and vice versa.   Dorothy Parker

It's always a business doing pleasure with you.   Dolly Parton

Love flies out the door when money comes innuendo.   Groucho Marx

All men are cremated equal.   Vern Partlow

DEFINITIONS

An acquaintance is a person whom we know well enough to borrow
from, but not well enough to lend to.   Ambrose Bierce

Admiration is our polite recognition of another's resemblance to
ourselves.   Ambrose Bierce

An agent is someone whom you pay to make bad blood between
yourself and your publisher.   Angela Thirkell

Ambition is but avarice on stilts.   Walter Savage Landor

An antique is a thing which has been useless for so long that it is
still in pretty good condition.   Martyn Harris

An archbishop is a Christian ecclesiastic of a rank superior to that
attained by Christ.   H.L. Mencken

An autobiography is an obituary in serial form with the last instalment
missing.   Quentin Crisp

A book is what they make a movie out of for television.   Leonard Levinson

Bigotry is being certain of something you know nothing about.

Mark Twain

A boss is a person who's early when you're late and late when you're early.

Herb Caen

A bore is someone who talks when you wish him to listen.   Ambrose Bierce

Carperpetuation: the act, when vacuuming, of running over a string at least a dozen times, reaching over and picking it up, examining it, then putting it back down to give the vacuum one last chance.   Rich Hall

A censor is a man who knows more than he thinks you ought to.

Laurence J. Peter

Chutzpah: that quality in a man who, having killed his mother and father, throws himself on the mercy of the court because he is an orphan.

Leo Rosten

A city is a place where you're least likely to get a bite from a wild sheep.

Brendan Behan

A class reunion is a meeting where two hundred people hold in their stomachs for five hours while writing down the names and addresses of friends they'll never contact.   Brenda Davidson

A committee is a group of people who individually can do nothing, but together decide that nothing can be done.   Fred Allen

A committee is a cul-de-sac into which ideas are lured and then quietly strangled.   John A. Lincoln

Genderplex: the predicament of a person in a restaurant who is unable to determine his or her designated restroom e.g. turtles or tortoises.

Rich Hall

Communist: one who has nothing, and is eager to share it with others.

Anon

A conference is a gathering of important people who singly can do nothing, but together can decide that nothing can be done.　Fred Allen

Conscience is a mother-in-law whose visit never ends.　H.L. Mencken

What is a cult? It just means not enough people to make a minority.

Robert Altman

Culture is what your butcher would have if he were a surgeon.

Mary Poole

A cynic is a man who knows the price of everything and the value of nothing.　Oscar Wilde

A cynic is just a man who found out when he was about ten that there wasn't any Santa Claus, and he's still upset.　James Gould Cozens

Cynicism is merely the art of seeing things as they are instead of as they ought to be.　Oscar Wilde

A door is what a dog is perpetually on the wrong side of.　Ogden Nash

Eloquence: the ability to describe Pamela Anderson without using one's hands.　Michael Harkness

Esplanade (v.), to attempt an explanation while drunk.　Anon

Flatulence (n.), the emergency vehicle that picks you up after you are run over by a steamroller.　Anon

Furbling: having to wander through a maze of ropes at an airport or bank even when you are the only person in line.　Rich Hall

A hotel is a place that keeps the manufacturers of 25-watt bulbs in business.　Shelley Berman

A library is a room where the murders take place. **J.B. Morton**

Gratitude, like love, is never a dependable international emotion.
Joseph Alsop

Home cooking: where many a man thinks his wife is. **Jimmy Durante**

A hypocrite is a person who – but who isn't? **Don Marquis**

Intuition is the strange instinct that tells a woman she is right, whether she is or not. Oscar Wilde

An idealist is one who, on noticing that a rose smells better than a cabbage, concludes that it will also make better soup. **H.L. Mencken**

Imagination is what prevents us from being as happy in the arms of a chambermaid as in the arms of a duchess. **Samuel Johnson**

Initiative is doing the right thing without being told. **Elbert Hubbard**

A legend is simply a lie that has attained the dignity of age. **Harry Oliver**

Liar: one who tells an unpleasant truth. **Oliver Herford**

Magnocartic: any automobile that, when left unattended, attracts shopping trolleys. **Rich Hall**

A misogynist is a man who hates women as much as women hate each other. **H.L. Mencken**

Multi-tasking is the ability to screw everything up simultaneously.
Jeremy Clarkson

Misfortune: the kind of fortune that never misses. **Ambrose Bierce**

Once (adv.): enough.   Ambrose Bierce

Original thought is like original sin: both happened before you were born to people you could not have possibly met.   Fran Lebowitz

Originality is when you remember something you hear but not the name of the person who said it.   Max Kauffmann

Perfume: any smell that is used to drown a worse one.   Elbert Hubbard

Pokémon: a Jamaican proctologist.   Anon

Political asylum: any governmental office.   Johnny Carson

Positive: being mistaken at the top of one's voice.   Ambrose Bierce

Rain: what makes flowers grow – and taxis disappear.   Hal Roach

Research means they are looking for the guy who lost the file.   Leonard Levinson

A recession is when your neighbour loses his job. A depression is when you lose yours.   Harry S. Truman

Remorse is the regret that one waited so long to do it.   H.L. Mencken

Self-evident: evident to one's self and to nobody else.   Ambrose Bierce

Sentimentality is what we call the sentiment we don't share.   Graham Greene

Serendipity means searching for a needle in a haystack and instead finding a farmer's daughter.   Anon

Snacktrek: the peculiar habit, when searching for a snack, of constantly returning to the refrigerator in hopes that something new will have materialized.   Rich Hall

Stress: what used to be called life.   Malcolm Burgess

Style is when they're running you out of town and you make it look like you're leading a parade.   William Battie

Teamwork: a chance to blame someone else.   Ambrose Bierce

GOLDWYNISMS

They say it's not as bad as they say it is.

It's spreading like wildflowers.

We'll jump off that bridge when we come to it.

Don't count your chickens before they cross the road.

You gotta take the sour with the bitter.

Gentlemen, include me out.

I'll give you a definite maybe.

I can answer in two words, im-possible.

Avoid clichés like the plague.

A verbal contract isn't worth the paper it's written on.

It's more than magnificent, it's mediocre.

Throw out all the old files but be sure and make a copy of everything before getting rid of it.

Directors are always biting the hand that lays the golden egg.

What we need is a story that starts with an earthquake and works its way up to a climax.

Do you want me to put my head in a moose?

Never let the bastard back into my office again – unless I need him.

Sam Goldwyn

INSULTS AND CURSES

He's not unlike Hitler, but without the charm.　Gore Vidal

I admire him, I freely confess. And when his time comes, I shall buy a piece of the rope for a keepsake.　Mark Twain

He hasn't been himself lately, so let's hope he stays that way.　Irvin S. Cobb

He is one of those people who would be enormously improved by death.

Saki

I treasure every moment that I do not see her.　Oscar Levant

What's on your mind – if you'll forgive the overstatement?　Fred Allen

The answer is in the plural and they bounce.　Edwin Lutyens

Unless you're served in a frosted glass, never come within four feet of my lips.　**Karen Walker**, *Will and Grace*

Who is one cell short of an amoeba?　Anne Robinson

When he said we were trying to make a fool of him, I could only murmur that the Creator had beat us to it.
Ilka Chase

It's probably the worst idea since Hitler's dad said to Hitler's mum, 'Come upstairs, Brünnhilde, I'm feeling saucy tonight.'
Hugo Horton, *The Vicar of Dibley*

I decided that the worst thing you can call Paul Keating, quite frankly, is Paul Keating.
John Hewson

If you give us any more trouble I shall visit you in the small hours and put a bat up your nightdress.
Basil Fawlty

—I've never been so insulted in my life.
—Well, it's early yet.
Groucho Marx

I described you in terms which were positively glowing, which is exactly how I'd like to see you in hell.
Lilith Sternin, *Frasier*

I shan't be taking my wife with me to Paris. You don't take a sausage roll to a banquet.
Winston Churchill

I would rather eat my own scrotum.
David Horton, *The Vicar of Dibley*

You have a brain like Einstein's – dead since 1955.
Gene Perret

If your IQ was any lower, we'd have to water you.
Anne Robinson

When you go to a mind-reader, do you get half price?
David Letterman

A hundred thousand sperm, and *you* were the fastest?
Jim Hightower

May the fleas of a thousand camels infest your armpits.
Arabic

May all your teeth fall out but one – to get toothaches.
Catalan

If you're going out of your mind, I suggest you pack light. It's a short trip.
Anne Robinson

Some guy hit my fender, and I told him, 'Be fruitful and multiply.'
But not in those exact words.   Woody Allen

When you said you went to university, presumably it was to be studied by others.
Anne Robinson

My last assistant left because I called her a cunt. Would that be a
problem for you?   Dawn Steel

Go take a flying fuck at a rolling doughnut.   Kelvin MacKenzie

I'll ruin you! You'll never waitress in Torquay again!   Basil Fawlty

I fart in your general direction! Your mother was a hamster and
your father smells of elderberries.   *Monty Python*

May you live in interesting times.   Anon

May your piles hang like a bunch of grapes.   Greek

May your left ear wither and fall into your right pocket.   Arabian

May you dig up your father by moonlight and make a soup out of his
bones.   Fijian

If I found you floating in my pool, I'd punish my dog.   Joan Rivers

When they circumcised you, they threw away the wrong bit.
David Lloyd George

I will make you shorter by a head.   Queen Elizabeth I

Goodbye, and don't think it hasn't been a little slice of heaven,
'cause it hasn't.   Bugs Bunny

And I hope your mother dies in a freak yachting accident.
Captain Blackadder to Captain Darling, *Blackadder Goes Forth*

I worship the ground he's buried in.   **Harry Cohn**

Don't torture yourself. That's my job.   **Morticia Addams, *The Addams Family***

I've had ear infections I'm fonder of.   **Luke Meyer**

I even hate the way you lick stamps.   **Danny de Vito**

Would thou wert clean enough to spit upon.   **William Shakespeare**

I wouldn't piss down your throat if your heart was on fire.   **James Carville**

My piles bleed for you.   **Herbert Beerbohm Tree**

I've had a wonderful evening – but this wasn't it.   **Groucho Marx**

Go, and never darken my towels again!   **Groucho Marx**

—You're fired.
—But, my lord, I've been in your family since 1532.
—So has syphilis. Now get out!   **Blackadder and Baldrick, *Blackadder II***

How many times do I have to flush before you go away?   **Stephen Fry**

You'd better beat it. You can leave in a taxi. If you can't get a
taxi, you can leave in a huff. If that's too soon, you can leave in
a minute and a huff.   **Groucho Marx**

I want loyalty. I want you to kiss my ass in Macy's window at high noon and tell me it smells like roses. I want your pecker in my pocket.   Lyndon B. Johnson

PUT-DOWNS AND COMEBACKS

—Hello, oh, great one.
—Are you talking to me or my ass?   **Artie and Larry Sanders**

—Can I ask a dumb question?
—Like no one else.   **Rose Martin and Sophia Petrillo,** *The Golden Girls*

—Would you say I'm selfish?
—No. Not to your face.   **Cher Horowitz and Dionne Davenport,** *Clueless*

—Why does everyone take an instant dislike to you?
—Saves time.   **Spike Milligan**

—I wouldn't be seen dead in that dress.
—You'd have to have been dead three months before you could even fit
in it.   **Lily Savage and Gayle Tuesday**

—Looking at how thin you are, people would think there was a famine
in England.
—And looking at how fat you are, people would think you were the
cause of it.   **Lord Northcliffe and George Bernard Shaw**

—Calvin Coolidge is dead.
—How can they tell?
—He had an erection.   **Dorothy Parker**

—Why did he shoot himself?
—I suppose nobody else would.   **Spike Milligan**

—Did you really pose for that calendar with nothing on?
—I had the radio on.   **Marilyn Monroe**

—What did you get on your SAT test?
—Nail polish.   **Jennifer Lopez**

—It's not a great work of art.
—Perhaps not, but then *you're* not a great work of nature.

Sitter for portrait and James McNeill Whistler

—Don't touch my painting! Can't you see, it's not dry yet.
—I don't mind. I have gloves on.   **James McNeill Whistler and Mark Twain**

—Would you like to request the orchestra to play anything in particular?
—Dominoes.   **Sir Thomas Beecham and George Bernard Shaw**

—I can't bear fools.
—Strange, your mother could.   **Dorothy Parker**

—What do you wear in bed?
—Chanel No. 5.   **Marilyn Monroe**

—Your singing is terrible. If you were to win American Pop Idol, you'd kill the American music industry stone dead.
—At least I'm from a country where people brush their teeth twice a day.

Simon Cowell and aspiring American pop idol

—I wouldn't vote for you if you were the Archangel Gabriel.
—If I were the Archangel Gabriel, you wouldn't be in my constituency.

Voter and Robert Menzies

—He's his own worst enemy.
—Not while I'm alive.   **Herbert Morrison and Ernest Bevin**

—Are you enjoying yourself?
—There's nothing else at this party to enjoy.

Hostess and George Bernard Shaw

—You've never written another novel as good as *Catch 22*.
—Who has?   **Joseph Heller**

—If I were your wife, I'd put poison in your coffee.
—If I were your husband, I'd drink it.

Nancy Astor and Winston Churchill

—Your accountant is dead. They say he blew his brains out.
—I'm amazed he was such a good shot.   **Noël Coward**

—What comes first, the music or the words?
—First comes the phone call.   **Sammy Cahn**

—Ah, Mr Wilde, I passed your house this afternoon.
—Thank you so much.   **Unknown woman and Oscar Wilde**

—Come on, Joan, tell us which husband was the best lover?
—Yours.   **Joan Rivers and Joan Collins**

NAMES

Groucho isn't my real name. I'm breaking it in for a friend.
                                                        Groucho Marx

Mr Ball? How very singular.   **Thomas Beecham**

Some people have difficulty deciding on a name for the new baby,
but others have rich relatives.   **Don McElroy**

If it's a girl, my wife wants to call her Sue – a lovely name, but
one which, for Jews, is generally a verb.   **Dennis Wolfberg**

Some names have class connotations. I was born on a council
estate but once I'd been called Jeremy, we had to move. **Jeremy Hardy**

Always end the name of your child with a vowel, so that when you
yell, the name will carry.   **Bill Cosby**

When a teacher calls a boy by his entire name, it means trouble.
                                                        Mark Twain

I don't know what my dog's real name is but I call him 'Rover'.
                                                        Stafford Beer

I went up to a woman in a bar and said, 'What's your name?'
She said, 'Don't even bother.' I said, 'Is that an Indian name,
because I'd sure like to meet Hot to Trot.'   **Garry Shandling**

—Surely you can't be serious?
—I am serious. And don't call me Shirley.
                                        Ted Striker and Doctor Rumack, *Airplane!*

I said to my husband, 'Why don't you call out my name when we we're
making love?' He said, 'I don't want to wake you up.'   **Joan Rivers**

The common Welsh name Bzjxxllwcp is pronounced Jackson.
                                                              Mark Twain

Fate tried to conceal him by naming him Smith.   **Oliver Wendell Holmes**

There are so many Smiths about because Smiths were very good
at picking chastity belts.   **Brendan Cooper**

If your surname is Toblerone you should always take along an
empty Toblerone chocolate box when attending interviews for office
jobs. This would save your potential employer the expense of having
to make a name plaque for your desk, and therefore increase your
chances of getting the job.   **Top tip, *Viz***

I am convinced the name Ursula Andress is a spoonerism.   **John Simon**

The batsman's Holding, the bowler's Willey.   **Brian Johnson**

Aziz Ezzet, a gentleman of importance in Egypt, says his name can
be pronounced by opening a soda bottle slowly.   **Harry Wade**

—How do you do, Margot.
—The *t* is silent, as in 'Harlow'.   **Jean Harlow and Margot Asquith**

I have a poor memory for names, but I never remember a face.   **W.C. Fields**

It ain't what they call you, it's what you answer to.   **W.C. Fields**

Arianna Stassinopoulos is so boring you fall asleep halfway through
her name.   **Alan Bennett**

They named an airport after John Lennon. I wouldn't want an airport
named after me, but I wouldn't mind a luggage carousel.   **Ringo Starr**

—Of course, Mick Jagger isn't his real name, you know.
—Mick Jagger isn't whose real name?   **Two people at a Rolling Stones concert**

Suppose our word for rose had come from the Netherlands, anglicized as
'stinkbloom'. What follows? 'My love is like a red, red stinkbloom.'
                                                            Arthur Marshall

PUBLIC SPEAKING

A survey shows that the number one fear of people is public
speaking. Number two is death. That means that at a funeral the
average person would rather be in the casket than doing the eulogy.
                                                            Jerry Seinfeld

The human brain starts working the moment you are born and never
stops until you stand up to speak in public.   **George Jessel**

—I've got to make a speech to my old school, and talk to them
about racing. What shall I tell them?
—Tell them you've got flu.   **Jeffrey Bernard and Lester Piggott**

A typical speech by Margaret Thatcher sounds like the Book of
Revelation read out over a railway station public address system
by a headmistress of a certain age wearing calico knickers.   **Clive James**

When I hear a man preach, I like to see him act as if he were
fighting bees.   **Abraham Lincoln**

Father Clippit says a good long sermon. Four hours he does.
Since his stroke.   *Father Ted*

—What did the priest have to say about sin in his sermon?
—He was against it.   Calvin Coolidge

The head cannot take in more than the seat can endure.   Winston Churchill

A good sermon should be like a woman's skirt: short enough to
rouse the interest, but long enough to cover the essentials.   Ronald Knox

If you haven't struck oil in your first three minutes, *stop boring*!
                                                      George Jessel

I do not object to people looking at their watches when I am
speaking. But I do mind their holding it up to their ears.   James Sidgwick

I will be so brief I have already finished.   Salvador Dali, entire speech

No man should presume to stand up and speak in public for longer
than he can lie down and make love in private.   Godfrey Smith

Making a speech on economics is a lot like pissing down your leg.
It seems hot to you, but it never does to anyone else.   Lyndon B. Johnson

Winston Churchill devoted the best years of his life to preparing his
impromptu speeches.   F.E. Smith

I listened to Richard Nixon's speech. I may not know much, but
I know chicken shit from a chicken salad.   Lyndon B. Johnson

'In conclusion' – the phrase that wakes up the audience.
                                                   Herbert Prochnow

TALK AND SILENCE

A gossip is one who talks to you about others; a bore is one who
talks to you about himself; and a brilliant conversationalist is one
who talks to you about yourself.   Lisa Kirk

How time flies when it's you who's doing all the talking.   **Harvey Fierstein**

I've just spent an hour talking to Tallulah Bankhead for a few minutes.
                                                          Fred Keating

There's nothing so annoying as to have two people go right on talking
when you're interrupting.   **Mark Twain**

No one really listens to anyone else, and if you try it for a while,
you will see why.   **Mignon McLaughlin**

Madam, don't you have any unexpressed thoughts?   **George S. Kaufman**

Jonathan Ross's wife is an excellent listener and God knows, she's
had plenty of practice.   **Phill Jupitus**

There's now a support group for compulsive talkers. It's called
On Anon Anon.   **Paula Poundstone**

I think the point at which we fell out was when he said, 'I think,'
and I said, 'I don't give a fuck what you think.'   **Kelvin MacKenzie**

I'll not listen to reason. Reason always means what someone else
has got to say.   **Elizabeth Gaskell**

To cut a long story short, there's nothing like having the boss walk in.
                                                          Doris Lily

He had occasional flashes of silence, which make his conversation
perfectly delightful.   **Sydney Smith**

I like to do all the talking myself.
It saves time and prevents arguments.

Oscar Wilde

Although there exists many thousand subjects for elegant conversation, there are persons who cannot meet a cripple without talking about feet.

Ernest Bramah

The opposite of talking isn't listening. The opposite of talking is waiting.

Fran Lebowitz

Better to keep your mouth shut and appear stupid than to open it and remove all doubt.

Mark Twain

If only these old walls could talk. How boring they would be.

Robert Benchley

Drawing on my fine command of language, I said nothing.

Robert Benchley

He talks so fast that listening to him is like trying to read *Playboy* magazine with your wife turning the pages.

Barry Goldwater

Silence is the unbearable repartee.

G.K. Chesterton

Silence is not only golden, it's seldom misquoted.

Bob Monkhouse

'Shut up,' he explained.

Ring Lardner

You can get away with saying anything stupid, so long as you attribute it to Samuel Johnson, Marcus Aurelius or Dorothy Parker.

George Mikes

SCIENCE
AND
TECHNOLOGY

SCIENCE

Okay, so what's the speed of dark?   Steven Wright

Oh, there's so much I don't know about astrophysics. I wish I'd
read that book by that wheelchair guy.   Homer Simpson

Science is a lot of little guys in tweed suits cutting up frogs on
foundation grants.   Woody Allen

Scientists are rarely to be counted among the fun people. Awkward at
parties, shy with strangers, deficient in irony – they have no choice but
to turn their attention to the close study of everyday objects. Fran Lebowitz

If a scientist were to cut his ear off, no one would take it as evidence of a
heightened sensibility.   Peter Medawar

Quantum mechanics: the dreams stuff is made of.   Steven Wright

In order to make an apple pie from scratch, you must first create the
universe.   Carl Sagan

The real goal of physics is to come up with an equation that could
explain the universe but still be small enough to fit on a T-shirt.

Leon Lederman

Your equation isn't right. It isn't even wrong.   Wolfgang Paul

If it squirms, it's biology; if it stinks, it's chemistry; if it doesn't work,
it's physics and if you can't understand it, it's mathematics.   Magnus Pyke

If those scientists are so smart, why do they all count backwards?

Robert Orben

That's 24 points for Schumacher and 23 points for Hill, so there's only
one point between them if my mental arithmetic is correct.

Murray Walker

I once dated a guy who was so dumb he couldn't count to twenty-one
unless he was naked.

Joan Rivers

—Let's try this again, shall we? I have two beans, then I add two more
beans. What does that make?
—A very small casserole.

Blackadder and Baldrick, *Blackadder II*

I'm not good at math. I've never been good at math. I accepted it
from an early age. My teacher would hand me a math test. I'd just
write on it, 'I'm going to marry someone who can do this.'

Rita Rudner

The metric system did not really catch on in the States, unless you
count the increasing popularity of the nine-millimetre bullet.

Dave Barry

Few persons invent algebra on their own.

Frederick Mosteller

Stand firm in your refusal to remain conscious during algebra.
In real life, I assure you, there is no such thing as algebra.

Fran Lebowitz

A man has one hundred dollars and you leave him with two dollars,
that's subtraction.

Mae West

Mathematics was always my worst subject. I couldn't convince my
teachers that many of my answers were meant ironically.

Calvin Trillin

I love mathematics. Add a bed, subtract our clothes, divide our legs,
and multiply!

Mel Brooks

If the universe is expanding, why can't I find a parking space?

Woody Allen

Living on Earth may be expensive, but it includes an annual free
trip around the sun.

Ashleigh Brilliant

Only two things are infinite – the universe and human stupidity
and I'm not sure about the former.

Albert Einstein

If you're not part of the solution, you're part of the precipitate.

Anon

There is speculation. Then there is wild speculation. Then there is
cosmology.   **Martyn Harris**

A friend sent me a postcard with a satellite picture of the entire planet
taken from space. On the back it said, 'Wish you were here.'
                                                        Steven Wright

Space isn't remote at all. It's only an hour's drive away if your car
could go straight upwards.   **Fred Hoyle**

As I hurtled through space, one thought kept crossing my mind –
every part of this rocket was supplied by the lowest bidder.   **John Glenn**

Buzz Aldrin, tell me the truth, were you really mad when you were
beaten to the moon by Louis Armstrong?   **Ali G**

The Chinese just put a man in space. They didn't use a rocket: they stood
on each other's shoulders and passed him up.   **Al Murray**

Outer space is no place for a person of breeding.   **Violet Bonham Carter**

I don't think there's intelligent life on other planets. Why should
other planets be any different from this one?   **Bob Monkhouse**

The surest sign that intelligent life exists elsewhere in the universe
is that it has never tried to contact us.   **Bill Watterson**

According to modern astronomers, space is finite. This is a very
comforting thought, particularly for people who can never remember
where they have left things.   **Woody Allen**

Scientists have discovered a noise made just prior to the Big Bang
that sounds something like 'oops'.   **Cully Abrell**

The Smithsonian Museum found my wife's shoe. On the basis of its
measurements, they constructed a dinosaur.   **Woody Allen**

My theory of evolution is that Darwin was adopted.   **Steven Wright**

Apparently, the difference between a stink bomb and a Level 3 Toxin Biohazard is two extra drops of sulphur textraoxide. I am totally suing that website.   **Malcolm, *Malcolm in the Middle***

Not all chemicals are bad. Without hydrogen or oxygen, for example, there would be no way to make water, a vital ingredient in beer.
Dave Barry

Scientists think they can now clone an all-white zebra. Now, I'm no expert, but isn't that a horse?   **Jay Leno**

Dolly the cloned sheep got pregnant in the old-fashioned, conventional way – by a shepherd.   **Bill Maher**

I can't wait till they start cloning humans. I could have sex with my underage clone. **Will Self**

Scientists have enlarged the brains of mice, so you know what that means? Smarter hot dogs.   **Jay Leno**

I worry about scientists discovering that lettuce has been fattening all along.   **Erma Bombeck**

My suspicion is that the universe is not only queerer than we suppose, but queerer than we *can* suppose.   **J.B.S. Haldane**

It is more comfortable to believe that we are a slight improvement on a monkey than such a falling off from the angels.   **Finley Peter Dunne**

If Darwin's theory of evolution was correct, cats would be able to operate a can-opener by now.   **Larry Wright**

The scientific theory I like best is that the rings of Saturn are composed entirely of lost airline luggage.   **Mark Russell**

If toast always lands butter-side down, and cats always land on their feet,
what happens if you strap toast on the back of a cat and drop it?

Steven Wright

The greatest unsolved scientific problem is: how can you be sitting on
a damp towel for half an hour and not realize it until you stand up?

Patrick Murray

When a man sits with a pretty girl for an hour, it seems like a minute.
But let him sit on a hot stove for a minute, and it's longer than
any hour. That's relativity.

Albert Einstein

A good scientific theory should be explicable to a barmaid.

Ernest Rutherford

I tried to imagine the easiest way God could have done it.

Albert Einstein

A stitch in time would have confused Einstein.

Steven Wright

Everything that goes up must come down. But there comes a time
when not everything that's down can come up.

George Burns

It's a good thing we have gravity, or else when birds die they would
stay up there.

Steven Wright

The public is not really concerned with atomic fallout, because so
far it has not affected television reception.

Dennis Miller

Let's be frank, the Italians' technological contribution to humankind
stopped with the pizza oven.

Bill Bryson

It's called a pen. It's like a printer, hooked straight to my brain.

Dale Dauten

How do you get that non-stick stuff to stick to frying pans?

Steven Wright

Inanimate objects are classified scientifically into three major categories – those that don't work, those that break down and those that get lost.

Russell Baker

Normal people believe that if it ain't broke, don't fix it. Engineers believe that if it ain't broke, it doesn't have enough features yet.

Scott Adams

You can stop almost anything from functioning by hitting it with a large rock.

Russell Bell

The thing with high-tech is that you always end up using scissors.

David Hockney

Automatic simply means that you cannot repair it yourself.

Jed Larson

The first rule of intelligent tinkering is to save all the parts.

Paul Ehrlich

Every great scientific truth goes through three stages. First, people say it conflicts with the Bible. Next, they say it has been discovered before. Lastly, they say they have always believed it.

Louis Agassiz

And God said, 'Let there be light,' and there was light, but the Electricity Board said he would have to wait till Thursday to be connected.

Spike Milligan

I've had all the electric leads in my house shortened to save on electricity.

Gracie Allen

I am an expert on electricity. My father occupied the chair of applied electricity at the State Prison.

W.C. Fields

I have a telescope on the peephole of my door so that I can see who's at the door for 200 miles.

Steven Wright

The last time I came up with an invention, I passed the sketch round the pub and I never got the bit of paper back. Three years later … Microsoft Word for Windows.

Harry Hill

My wife insisted on looking through the telescope. She heard a nasty rumour that the star I bought for her birthday imploded.

Niles Crane, *Frasier*

The telescope is a device having a relation to the eye similar to that of the telephone to the ear, enabling distant objects to plague us with a multitude of needless details. Luckily, it is unprovided with a bell summoning us to the sacrifice.

Ambrose Bierce

If you build a better mousetrap, you will catch better mice.

George Gobel

He's a millionaire. He made all his money designing the little diagrams that tell you which way to put batteries in.

Steven Wright

It's the greatest thing since they reinvented unsliced bread.

William Keegan

My father invented the burglar alarm, but it was stolen from him.

Victor Borge

I'm lazy. But it's the lazy people who invented the wheel and the bicycle because they didn't like walking or carrying things.

Lech Walesa

The guy who invented the first wheel was an idiot, but the guy who invented the other three, now he was a genius.

Sid Caesar

You can't make anything idiot proof because idiots are so ingenious.

Ron Burns

When I die, I'm going to leave my body to science fiction.

Steven Wright

Statistics are like loose women; once you get your hands on them you can do anything you like with them.

Walt Michaels

He uses statistics as a drunken man uses lampposts – for support rather than illumination.

Andrew Lang

Statistics are figures that prove the best time to buy anything was last year.

Jack Benny

There are two kinds of statistics: the kind you look up, and the kind you make up.

Bob Mortimer

A newspaper has come out with a new survey. Apparently, three out of four people make up 75 per cent of the population.

David Letterman

50 per cent of the public don't actually know what the term 50 per cent means.

Patricia Hewitt

If Sigismund Unbuckle had taken a walk in 1426 and met Wat Tyler, the Peasants' Revolt would never have happened and the motor car would not have been invented until 2026, which would have meant that all the oil could have been used for lamps, thus saving the electric light bulb and the whale, and nobody would have caught Moby Dick or Billy Budd.

Mike Harding

Modern science was conceived largely as an answer to the servant problem.

Fran Lebowitz

Ketchup left overnight on dinner plates has a longer half-life than radioactive waste.

Wes Smith

The most useful and least expensive household repair tool is the telephone.

Wes Smith

The truth is that our race survived ignorance; it is our scientific genius that will do us in.

Stephen Vizinczey

COMPUTER

A computer is like an Old Testament God – lots of rules and no mercy.

Joseph Campbell

No matter which computer you buy, no matter how much money you spend, by the time you get it back to your car, it's an eight-track tape player.

Dennis Miller

To err is human, but to really foul things up you need a computer.

Paul Ehrlich

To err is human and to blame it on the computer is even more so.

Robert Orben

To Start Press Any Key. Where's the ANY key? Common query to computer helplines

Computers don't poop, fart, fuck or laugh, and cannot detect irony. These, then, are the distinguishing characteristics of humanity.

Eric Idle

A computer lets you make more mistakes faster than any invention in human history, with the possible exception of handguns and tequila.

Mitch Ratcliffe

In view of all the deadly computer viruses that have been spreading lately, I would like to remind you: when you link up to another computer, you're linking up to every computer that that computer has ever linked up to.

Dennis Miller

I got a computer. I wrote an apology note to my VCR for ever thinking it was difficult. You find someone in this country who can print out an envelope.

Elayne Boosler

I don't know anything about computers. I don't even know how often to change the oil.

Buzz Nutley

Computers are like humans – they do everything except think.

John Von Neumann

Bill Gates declared to the world, 'I am Microsoft.' Mrs Gates had no comment.

Whoopi Goldberg

I have emerged unscathed from the information explosion. **Henry Martin**

Bill Gates is only a white Persian cat and a monocle away from
being the villain in a James Bond movie.

Dennis Miller

A computer once beat me at chess, but it was no match for me at
kickboxing.

Emo Philips

How do I set my laser printer to stun?

Chris Moyles

When I log on to AOL it says, 'You've got problems.'

Richard Lewis

Getting information from the Internet is like trying to get a glass
of water from Niagara Falls.

Arthur C. Clarke

The Internet is so big, so powerful and so pointless that for some
people it is a complete substitute for life.

Andrew Brown

They call it 'surfing' the net. It's not surfing. It's typing in your
bedroom.

Jack Dee

The Web brings people together because no matter what kind of
twisted sexual mutant you happen to be, you've got millions of pals
out there. Type in, 'Find people that have sex with goats that are
on fire,' and the computer will say, 'Specify type of goat.'

Richard Jeni

The trouble with the Internet is that it is replacing masturbation
as a leisure activity.

Patrick Murray

We used to have lots of questions to which there were no answers.
Now, with the computer, there are lots of answers to which we
haven't thought up the questions.

Peter Ustinov

The council election in Bolton has been done by e-mail, and was won by Click Here For Penis Enlargement.

Armando Ianucci

UNIVERSAL LAWS

If anything can go wrong, it will.   **Murphy's Law**

Everything takes longer than it should except sex.   **Murphy's Law**

If you play with anything long enough it will break.   **Murphy's Law**

If something is adjustable, sooner or later it will need adjusting.

Max Frisch

If it flies, floats or fucks, it's always cheaper to rent than to buy.   **Anon**

Anything you buy will be in the sale next week.   **Erma Bombeck**

If it's good, they'll stop making it.   **Herbert Block**

90 per cent of anything is crap.   **Theodore Sturgeon**

When it comes to foreign food, the less authentic the better.

Gerald Nachman

When ripping an article from a newspaper, the tear is always into
and never away from the required article.   **Alan Fraser**

When you give a child a hammer, everything becomes a nail.   **Leo Kaplan**

When a man says his word is as good as his bond, always take
his bond.   **Hugo Vickers**

Every household has a box of odd keys. None of them will ever be
found to fit any lock.   **Pam Brown**

Preudhomme's Law of Window Cleaning: it's on the other side.

Winston Preudhomme

Everything tastes more or less like chicken.   **Paul Dickson**

However much a shower control may rotate, the degree of rotation required to change from ice-cold to scalding is never more than one millimetre.

Joe Bennett

The larger the German body, the smaller the German bathing suit.

Jed Larson

More always means worse.

Kingsley Amis

Once you start buying first-aid kits you start having accidents.

George Mikes

The first piece of luggage on the airport carousel never belongs to anyone.

George Roberts

Every decision you make is a mistake.

Edward Dahlberg

The less one has to do, the less time one finds to do it in.

Lord Chesterfield

Gunter's Second Law of Air Travel: the strength of the turbulence is directly proportional to the temperature of the coffee.

Nicholas Gunter

Any tool dropped while repairing a car will roll beneath the vehicle to its exact centre.

Murphy's Law of car repair

There are no exceptions to the rule that everybody likes to be an exception to the rule.

William F. Buckley

No matter how many good tables are free, you will always be given the worst available.

Jonathan Yardley

Hofstadler's Law: it always takes longer than you expect, even when you take Hofstadler's Law into account.

Hofstadler

At bank, post office or supermarket, there is one universal law which you ignore at your own peril: the shortest line moves the slowest.

Bill Vaughan

Wood burns faster when you have cut and chopped it yourself.

Harrison Ford

Nothing is so simple it cannot be misunderstood.   **Albert Einstein**

Two wrongs don't make a right, but they make a good excuse.

Thomas Szasz

The easiest way to find something you have lost is to buy a
replacement.   **Rosenbaum's Law**

Anyone who says he isn't going to resign four times, definitely will.

J.K. Galbraith

87 per cent of all people in all professions are incompetent.   **John Gardner**

A shortcut is the longest distance between two points.   **Charles Issawi**

When your cat has fallen asleep on your lap and looks utterly content
and adorable you will suddenly have to go to the bathroom.   **Anon**

When all else fails, read the instructions.   **Anon**

When all else fails, and the instructions are missing – kick it.   **Anon**

It works better if you plug it in.   **Sattinger's Law**

TRANSPORT

—Would you call me a cab?
—Yes, but not a hansom one.   **James Agate**

I phoned my local cab firm and said: 'Can you please send me a
big fat racist bastard with a personal hygiene problem some time
before I have my menopause?'   **Jo Brand**

I have done almost every human activity inside a taxi which does not require main drainage.   Alan Brien

Everywhere in life is somewhere else and you get there in a car.
                                                              E.B. White

—I was driving along and I saw you through the window.
—Oh, do you have a car?
—Well, I don't just have the window.
          Bob Ferris and Terry Collier, *Whatever Happened to the Likely Lads?*

It's fast, my Cortina. You could drive 50 miles for a bag of chips in this car and they'd still be warm when you got home.   Rigsby, *Rising Damp*

What's the fastest car in the world? A rental car.   P.J. O'Rourke

Whenever I rent a car, in order to cut down on the mileage rate,
I reverse everywhere.   Woody Allen

My father told me that if I saw a man in a Rolls-Royce, you could be sure he was not a gentleman unless he was a chauffeur.   Earl of Arran

A pedestrian is someone who thought he had put petrol in his tank.
                                                            Sam Levinson

A motorist is a person who, after seeing a serious wreck, drives carefully for several blocks.   Jane Pickens

Until you've learned to drive, you've never really learned how to swear.
                                                            Robert Paul

I was getting into my car, and this bloke says to me, 'Can you give me a lift?' I said, 'Sure, you look great, the world's your oyster. Go for it.'
                                                           Tommy Cooper

I think all cars should have car phones in them and their licence plates should be their phone number so you can call them up and tell them to get the hell out of the way.   John Mendoza

Driving hasn't been the same since I installed funhouse
rear-view mirrors.   Steven Wright

My licence plate says PMS. Nobody cuts me up.   Wendy Liebman

That's okay, we can walk to the kerb from here.   Woody Allen

Save money on expensive personalized car number plates by simply
changing your name to match your existing plate.   STG 400H

Somebody actually complimented me on my driving today. They left
a note on the windscreen, it said, 'Parking Fine'.   Tommy Cooper

Anybody going slower than you is an idiot, and anybody going faster
than you is a maniac.   George Carlin

What about those red balls they have on car aerials so you can spot
your car in a car park. I think all cars should have them.   Homer Simpson

I went down to campaign against the bypass scheme, but I got stuck
in traffic.   Harry Hill

SLOW, NO HOSPITAL   Road sign, USA

I was pulled over by a cop for running a stop sign. He said, 'Didn't you
see the stop sign?' I said, 'Sure, but I don't believe everything I read.'
                                                              Steven Wright

I drive way too fast to worry about cholesterol.   Steven Wright

CAUTION: Water on Road During Rain   Road sign, USA

We bought a Suzuki jeep and the wife turned it over. I said, 'How did it
happen?' She said, 'There was a pine tree, and I went to the left and it
swung to the left, I went to the right and it swung to the right.' I said,
'It was the air-freshener, you twat.'   Roy Chubby Brown

Parking is such street sorrow.   Herb Caen

I heard most accidents happen within five miles of home, so I've
moved ten miles away. **Jenny Abrams**

The quickest way to make a red light turn green is to try to find
something in the glove compartment. **Billy Connolly**

I've just solved the parking problem. I bought a parked car. **Henny Youngman**

Parking space: an unoccupied place on the other side of the street. **Pete Hagan**

Finding a parking space is like going to a prostitute: why pay for
one when if you apply yourself you can get it for free? **George Costanza, *Seinfeld***

Robinson's Law: the guy you beat out of a prime parking space is
the one you have to see for a job interview. **Cal Robinson**

When I get real bored, I like to drive downtown and get a great
parking spot, then sit in my car and count how many people ask
me if I'm leaving. **Steven Wright**

The slowest drivers in the world are those people who are getting
out of the parking space you want to get into. **Miles Kington**

I'd marry a midget just for the handicapped parking. **Kathleen Madigan**

Stupidity is not a handicap. Park elsewhere. **Anon**

Avoid parking tickets by leaving you windscreen wipers turned to
'fast wipe' whenever you leave your car parked illegally. **Top tip, *Viz***

A car is just a moving, giant handbag. You never have actually to
carry groceries, or dry cleaning, or anything. You can have five
pairs of shoes with you at all times. **Cynthia Heimel**

I went to court for a parking ticket. I pleaded insanity.   Steven Wright

One way to solve all the traffic problems would be to keep all the
cars that aren't paid for off the streets.   Will Rogers

I've called my car Flattery because it gets me nowhere.   Henny Youngman

I drove my car up to a toll bridge. The man said, '50 cents.' I said, 'Sold.'
        Slappy White

If the automobile had followed the same development pattern as
the computer, a Rolls-Royce would today cost a thousand dollars,
do a million miles to the gallon, and explode once a year killing
everyone inside.   Robert X. Cringely

What do I think of Volkswagens?
I've been in bigger women.   Harry Kurnitz

Do they need tinted windows in limousines? You see a limo go by,
you know it's either a rich guy or fifty prom kids with a couple of
dollars each.   Jerry Seinfeld

Whenever I pick up a hitchhiker I say, 'Buckle your seat belt, buddy,
I want to try something I saw in a cartoon.'   Steven Wright

My garage's motto seems to be, 'If it ain't broke, we'll break it.'
        Jerry Seinfeld

My wife came home and said she had some good news and some
bad news about the car. I said, 'What's the good news?' She said,
'The airbag works.'   Roy Chubby Brown

The only way of catching a train I ever discovered is to miss the
train before.   G.K. Chesterton

The next train has gone ten minutes ago.   *Punch* magazine

A friend of mine was so fed up with the train delays and cancellations that he threw himself onto the track. Died of exposure. **Jack Dee**

A survey has shown that the average man has had sex in a car 15 times. Something to keep in mind next time you're looking for a used car.

Jay Leno

When buying a used car, punch the buttons on the radio. If all the stations are rock 'n' roll, there's a good chance the transmission is shot.

Larry Lujac

Wouldn't it be nice if the wattage of a car stereo could not exceed the IQ of the driver? **Robert Maine**

Did you hear about the American Siamese twins who came to England so that the other one could drive? **Anon**

If you can read this, the bitch fell off.

Slogan on the back of a motorcycle jacket

So I said to the train driver, 'I want to go to Paris.' He said, 'Eurostar?' I said, 'Well, I've done a bit of telly, but I'm no Dean Martin.' **Tim Vine**

On Sunday, I took a train, which didn't seem to want to go to Newcastle. **J.B. Priestley**

Sir, Saturday morning, although recurring at regular and well-foreseen intervals, always seems to take this railway station by surprise.

W.S. Gilbert

Probably the most common of all antagonisms arises from a man taking a seat beside you on a train. **Robert Benchley**

When I'm on the train, why do I always end up sitting next to the woman who's eating the individual fruit pie by sucking the filling out through the hole in the middle? **Victoria Wood**

A sure cure for seasickness is to sit under a tree. **Spike Milligan**

Public transport should be avoided with precisely the same zeal that
one accords Herpes II.   **Fran Lebowitz**

Being in a ship is like being in a jail, with the option of drowning.
                                                                Samuel Johnson

A girl never really looks as well as she does on board a steamship,
or even a yacht.   **Anita Loos**

The transatlantic crossing was so rough that the only thing I could
keep on my stomach was the first mate.   **Dorothy Parker**

Seasickness comes in two stages – in the first, you're afraid you're going
to die, in the second, you're afraid you're not going to.   **Sandi Toksvig**

Motto of the US airline industry: 'We're Hoping to Have a Motto
Announcement in About an Hour.'   **Dave Barry**

How difficult can it be to fly a plane? I mean, John Travolta
learned how.   **Graham Chapman**

Flying a plane is no different from riding a bicycle. It's just a lot harder
to put baseball cards in the spokes.   **Captain Rex Kramer, *Airplane!***

Airline pilots don't need much of an excuse for a celebration drink.
If it isn't someone's birthday, they'll celebrate the fact that all the
lifts in the hotel are working.   **Anonymous British Airways source**

If God had intended us to fly, he would have sent us tickets.   **Mel Brooks**

Experts say you're more likely to get hurt crossing the street than
you are flying, but that doesn't make me feel any less frightened
of flying. If anything, it makes me more afraid of crossing the street.
                                                                Ellen DeGeneres

I knew I'd chosen the wrong airline when the flight attendant warned
us to keep our hands and arms inside the aircraft while it was in
motion. The airsick bag was printed with the Lord's Prayer.   **Les Dawson**

There ought to be a requirement that crying babies have to go into the overhead compartment.

Bobby Slayton

I like terra firma. The more firma, the less terra.

George S. Kaufman

If God had intended us to fly, he would have made it easier to get to the airport.

Jonathan Winters

You know the oxygen on airplanes? I don't think there's really any oxygen. I think they're just to muffle the screams.

Rita Rudner

—Superman don't need no seat belt.
—Superman don't need no airplane, either.

Muhammad Ali and flight attendant

The ship is sinking. We must try and save it. Help me get it into the lifeboat.

Spike Milligan

I always sit in the tail end of a plane, always, 'cos you never hear of a plane backing into a mountain.

Tommy Cooper

My inclination to go by Air Express is confirmed by the crash they had yesterday, which will make them careful in the immediate future.

A.E. Housman

The nice thing about a plane crashing at an air show is that they always have good video footage of the actual crash.

George Carlin

Jumping into the sea is a certain cure for seasickness.

John Ruskin

When I'm on a plane, I can never get my seat to recline more than a couple of centimetres, but the guy in front of me – his seat comes back far enough for me to do dental work on him.

Ellen DeGeneres

Why not give your son a motorcycle for his last birthday?

Colin Bowles

Try flying on any plane with a baby if you want a sense of what it must have been like to be a leper in the fourteenth century.   Nora Ephron

Riding a moped is like being on a hairdryer. Dogs are walking faster than you're going.   Eddie Izzard

I know what you're thinking, you're thinking, what's the best way to transport an owl?   Harry Hill

Doctors have a name for motorcyclists: organ donors.   Cheryl Atkin

COMMUNICATION

You can e-mail me, but I prefer letters that come through conventional mail. I like letters that have been licked by strangers.   David Letterman

There is a kind of person who will sit down and compose an answer to a family letter directly it has been received.   E.V. Knox

I believe in opening my mail once a month – whether it needs it or not.
     Bob Considine

Good news rarely comes in a brown envelope.   Henry Goldsmid

Never answer a letter until you get a second one on the same subject from the same person.   Michael O'Hagan

Ever get a letter and you aren't sure who it's from? Run after the postman and shout, '1471'. He'll have to tell you.   Harry Hill

One of the pleasures of reading old letters is the knowledge that they need no answer.   Lord Byron

Correspondences are like knickers without elastic. It is impossible to keep them up.   Anon

In my life, I have received no more than one or two letters that
were worth the postage. Henry David Thoreau

Nine-tenths of the letters in which people speak unreservedly of their
inmost feelings are written after ten at night. Thomas Hardy

A woman seldom writes her mind but in her postscript. Richard Steele

A real love letter is absolutely ridiculous to everyone except the writer
and the recipient. Myrtle Reed

To write a love letter we must begin without knowing what we intend to
say, and end without knowing what we have written. Jean Jacques Rousseau

Sending your girlfriend's love letters to your rival after he has married
her is one form of revenge. Ambrose Bierce

I have e-mail, a pager, a cell phone, a fax. I've got an answering machine,
three phone lines at home, one in my purse, and a phone in my car.
The only excuse I have if I don't return your call is I just don't like you.
Alicia Brandt

I don't answer the telephone because I have this feeling there is going
to be somebody on the other end. Fred Couples

What fresh hell is this? Dorothy Parker, answering the phone

All phone calls are obscene. Karen Elizabeth Gordon

Hi, this is Sylvia. I'm not home right now, so when you hear the
beep ... hang up. Nicole Hollander

I like to leave a message before the beep.
Steven Wright

Old women with mobile phones look wrong. Peter Kay

I climbed a mountain and hollered, 'Hellooo!' A voice came back,
'The echo is busy at the moment. Leave a message at the beep, and
we'll get back to you.'
Eddie Izzard

Hello, this is Harris. I'm in right now, so you can talk to me personally.
Please start talking at the sound of the beep.
Harris K. Telemacher

You're at home you're on the phone, you're in the car you're makin'
calls, you get to work, 'Any messages for me?' You've got to give
people a chance to miss you a little bit.
Jerry Seinfeld

Mobile phones are the only subject on which men boast about who's
got the smallest.
Neil Kinnock

You need a mobile phone. How else can you let people know that
you are on the train?
Rob Moseley

When I'm on a train and someone starts to bellow into their mobile
phone I shout, 'Quiet! I'm trying to travel.'
Maureen Lipman

The concept behind the mobile phone is that you have absolutely nothing to say and you've got to talk to someone about it right now.
Jerry Seinfeld

New York is the first state to ban talking on hand-held cell phones
while driving. First-time violators could receive a fine of $100, with
an additional mandatory six-month jail sentence if your ring tone
plays a Latin theme novelty song.
Jon Stewart

The cell phone people say there's absolutely no danger from cell phone
radiation. Boy, it didn't take those tobacco executives long to find new
jobs, did it?
Bill Maher

I need a mobile phone like I need a hole in the head. Which may turn out to be the same thing.

William Barrett

At the end of every year, I add up the time that I have spent on the phone on hold and subtract it from my age. I don't count that time as really living. By the time I die, I'm going to be quite young.

Rita Rudner

Have you ever noticed that wrong numbers are never engaged?

Steven Wright

Every improvement in communication makes the bore more terrible.

Frank Moore

I don't own a cell phone or a pager. I just hang around everyone I know, all the time. If someone needs to get ahold of me they just say, 'Mitch,' and I say, 'What?' and turn my head slightly.

Mitch Hedberg

The technological advance I'm waiting for on my phone is the 'get to the point' button.

Alicia Brandt

Only a man will think of a burp as a greeting for another man.

Tim Allen

—I'm sure you remember my number.
—Still 666?

Bebe Glazer and Frasier Crane, *Frasier*

The mobile phone ... the fax machine ... the e-mail. Call me old-fashioned, but what's wrong with a chain of beacons?

Harry Hill

SOCIETY
AND
POLITICS

POWER

I see nothing wrong with power as long as I am the fellow who has it.

Cecil King

Being powerful is like being a lady. If you have to tell people you
are, you aren't.

Margaret Thatcher

I have seen three emperors in their nakedness, and the sight was not
inspiring.

Otto von Bismarck

The most powerful men in Russia is Tzar Nicholas II and the last
person who spoke to him.

Anon

Now I am no longer President, I find I no longer win every game
of golf I play.

George Bush Sr

POLITICS AND GOVERNMENT

Politics is Hollywood for ugly people.

Jay Leno

Politics is just like show business, you have a hell of an opening,
coast for a while, and then have a hell of a close.

Ronald Reagan

Politics is the art of looking for trouble, finding it everywhere,
diagnosing it wrongly and applying unsuitable remedies.

Groucho Marx

The only difference between the Republican and Democratic parties
is the velocity with which their knees hit the floor when corporations
knock on their door.

Ralph Nader

Being in politics is like being a football coach. You have to be smart
enough to understand the game, and dumb enough to think it's
important.

Eugene McCarthy

Politics is derived from two words – poly, meaning many, and tics, meaning small blood-sucking insects.

Chris Clayton

Politics is the systematic organization of hatred.

Henry Adams

I've decided to take up a life of crime, but I can't decide which political party to join.

Roy Chubby Brown

The reason there are so few female politicians is that it is too much trouble to put make-up on two faces.

Maureen Murphy

Politics are almost as exciting as war and quite as dangerous. In war, you can only be killed once, but in politics – many times.

Winston Churchill

Politics ain't worrying this country one-tenth as much as where to find a parking space.

Will Rogers

—Have you ever taken a serious political stand on anything?
—Yes, for 24 hours I refused to eat grapes.

Woody Allen

I'm a political activist. I support lots of causes. I don't wear leather. I don't wear Nike trainers. I boycott Nestlé – apart from KitKats, obviously.

Bunk Bed Boy

A politician is a fellow who will lay down your life for his country.

Texas Guinan

Politicians are people who, when they see the light at the end of the tunnel, order more tunnel.

John Quinton

I did not become a politician because I could not stand the strain of having to be right all the time.

Peter Ustinov

A politician never believes anything he says, so he is always amazed when other people do.

Charles de Gaulle

Ronald Reagan won the election because he ran against Jimmy Carter. Had Reagan run unopposed, he would have lost.

Mort Sahl

Generally speaking, politicians are generally speaking.   **John Sergeant**

Mr Speaker, I withdraw my statement that half the cabinet are asses –
half the cabinet are not asses.   **Benjamin Disraeli**

Politics is so corrupt, even the dishonest people get screwed.

George Carlin

Government is to life what pantyhose are to sex.   **P.J. O'Rourke**

I have orders to be awakened at any time in case of a national
emergency, even if I'm in a cabinet meeting.   **Ronald Reagan**

I'm offended by political jokes. Too often they get elected.   **Will Rogers**

The White House is giving George W. Bush intelligence briefings.
You know, some jokes just write themselves.   **David Letterman**

George W. Bush has taken a urine test. But beforehand he wrote
the answers on his hand.   **Conan O'Brien**

Bush says he's being stalked. He says wherever he goes, people are
following him. Finally someone told him, 'Psst. That's the Secret Service.'

Jay Leno

I think the voters misunderestimate me.   **George W. Bush**

You can't have it both ways. You can't take the high horse and then claim
the low road.   **George W. Bush**

One suspects George W. Bush only stood for election because he misread
the word as 'electrocution' and knew that was something he liked.

Jeremy Hardy

George W. Bush went into a think tank this week and almost drowned.

Jay Leno

Nothing is so admirable in politics as a short memory.   **J.K. Galbraith**

The whole aim of practical politics is to keep the populace alarmed (and hence clamorous to be led to safety) by menacing it with an endless series of hobgoblins, all of them imaginary.　　　H.L. Mencken

It's clearly a budget. It's got a lot of numbers in it.

George W. Bush

If you want to rise in politics in the United States there is one subject you must stay away from, and that is politics.　　　Gore Vidal

There ought to be one day, just one, when there is open season on senators.　　　Will Rogers

Political skill is the ability to foretell what is going to happen tomorrow, next week, next month and next year. And to have the ability afterwards to explain why it didn't happen.　　Winston Churchill

When there is a great cry that something should be done, you can depend on it that something remarkable silly probably will be done.　　Tony Benn

Three people marooned on a desert island would soon reinvent politics.

Mason Cooley

I never did give anybody hell. I just told the truth and they thought it was hell.　　　Harry S. Truman

Gerald Ford looks like the guy in a science-fiction movie who is first to see the Creature.　　　David Frye

University politics make me long for the simplicity of the Middle East.

Henry Kissinger

A fool and his money are soon elected.　　　Will Rogers

If God had wanted us to vote, he would have given us candidates.

Jay Leno

The cardinal rule of politics: never get caught in bed with a dead
girl or a live boy.
Edwin W. Edwards

Being criticized by Geoffrey Howe is like being savaged by a dead sheep.
Denis Healey

Under capitalism, man exploits man. Under communism, it's precisely the opposite.
J.K. Galbraith

The Lord Privy Seal is neither a lord, nor a privy, nor a seal.
S.D. Bailey

Jeffrey Archer, is there no beginning to your talents?
Clive Anderson

—Shred that document! No one must ever be able to find it again!
—In that case, Minister, I think it's best that I file it.
Jim Hacker and Bernard Woolley, *Yes, Minister*

If there is anything a public servant hates to do it's doing something
for the public.
Kin Hubbard

Tories are not always wrong, but they are always wrong at the right
moment.
Violet Bonham Carter

I don't object to Gladstone always having the ace of trumps up his sleeve,
but merely to his belief that God Almighty put it there.
Henry Labouchère

The public say they are getting cynical about politicians. They should
hear how politicians talk about them.
George Walden

Politicians are interested in people in the same way that dogs are
interested in fleas.
P.J. O'Rourke

We started off trying to set up a small anarchist community, but
people wouldn't obey the rules.
Alan Bennett

There is nothing in socialism that a little age or a little money will
not cure. **Will Durant**

She said, 'What do you think of Marx?' I said, 'I think their pants
have dropped off but you can't fault their broccoli.' **Victoria Wood**

I am a Marxist – of the Groucho tendency. **Anon**

You can't get good Chinese takeout in China, and Cuban cigars are
rationed in Cuba. That's all you need to know about communism.

P.J. O'Rourke

No one grows up wanting to be a junkie, eating Utterly Butterly or
listening to Phil Collins but capitalism wears you down. **Jeremy Hardy**

It's easy to be politically correct and a liberal when you live in
a gated community. **Bobcat Goldthwait**

Ninety per cent of politicians give the other ten per cent a bad reputation.
Henry Kissinger

Minorities are almost always in the right. **Sydney Smith**

Governments are like underwear. They need to be changed often
and for the same reason. **Italian proverb**

Prime ministers are wedded to the truth, but like other married couples
they sometimes live apart. **Saki**

If I saw Mr Haughey buried at midnight at a crossroads, with a stake
driven through his heart – politically speaking – I should continue to
wear a clove of garlic round my neck, just in case. **Conor Cruise O'Brien**

Giving money and power to government is like giving whiskey and
car keys to teenage boys. **P.J. O'Rourke**

Working in Westminster is like having the nutters on the bus beside
you every day. **Amanda Platell**

If you would know the depth and meanness of human nature, you have got to be a prime minister running a general election.   **John A. MacDonald**

He's going around the country stirring up apathy.   **William Whitelaw**

The US presidency is a Tudor monarchy plus telephones.   **Anthony Burgess**

In America any boy may become President and I suppose it's just one of the risks he takes.   **Adlai Stevenson**

When I was a boy, I was told that anybody could become President. I'm beginning to believe it.   **Clarence Darrow**

Politics has become so expensive that it takes a million dollars even to be defeated.   **Will Rogers**

Anyone who is capable of getting themselves made President should on no account be allowed to do the job.   **Douglas Adams**

If Presidents don't do it to their wives, they do it to the country.   **Mel Brooks**

Being President is like running a cemetery: you've got a lot of people under you and nobody's listening.   **Bill Clinton**

We've never had a president named Bob. I think it's about time we had one.   **Bob Dole**

I discovered that being a president is like riding a tiger. A man has to keep on riding or be swallowed.   **Harry S. Truman**

Am I the only one to think that John F. Kennedy was killed by a peanut allergy?   **Harry Hill**

A fascist is anyone who disagrees with you.

John Koski

Dan Quayle taught the kids a valuable lesson: if you don't study you could wind up as Vice-President.   **Jay Leno**

If a tree fell in a forest, and no one was there to hear it, it might sound like Dan Quayle looks.   **Tom Shales**

The government solution to any problem is usually at least as bad as the problem.   Milton Friedman

Republicans don't understand the importance of bondage between a mother and daughter.   **Dan Quayle**

The Vice-Presidency ain't worth a pitcher of warm spit.   **John Nance Garner**

The Vice-Presidency is sort of like the last cookie on the plate. Everybody insists he won't take it, but somebody always does.
                                        Bill Vaughan

The Vice-President is a man who sits in the outer office of the White Office, hoping to hear the President sneeze.   **H.L. Mencken**

Too bad all the people who know how to run the country are busy driving cabs or cutting hair.   **George Burns**

It will be a clash between the political will and the administrative won't.
                                        Jonathan Lynn

Many journalists have fallen for the conspiracy theory of government. They would produce more accurate work if they adhered to the cock-up theory.   **Bernard Ingham**

Bill Clinton gets so much in speaking fees these days that when I saw him in New York the other day and said hello to him he said, 'That'll be $10.'   **Bob Dole**

I always have one golden rule for such occasions – I ask myself what
Nanny would have expected me to do.   **Lord Carrington**

He handles political crises with all the confidence of a man dialling his
own telephone number.   **John Bell**

The forest fires are the worst disaster in California since I was elected.

Arnold Schwarzenegger

There's nothing so improves the mood of the party as the imminent
execution of a senior colleague.   **Alan Clark**

Bill Clinton's foreign policy stemmed mainly from having breakfast
at the International House of Pancakes.   **Pat Buchanan**

My husband is a hard dog to keep on the porch.   **Hillary Rodham Clinton**

The biggest mistake Bill Clinton made was not getting Teddy Kennedy
to drive Monica Lewinsky home.   **Denis Leary**

Did you sleep with Bill Clinton? No, neither did I. Small world, isn't it?
Marty Allen

Clinton's problem was that he misunderstood the role of the
President, which is to screw the country as a whole, not individually.
Betsy Salkind

The only reason I'm not running for President is that I'm afraid no
woman will come forward and say she's slept with me.   **Garry Shandling**

Today, the *LA Times* accuse Arnold Schwarzenegger of groping six
women. I'm telling you, this guy is presidential material. **David Letterman**

The duty of an opposition is very simple: to oppose everything, and
propose nothing.   **Lord Derby**

There cannot be a world crisis next week, my schedule is full.

Henry Kissinger

Richard Nixon is the kind of politician who would cut down a redwood tree, and then mount the stump and make a speech on conservation.

Adlai Stevenson

I would have made a good Pope.

Richard Nixon

Nixon's motto is, if two wrongs don't make a right, try three.

Laurence J. Peter

Nixon could tell two separate lies out of different corners of his mouth at the same time.

Anon

Politicians are the same all over. They promise to build a bridge even when there is no river.

Nikita Kruschev

How the hell would I know why there are Nazis? I don't even know how a can opener works.

Woody Allen

A liberal is a man too broad-minded to take his own side in a quarrel.

Robert Frost

A liberal is a person whose interests aren't at stake at the moment.

Willis Player

Reader, suppose you were an idiot. And suppose you were a member of Congress. But I repeat myself.

Mark Twain

Let him join our campaign. I'd rather have him inside our tent pissing out than outside our tent pissing in.

Lyndon B. Johnson

The senator got so tired on the campaign trail that he started kissing hands and shaking babies.

David Letterman

Rhodes Boyson looks like a character out of an unpublished novel by Charles Dickens.

Anon

A politician will always be there when he needs you.　　　Ian Walsh

Politics is supposed to be the second oldest profession. I have come to realize that it bears a very close resemblance to the first.　　Ronald Reagan

A politician will double-cross that bridge when he comes to it.
　　　　　　　　　　　　　　　　　　　　　　　Oscar Levant

If you walk like a duck, and you quack like a duck, and you say you're a duck, you're a duck.　　　　　　　　　　　　　　George Bush Sr

Gerald Ford is so dumb he can't fart and chew gum at the same time.
　　　　　　　　　　　　　　　　　　　　　　Lyndon B. Johnson

George Bush reminds every woman of her first husband.　　Jane O'Reilly

Sometimes I look at Billy and Jimmy and I say to myself 'Lilian, you should have stayed a virgin.'　　　　　　　　　　　Lilian Carter

That one never asks a question unless one knows the answer is basic to parliamentary questioning.　　　　　　　　　　John Diefenbaker

A government which robs Peter to pay Paul can always depend on the support of Paul.　　　　　　　　　　　　　George Bernard Shaw

I like Republicans, and I would trust them with anything in the world except public office.　　　　　　　　　　　　Adlai Stevenson

One could drive a prairie schooner through any part of the arguments of William Jennings Bryan and never scrape against a fact.　　David Huston

Clement Atlee is a modest little man with much to be modest about.
　　　　　　　　　　　　　　　　　　　　　　Winston Churchill

Clement Atlee reminds me of a dead fish before it has had time to stiffen.
　　　　　　　　　　　　　　　　　　　　　　　George Orwell

I never vote *for* anybody; I always vote *against*.　　　W.C. Fields

It is not enough to have every intelligent person in the country voting for me – I need a majority.

Adlai Stevenson

Poor George Bush, he can't help it – he was born with a silver foot in his mouth.

Ann Richard

When you say that you agree to a thing in principle you mean that you have not the slightest intention of carrying it out in practice.

Otto von Bismarck

They couldn't pour piss out of a shoe if the instructions were written on the heel.

Lyndon B. Johnson

One-fifth of the people are against everything all the time.   Robert Kennedy

The voters have spoken – the bastards.

Richard Nixon

The vote means nothing to women. We should be armed.

Edna O'Brien

Who sleeps with whom is intrinsically more interesting than who votes for whom.

Malcolm Muggeridge

If voting changed anything, they'd abolish it.

Ken Livingstone

One day the don't-knows will get in, and then where will we be?

Spike Milligan

It's not the voting that's democracy, it's the counting.

Tom Stoppard

Any political party that includes the word 'democratic' in its name, isn't.

Patrick Murray

The largest turnout at elections is always where there is only one candidate.

Peter Ustinov

All politics are based on the indifference of the majority.   James Reston

Democracy is a process by which the people are free to choose the man who will get the blame.   Laurence J. Peter

Democracy is the name we give the people whenever we need them.   Marquis de Flers

The best argument against democracy is a five-minute conversation with the average voter.   Winston Churchill

Democracy is the theory that the common people know what they want, and deserve to get it good and hard.   H.L. Mencken

You have to remember one thing about the will of the people – it wasn't so long ago that we were swept away by the Macarena.   Jon Stewart

You realize you're no longer in government when you get in the back of your car and it doesn't go anywhere.   Malcolm Rifkind

The ideal form of government is democracy tempered with assassination.   Voltaire

In Pierre Trudeau, Canada has at last produced a political leader worthy of assassination.   Irving Layton

Assassination is the extreme form of censorship.   George Bernard Shaw

He's a sheep in sheep's clothing.   Winston Churchill

Margaret Thatcher is the sort of woman who wouldn't give you your ball back.   Mike Harding

I believe in benevolent dictatorships, provided I am the dictator.   Richard Branson

When smashing monuments, save the pedestals – they always come in handy.   Stanislaw J. Lec

Dictators always look good until the last minutes.   **Thomas Masaryk**

He may be a son of a bitch, but at least he's our son of a bitch.   Franklin Roosevelt

I must follow them for I am their leader.   **Alexandre Ledru-Rollin**

If you want to be a leader with a large following, just obey the speed limit on a winding, two-lane road.   **Charles Barr**

I have not met Norman Scott face to face for many years.

Jeremy Thorpe

An honest politician is one who when he is bought will stay bought.

Simon Cameron

When a politician addresses you, all you have to ask yourself is, 'Why is this bastard lying to me?'   **Claud Cockburn**

I don't mind how much my ministers talk, so long as they do what I say.

Margaret Thatcher

In politics while there is death, there is hope.   **Harold Laski**

If, one morning, I walked over the River Thames, the headline that afternoon would read, 'Prime Minister Can't Swim.'   **Margaret Thatcher**

Margaret Thatcher behaved with all the sensitivity of a sex-starved boa constrictor.   **Anonymous MP**

I keep a video of Tony Blair reading Corinthians at Princess Diana's funeral and threaten to show it to anyone who is impressed by the Prime Minister's sincerity.   **Bob Marshall-Andrews**

Margaret Thatcher is democratic enough to talk down to anyone.

Austin Mitchell

Margaret Thatcher even dresses to the right.

Patrick Murray

As God once said, and I think rightly...

Margaret Thatcher

—Do you know why Mrs Thatcher dislikes you?
—I am not a doctor.

Edward Heath

Tony Blair has as much charisma as a pair of dentures grinning in a glass of water.

Trevor Bayliss

—I think the Prime Minister wants to govern Britain.
—Well, stop him, Bernard.

Bernard Woolley and Sir Humphrey Appleby, *Yes, Minister*

Tony Blair is only Bill Clinton with his zip done up.

Neil Hamilton

Peter Mandelson is someone who can skulk in broad daylight.

Simon Hoggart

When Gordon Brown leaves a room, the lights go on.

Anon

John Prescott has the face of a man who clubs baby seals to death.

Denis Healey

Burly and greasy-haired, John Prescott looks rather like one of those plain-talking policemen who, during the late 1970s, were always being photographed on yachting holidays with villains somewhere in the Mediterranean.

Craig Brown

When Ann Widdecombe read out the Ten Commandments at Westminster Cathedral it sounded as though she had written them herself.

Father Michael Seed

—The trouble with England is it's being governed by cunts.
—Quite frankly, old man, there're an awful lot of cunts in England, and they deserve representation.

Rex Harrison and unnamed MP

When Roy Hattersley is with his dog, it's like a Womble taking Cerberus for a walk.

Will Cohn

I wish my flat was filled with one big man in his blue underpants.

Edwina Currie on John Major

At least it wasn't Ann Widdecombe.

Pat Dessoy, John Major's sister

DIPLOMACY

A diplomat is a man who always remembers a woman's birthday but never remembers her age.

Robert Frost

A diplomat is person who can be disarming, even if his country isn't.

Sidney Brody

Diplomacy – lying in state.

Oliver Herford

Diplomacy is the art of saying 'nice doggie' until you can find a rock.

Will Rogers

The chief distinction of a diplomat is that he can say no in such a way that it sounds like yes.

Lester Bowles Pearson

A diplomat is a person who can tell you to go to hell in such a way that you actually look forward to the trip.

Caskie Stinnett

To say nothing, especially when speaking, is half the art of diplomacy.

Will Dufant

I was rejected by the Diplomatic Corps. I was wisely seen as unsuitable.

Jeremy Paxman

Progress in the Foreign Service is either vaginal or rectal. You either marry the boss's daughter or you crawl up his backside.

Nicholas Monsarrat

A real diplomat is one who can cut his neighbour's throat without
having his neighbour notice it.   Trygve Lie

American diplomacy is like watching somebody trying to do joinery
with a chainsaw.   James Hamilton-Paterson

The French are masters of 'the dog ate my homework' school of
diplomatic relations.   P.J. O'Rourke

An ambassador is an honest man sent to lie abroad for the good
of his country.   Henry Wotton

An ambassador is a man sent abroad to eat for his country.   Clark T. Rand

—Who knows Foreign Office secrets, apart from the Foreign Office?
—Only the Kremlin.   Jim Hacker and Bernard Woolley, *Yes, Minister*

The British Secret Service was staffed at one point almost entirely by
alcoholic homosexuals working for the KGB.   Alan Bennett

ROYALTY

—Are you of royal stock?
—No, my father was a grocer. I'm of vegetable stock.   Morecambe and Wise

—You look awfully like the Queen.
—How frightfully reassuring.   Person in crowd and Queen Elizabeth II

I declare this thing open – whatever it is.   Prince Philip

—You look like Princess Anne.
—I think I'm a bit better looking than she is.
                                    Horse-show spectator and Princess Anne

When I appear in public people expect me to neigh, grind my teeth,
paw the ground and swish my tail – none of which is easy.   Princess Anne

Nobody has any business to go around looking like a horse and behaving as if it were all right. You don't catch horses going around looking like people do you?

Dorothy Parker

Princess Diana? Henry VIII would have known how to deal with her.

Max Blane

The tragedy about Diana's death was she was just getting her hair right.

Unidentified hairdresser

Princess Anne is so outdoorsy. She loves nature in spite of what nature did to her.

Bette Midler

I couldn't believe it when I picked up a newspaper and read that 82 per cent of men would rather sleep with a goat than me.   Sarah Ferguson

If you find you are to be presented to the Queen, do not rush up to her. She will eventually be brought around to you, like a dessert trolley at a good restaurant.

Anon

—Will there be another Royal Jubilee Concert?
—Not in my garden.   Paul McCartney and Queen Elizabeth II

Buckingham Palace isn't ours. It's a tied cottage.   Prince Philip

When royalty leaves the room, it is like getting a seed out of your tooth.

Mrs Paul Phipps

Do you know they have eating dogs for the anorexic now?

Duke of Edinburgh to a blind woman with a guide dog

For seventeen years, George V did nothing at all but kill animals and stick in stamps.

Harold Nicholson

The closest thing that we have to royalty in America are the people that get to ride in those little carts through the airport. When cart people drive by we all scurry out of the way like worthless peasants.

Jerry Seinfeld

How different from the home life of our own dear Queen! **Anon**

—Where's the egg-timer?
—It's his day off. **The Queen and Prince Philip, attributed**

Queen Elizabeth II is head of a dysfunctional family. If she lived on a council estate in Sheffield, she'd probably be in council care. **Michael Parkinson**

I left England when I was four because I found out I could never be King. **Bob Hope**

CLUB

I've a good mind to join a club and beat you over the head with it. **Groucho Marx**

Every Englishman is convinced of one thing: that to be an Englishman is to belong to the most exclusive club there is. **Oscar Wilde**

The essence of an English club is that we would prefer a silver salt cellar that doesn't work to a plastic one that does. **Evelyn Waugh**

To qualify as a member of the Women's Royal Voluntary Service you need to be able to wear a twin set and pearls and to have had a hysterectomy. **Stella Reading**

My advice to the women's clubs of America is: raise more hell and fewer dahlias. **James McNeill Whistler**

I got kicked out of Scouts for eating a Brownie. **Ross Noble**

Please accept my resignation. I don't care to belong to any club that will accept me as a member. **Groucho Marx**

You're not a proper member of an Irish club until you've been barred. **Michael Davitt**

LAW AND LAWYERS

Make crime pay. Become a lawyer.

Will Rogers

I urge you to study law. A man who never graduated from school might steal from a freight car. But a man who graduates as a lawyer might steal the whole railroad.

Theodore Roosevelt

Show me a Jewish boy who doesn't go to medical school and I'll show you a lawyer.

Milton Berle

A lawyer is the larval stage of a politician.

Ambrose Bierce

A lawyer is a person who writes a ten-thousand-word document and calls it a brief.

Franz Kafka

Lawyers are like rhinoceroses – thick-skinned, short-sighted, and always ready to charge.

David Mellor

Let's find out what everyone is doing, and then stop everyone from doing it.

A.P. Herbert

However harmless a thing is, if the law forbids it most people will think it wrong.

Somerset Maugham

The less people know about how sausages and laws are made, the better they'd sleep at night.

Otto von Bismarck

It is impossible to obtain a conviction for sodomy from an English jury. Half of them don't believe that it can physically be done, and the other half is doing it.

Winston Churchill

My attorney is brilliant. He didn't bother to graduate from law school. He settled out of class.

Milton Berle

No brilliance is needed in the law, except common sense, and relatively clean fingernails.

John Mortimer

You can tell an attorney by all the books of equal height on his shelf.

Dave Barry

Criminal lawyer. Or is that redundant?   **Will Durst**

The one great principle of the English law is to make business for itself.

Charles Dickens

There is nothing like a solemn oath. People always think you mean it.

Norman Douglas

I had inherited what my father called the art of the advocate, or the irritating habit of looking for the flaw in any argument.   **John Mortimer**

—Did you ever sleep with him in New York?
—I refuse to answer the question.
—Did you ever sleep with him in Chicago?
—I refuse to answer the question.
—Did you ever sleep with him in Miami?
—No.   **Genuine court transcript**

I have the kind of lawyer you hope the other fellow has.

Raymond Chandler

I broke a mirror in my house, which is supposed to be seven years' bad luck. My lawyer thinks he can get me five.   **Steven Wright**

The only difference between a dead skunk lying in the road and a dead lawyer lying in the road is that there are skid marks around the skunk.

Anon

In Washington DC, there are more lawyers than people.   **Jed Larson**

My definition of total waste is a coach load of lawyers going over a cliff with three empty seats.   **Lamar Hunt**

I hate lawyers, but they do make excellent psychiatric patients. They have excellent health insurance, and they never get better.   **Niles Crane, *Frasier***

I have come to regard the law courts not as a cathedral but rather
as a casino.
Richard Ingrams

A lawyer will do anything to win a case. Sometimes, he will even tell the truth.

Patrick Murray

—You're a high-priced lawyer! If I gave you £500, will you answer two
questions for me?
—Absolutely. What's the second question?
Hal Burton

The ideal client is the very wealthy man in very great trouble. John Sterling

As your attorney, it is my duty to inform you that it is not important
that you understand what I'm doing or why you're paying me so much
money. What's important is that you continue to do so.
Hunter S. Thompson

Lawyers believe a man is innocent until proven broke.
Robin Hall

An incompetent lawyer can delay a trial for months or years.
A competent lawyer can delay one even longer.
Evelle J. Younger

I don't want to know what the law is, I want to know who the judge is.
Roy M. Cohn

A jury consists of twelve persons chosen to decide who has the better
lawyer.
Robert Frost

Remember at the Preston A. Mantis Consumers Retail Law Outlet,
our motto is: 'It is very difficult to disprove certain kinds of pain.'
Dave Barry

Only lawyers and mental defectives are automatically exempt from
jury duty.
George Bernard Shaw

We find the defendants incredibly guilty.   Mel Brooks

Some circumstantial evidence is very strong, as when you find a
trout in the milk.   Henry David Thoreau

The Scottish verdict 'not proven' means, 'guilty, but don't do it again'.
                                                Winifred Duke

In England, justice is open to all, like the Ritz Hotel.   James Mathew

Justice must not only be seen to be done but has to be seen to be
believed.   J.C. Morton

CRIME AND PUNISHMENT

Kill my boss? Do I dare live out the American Dream?   Homer Simpson

Every normal man must be tempted at times to spit upon his hands,
hoist the black flag, and begin slitting throats.   H.L. Mencken

Mass murderers are simply people who have had enough.   Quentin Crisp

My wife and I have just celebrated our thirtieth wedding anniversary.
If I had killed her the first time I thought about it, I'd be out of
prison by now.   Frank Carson

Did you hear about the woman who stabbed her husband 37 times?
I admire her restraint.   Roseanne

One prefers, of course, on all occasions to be stainless and above
reproach, but, failing that, the next best thing is unquestionably
to have got rid of the body.   P.G. Wodehouse

Salome, dear, *not* in the fridge!   Marion Hill

I'd horsewhip you if I had a horse.   Groucho Marx

I'm all for bringing back the birch, but only between consenting adults.

Gore Vidal

I've never struck a woman in my life, not even my own mother.

W.C. Fields

He wouldn't hurt a fly. Not if it was buttoned up.   **Dorothy Parker**

I was going to thrash them within an inch of their lives but I didn't
have a tape measure.   **Groucho Marx**

Violence is the repartee of the illiterate.   **George Bernard Shaw**

A criminal is a person with predatory instincts who has not sufficient
capital to form a corporation.   **Howard Scott**

Many a man may look respectable, and yet be able to hide at will
behind a spiral staircase.   **P.G. Wodehouse**

He's so crooked that if he swallowed a nail he'd shit it corkscrewed.

Gerald Templer

If you're going to do something wrong, at least enjoy it.   **Leo Rosten**

I was arrested for selling illegal-sized paper.   **Steven Wright**

Statisticians estimate that crime among good golfers is lower than in
any class of the community except possibly bishops.   **P.G. Wodehouse**

I was walking down Fifth Avenue today and I found a wallet with
$150 in it. I was going to return it, but I thought that if I lost $150,
how would I feel? And I realized I would want to be taught a lesson.

Emo Philips

Getting mugged was one of the worst experiences I ever had. They
got my wallet and my driving licence with a really good picture of
me. What are the chances of me duplicating that photo?   **Janeane Garofalo**

Last week some guy pulled a knife on me, but I could tell it wasn't a real professional job. There was still butter on it.   **Rodney Dangerfield**

Police arrested two children yesterday, one was drinking battery acid, the other was eating fireworks. They charged one and let the other one off.
Tommy Cooper

If a mime gets arrested is he informed of his right to remain silent?
Jay Leno

Are you going to come quietly or do I have to use earplugs?
Spike Milligan

Hello, I'm a convicted paedophile looking to insure my ice-cream van...
Danny Bhoy

The way the girls dress these days I can't tell a 13-year-old from a 10-year-old.   **Pretty Paul Parson**

—Joey, you ever been in a cockpit before?
—No, sir, I've never been in a plane before.
—Joey, have you ever seen a grown man naked?
Joey Hammen and Captain Oveur, *Airplane!*

I already get the Cartoon Network, and I heard if you have that and the Sex Channel, they put you in some sort of file.   **Drew Carey**

Joey, have you ever been in a Turkish prison?   **Captain Oveur, *Airplane!***

Child sex abuse seems to have happened to so many people, but after I was born, my parents were hardly interested in having sex with each other, let alone me.   **Garry Shandling**

Joey, do you like movies about gladiators?   **Captain Oveur, *Airplane!***

I have six locks on my door, all in a row. When I go out, I lock every other one. I figure no matter how long somebody stands there picking the locks, they are always locking three.   **Elayne Boosler**

The Catholic Church has a tough new policy on child molesters: three strikes and you're a cardinal.   **David Letterman**

Everyone in public life should be arrested at least once. It's an education.
                                                                Alan Clark

Please, if you ever see me getting beaten up by the police, please put your video camera down and help me.   **Bobcat Goldthwait**

Women call it stalking. It's just selective walking.   **Otis Lee Crenshaw**

You've got to get up early in the morning to catch me peeking through your bedroom window.   **Emo Philips**

My friend Larry's in jail now. He got 25 years for something he didn't do. He didn't run fast enough.   **Damon Wayans**

The only thing more suspicious than a black man running is a black man tippy-toeing.   **Dave Chappelle**

When an estate agent gets mugged, do you think the police actually believe their description of what went on? 'Yes, officer, I was pushed into quite a spacious alley, only two miles from the train station. I was then punched in my face, which still retains some of its original features.'
                                                                Sean Meo

If you want to be safe on the streets at night, carry a projector and slides of your latest vacation.   **Helen Mundis**

One way to discourage burglars is by wearing an old policeman's uniform and standing outside your house all day and night.   **George Byker**

Our kid is on parole. She was caught shoplifting – from the Pound Shop.
                                                                Lily Savage

A woman arrested for shoplifting had a whole salami in her knickers.
When asked why, she said it was because she was missing her Italian
boyfriend.   **Reuters news agency**

Has anyone here been caught thieving in the Middle East? Let's have a
show of hands.   **Jimmy Carr**

We ought never do wrong when people are looking.

Mark Twain

Why would anyone steal a shopping cart? It's like stealing a two-year-old.

Erma Bombeck

I can't stay long. I've left my Mercedes parked outside and you know
what they're like on this estate. They'd have the wheels off a jumbo
if it flew too low.   **Boycey**, *Only Fools and Horses*

Kids today – they can swipe the hubcaps off moving cars.   **Woody Allen**

When you speak of the Great Train Robbery, this, in fact, involved no
loss of train. It's merely what I like to call the contents of the train which
were pilfered. We haven't lost a train since 1946, the year of the great
snows. We mislaid a small one.   **Peter Cook**

Vinnie Jones has been sentenced to 120 hours community service, but this
was reduced to 80 hours on appeal – from the community.

Angus Deayton

I once sent a dozen of my friends a telegram saying: FLEE AT ONCE –
ALL IS DISCOVERED. They all left town immediately.   **Mark Twain**

Vouchsafe O Lord, to keep us this day without being found out.

Samuel Butler

It's not the people who are in prison that worry me; it's the people
who aren't.   **Arthur Gore**

Outside of the killings, Washington has one of the lowest crime rates in the country.

Marion Barry, Mayor of Washington

If one is shot dead, it is a great consolation to know that it was with a legally held firearm.

Margaret Thatcher

They say, 'Guns don't kill people, people kill people.' Well, I think the gun helps. If you just stood there and yelled BANG, I don't think you'd kill too many people.

Eddie Izzard

One of my friends went on a Murder Weekend. Now he's doing life for it.

Jack Dee

Murder, like talent, seems occasionally to run in families.

George Lewis

Murder is always a mistake. One should never do anything that one cannot talk about after dinner.

Oscar Wilde

I have never killed a man, but I have read many obituaries with a lot of pleasure.

Clarence Darrow

By the argument of counsel it was shown that at 10.30 in the morning on the day of the murder the defendant became insane, and remained so for eleven and a half hours exactly.

Mark Twain

I just don't buy temporary insanity as a murder defence. Breaking into someone's home and ironing all their clothes – *that's* temporary insanity.

Sue Kolinsky

The person by far the most likely to kill you is yourself.

Jock Young

Getting caught is the mother of invention.

Robert Byrne

Kill one man and you are a murderer. Kill millions and you are a conqueror. Kill all and you are a God.

Jean Rostand

O.J. Simpson swears he's going to spend the rest of his life searching
for the real killer. He apparently thinks a caddie did it.   Dennis Miller

An eye for an eye and a tooth for a tooth! And then the whole world
would be blind and toothless.   Sheldon Harnick

If you shoot a mime, should you use a silencer?   Steven Wright

Arson cannot be considered a crime. There are many buildings that
deserve to be burned down.   H.G. Wells

It was beautiful and simple as all truly great swindles are.   O. Henry

'I will only shake my finger at him,' he said, and placed it on the trigger.
        Stanislaw J. Lec

Thirty years ago, a juvenile delinquent was a kid with an overdue
library book.   Harry Hershfield

We live in an age when pizza gets to your house before the police do.
        Jeff Marder

I never came across a situation so dismal that a policeman couldn't
make it worse.   Brendan Behan

Rain is the best policeman of all. Criminals don't like getting wet.
        John Stalker

Curiosity killed the cat, but for a while, I was a suspect.   Emo Philips

I believe capital punishment to be an appropriate remedy for anyone
who does me injury, but under no other circumstances.   F.L. Bailey

I'm for a stronger death penalty.   George Bush

The death penalty is almost a way of life in the USA.   Dennis Miller

If there was no capital punishment, there'd be no Easter.   Bill Hicks

People who deserve it always believe in capital punishment.   **Lincoln Steffens**

Capital punishment would be more effective as a preventative measure if it were administered prior to the crime.   **Woody Allen**

You know the good thing about all the executions in Texas? Fewer Texans.   **George Carlin**

When a man knows that he is to be hanged in a fortnight, it concentrates his mind wonderfully.   **Samuel Johnson**

Nothing is more annoying than to be obscurely hanged.   **Voltaire**

—Have you any last requests before you're hanged?
—Yes, I'd like to see Paris before I die.   **W.C. Fields**

I'm to be executed tomorrow at dawn. It's okay, it's not for anything serious.   **Ronnie Corbett**

WAR AND PEACE

War? My dear boy, it's awful – the noise, and the people!   **W.H. Auden**

Like German opera, war is too long and too loud.   **Evelyn Waugh**

How do wars start? Diplomats tell lies to journalists and then believe what they read.   **Karl Kraus**

Ready, fire, aim.   **Spike Milligan**

War is like love, it always finds a way.   **Bertolt Brecht**

The recruiting officer asked me, 'Why the tank corps?' I replied that I preferred to go into battle sitting down.   **Peter Ustinov**

Usually, when a lot of men get together, it's called war.   **Mel Brooks**

Join the army and see the next world. Dylan Thomas

How long was I in the army? Five foot eleven. Spike Milligan

Nothing in life is so exhilerating as to be shot at without result.
Winston Churchill

I don't worry about terrorism.
I was married for two years. Sam Kinison

—If we do happen to tread on a mine, sir, what do we do?
—Normal procedure, lieutenant, is to jump 200 feet in the air
and scatter oneself over a wide area.
Lieutenant George and Captain Blackadder, *Blackadder Goes Forth*

We are not retreating; we are advancing in another direction.
General Douglas MacArthur

The best defence against the atom bomb is not to be there when
it goes off. Winston Churchill

If there's an atomic war, this country will be flattened in three minutes.
Good. Time to fuck the wife. Twice. Roy Chubby Brown

Experts have spent years developing weapons which can destroy people's
lives but leave buildings intact. They're called mortgages. Jeremy Hardy

I don't know what weapon will be used in World War III, but I know
that World War IV will be fought with wooden sticks. Albert Einstein

Given a choice of weapons with you, sir, I should choose grammar.
Halliwell Hobbes

War doesn't determine who's right – only who's left. Bertrand Russell

An appeaser is one who feeds a crocodile, hoping that it will eat him last.
Winston Churchill

—For all we know, he could be part of al-Qaeda.
—Don't be stupid. Does he look like he works in a furniture store?
Rodney and Del Boy Trotter, *Only Fools and Horses*

Peace is when nobody's shooting. A 'just peace' is when your side
gets what it wants.
Bill Mauldin

I can picture in my mind a world without war, a world without hate.
And I can picture us attacking that world, because they'd never expect it.
Jack Handey

Everybody's a pacifist between wars. It's like being a vegetarian
between meals.
Colman McCarthy

They still haven't found Osama Bin Laden. Why don't they give his name
to the Child Support Agency, they'll find him.
Roy Chubby Brown

Procedure in the event of a bomb warning: in the built-up area, take
cover inside the nearest building; inside rooms, open windows and close
curtains; on the playing fields, continue games.
Eton College Diary, 1988

China sent a message to George W. Bush, that US missile defence
proposals will have 'a formidable adverse global impact and they're
poisoning the trend of multipolarity'. In response, George W. Bush
said, 'What?'
Conan O'Brien

Going to war over religion is basically killing each other to see who's
got the better imaginary friend.
Richard Jeni

The first step in having any successful war is getting people to fight it.
Fran Lebowitz

—Maybe he's agoraphobic.
—Jack? Afraid of fighting? I don't think so.
Father Ted and Father Dougal, *Father Ted*

If Kitchener was not a great man, he was at least a great poster.
Margot Asquith

To hear Alice talk about her escape from France, one would have thought she had swum the Channel with her maid between her teeth.

Mrs Ronald Greville

Join the army, meet interesting people, and kill them.

Anon

The Army is a place where you get up early in the morning to be yelled at by people with short haircuts and tiny brains.

Dave Barry

During the Second World War, a German prisoner of war was sent each week to tend my garden. He always seemed a nice friendly chap, but when the crocuses came up in the lawn in February, 1946, they spelt out 'Heil Hitler'.

Irene Graham

The Japanese Prime Minister has apologized for Japan's part in World War II. However, he still hasn't mentioned anything about karaoke.

David Letterman

This war, like the next war, is a war to end all wars.

David Lloyd George

I don't know what effect these men will have upon the enemy, but, by God, they frighten me.

Duke of Wellington

Why can't they have gay people in the US army? Personally, I think they're just afraid of a thousand guys with M-16s going, 'Who'd you call a faggot?'

Jon Stewart

When I was in the military, they gave me a medal for killing two men, and a discharge for loving one.

Leonard Matlovitch

Colonel Cathcart had courage and never hesitated to volunteer his men for any target available.

Joseph Heller

UN inspectors haven't yet found any weapons of mass destruction in Iraq. The most they've done is close down a coffee shop in Baghdad, because the fry cook wasn't wearing a hair net.

Bill Maher

The quickest way to end a war is to lose it.

George Orwell

I do not believe in using women in combat, because females are too
fierce.
Margaret Mead

The object of war is not to die for your country, but to make the
other bastard die for his.
General George Patton

I don't understand why gay people want to be in the military because
they only get one outfit to wear.
Kevin Maye

I am not fighting in the war to defend civilization, because I am the
civilization they are fighting to defend.
Heathcote William Garrod

The Falklands War was two bald men arguing over a comb.
Jorge Luis Borges

One way to avoid war is to give Bush and Saddam a toddler each
to look after with no help.
Rory Bremner

It's too late to prevent the war. I've already paid a month's rent on the
battlefield.
Groucho Marx

All the same, sir, I should put some of the colonies in your wife's name.
Chief Rabbi to George VI, 1940

Fighting for peace is like fucking for virginity.
Anon

My only qualification for being put at the head of the navy is that
I am very much at sea.
Edward Carson

Don't talk to me about naval tradition. It's nothing but rum, sodomy,
and the lash.
Winston Churchill

Obesity is now a problem in the navy. They've created a new rank:
Really Big Rear Admiral.
David Letterman

The general was essentially a man of peace, except in his domestic life.

Oscar Wilde

Generals detest generals on their own side far more than they dislike the enemy.

Peter Ustinov

In a civil war, a general must know exactly when to move over to the other side.

Henry Reed

I'm really a timid person. I was beaten up by Quakers.

Woody Allen

Whenever I hear about a 'peace-keeping force', I start wondering – if they're so interested in peace, why do they use force?

George Carlin

Sometime they'll give a war and nobody will come.

Carl Sandburg

Sometimes I think war is God's way of teaching us geography.

Paul Rodriguez

They couldn't hit an elephant at this dist...

General John Sedgwick

Always forgive your enemies. Nothing annoys them so much.

Oscar Wilde

No one ever forgets where he buried the hatchet.

Kin Hubbard

I think we should attack Russia now. They'd never be expecting it.

George Carlin

BUSINESS

The quickest way to make a million? Marry it.

Zsa Zsa Gabor

No woman marries for money: they are all clever enough, before marrying a millionaire, to fall in love with him first.

Cesare Pavese

If you see a bandwagon, it's too late.

James Goldsmith

Don't worry, Homer, nine out of ten religions fail in their first year.   **God**

The quickest way to make a million in musical theatre is to start
with two million.   **Andrew Lloyd Webber**

I made my first million the old-fashioned way. I made a hundred million for somebody else.   Roseanne

Nobody ever went broke underestimating the taste of the American
public.   **H.L. Mencken**

The first rule of business is: do other men for they would do you.
Charles Dickens

If an object is old and you are trying to sell it, it's obsolete; if you're
trying to buy it, it's a collector's item.   **Frank Ross**

A study of economics usually reveals that the best time to buy anything
was last year.   **Marty Allen**

The only function of economic forecasting is to make astrology look
respectable.   **J.K. Galbraith**

My dog is worried about the economy because his dog food is up to
99 cents a can. That's almost 7 dollars in dog money.   **Joe Weinstein**

Business is the art of extracting money from another man's pocket
without resorting to violence.   **Max Amsterdam**

The art of management is the art of taking credit for other people's work.
Germaine Greer

Gentlemen prefer bonds.   **Andrew Mellon**

In the business world, an executive knows something about everything, a technician knows everything about something, and the switchboard operator knows everything.   Harold Coffin

I think it's wrong that only one company makes the game Monopoly.
                                                      Steven Wright

There are two times in a man's life when he should not speculate: when he can't afford it, and when he can.   Mark Twain

There is hardly anything in the world that some man cannot make a little worse and sell a little cheaper.   John Ruskin

Insider trading is just another way of saying 'stealing too fast'.
                                                      Calvin Trillin

Elbert Gary of the United Steel Company never saw a blast furnace until after he was dead.   Benjamin Stolberg

ADVERTISING

Titanic Beer: goes down better than the real thing.   **Advert for Titanic Beer**

Death: bit of a worry, isn't it?   **Advert outside a church**

'Kiss your haemorrhoids goodbye,' the commercial said. Not even I could do that.   John Mendoza

Why did anyone think a camel is a good product image for a cigarette? I think each one is the equivalent tar of smoking an actual camel.
                                                      Jerry Seinfeld

Following the success enjoyed by French Connection after they became known as FCUK, I was wondering if I could market the strip used by my son's rugby team. He plays for the Chipping Norton Under Tens.
                                                      Jeremy Clarkson

The general advertiser's attitude would appear to be: if you are a lousy, smelly, idle, underprivileged and over-sexed status-seeking neurotic moron, give me your money.   **Kenneth Bromfield**

All commercials cost a fortune. Some commercials look as if they cost twice as much as you think. They're the ones that cost five times as much as you think.   **Clive James**

Promoting orange juice as 'cholesterol-free' is like saying 'Fly United Airlines – it's dandruff-free.'   **Leslie Savan**

Today I met a subliminal advertising executive just for a second.   **Steven Wright**

—A subliminal idea can be planted in your mind without you even knowing it.
—Lisa, that's a load of rich, creamy butter.   **Lisa and Homer Simpson**

Half the money I spend on advertising is wasted. The trouble is I don't know which half.   **Viscount William Leverhulme**

Advertising is the rattle of a stick inside a swill bucket.   **George Orwell**

I think that I shall never see a billboard lovely as a tree.   **Ogden Nash**

The consumer isn't a moron; she is your wife.   **David Ogilvy**

A suicide hotline is where they talk to you until you don't feel like killing yourself. Exactly the opposite of telemarketing.   **Dana Snow**

MONEY

Three things have helped me through the ordeals of life: an understanding husband, a good analyst, and millions of dollars.

Mary Tyler Moore

Some people get so rich they lose all respect for humanity. That's how rich I want to get.

Rita Rudner

One can never be too thin or too rich.

Wallis Simpson

I'm filthy stinking rich – well, two out of three ain't bad.

Emo Philips

Money is exactly like sex: you think of nothing else if you don't have it and other things if you do.

James Baldwin

If you would know what the Lord God thinks of money, you have only to look at those to whom he gives it.

Maurice Baring

All I ask is a chance to prove that money can't make me happy. Spike Milligan

Wealth is any income that is at least 100 dollars a year more than the income of one's wife's sister's husband.

H.L. Mencken

Money isn't the most important thing in the world. Love is. Fortunately, I love money.

Jackie Mason

Few of us can stand prosperity. Another man's, I mean.

Mark Twain

It is the wretchedness of being rich that you have to live with rich people.

Logan Pearsall Smith

There is nothing in the world more reassuring than an unhappy lottery winner.

Tony Parsons

For one person who dreams of making fifty thousand pounds, a hundred people dream of being left fifty thousand pounds.

A.A. Milne

They don't put indicators on your car in Beverly Hills. They figure if you're that rich you don't have to tell no one where you're going.

Bette Midler

You can name your own salary in this business. I call mine Fred.

Rodney Dangerfield

They offered me a handshake of £10,000 to settle amicably.
I told them that they would have to be a lot more amicable than that.

Tommy Docherty

Money doesn't make you happy. I have $50 million but I was just as
happy when I had $48 million. **Arnold Schwarzenegger**

Things could be much worse. I could be one of my creditors.

Henny Youngman

—The rich are different from you and me.
—Yes, they have more money. **F. Scott Fitzgerald and Ernest Hemingway**

A rich man is one who isn't afraid to ask the salesperson to show him
something cheaper. Jack Benny

Rod Stewart was so mean, it hurt him to go to the bathroom.

Britt Ekland

When Jack Benny has a party, you not only bring your own Scotch,
you bring your own rocks. George Burns

—Your money or your life!
—…I'm thinking it over. **Mugger and Jack Benny**

He's so tight that if you stuck a piece of coal up his ass in two weeks
you'd have a diamond. **Matthew Broderick**

A builder's estimate is a sum of money equal to half the final cost.

Neil Collins

A rich man is nothing but a poor man with money. W.C. Fields

If someone says, 'It's not the money, it's the principle,' it's the money.

Kin Hubbard

Money is the poor man's credit card.   Marshall McLuhan

I was feeling very irritable and moody. It was that difficult time of the
month when the credit card statement arrives.   Julie Walters

My last credit card bill was so big, before I opened it I actually heard
a drum roll.   Rita Rudner

I had my credit card stolen, but I didn't report it because whoever
stole it is spending less than my wife.   Henny Youngman

Why is there so much month left at the end of the money?
                                                       John Barrymore

In the midst of life, we are in debt.   Ethel Watts Mumford

The cost of living has gone up another dollar a quart.   W.C. Fields

I put a dollar in a change machine. Nothing changed.   George Carlin

When you've got them by their wallets, their hearts and minds will
follow.   Fern Naito

The rich are different from you and me. They have more credit.
                                                        John Leonard

I handed one of my creditors an IOU and thought thank heavens
that's settled.   Richard Sheridan

Can you lend me five thousand dollars? I'd rather do anything than
beg you for money, but you're the only person I know that can't
possibly think any less of me.   Dan Conner, *Roseanne*

The difference between outlaws and in-laws is that outlaws don't
promise to pay it back.   Kin Hubbard

I lent a friend of mine ten thousand dollars for plastic surgery and
now I don't know what he looks like.   Emo Philips

Borrowing, like scratching, is only good for a while.   **Jewish saying**

If there is anyone to whom I owe money, I am prepared to forget it if
they are.   **Errol Flynn**

Money can't buy everything.
That's what credit cards are for. Ruby Wax

Nothing dispels enthusiasm like a small admission fee.   **Kin Hubbard**

She tipped him her nickel with the manner of one presenting a park
to the city.   **Dorothy Parker**

A bellperson carries my luggage – one small gym-style bag, and I tip
him $2, which he takes as if I am handing him a jar of warm sputum.
                                                                Dave Barry

I once gave a waiter a tip – I told him never to step off a moving bus.
                                                                Groucho Marx

If someone was stupid enough to offer me a million dollars to make
a picture, I was certainly not dumb enough to turn it down.
                                                                Elizabeth Taylor

Money makes money and the money money makes makes money.
                                                                Benjamin Franklin

The trick is not to live off the interest on one's capital, but off the
interest on the interest.   **Alan Clark**

My problem is how to reconcile my net income with my gross habits.
                                                                Errol Flynn

Today you can go to a gas station and find the cash register open and the
toilets locked. They must reckon toilet paper is worth more than money.
                                                                Joey Bishop

I gave him an unlimited budget and he exceeded it.   Edward Williams

I must have blown a fortune during my career. Part of the loot went on booze, part on horses and part on women. The rest I spent foolishly.

George Raft

The difference between a taxidermist and a tax collector is that the taxidermist takes only your skin.

Mark Twain

Never underestimate the effectiveness of a straight cash bribe.

Claud Cockburn

When a man tells you he got rich by hard work, ask him whose.

George Bernard Shaw

It is better to have a permanent income than to be fascinating.

Oscar Wilde

It doesn't matter whether you're rich or poor as long as you have money.

Max Miller

To suppose, as we all suppose, that we could be rich and not behave as the rich behave, is like supposing that we could drink all day and keep absolutely sober.   Logan Pearsall Smith

Saving is a fine thing – especially when your parents have done it for you.

Winston Churchill

Save a little money each month, and at the end of the year, you'll be surprised at how little you have.   Ernest Haskins

I've got all the money I'll ever need if I die by four o'clock.

Henny Youngman

If you have to ask the price, you can't afford it.   J.P. Morgan

'Imagine no possessions,' sang John Lennon who owned a luxury
apartment in New York solely to house his clothes.   Arthur Smith

I've been rich and I've been poor. Believe me, honey, rich is better.
                                                            Sophie Tucker

Bob Hope's got more money on him than I have in the bank.
                                                             Bing Crosby

That money talks, I'll not deny; I heard it once, it said, 'Goodbye.'
                                                           Richard Armour

I'm spending a year dead for tax reasons.   Douglas Adams

The Tax Office has streamlined its tax form this year. It goes like this:
(a) How much did you make last year? (b) How much have you got left?
(c) Send (b).   Henny Youngman

I told the Inland Revenue I didn't owe them a penny because I lived
by the seaside.   Ken Dodd

When they fire a rocket at Cape Canaveral, I feel as if I own it.
                                                           William Holden

Income tax has made more liars out of the American people than golf.
                                                              Will Rogers

The hardest thing in the world to understand is income tax.
                                                           Albert Einstein

Why does a slight tax increase cost you 200 dollars and a substantial
tax cut save you 30 cents?   Peg Bracken

We contend that for a nation to try to tax itself into prosperity is like
a man standing in a bucket and trying to lift himself up by the handle.
                                                         Winston Churchill

Everyone should pay their income tax with a smile. I tried it but they
demanded cash.   Jackie Mason

A banker is a fellow who lends you his umbrella when the sun is
shining and wants it back the minute it begins to rain.   Mark Twain

If you owe the bank a hundred dollars, that's your problem. If you owe
the bank a million dollars, that's the bank's problem.   James Goldsmith

I went to see my bank manager. I said, 'Tell me, how does my account
stand?' He said, 'I'll toss you for it.'   Les Dawson

I wouldn't trust a bank that would lend money to such a poor risk as me.
                                                        Robert Benchley

I've written to the bank and told them if they send me any more nasty
letters I shall take my overdraft elsewhere.   Jed Larson

They usually have two tellers in my local bank. Except when it's very
busy, when they have one.   Rita Rudner

Banks have this new image of being your friend. If they're so friendly,
how come they chain down the pens?   Alan King

I wish the banks would just say, 'Look, you shits, line up there, we don't
give a fuck about your miserable little bank accounts.'   Paul Fussell

—Why do you persist in robbing banks?
—Because that's where the money is.   Willie Sutton

If economists were any good at business, they would be rich men
instead of advisers to rich men.   Kirk Kerkorian

I was born in very sorry circumstances. My mother was sorry and
my father was sorry as well.   Norman Wisdom

I worked myself up from nothing to a state of extreme poverty.
                                                          Groucho Marx

I never had a penny to my name. So I changed my name.

Rodney Dangerfield

We were so poor when I was growing up, if we wanted a Jacuzzi,
we had to fart in the tub.

Eddie Murphy

We were so poor we couldn't even afford a proper lavatory brush.
We had to tie my pet hedgehog to a stick and tell him to hold his breath.

Roy Chubby Brown

We couldn't afford a proper bath. We just had a pan of water and
we'd wash down as far as possible and we'd wash up as far as
possible. Then, when somebody'd clear the room, we'd wash possible.

Dolly Parton

We were so poor that if we woke up on Christmas day without an
erection, we had nothing to play with.

Frank McCourt

My family was so poor that blues singers used to come to our house
when they had writers' block.

Otis Lee Crenshaw

My family was so poor that the lady next door gave birth to me.

Lee Trevino

I was once so poor I didn't know where my next husband was coming from. Mae West

One of the strangest things about life is that the poor, who need money
the most, are the very ones that never have it.

Finley Peter Dunne

The rich would have to eat money, but luckily the poor provide food.

Russian proverb

Money is better than poverty, if only for financial reasons.

Woody Allen

The lack of money is the root of all evil.

Mark Twain

They had absolutely nothing. But they were willing to risk it all.

Tagline, *The Commitments*

If only God would give me some clear sign! Like making a large deposit in my name at a Swiss bank.

Woody Allen

October. This is one of the peculiarly dangerous months to speculate in stocks. Other dangerous months are July, January, September, April, November, May, March, June, December, August and February.

Mark Twain

I started out with nothing and I've still got most of it left.   Groucho Marx

To force myself to earn more money, I determined to spend more.

James Agate

I'm living so far beyond my income that we may almost be said to be living apart.

Saki

The safest way to double your money is to fold it over once and put it in your pocket.

Kin Hubbard

There are few sorrows, however poignant, in which a good income is of no avail.

Logan Pearsall Smith

Now that he was rich he was not thought ignorant any more, but simply eccentric.

Mavis Gallant

I have enough money to last me the rest of my life – unless I have to buy something.

Jackie Mason

All your life I gave you nothing, and still you ask for more.

Gilbert and George

Any man who has ten thousand dollars left when he dies is a failure.

Errol Flynn

The rich are different from you and me. They pay less taxes.   Peter de Vries

CHARITY

We are here on earth to do good for others; what the others are here
for I have no idea.
                                                              W.H. Auden

'Please, sir,' pleaded the stranger, 'would you be so kind as to help
a poor unfortunate fellow who is hungry and can't find work?
All I have in the world is this gun.'
                                                            Martin Latham

Victoria Beckham gives away all her old clothes to starving children.
Well, who else are they going to fit?
                                                             Pauline Calf

I can't give away my old clothes to the poor. They have enough to
put up with without the added humiliation of wearing last season.
                                           Edina Monsoon, *Absolutely Fabulous*

During the festive season we must not forget those who are less fortunate
than ourselves – the poor. They may attempt to burgle your house while
you are at church.   Mr Cholmondley-Warner, *Harry Enfield and Chums*

Would the congregation please note that the bowl at the back of the
church labelled 'For the Sick' is for monetary donations only.
                                              Churchtown parish magazine

It is ungentlemanly to include more than one foreign coin in
contributions to the church collection.
                                                             George Moor

—What was it Father Jack used to say about the needy? He had a term
for them.
—Shower of bastards.   Father Ted and Father Dougal, *Father Ted*

When it comes to giving to others, I stop at nothing.   Roger Price

I don't get paid enough to care.   Conan O'Brien

A homeless person said, 'I haven't had anything to eat for two days.'
I said, 'I wish I had your willpower.'
                                                          Roy Chubby Brown

I was harpooned by a Lifeboat Institute flag seller in the High Street.
That pin gave me an infection. They owe me a few deep-sea rescues
that lot do.   **Rigsby, *Rising Damp***

A woman with a clipboard stopped me in the street. She said,
'Could you spare a couple of minutes for cancer research?' I said,
'All right, but we won't get much done.'   **Jimmy Carr**

I'm sorry, my good fellow, but all my money is tied up in currency.
                                                            W.C. Fields

In Palm Springs, they think homelessness is caused by bad divorce
lawyers.   **Gary Trudeau**

I'd like to help the homeless but they're never home.
Lenny Clarke

Homelessness is homelessness no matter where you live.   **Glenda Jackson**

The worst thing about being homeless is that you'll never be able
to enjoy camping.   **Paul Rodriguez**

I always give homeless people money, and my friends shout at me,
'He's only going to buy more alcohol and cigarettes.' And I'm
thinking, 'Oh, like I wasn't.'   **Kathleen Madigan**

—Our benefit show is being held in aid of a very good cause.
—A rest home for pirates?   **Homer Simpson**

Some charity asked me to take part in a fund-raising programme in
support of imprisoned writers. I declined on the grounds that, on the
whole, I think all writers should be in prison.   **Ralph Richardson**

Sex Appeal – please give generously.   **Bumper sticker**

If things get worse, I'll have to ask you to stop helping me.   **Roseanne**

I only give to one charity, the F.E.B.F – Fuck Everybody But Fields.

W.C. Fields

He was so benevolent, so merciful a man that he would have held
an umbrella over a duck in a shower of rain. **Douglas Jerrold**

Philanthropic people lose all sense of humanity. It is their distinguishing
characteristic. **Oscar Wilde**

Billy Connolly gives away money as silently as a waiter falling down a
flight of stairs with a tray of glasses. **Anon**

His wallet is more capacious than an elephant's scrotum and just as
difficult to get your hands on. *Blackadder II*

He threw his money around like a man with no arms. **Anon**

If I knew that a man was coming to my house with the conscious
design of doing me good, I should run for my life. **Henry David Thoreau**

No good deed ever goes unpunished. **Clare Boothe Luce**

When you are in trouble, people who call to sympathize, are really
only looking for more details. **Edgar W. Howe**

He's so generous, he'll go out, get two blowjobs, come back and
give you one of them. **Milton Berle**

—I want to do something for humanity.
—How about sterilization? **Cher Horowitz and Josh Lucas,** *Clueless*

NATIONS

COUNTRIES AND NATIONALITIES

I have the world's oldest globe. It's flat.   **Buzz Nutley**

I showed my appreciation of my native land in the usual way by getting
out of it as soon as I possibly could.   **George Bernard Shaw**

Patriotism is the conviction that your country is superior to all others
because you were born in it.   **George Bernard Shaw**

Sometimes I wonder if I am patriotic enough. Sure, I want to kill people.
But on both sides.   **Jack Handey**

Ask not what you can do for your country, for they are liable to tell you.
                                                          Mark Steinbeck

The importance of a country is inversely proportional to the length
of its national anthem.   **Allen Otter**

You can't be a real country unless you have a beer and an airline.
It helps if you have some kind of football team, or some nuclear
weapons, but at the very least you need a beer.   **Frank Zappa**

Addresses are given to us to conceal our whereabouts.   **Saki**

Welcome to Mudville. There is no joy, but we've got a Starbucks.
                                                          Gregory Mills

—What state do you live in?
—Denial.   **Anon**

You're not in Hell, you're just in Langford. Same zip code though.
                                                             Roseanne

Where's the Cannes Film Festival being held this year?   **Christina Aguilera**

My hometown is so dull that the drugstore sells picture postcards of other towns.

Milton Berle

I hate small towns because once you've seen the cannon in the park, there's nothing else to do.

Lenny Bruce

'Christ,' said Gunner White, 'I *must* be bored. I just thought of Catford.'

Spike Milligan

Never ask a man if he's from Yorkshire. If he is, he'll already have told you. If he isn't, why embarrass him?

Roy Hattersley

If you're going to have a north/south divide in England, you really should police it.

Jimmy Carr

—Have you lived here all your life?
—Not yet.

Lee Evans

So, you're from Windsor. They have some lovely homes there.
Do you live near any of them?

Dame Edna Everage

There's no shame in being from Texas. The only shame is having to go back.

Kinky Friedman

When the white missionaries came to Africa they had the Bible, and we had the land. They said, 'Let us pray.' We closed our eyes. When we opened them we had the Bible and they had the land.

Archbishop Desmond Tutu

I have to choose between the world, the next world and Australia.

Oscar Wilde

Australians are just British people who are happy.   Craig Hill

To live in Australia permanently is rather like going to a party and
dancing all night with your mother.   **Barry Humphries**

Belgium is a country invented by the British to annoy the French.
                                                    Charles de Gaulle

Apart from cheese and tulips, the main product of Holland is advocaat,
a drink made from lawyers.   **Alan Coren**

Apparently, one in five people in the world are Chinese. And there
are five people in my family, so it must be one of them. It's either my
mum or my dad. Or my older brother, Colin. Or my younger brother,
Ho-Cha-Chu. But I think it's Colin.   **Tommy Cooper**

America: the land of the dull and the home of the literal.   **Gore Vidal**

America is the only country where a significant proportion of the
population believes that professional wrestling is real but the moon
landing was faked.   **David Letterman**

The trouble with America is that there are far too many wide-open
spaces surrounded by teeth.   **Charles Luckman**

Illegal aliens have always been a problem in the United States.
Ask any Indian.   **Robert Orben**

Of course, America had often been discovered before Columbus, but it had always been hushed up. Oscar Wilde

One of the reasons Britain is such a steady and gracious place is the
calming influence of the football results and shipping forecasts.
                                                        Bill Bryson

I support making deportation for illegal immigration retroactive,
and shipping the Anglos back home.   Paul Rodriguez

Never criticize Americans. They have the best taste money can buy. Miles Kington

I don't believe there's any problem in this country, no matter how
tough it is, that Americans, when they roll up their sleeves, can't
completely ignore.   George Carlin

America is the only nation in the world where all our poor people are fat.
                                                         Al Franken

Americans will put up with anything provided it doesn't block traffic.
                                                         Dan Rather

Americans are people who laugh at African witch doctors and spend
100 million dollars on fake diets.   L.L. Levinson

The thing that impresses me most about America is the way parents
obey their children.   Edward VIII

America is the only nation in history which miraculously has gone from
barbarism to degeneration without the usual interval of civilization.
                                                   Georges Clemenceau

Why is America such a violent country? Because their wallpaper is
so hideous.   Oscar Wilde

You cannot underestimate the intelligence of the American people.
                                                       H.L. Mencken

It's an appropriate coincidence that the word 'American' ends in 'I can.'
                                                   Alexander Animator

I went to San Francisco. I found someone's heart.   Steven Wright

The motto for Cleveland should be, 'You gotta live somewhere.'

Jimmy Brogan

I have just returned from Boston. It is the only thing to do if you find yourself there.

Fred Allen

It is a scientific fact that if you live in California you lose one point of your IQ every year.

Truman Capote

Woy-Woy is the only above-ground cemetery in the world.

Spike Milligan

If I owned Texas and Hell, I'd rent out Texas and live in hell.

Philip Sheridan

The United States, I understand, are under the impression that they are twenty years in advance of Britain; whilst, as a matter of actual verifiable fact, they are just about six hours behind it.

Harold Hobson

California is a fine place to live – if you happen to be an orange.

Fred Allen

If we destroy Kansas, the world may not hear about it for years.

Sean Connery

In Las Vegas, you'll find all kinds of gambling devices – roulette tables, slot machines, wedding chapels.

Stanley Davis

Los Angeles is a big hard-boiled city with no more personality than a paper cup.

Raymond Chandler

LA – any town that's got an all-night, drive-in taxidermist has got to be weird.

Billy Connolly

Britain: the land of embarrassment and breakfast.

Julian Barnes

Los Angeles is a very transient town. It's the only place I know where you can actually rent a dog.

Rita Rudner

Los Angeles: I wouldn't want to live in a city where the only cultural advantage is that you can make a right turn on a red light.

Woody Allen

The difference between Los Angeles and yoghurt is that yoghurt has real culture.

Tom Taussik

I moved to Los Angeles, and I miss so many things from the real world that they don't have here, like ageing, pride, and dignity.

Greg Proops

If you live in New York, even if you're Catholic, you're Jewish.

Lennie Bruce

New York: Skyscraper National Park.

John Updike

New York now leads the world's great cities in the number of people around whom you shouldn't make a sudden move.

David Letterman

When you're in New York City, always keep your money and other valuables in a safe place, such as Switzerland.

Dave Barry

New York is an exciting town where something is happening all the time, most of it unsolved.

Johnny Carson

I once spent a year in Philadelphia. I think it was on a Sunday.

W.C. Fields

Why do I continue to live in America? Why do men go to zoos?

H.L. Mencken

Always remember that you are an Englishman and therefore have drawn first prize in the lottery of life. Cecil Rhodes

When we win an Olympic medal, we're English; when we riot and
throw petrol bombs, we're West Indian.   **Winston Price**

'England for the English,' as we used to say about India.
                        Audrey fforbes-Hamilton, *To the Manor Born*

The English are best explained in terms of tea, roast beef and rain.
A people is first what it eats, drinks and gets pelted with.   **Pierre Daninos**

Continental people have sex lives; the English have hot-water bottles.
                                                          George Mikes

The old English belief that if a thing is unpleasant it is automatically
good for you.   **Osbert Lancaster**

The English really aren't interested in talking to you unless you've been
to school or to bed with them.   **Lady Nancy Keith**

I would like to live in Manchester, England. The transition between
Manchester and death would be unnoticeable.   **Mark Twain**

I have no great hopes from Birmingham. I always say there is something
direful in the sound.   **Jane Austen**

They say that men become attached even to Widnes.   **A.J. Taylor**

Brighton has the perennial air of being in a position to help the police
with their inquiries.   **Keith Waterhouse**

When a man is tired of London, he is tired of life; for there is in London
all that life can afford.   **Samuel Johnson**

May I ask what you were hoping to see out of a Torquay bedroom
window? Sydney Opera House, perhaps? The Hanging Gardens of
Babylon? Herds of wildebeest sweeping majestically by?   **Basil Fawlty**

The English never smash in a face. They merely refrain from asking
it to dinner.   **Margaret Halsey**

I like the English. They have the most rigid code of immorality in the world.
Malcolm Bradbury

In England I would rather be a man, a horse, a dog or a woman, in that order. In America I think the order would be reversed.
Bruce Gould

Philip Larkin was so English that he didn't even care much about Britain, and he rarely mentioned it.
Clive James

It's no longer true that continental people have sex lives whereas the English have hot-water bottles – the English now have electric blankets.
George Mikes

Contrary to popular belief, English women do not wear tweed nightgowns.
Hermione Gingold

The Englishwoman is so refined, she has no bosom and no behind.
Stevie Smith

If an Englishman gets run down by a truck he apologizes to the truck.
Jackie Mason

An Englishman, even if he is alone, forms an orderly queue of one.
George Mikes

He is a typical Englishman, always dull and usually violent.
Oscar Wilde

The Englishman has all the qualities of a poker except its occasional warmth.
Daniel O'Connell

An Englishman's mind works best when it is almost too late.
Lord D'Abernon

The English have an extraordinary ability for flying into a great calm.
Alexander Woollcott

Canada is a country so square that even the female impersonators are women.

Richard Brenner

Boasting about modesty is typical of the English. George Bernard Shaw

Even crushed against his brother in the tube, the average Englishman pretends desperately that he is alone. Germaine Greer

An Englishman's real ambition is to get a railway compartment to himself. Ian Hay

The perfidious, haughty, savage, disdainful, stupid, slothful, inhospitable, inhuman English. Julius Caesar Scaliger

There'll always be an England, even if it's in Hollywood. Bob Hope

I'm Canadian. That's like American but without the guns. Dave Foley

Canadians are Americans with no Disneyland. Margaret Mahy

I've been to Canada, and I've always gotten the impression that I could take the country over in two days. Jon Stewart

Canada is all right really, though not for the whole weekend. Saki

Canadians are generally indistinguishable from Americans and the surest way of telling the two apart is to make this observation to a Canadian. Richard Starnes

Canada is an entire country named Doug. Greg Proops

Edmonton isn't exactly the end of the world, but you can see it from there. Ralph Klein

What has China ever given the world? Can you really respect a nation that's never taken to cutlery? Victoria Wood

I can't figure out why Columbia isn't a superpower by now.
They produce coffee and cocaine, so it's not like they can't figure
out how to motivate the workforce.   **Margot Black**

If I were God and I were trying to create a nation that would get up
the nostril of the Englishman, I would create the French.   **Julian Barnes**

The Americans have called the French, 'cheese-eating surrender monkeys',
a description I totally disagree with. They left out, 'wine-guzzling'.
                                                      William Hague

France: how can you unite a country that produces 263 kinds of cheese?
                                                      Charles de Gaulle

—What's the capital of France?
—F.   **Reverend Geraldine Granger and Alice Tinker,** *The Vicar of Dibley*

No matter how politely or distinctly you ask a Parisian a question he
will persist in answering you in French.   **Fran Lebowitz**

The best view in Paris is the one from the Eiffel Tower, because it is
the only place in Paris from which you can't see the damn thing.
                                                      William Morris

It is unthinkable for a Frenchman to arrive at middle age without having both syphilis and the Cross of the Legion of Honour. André Gide

Going to war without France is like going deer hunting without an
accordion.   **General Norman Scharwzkopf**

The problem with the French is that they don't have a word for
entrepreneur.   **George W. Bush**

How can you identify a French infantryman? Sunburned armpits. **Anon**

A bad liver is to a Frenchman what a nervous breakdown is to an American. Everyone has had one and everyone wants to talk about it.
Art Buchwald

Going to the loo in a yacht in a French harbour is not so much goodbye as au revoir. **Noël Coward**

The best thing that can be said for France is that it's not Germany. **Anon**

The Germans are a cruel race. Their operas last for six hours and they have no word for 'fluffy'. **Captain Blackadder**, *Blackadder Goes Forth*

You can always reason with a German. You can always reason with a barnyard animal, too, for all the good it does. **P.J. O'Rourke**

My sister married a German. He complained he couldn't get a good bagel back home. I said, 'Well, whose fault is that?' **Emo Philips**

India: done the elephants, done the poverty. **Phil Tufnell**

What I look forward to most on returning from a long tour of India is a dry fart. **Phil Edmonds**

I think Iraq and Iran should be combined into one country called Irate. All the pissed-off people live in one place and get it over with.
Denis Leary

The Irish are a race of people who don't know what they want and are prepared to fight to the death to get it. **Sidney Littlewood**

When I told the people of Northern Ireland that I was an atheist, a woman in the audience stood up and asked if the God I did not believe in was Protestant or Catholic. **Quentin Crisp**

Put an Irishman on the spit, and you can always get another Irishman to turn him. **George Bernard Shaw**

Where would the Irish be without someone to be Irish at?   **Elizabeth Bowen**

I like the Irish but what I cannot understand is that when I say,
'I'm from London,' in a Dublin pub, this tends to be heard as,
'I am Oliver Cromwell.'   **Jo Brand**

Our Irish ancestors believed in magic, prayers, trickery, browbeating and
bullying. I think it would be fair to sum that list up as 'Irish politics'.
                                                          Flann O'Brien

I once saw a sign on a lift in Dublin that said: 'Please do not use this
when it is not working.'   **Spike Milligan**

I'm Irish. We think sideways.   **Spike Milligan**

The Irish is one race of people for whom psychoanalysis is of no use
whatsoever.   **Sigmund Freud**

The Italians are the most civilized people. And they're very warm.
Basically, they're Jews with great architecture.   **Fran Lebowitz**

What's the difference between toast and Italians? You can make soldiers
out of toast.   **Peter Ball**

I spat right in the face of an Italian girl and she thanked me. Her moustache was on fire. **Jackie Martling**

Rome reminds me of a man who lives by exhibiting to travellers his
grandmother's corpse.   **James Joyce**

Venice is a Renaissance Disneyland with entrance fees only the very rich
can afford.   **Richard Ingrams**

I couldn't settle in Italy. It was like living in a foreign country.   **Ian Rush**

In Britain, a dog is for Christmas. In Korea, it could be for breakfast, lunch or dinner.

Anon

New Zealand is a country of thirty thousand million sheep, three million of whom think they're human.

Barry Humphries

I find it hard to offer an opinion on New Zealand because when I was there it seemed to be shut.

Clement Freud

I don't like Norwegians at all. The sun never sets, the bar never opens, and the whole country smells of kippers.

Evelyn Waugh

Russia is miles of cornfields, and ballet in the evening.

Alan Hackney

One Russian is an anarchist, two Russians are a chess game, three Russians are a revolution, and four Russians are the Budapest String Quartet.

Jascha Heifetz

The way I understand it, the Russians are a sort of combination of incompetence and evil – sort of like the Post Office with tanks.

Emo Philips

Scottish-Americans tell you that if you want to identify tartans, it's easy: you look under the kilt, and if it's a quarter-pounder, it's a McDonald's.

Billy Connolly

A Scotsman is a man who, before sending his pyjamas to the laundry, stuffs a sock in each pocket.

Ambrose Bierce

I have been trying all my life to like Scotchmen, and am obligated to desist from the experiment in despair.

Charles Lamb

It is never difficult to distinguish between a Scotsman with a grievance and a ray of sunshine.

P.G. Wodehouse

Sweden is where they commit suicide and the king rides a bicycle.

Alan Bennett

In Italy for thirty years under the Borgias, they had warfare, terror, murder, bloodshed – they produced Michelangelo, Leonardo da Vinci, and the Renaissance. In Switzerland, they had brotherly love, five hundred years of democracy and peace and what did they produce? The cuckoo clock.

Orson Welles

The only interesting thing that can happen in a Swiss bedroom is suffocation by a feather pillow.

Nunnally Johnson

Switzerland is the land of peace, understanding, milk chocolate, and all those lovely snow-capped tax benefits.

David Niven

Switzerland is one bloody picture postcard after the other. Nothing but views.

Francis Bacon

I am moving to Switzerland because I am devoted to chocolate.

Noël Coward

When in Turkey, do as the turkeys do.

Honoré de Balzac

In Istanbul I was known as 'English Delight'.

Noël Coward

Wales is a country where Sunday starts early, and lasts several years.

Peg Bracken

The Welsh are always so pleased with themselves. I've never taken to them. What are they *for*?

Anne Robinson

The Welsh – all they've ever been systematically lumbered with are copious Giros and repeat prescriptions of pessaries for ovine cystitis.

A.A. Gill

Wales is a ghastly place. Huge gangs of sinewy men roam the valleys terrorizing people with their close-harmony singing. You need half a pint of phlegm in your throat just to pronounce the place names. *Blackadder III*

When asked his opinion of Welsh nationalism, Mr Thomas replied in three words, two of which were 'Welsh nationalism'.   Dylan Thomas

Wales is the land of my fathers. And my fathers can have it. Dylan Thomas

TRAVEL

Never go abroad. It's a dreadful place.   Earl of Cardigan

I don't hold with abroad and think that foreigners speak English when our backs are turned.   Quentin Crisp

I like my 'abroad' to be Catholic and sensual.   Chips Cannon

They say travel broadens the mind; but you must have the mind.   G.K. Chesterton

At my age, travel broadens the behind.   Stephen Fry

Last week I went to a travel agent to see about my holidays. There was a big poster of Majorca on the office wall. I said, 'I want to go there,' so she pinned me to the wall.   Tommy Cooper

The wife and I have been arguing about where to go on our holidays. I want to go to Tenerife. And she wants to come with me.   Roy Chubby Brown

I wouldn't mind seeing China if I could come back the same day.   Philip Larkin

If you look like your passport photo, you're too ill to travel. Will Kommen

A passport picture is a photo of a man that he can laugh at without realizing that it looks exactly the way his friends see him.   Phyllis Diller

Why is it called tourist season if we can't shoot them?   George Carlin

They've started giving passports to animals now. My cat has a passport. Do you know how that makes Mohammad Al Fayed feel?   **Jeff Green**

We're gonna see America. Gonna go west, where the air is fresh, the sky is big, and a man can still kill his dinner with his car.

Al Bundy, *Married ... With Children*

A tourist is someone who goes 3000 miles to get a photograph of themselves in front of their car.   **Robert Benchley**

All my wife has ever taken from the Mediterranean – from the whole vast intuitive culture – are four bottles of Chianti to make into lamps.

Peter Shaffer

To be a Frenchman abroad is to be miserable; to be an American abroad is to make other people miserable.   **Ambrose Bierce**

I have recently been all round the world and have formed a very poor opinion of it.   **Thomas Beecham**

I hate views. They are only made for bad painters.   **Oscar Wilde**

In hotel rooms, I worry. I think, I can't be the only guy who sits on the furniture naked.   **Jonathan Katz**

It is not worthwhile to go round the world to count the cats in Zanzibar.

Henry David Thoreau

I have found that there ain't no surer way to find out whether you like people or hate them than to travel with them.   **Mark Twain**

I went to Switzerland and got an obscene yodel.   **Rodney Dangerfield**

My first rule of travel is never to go to a place that sounds like a medical condition and Critz is clearly an incurable disease involving flaking skin.

Bill Bryson

When embarking on a polar expedition, begin with a clear idea which pole you are dashing at, and try to start facing the right way. Choose your companions carefully – you may have to eat them.

W.C. Sellar and R.J. Yeatman

Jews don't go camping.
Life is hard enough as it is.

Carol Siskind

Camping is nature's way of promoting the motel business.

Dave Barry

I've just been to Africa. Now I know how white people feel in America. Relaxed.

Richard Pryor

I've just been on holiday by mistake to the Norfolk B-roads.

Peter Kay

We also saw Haworth, which surpassed even my appetite for gloomy churchyards. Glutted, is the only word for it.

Sylvia Townsend Warner

To the question on the US visa form, 'Is it your intention to subvert the Government of the United States by force?' I answered: Sole purpose of visit.

Gilbert Harding

Always choose the oldest customs official. No chance of promotion.

Somerset Maugham

In America, there are two classes of travel – first class, and with children.

Robert Benchley

I have nothing to declare except my genius.

Oscar Wilde

I went to America to continue my life-long quest for naked women in wet mackintoshes.

Dylan Thomas

What I gained by being in France was learning to be better satisfied with my own country.

Samuel Johnson

True, you can sit outside in Paris and drink little cups of coffee, but why this is more stylish than sitting inside drinking large glasses of whiskey I don't know.

P.J. O'Rourke

You go Uruguay, and I'll go mine.

Groucho Marx

Don't you love looking at your friends' vacation pictures? Especially when they owe you money.

J. Chris Newberg

No man needs a vacation so much as the person who has just had one.

Elbert Hubbard

THE WORLD

All the world's a stage, and most of us are desperately unrehearsed.

Sean O'Casey

It's a small world, but I wouldn't want to paint it.   Steven Wright

The world is like a safe to which there is a combination – but the combination is locked up in the safe.   Peter de Vries

You know the world is crazy when the best rapper is a white guy, the best golfer is a black guy, and Switzerland holds the America's Cup.

Chris Rock

The quietest place in the world is the complaints department at the parachute packing plant.   Jackie Martling

Do you ever feel like the world's a tuxedo and you're a pair of brown shoes?   George Gobel

All the world is queer save thee and me, and even thou art a little queer.

Robert Owen

Cough and the world coughs with you; fart and you fart alone.

Trevor Griffiths

The world is like a cucumber – today it's in your hands, tomorrow it's up your arse.   Arab saying

We are living in a world today where lemonade is made from artificial flavours and furniture polish is made from real lemons.   Alfred Newman

LIFE

Life is full of misery, loneliness, unhappiness and suffering, and it's over much too soon.
Woody Allen

I read *The Times* each morning and if my name does not appear in the obituaries, I go on to enjoy the day.
Noël Coward

Some mornings, it's just not worth chewing through the leather straps.
Emo Philips

I long ago came to the conclusion that all life is 6 to 5 against.
Damon Runyon

Ducking for apples. Change one letter and it's the story of my life.
Dorothy Parker

Life is a cement trampoline.
Harold Nordberg

Life is anything that dies when you stomp on it.
Dave Barry

Life is a whim of several billion cells to be you for a while.
Anon

Life is something to do when you can't get to sleep.
Fran Lebowitz

Life is a sexually transmitted disease and the mortality rate is one hundred per cent.
R.D. Laing

Life is good and bad. Mostly and.
Diogenes

Nothing in life ever looks as good as it does on the seed packet.
Kinky Friedman

That's the trouble with life – crap dialogue and bad lighting.
Elizabeth Taylor

The living are just the dead on holiday.
Maurice Maeterlinck

Life is intrinsically boring and dangerous at the same time. At any given moment, the floor may open up. Of course, it almost never does; that's what makes it boring.
                                                            Edward Gorey

It may be that your sole purpose in life is to serve as a warning to others.
                                                            Anon

God writes the script, sweetie, I just say the lines.   Vic Grassi

Life – with a capital F.   Lilian Baylis

'Life is like that, dear,' she would sometimes say, but she would never say what it was that life was like.   Ronald Firbank

If life was fair, Elvis would be alive today and all the impersonators would be dead.   Johnny Carson

Life is generally something that happens elsewhere.   Alan Bennett

Life's a beach, and then you drown.   Anon

Life's a bitch, and then you marry one.
                                                            Anon

Life is a rollercoaster. Eat a light lunch.   David Schmaltz

If I had my life to live over again, I would do everything the exact same way, with the possible exception of seeing the movie remake of *Lost Horizon*.   Woody Allen

Remember, we're all in this alone.   Lily Tomlin

Life is like a sewer. What you get out of it depends upon what you put in.
                                                            Tom Lehrer

Life is like playing a violin solo in public and learning the instrument as one goes on.   Edward Bulwer-Lytton

Some things in life are certain: when you write a message on the fridge door with the magnetic letters on it, there are never enough vowels; cinemas and theatres, like Doctor Who's Tardis, are always bigger inside than they are outside; at least one line in every person's address is unnecessary.

Miles Kington

Life is stepping down a step or sitting in a chair – and it isn't there.

Ogden Nash

Life is a bowl of pits.

Rodney Dangerfield

In Greek myth, Icarus flew too high and his wings melted. What is the moral? Don't fly too close to the sun? Or is it, as I choose to believe: build better wings.

Stanley Kubrick

He never lived his life at all; only stayed and lunched with it occasionally.

A.C. Benson

Life is like a dog-sled team. If you ain't the lead dog, the scenery never varies.

Lewis Grizzard

When I hear someone sigh, 'Life is hard,' I am always tempted to ask, 'Compared to what?'

Sydney Harris

Life without you was like a broken pencil – pointless.

Lord Blackadder to Elizabeth I, *Blackadder II*

There are three things in life you can do nothing about: getting AIDS, getting clamped, and running out of Château Lafite '45. **Alan Clark**

When life hands you lemons, make whisky sours. **W.C. Fields**

On the keyboard of life, always keep one finger on the escape key.

Scott Adams

—Oh, great guru, tell me, what is the secret of life?
—The secret of life is abstinence from alcohol, women and sex.
—Is there anyone else here I can talk to? **Hagar the Horrible**

When life hands you lemons, make lemonade, pee in it, and serve it to the people that piss you off. **Jack Handey**

If I had my life to live over, I don't think I'd have the strength.
Flip Wilson

If I had my life to live over, I'd live over a saloon. **W.C. Fields**

Life is rather like opening a tin of sardines. We're all of us looking for the key. **Alan Bennett**

—How's life treating you, Norm?
—Like it caught me sleeping with its wife.
Coach Pantusso and Norm Peterson, *Cheers*

My only regret in life is that I'm not someone else. **Woody Allen**

Some people go to India to find the mystery of life. I'm still trying to figure out how to start my car. **Rodney Dangerfield**

Just when I discovered the meaning of life, they changed it. **George Carlin**

What if the hokey-cokey really is what it's all about? **Bob Monkhouse**

I hope life isn't a big joke, because I don't get it. **Jack Handey**

—How's life treating you, Norm?
—Like I just ran over its dog. **Coach Pantusso and Norm Peterson,** *Cheers*

The meaning of life is that it stops. **Franz Kafka**

Life doesn't imitate art. It imitates bad television. **Woody Allen**

The only thing in my life that I regret is that I once saved David Frost from drowning. I had to pull him out, otherwise nobody would have believed I didn't push him in.

Peter Cook

Three little sentences will get you through life. Number one: Cover for me. Number two: Oh, good idea, boss. Number three: It was like that when I got here.

Homer Simpson

One's real life is so often the life that one does not lead.

Oscar Wilde

Some days you're the pigeon, and some days you're the statue.

David Brent, *The Office*

As life goes on, don't you find that all you need is about two real friends, a regular supply of books, and a Peke?

P.G. Wodehouse

I think it was John Lennon who said, 'Life is what happens while you're making other plans,' and that's how I feel. Although he also said, 'I am the walrus, I am the eggman,' so I don't know what to believe.

David Brent, *The Office*

In New York, life is what happens while you're waiting for a table.

Carrie Bradshaw, *Sex and the City*

Yesterday was the first day of the rest of your life and you messed it up again.

Patrick Murray

It's a dog eat dog world and I'm wearing Bonio underwear.

Norm Peterson, *Cheers*

Don't worry about the world ending today: it's already tomorrow in Australia.

Steven Wright

My wife and I took out life insurance policies on one another, so now it's just a waiting game.

Bill Dwyer

There are three things you just can't do in life: you can't beat the phone company, you can't make a waiter see you until he's ready, and you can't go home again.
                                                                    Bill Bryson

Life is just one damned thing after another.   **Elbert Hubbard**

The day after tomorrow is the third day of the rest of your life.
                                                                    George Carlin

The biggest conspiracy has always been that there is no conspiracy. Nobody's out to get you. Nobody gives a shit whether you live or die. There, you feel better now?   **Dennis Miller**

In spite of the cost of living, it's still popular.   **Kathleen Norris**

BELIEFS

All those who believe in telekinesis, raise my hand.   **Emo Philips**

I can believe in anything, provided that it is quite incredible.   **Oscar Wilde**

There are some ideas so wrong that only a very intelligent person could believe in them.   **George Orwell**

—Have you any concrete evidence of ghosts?
—No. Very few ghosts are made of concrete.   **Michael Bentine**

Vampires are make-believe, just like elves, gremlins and Eskimos.
                                                        Homer Simpson

I don't believe in fairies, even if they exist.   **Brendan Behan**

I distrust all beliefs, most thought and anything ending in *ism*.   **Joe Bennett**

I don't believe in astrology. I'm a Sagittarian and we're sceptical.
                                                        Arthur C. Clarke

People will believe anything if you whisper it.   Karl Kraus

Tell a man there are 300 billion stars in the universe and he'll believe you.
Tell him a bench has wet paint on it and he'll have to touch it to be sure.
                                                                  Herb Cohen

My husband has two beliefs in life. He believes in God, and he believes
that when the gas gauge is on empty, he still has a quarter of a tank.
                                                                  Rita Rudner

In Texas, we grew up believing two things: God loves you and he's
going to send you to hell, and sex is bad and dirty and nasty and
awful and you should save it for the one you love.   Butch Hancock

There are three statements you should never believe: the cheque is
in the post; I am from the government and I am here to help you;
I promise I won't come in your mouth.   Bill Hicks

Puritanism is the haunting fear that someone, somewhere, may be happy.
                                                             H.L. Mencken

No matter how cynical you get, it's impossible to keep up.   Lily Tomlin

Believe nothing until it has been officially denied.   Claud Cockburn

Feng Shui is the ancient Chinese art of getting men to put the toilet
lid down.   Jeff Green

I don't believe in mathematics.   Albert Einstein

When men cease to believe in God, they will not believe in nothing,
they will believe in anything.   G.K. Chesterton

I don't believe in God, but I do believe that you shouldn't step on the
cracks in the sidewalk.   Jonathan Katz

Everybody should believe in something; I believe I'll have another drink.
                                                           Robert Benchley

GOD AND RELIGION

—Do you think there is a God?
—Well, *somebody*'s out to get me.

Bill Watterson

God is love – but get it in writing.

Gypsy Rose Lee

How cruel God would be, if he were not so great.

Alphonse de Lamartine

Men don't get cellulite. God might just be a man.

Rita Rudner

If God did not exist, it would be necessary to invent him.

Voltaire

I don't believe in God. I believe in sex and death. Two things that
come once in a lifetime. But at least after death you're not nauseous.

Woody Allen

Not only is there no God, but try getting a plumber on weekends.

Woody Allen

God may be dead, but 50,000 social workers have risen to take his place.

J.D. McCoughey

Only one thing is impossible for God: to find any sense in any copyright
law on the planet.

Mark Twain

In real life, Diane Keaton believes in God. But she also believes that the
radio works because there are tiny people inside it.

Woody Allen

The question I'd like to ask God isn't the usual, 'Why is there pain
and suffering?' sort of thing. What I want to know is, what was the
biggest, grossest bug that ever crawled on anyone and they didn't
notice, and then it crawled away?

Julia Sweeney

When I was a kid, I used to pray every night for a new bicycle.
Then I realized that the Lord doesn't work that way, so I stole one
and asked him to forgive me.

Emo Philips

Some people say there is a God. Others say there is no God. The truth probably lies somewhere in-between.   **W.B. Yeats**

Our only hope rests on the off-chance that God does exist.
                                                    Alice Thomas Ellis

Many people believe they are attracted by God, or by Nature, when they are only repelled by man.   **W.R. Inge**

Give a man a fish, and you'll feed him for a day. Give him a religion, and he'll starve to death while praying for a fish.   **Timothy Jones**

If you talk to God, you are praying; if God talks to you, you have schizophrenia.   **Thomas Szasz**

I don't believe in God. I believe in cashmere.   **Fran Lebowitz**

If you want to make a man very angry, tell him you are going to pray for him.   **Edgar W. Howe**

My church accepts all denominations – fivers, tenners, twenties.
                                                    Patrick O'Connell

The one thing father always gave up for Lent was going to church.
                                                    Clarence Day

I know God is a man. Because if God was a woman She would have made sperm taste like chocolate. **Carrie Snow**

I once saw a miracle – just when we could have done without one.
                                                    Stanislaw J. Lec

It would have approached nearer to the idea of a miracle if Jonah had swallowed the whale.   **Thomas Paine**

If God loves us all so much, how come he never makes rain taste minty?
So everyone can have fresh breath.   Bob Odenkirk

After washing twelve pairs of feet, the crucifixion must have been a
pushover.   Alan Bennett

Here's the church, here's the steeple, look inside … yeah, not as popular
as it used to be, is it?   Harry Hill

Never read the Bible as if it means something. Or at any rate don't
try to mean it. Nor prayers. The liturgy is best treated and read as if
it's someone announcing the departure of trains.   Alan Bennett

Taking Reservations For Eternity. Smoking or Non-Smoking.
                                                              Sign outside church

The Bible? Talk about a preachy book. Everybody's a sinner!
Except this one guy.   Homer Simpson

My favourite characters in the Bible are King David, Delilah and
Charlton Heston.   Milton Berle

If you drop a Bible from a great height, you can kill a fieldmouse.
So maybe the Bible isn't all good.   Harry Hill

So, what's with this guy, Gideon, anyway? And why can't he ever
remember his Bible?   Rob Turner

The New English Bible: even the end of the world is described as if it were only an exceptionally hot afternoon.

                                                                     Peter Mallen

The best prayer I ever heard was, 'Dear Lord, please make me the kind
of person my dog thinks I am.'   Reverend Warren J. Keating

I do want to have Brooklyn christened, but I'm not sure which religion.

David Beckham

Jews know two things: suffering, and where to find great Chinese food.

Mark Linn-Baker

What religion am I? I'm the one with all the well-meaning rules that don't work out in real life, uh, Christianity.   **Homer Simpson**

A Christian is a man who feels repentance on a Sunday for what he did on Saturday and is going to do on Monday.   **Thomas Ybarra**

People may say what they like about the decay of Christianity; the religious system that produced green Chartreuse can never really die.   **Saki**

—Are you Jewish?
—No, a tree fell on me.   **Spike Milligan**

I'm an Anglo-Jew: I do believe I was personally chosen by God, but I don't like to make a fuss about it.   **Chris Addison**

Jesus was Jewish – but only on his mother's side.   **Archie Bunker**

I was raised in the Jewish tradition, taught never to marry a Gentile woman, shave on a Saturday night and, most especially, never to shave a Gentile woman on a Saturday night.   **Woody Allen**

The Jews were a proud people and throughout history they had trouble with the unsympathetic Genitals.   **Schoolboy howler**

My grandfather was a Jewish juggler. He used to worry about six things at once.   **Richard Lewis**

My mother is a typical Jewish mother. One time she was on jury duty and they sent her home. She insisted *she* was guilty.   **Cathy Ladman**

I was banned from the Beverly Hills Swimming Club because I'm Jewish. 'My son's only half Jewish,' I said, 'so could he go in up to his waist?'

Groucho Marx

The only advantage I have found to being Jewish is that I can be openly anti-Semitic.

Kirk Douglas

An anti-Semite is a person who hates Jews more than is absolutely necessary.

Jewish proverb

My parents worshipped old-world values: God and carpeting.   Mel Brooks

I don't believe in miracles. I rely on them.

Brendan Behan

I'm half-Catholic and half-Jewish. When I go to confession, I take my lawyer with me.

Ed Mann

The Jews invented guilt and the Catholics turned it into an art form.

Jed Larson

Being a Catholic doesn't stop you from sinning. It just stops you from enjoying it.

Cleveland Amory

He is such a devout Catholic, he won't be happy until he is crucified.

John B. Keane

Catholicism – what can you say about a religion that makes a sin out of sex, and a sacred act out of drinking alcohol?

Anon

He was of the faith chiefly in the sense that the church he currently did not attend was Catholic.

Kingsley Amis

—What's so special about Jesus?
—His name's a swear word.

Reverend Geraldine Granger and child, The Vicar of Dibley

One of the opposums was St Matthew who was also a taximan.

Schoolboy howler

Does anyone exist more Catholic than the Devil? **Charles Baudelaire**

Methodism is not really a religion – it's just a sort of insurance policy
in case there does turn out to be a God. **Kenneth Haworth**

Tennessee Williams and I are the only constantly High Episcopalians
I know. **Tallulah Bankhead**

Just how many witnesses do they need before Jehovah's trial starts?

Tom Shields

Jehovah's Witnesses don't take part in Halloween because it's against
their religion. They don't like it when strangers come to their doors
and bother them. **Bruce Clark**

A religious group came to my door yesterday selling cosmetics.
They call themselves Jojoba's Witnesses. **Jeannie Dietz**

If there is reincarnation, I'd like to come back as Warren Beatty's fingertips.

Woody Allen

I spend money with reckless abandon. I spent $5,000 on a seminar
about reincarnation. I got to thinking, what the hell, you only live once.

Ronnie Shakes

If there is such a thing as reincarnation, knowing my luck I'll come
back as me. **Rodney Trotter, *Only Fools and Horses***

I have never been molested when travelling alone on trains. I just
have to say a few words and I am immediately left alone: 'Are you
a born-again Christian?' **Rita Rudner**

I do benefits for all religions. I'd hate to blow the hereafter on a
technicality.
Bob Hope

All religions are basically the same – guilt, with different holidays.
Cathy Ladman

I would be converted to any religion for a cigar and baptized in it
for a box of them.
Mark Twain

I'm not a religious woman, but I find if you say no to everything you can hardly tell the difference.
Enid Featherstone

I'm a dyslexic satanist. I worship the drivel.
Linda Smith

There is a remote tribe that worships the number zero. Is nothing sacred?
Les Dawson

—Are you religious?
—No, I'm Church of England.
Andy Hamilton

The Church of England is the perfect church for those who don't go
to church.
Gerald Priestland

If all the people who go to sleep in church were laid end to end,
they would be a lot more comfortable.
Roberta A. Taft

I don't go to church because I can pray better in fields.
Barbara Woodhouse

You can no more become a Christian by going to church than you
can become an automobile by sleeping in your garage.
Garrison Keillor

A converted cannibal is one who, on Fridays, only eats fishermen.
Max Kauffmann

My religion? I'm an alcoholic.   Brendan Behan

Once my friend told me that he had found Jesus. I thought to myself,
'Woohoo, we're rich!' It turns out he meant something different.
                                                                  Emo Philips

There's one born-again every minute.   P.J. O'Rourke

The problem with born-again Christians is that they're an even bigger
pain the second time around.   Denis Leary

I'd rather meet an axe-murderer than a born-again Christian. At least
the axe-murderer will eventually leave you alone.   Barry Steiger

People give themselves to God when the devil wants nothing more to
do with them.   Sophie Arnould

I am a communist by day and a Catholic after dark.   Brendan Behan

My wife converted me to religion. I never believed in hell till I
married her.   Hal Roach

Do you have to believe in God to become a nun?   Rosie O'Donnell

The easy confidence with which I know another man's religion is folly
teaches me to suspect that my own is also.   Mark Twain

There doesn't seem very much left for us agnostics not to believe in.
                                                                 Jed Larson

Reincarnation: Life sucks, then you die, then life sucks again.   Slogan on T-shirt

An evangelical minister has had to resign after pictures surfaced
showing him in a hot tub with two women. He claimed it was just a
baptism gone terribly wrong.   Jay Leno

A casual stroll through a lunatic asylum shows that faith does not prove anything.

Friedrich Nietzsche

When it is a question of money, everybody is of the same religion. Voltaire

I admire the Pope. I have a lot of respect for anyone who can tour without an album.

Rita Rudner

I do not accept the word of the slanderous bachelor who lives on the banks of the Tiber.

Ian Paisley

The Vatican have come down with a ruling against surrogate mothers. Good thing they didn't make this rule before Jesus was born.

Elayne Boosler

I'm not a fascist. I'm a priest. Fascists dress up in black and tell people what to do. Whereas priests...

Father Ted

Priests – no chicks, no money ever. What could go wrong? Dennis Miller

When it comes to gay priests, even the tabloids suddenly find they have a religious affairs correspondent.

David Hare

It is no accident that the symbol of a bishop is a crook and the symbol of an archbishop is a double-cross.

Gregory Dix

Can bishops only move diagonally?

Lester Wood

I have always believed that a cherubim was a seraphim beneath the age of consent.

G.K. Chesterton

Forgive, O Lord, my little jokes on Thee, and I'll forgive Thy great big one on me.

Robert Frost

There are no atheists on a turbulent aircraft.

Erica Jong

God is always on the side that has the best football coach.

Heywood Broun

God will pardon me. It is his job.

Heinrich Heine

Thank God, I am an atheist.

Luis Buñuel

To you I'm an atheist; to God, I'm the loyal opposition.

Woody Allen

I would join a monastery that would take unbelievers.

Anton Chekhov

I'd rather be Frank Capra than God. If there is a Frank Capra.

Garson Kanin

To the lexicographer, God is simply the word that comes next to go-cart.

Samuel Butler

If triangles invented a god, they would make him three-sided.

Baron de Montesquieu

Man is a dog's idea of what God should be.

Holbrook Jackson

What do you say to God when he sneezes?

Henny Youngman

How do you make God laugh? Tell him your plans.

Woody Allen

Dear God: if You forgive us, we will forgive You.

Leo Rosten

IMMORTALITY

If Einstein and Shaw couldn't beat death, what chance have I got?
Practically none.

Mel Brooks

Millions long for immortality who do not know what to do with
themselves on a rainy Sunday afternoon.

Susan Ertz

If you don't believe in the resurrection of the dead, look at any office at quitting time.

Robert Townsend

Immortality is a long shot, but somebody has to be first.   Whoopi Goldberg

Jim Morrison is dead now and that's a high price to pay for immortality.

Gloria Estefan

I don't want to live on in my work. I want to live on in my apartment.

Woody Allen

I intend to live for ever. So far, so good.

Steven Wright

I will live for ever or die in the attempt.

Joseph Heller

If man were immortal, do you realize what his meat bills would be?

Woody Allen

HEAVEN AND HELL

The Catholic idea of heaven and hell is full of extremes. It's either eternal bliss, walking around on clouds playing table tennis with Mozart and Cary Grant, or eternal damnation where you have to light Hitler's cigars.

Paul Merton

Life after death is as improbable as sex after marriage.   Madeleine Kahn

Of course I believe in life after death. I'm in show business, I see it happen all the time.

Dale Winton

I do not believe in an afterlife, although I am bringing a change of underwear.

Woody Allen

Is there an afterlife? Well, there's an afterbirth, so why shouldn't there be an afterlife?

Kevin MacAleer

Heaven goes by favour. If it went by merit, you would stay out and your dog would go in.

Mark Twain

Heaven for climate; hell for society.

Mark Twain

They say that hell is hot, but is it humid? Because I can take the heat; it's the humidity I can't stand.

Ronnie Shakes

Either heaven or hell will have continuous background music. Which one you think it will be says a lot about you.

Bill Vaughan

From heaven, even the most miserable life will look like one bad night at an inconvenient hotel.

Saint Theresa

In heaven when the blessed use the telephone they will say what they have to say and not a word besides.

Somerset Maugham

My idea of heaven is eating *pâté de foie gras* to the sound of trumpets.

Sydney Smith

When I think of Indonesia – a country on the equator with 180 million people, a median age of 18, and a Muslim ban on alcohol, I know what heaven looks like.

Coca-Cola official

Heaven is largely a matter of digestion.

Elbert Hubbard

A worm in a jar of horseradish thinks he's in heaven.

Jewish saying

Heaven, as conventionally conceived, is a place so inane, so dull, so useless, so miserable, that nobody has ever ventured to describe a whole day in heaven, though plenty of people have described a day at the seaside.

George Bernard Shaw

Heaven is an English policeman, a French cook, a German engineer, an Italian lover and everything organized by the Swiss. Hell is an English cook, a French engineer, a German policeman, a Swiss lover and everything organized by the Italians.
                                                                John Elliot

I have a feeling that there is an afterlife but no one will know where it's being held.
                                                                Woody Allen

I shall be happy in heaven provided the angels are beautifully attired and wear their halos at a tilt.
                                                                Yves Saint Laurent

May you get to heaven a half-hour before the Devil knows you're dead.
                                                                Irish saying

A perpetual holiday is a good working definition of hell.
                                                                George Bernard Shaw

Maybe there is no actual place called hell. Maybe hell is just having to listen to our grandparents breathe through their noses when they're eating sandwiches.
                                                                Jim Carrey

Hell is full of musical amateurs.   George Bernard Shaw

The people in hell – where do they tell people to go?   Red Skelton

Maybe this world is another planet's hell.   Aldous Huxley

Here's to hell! May we have as good a time being there as we had getting there.
                                                                Yussel Shnook

It is a curious thing that every creed promises a paradise which will be absolutely uninhabitable for anyone of civilized taste.

Evelyn Waugh

HISTORY

Pearl Harbour, who's she?

Anon

She is an excellent creature, but she never can remember which came first, the Greeks or the Romans.

Benjamin Disraeli

'How wonderful it must have been for the Ancient Britons,' my mother said once, 'when the Romans arrived and they could have a hot bath.'

Katharine Whitehorn

—All right, but apart from sanitation, medicine, education, wine, public order, irrigation, roads, the fresh water system, and public health, what have the Romans ever done for us?
—Brought peace?
—Oh, peace. Shut up.

Life of Brian

He was an interesting character, Hadrian. He had a wife and a husband. And he built this enormous wall. I'd never thought of him as a gay bricklayer before.

Billy Connolly

Charlemagne either died or was born or did something with the Holy Roman Empire in 800.

Robert Benchley

They all laughed at Joan of Arc, but she went right ahead and built it.

Gracie Allen

Alexander III of Macedonia is known as Alexander the Great because he killed more people of more different kinds than any other man of his time.

Will Cuppy

My hunch is the gays started the Renaissance. Two gay guys at a party go, 'Say, wouldn't it be fun to make religious paintings of hot naked guys, and sell them to churches?'

Bob Smith

Say what you like about Genghis Khan but when he was around, old ladies could walk the streets of Mongolia safely at night.

Jo Brand

The Ottoman Empire was a civilization based on putting one's feet up.

Jerry Seinfeld

I have never been able to understand why anybody agreed to go on being a rustic after about 1400.

Kingsley Amis

If you think you have it tough, read history books.

Bill Maher

How many people died in the Irish Famine? I mean, if it was just the potatoes that were affected, at the end of the day, you will pay the price if you're a fussy eater.

Alan Partridge

I think Hitler had a fatal flaw. If I invented my own supreme race, I'd want them to look like me, or worse.

Buzz Nutley

Why did Hitler kill himself? He got his gas bill.

Jewish joke

France was discovered by Charlemagne in the Dark Ages. Other important historical figures are Louis XIV, the Huguenots, Joan of Arc, Jacques Cousteau and Charles de Gaulle, who was President for many years, and is now an airport.

Terry Jones

—What do you think has been the effect of the French Revolution?
—It is too soon to tell.

Chairman Mao, 1970

Why did Napoleon behave in the way he did? First of all, by all accounts, he was a bit of a short-arse and you know what they say about small men. They only come up to your Adam's apple and don't like it so they have to compensate by becoming Emperor of France.

Jo Brand

After you've heard two eyewitness accounts of an accident, it makes you wonder about history.

Dave Barry

No matter what happens, there is someone who knew it would.

Anon

During the Middle Ages, probably one of the biggest mistakes was not putting on your armour because you were just 'popping round the corner'.

Jack Handey

I think we agree, the past is over.

George W. Bush

Does Magna Carta mean nothing to you? Did she die in vain?

Tony Hancock

Gladstone spent his declining years trying to guess the answer to the Irish Question; unfortunately, whenever he was getting warm, the Irish secretly changed the Question.   W.C. Sellar and R.J. Yeatman

We owe to the Middle Ages the two worst inventions of humanity: gunpowder and romantic love. André Maurois

Had Cleopatra's nose been shorter, the whole history of the world would have been different.

Blaise Pascal

Over 90 per cent of high school students think BC means Before Cable.

Argus Hamilton

The Schleswig-Holstein question is so complex that only three men have ever fully understood it. The first is Prince Albert, who is dead. The second is a Danish professor, who became insane. The third is myself, and I have forgotten it.   Viscount Palmerston

Very few things happen at the right time, and the rest do not happen at all. The conscientious historian will correct these defects.   Herodotus

—What would have happened in 1963, had Khrushchev and not Kennedy been assassinated?
—With history, one can never be certain, but I think I can safely say that Aristotle Onassis would not have married Mrs Khrushchev.   Gore Vidal

People in the seventh century before Christ had no idea they were living in the seventh century before Christ.   Joseph Heller

The Holy Roman Empire was neither holy, nor Roman, nor an Empire.

Voltaire

If you remember the 1960s, you weren't there.   **George Harrison**

The sixties are now considered a historical period, just like the Holy
Roman Empire.   **Dave Barry**

The permissive society never existed. I should know, I've looked for it.

Rigsby, *Rising Damp*

Does history repeat itself, the first time as tragedy, the second time as
farce? No, that's too grand. History just burps, and we taste again the
raw-onion sandwich it swallowed centuries ago.   **Julian Barnes**

Perhaps in time the so-called Dark Ages will be thought of as including
our own.   **Georg Christoph Lichtenberg**

PROGRESS AND
THE FUTURE

—What do you think of modern civilisation?
—I think it would be a good idea.   **Mahatma Gandhi**

You can't say civilization don't advance for in every war they kill you
in a new way.   **Will Rogers**

I hate everything about the twentieth century except its dentistry.

A.L. Rowse

Progress is the exchange of one nuisance for another.   **Havelock Ellis**

In times like these, it is helpful to remember that there have always
been times like these.   **Paul Harey**

Is it progress if a cannibal uses a knife and fork?   Stanislaw J. Lec

Behold the turtle. He makes progress only when he sticks his neck out.
                                            James Bryant Conant

The future is not what it used to be.   Yogi Berra

What we anticipate seldom occurs; what we least expected generally
happens.   Benjamin Disraeli

Let others praise ancient times, I am glad I was born in these.
                                            Ovid (43 BC–AD 18)

More than any other time in history, mankind faces a crossroads.
One path leads to despair and utter hopelessness. The other, to total
extinction. Let us pray we have the wisdom to choose correctly.
                                            Woody Allen

These are the good old days. Just you wait and see.   Steve Turner

THE BODY

GENERAL APPEARANCE

Gussie, a glutton for punishment, stared at himself in the mirror.

P.G. Wodehouse

I never forget a face, but in your case I'll make an exception.

Groucho Marx

The face is familiar, but I can't remember my name.   Robert Benchley

I'm so obsessive about the way I look. I spend a lot of time just staring in the mirror. No wonder I get in so many traffic accidents.   Tanya Luckerath

It is only shallow people who do not judge by appearances.   Oscar Wilde

I was photographed on one occasion, sitting up in an over-elaborate bed looking like a heavily doped Chinese illusionist.   Noël Coward

Now must I look like as sober and demure as a whore at a christening.

George Farquhar

People on horses look better than they are. People in cars look worse than they are.   Marya Mannes

He looks as if someone has just poured cold porridge in his wellingtons.

Anon

He looks like the boy next door, which is unfortunate because where we live the boy next door is in fact a screaming queen who breeds hamsters.

Anon

If you are bored with your present enemies and want to make some new ones, tell two of your women friends that they look alike.

Mignon McLaughlin

Any girl can be glamorous. All you have to do is stand still and look stupid.   Hedy Lamarr

One girl can be pretty – but a dozen are only a chorus.   F. Scott Fitzgerald

Glamour is that indefinable something about a girl with a big bosom.
Abe Burrows

She was as inconspicuous as a nun at Hugh Hefner's dinner table.
Joe Joseph

I'm an intensely shy and vulnerable woman. My husband Norm has never seen me naked. Nor has he ever expressed the least desire to do so.
Dame Edna Everage

Naked, I had a body that invited burial.   Spike Milligan

I don't have an Achilles heel. I have an Achilles body.   Woody Allen

I don't have a photograph, but you can have my footprints. They are upstairs in my socks.   Groucho Marx

Charles de Gaulle looks like a female llama surprised in her bath.
Winston Churchill

Thomas Gray walks as if he had fouled his small-clothes, and looks as if he smelt it.   Christopher Smart

He looked like a man who's just realized that he's posted a love letter in the wrong envelope.   Hugh Laurie

André Gide was very bald with the general look of an elderly fallen angel travelling incognito.   Peter Quennell

Aunt Agatha's demeanour was rather like that of one who, picking daisies on the railway, has just caught the down express in the small of the back.   P.G. Wodehouse

Guy Burgess had the look of an inquisitive rodent emerging into daylight from a drain.

Harold Nicholson

His mouth had the coldly forbidding look of the closed door of a subway express when you have just missed the train.

P.G. Wodehouse

My father used to tell me I looked like a tramp peering out of a hayloft.

Billy Connolly

When he sits down, his ears pop.

Don Nelson

The thing is not a nose at all, but a bit of primordial chaos clapped on my face.

H.G. Wells

My genitals are like a sort of travel version of Linford Christie's.

Frank Skinner

If Woody Allen didn't exist then somebody would have knitted him.

Lesley White

Woody Allen has a face that convinces you that God is a cartoonist.

Jack Kroll

Ian Hislop looks rather like King Edward – the potato not the monarch.

Paul Merton

He's weird, and like all the most seriously weird people he looks perfectly ordinary.

Lynn Barber

Rumpers was a little man. He made no secret of his height.

Alan Bennett

When I go to the beach, I don't tan, I stroke.

Woody Allen

He had a smile on his face but it was about as thin as airline coffee.

Kinky Friedman

Barbara Cartland's eyes were twin miracles of mascara and looked like the corpses of two small crows that had crashed into a chalk cliff.

Clive James

Where lipstick is concerned, the important thing is not colour, but to accept God's final word on where your lips end. Jerry Seinfeld

He had but one eye, and the popular prejudice runs in favour of two.

Charles Dickens

He looks like the bridegroom on the wedding cake. Grace Hodgson Flandrau

He looked like a letter delivered to the wrong address.

Malcolm Muggeridge

My face looks like a wedding cake left out in the rain. W.H. Auden

HAIR

Why don't you get a haircut? You look like a chrysanthemum.

P.G. Wodehouse

Hair is another name for sex. Vidal Sassoon

She was a brunette by birth but a blonde by habit. Arthur Baer

It was a blonde. A blonde to make a bishop kick a hole in a stained glass window. Raymond Chandler

No one ever sounded as blonde as Marilyn Monroe did. Billy Wilder

What do blondes and spaghetti have in common? They both wriggle when you eat them. Anon

I'm not offended by dumb blonde jokes because I know I'm not dumb, and I know I'm not blonde.

Dolly Parton

Americans invented the dumb blonde as the English perfected the gun dog.

John Osborne

He wore his baldness like an expensive hat.

Gloria Swanson

There's one good thing about being bald: it's neat.

Milton Berle

Mom, I've accepted that you've had sex. I am not ready to know that you had Farrah hair.

Buffy the Vampire Slayer

My wife said to me, 'Do you mind if I wear my hair in a bun?' I said, 'I don't care if you wear it in a loaf of bread.'

Tommy Cooper

John McEnroe has hair like badly turned broccoli.

Clive James

She lived high up in a grey block of flats, as accessible as a bald Rapunzel.

William McIlvanney

The most delightful advantage of being bald – one can *hear* snowflakes.

R.G. Daniels

How long does it take me to have my hair done? I don't know. I'm never there.

Dolly Parton

When red-haired people are above a certain social grade, their hair is auburn.

Mark Twain

Her hair lounges on her shoulders like an anaesthetized cocker spaniel.

Henry Allen

I've got a hair in my mouth. That takes me back.

Lily Savage

—Are you asking for a lock of my hair?
—I'm letting you off lightly. I was going to ask for the whole wig.

Margaret Dumont and Groucho Marx

The French invented the only known cure for dandruff. It is called the guillotine. P.G. Wodehouse

Frankie Howerd's wig looked as if it had its own dandruff.

Nancy Banks-Smith

—How would you like your hair cut?
—In silence.

Archelaus

My barber is an authority on everything except how to cut hair properly.

William H. Roylance

I knew I was going bald when it was taking longer and longer to wash my face.

Harry Hill

Madonna is so hairy – when she lifted her arm, I thought it was Tina Turner in her armpit.

Joan Rivers

He looks like an explosion in a pubic hair factory.

Jonathan Miller

I love a man with a moustache. And luckily for me, I've found a man who loves a woman with one.

Barbara Pike

I refuse to think of them as chin hairs. I think of them as stray eyebrows.

Janette Barger

She was a redhead. No hair, just a red head.

Les Dawson

My pubic hair is all over the place, like some bloody rockery plant.

Victoria Wood

The last time I saw anything like that on a top lip, the whole herd had to be destroyed.   Eric Morecambe

Yes, my hair should make a statement. Just as long as it doesn't say, 'Thank you for the Country Music Award.'   Gracie Hart, *Miss Congeniality*

TATTOOS AND PIERCINGS

I always look for a woman who has a tattoo. I see a woman with a tattoo and I'm thinking, 'Okay, here's a girl who's capable of making a decision she'll regret in the future.'   Richard Jeni

A lot of people are into body piercing. They end up looking like they've been mugged by a staple gun.   Robin Williams

A friend of mine wants to get tattooed with the name of his girl. I told him, marry her, have a few kids, but a tattoo – man, that's so permanent.
                                                                    Drake Sather

My nan has a picture of the United Kingdom tattooed over her whole body. Some people think it's weird but you can say what you like about my nan, at least you know where you are with her.   Harry Hill

Men who have a pierced ear are better prepared for marriage. They've experienced pain and bought jewellery.   Rita Rudner

Thinking about getting a metal stud put through your tongue, or in your genitals? Don't forget to take lightning into account.   Dennis Miller

Grandmother used to take my mother to the circus to see the fat lady and tattooed man. Now they're everywhere.   Joan Collins

COSMETIC SURGERY

She got her looks from her father – he's a plastic surgeon.   **Groucho Marx**

The only parts left of my original body are my elbows.   **Phyllis Diller**

A woman went to a plastic surgeon and asked him to make her like Bo Derek. He gave her a lobotomy.   **Joan Rivers**

—Look at me. Do I need plastic surgery?
—Yes. Get your mouth sewn up.
Saffy and Edina Monsoon, *Absolutely Fabulous*

Look at Cher. One more face lift and she'll be wearing a beard.
Jennifer Saunders

Liza Minnelli looks like a *very old* 13.   **Jonathan Ross**

I did consider liposuction at one point, but then I heard they can accidentally vacuum out internal organs that you're using.   **Rita Rudner**

When they tell me to get my nose fixed I tell 'em to take a hike, I can smell just swell with the one I got.   **Robert Mitchum**

Sylvester Stallone's mother's plastic surgery looks so bad it could have been bought through a mail order catalogue.   **Graham Norton**

A boob job is the gift that keeps on giving. My ex bought them and my new guy enjoys them.   Elaine Pelino

—I paid four grand a breast for my wife's boob job.
—How much did that cost you then?
Boycey and Trigger, *Only Fools and Horses*

My wife's cosmetic surgery cost $20,000. For an extra five grand, I could have had a whole new wife from the Philippines. **Niles Crane,** *Frasier*

I don't need plastic surgery. I need Lourdes. **Paul O'Grady**

In Los Angeles, you have to have breast implants. An A-cup entitles you to park in a handicapped spot. **Jeannie Dietz**

My wife had plastic surgery. I cut up all her credit cards. **Henny Youngman**

How to look twenty years younger instantly: stand further away. **Jeff Green**

Why fear terrorists? With treatments like botox, women are waging germ warfare on themselves at £250 a pop. **Kathie Lette**

LOOKS

Why do you sit there looking like an envelope without any address on it? **Mark Twain**

He gave her a look that you could have poured on a waffle. **Ring Lardner**

We looked at each other with the clear innocent eyes of a couple of used-car salesmen. **Raymond Chandler**

He looked at me like I was a skid mark on a hotel towel. **Lily Savage**

Don't look at me in that tone of voice. **Dorothy Parker**

He looked at me as if I was a side dish he hadn't ordered. **Ring Lardner**

BEAUTY AND UGLINESS

My dear, you look like Helen of Troy after a good facial.

P.G. Wodehouse

The way I look at it, I'm a human being first and gorgeous second.

Harvey Fierstein

—Are you going to spend the rest of you life in front of that mirror?
—If I possibly can.

Quentin Crisp

A narcissist is someone better looking than you are.

Ambrose Bierce

I'm tired of all this nonsense about beauty being only skin-deep.
That's deep enough. What do you want – an adorable pancreas?

Jean Kerr

Beauty is only sin deep.

Saki

The most beautiful things in the world are the most useless – peacocks
and lilies for instance.

John Ruskin

All heiresses are beautiful.

John Dryden

You're the most beautiful woman I've ever seen, which doesn't say
much for you.

Groucho Marx

She looked more like Marilyn Monroe than anything human.

P.G. Wodehouse

The definition of a beautiful woman is one who loves me.

Sloan Wilson

The problem with beauty is that it's like being born rich and getting progressively poorer.

Joan Collins

All women are beautiful, like a toilet bowl, when you need one.

John Updike

Why is it that the winner of the Miss Universe contest always comes from earth?

Rich Hall

I was so handsome that women became spellbound when I came into view. In San Francisco, in rainy seasons, I was frequently mistaken for a cloudless day.

Mark Twain

Alain Delon is beautiful, but so is the Louis XVI commode I have.

Brigitte Bardot

It is better to be beautiful than to be good. But it is better to be good than to be ugly.

Oscar Wilde

Extreme Makeovers takes an ugly-ass person, and in an hour, they are beautiful. Isn't that what a six-pack of beer is for?

George Lope

I'm so ugly. I worked in a pet shop, and people kept asking how big I'd get.

Rodney Dangerfield

He was as ugly as a gargoyle hewn by a drunken stonemason for the adornment of a Methodist chapel in one of the vilest suburbs of Leeds or Wigan.

Max Beerbohm

I'm the only woman who can walk in Central Park at night and reduce the crime rate.

Phyllis Diller

After I was given a makeover on television, I knew I looked awful because my mother phoned and said I looked lovely.

Jo Brand

You know you're ugly when you go to the proctologist and he sticks his finger in your mouth.

Rodney Dangerfield

My face looks like a bouquet of elbows.

Phyllis Diller

Glenda Jackson has a face to launch a thousand dredgers.

Jack De Manio

She was a really bad-looking girl. Facially, she resembled Louis Armstrong's voice.

Woody Allen

She's what I call a 'two bagger' – you have to put a bag over her head and one over your own head in case hers breaks.

Mark Lamarr

I have a face like an elephant's behind.

Charles Laughton

He had a face like a collapsed lung.

Raymond Chandler

He looked like an extra from a crowd scene by Hieronymus Bosch.

Kenneth Tynan

I met my husband when a friend sent him over to my house to cure my hiccoughs.

Phyllis Diller

I stuck my head out of the window and got arrested for mooning.

Rodney Dangerfield

He looked like Rameses II with his wrappings off.

Hugh Fullerton

Beauty is only a light switch away.

Austin Powers

Your best side? My dear, you're sitting on it.

Alfred Hitchcock

PERSONAL HYGIENE

You're welcome to take a bath. You look like the second week of the
garbage strike.   Neil Simon

My grandmother took a bath every year, whether she needed it or not.
                                                        Brendan Behan

It may be December outside, ladies, but under your armpits, it is
always August.   John Snagge

—I have, on several occasions, been known to perspire a bit.
—We could grow rice.   Norm Peterson and Carla LeBec, *Cheers*

Armpits lead lives of quiet perspiration.   Patrick Murray

I'm as sweaty as Lucifer in leather leggings dancing at the disco inferno.
                                                        Anon

Why can't sweat smell good? It would be a different world. Instead
of putting laundry in the hamper, you'd put it in a vase. You'd have
a dirty sweatsock hanging from the rear-view mirror of your car.
And on a special night, maybe a little underwear coming out of your
breast pocket, just to show her she's important.   Jerry Seinfeld

I can confirm that Russell Crowe does not use deodorant. I understand
that in Australia it's known as animal magnetism.   Joan Rivers

The English think soap is civilization.   Heinrich von Treitschke

My mother is so neurotic. She spreads toilet paper on the seat even
at our relatives' house. At the dinner table.   Wendy Liebman

Some people sterilize a sweet dropped on the floor by blowing on it,
somehow assuming that this will remove the germs.   Diana Kent

Lady Badbreath, fresh as stilton…   Cyril Connolly

Why do they bother saying 'raw sewage'? Do some people cook the stuff?

George Carlin

A gentleman is someone who gets out of the bath to go to the toilet.

Freddie Truman

Ladies' bikini waxes now have fancy names like the 'Hollywood', the 'Landing Strip', and the 'Brazilian'. Personally, I prefer the 'Rainforest'.

Jim Davidson

Whenever I look at his fingernails, I thank God I don't have to look at his feet.

Athene Seyler

Whoever said girls are made of 'sugar and spice' obviously never saw one sniffing the crotch of her tights in the morning to see if she can get another wear out of them.

Jeff Green

You can have affection for a murderer or a sodomite, but you cannot have affection for a man whose breath stinks.

George Orwell

A former girlfriend of Bill Gates remembers him as having bad breath. He remembers her as not having a hundred billion dollars.

Conan O'Brien

I had a cab driver in Paris. The man smelled like a guy eating garlic-flavoured cheese while getting a perm inside the septic tank of a slaughterhouse.

Dennis Miller

They banned the movie *Psycho* in France for fear it might lead to copycat showers.

Craig Kilborn

On the day there was a full chamber pot under the breakfast table I decided to leave.

George Orwell

The man who has cured himself of BO and halitosis, has learned
French to surprise the waiter, and the saxophone to amuse the company,
may mind that people still avoid him because they do not like him.

Heywood Broun

Miss Debary, Susan and Sally made their appearance, and I was as
civil to them as their bad breath would allow me.

Jane Austen

FASHION

Looking good and dressing well are essential. A purpose in life is not.

Oscar Wilde

Some people are born with a sense of how to clothe themselves, others
acquire it, others look as if their clothes had been thrust upon them.   Saki

I base most of my fashion taste on what doesn't itch.

Gilda Radner

To my mind, following fashion is rather like masturbating or making
silent phone calls to ex-lovers after midnight.

Julie Burchill

I'm very important. I decide the direction of fashion. One snap of my
fingers and I can raise hemlines so high the whole world's your
gynaecologist.

Edina Monsoon, *Absolutely Fabulous*

Clothes make the man. Naked people have little or no influence in
society.

Mark Twain

I dress for women – and I undress for men.

Angie Dickinson

Here comes Ashley Judd in her no-yeast-infection-here Oscar gown...

Libby Gelman-Waxner

'Brevity is the soul of lingerie,' as the petticoat said to the chemise.

Dorothy Parker

Do you have bad credit or just bad taste? **Carson Kressley**

Your right to wear a mint-green polyester leisure suit ends where it meets my eyes. **Fran Lebowitz**

—Dad, stop fiddling with yerself.
—I'm not fiddling with meself. I paid a quid for these underpants and I've got 50 pence stuck up me arse.
Denise and Jim Royle, *The Royle Family*

Edible underwear? You wear them for a couple of days, they taste just like the other ones. **Tom Arnold**

I remember when pants were pants. You wore them for twenty years, then you cut them down for pan scrubs. **Victoria Wood**

I have no underwear because the pants haven't been built yet that'll take the job on. **Lord Flasheart,** *Blackadder Goes Forth*

Every time I'm about ready to go to bed with a guy, I have to look at my dad's name all over the guy's underwear. **Marci Klein, daughter of Calvin**

Why does everything you wear look as if it's bearing a grudge?
Edina Monsoon, *Absolutely Fabulous*

I got up one morning and couldn't find my socks, so I called the operator. I said, 'I can't find my socks.' She said, 'They're behind the couch.' And they were. **Steven Wright**

A woman's dress should be like a barbed-wire fence, serving its purpose without obstructing the view. Sophia Loren

Jeeves lugged my purple socks out of the drawer as if he were a vegetarian fishing a caterpillar out of his salad. **P.G. Wodehouse**

I was so self-conscious in my white suit – I felt like a sky-writer who can't spell.

Robert Benchley

His socks compelled one's attention without losing one's respect.   Saki

One of the few lessons I have learned in life is that there is invariably something odd about women who wear ankle socks.   Alan Bennett

Tell me the history of that frock, Janet. It's obviously an old favourite. You were wise to remove the curtain rings. I love that fabric. You were lucky to find so much of it.   Dame Edna Everage

Men love the suit so much, we've actually styled our pyjamas to look like a tiny suit. Our pyjamas have little lapels, little cuffs, simulated breast pocket. Do you need a breast pocket on your pyjamas? You put a pen in there, you roll over in the middle of the night, you kill yourself.

Jerry Seinfeld

I got some new underwear the other day. Well, new to me.   Emo Philips

The trick of wearing mink is to look as though you are wearing a cloth coat. The trick of wearing a cloth coat is to look as though you are wearing mink.   Pierre Balmain

I won't model a faux fur coat because it's cruel to the faux, which is a protected species.   Barbi Benton, model

My closet looks like a convention of multiple personality cases.

Anna Quindlen

My wife was looking through a fashion magazine, and she saw a fur coat. She said, 'I want that.' So I cut it out and gave it to her.   Tommy Cooper

Is there anything worn under the kilt? No, it's all in perfect working order.
Spike Milligan

I'm not a model and I'm okay with that because I don't want to look like a whippet or any other shaky dog.
Karen Kilgariff

Beware of the man who picks your dresses. He wants to wear them.
Erica Jong

The only way to atone for being a little over-dressed is by being always absolutely over-educated.
Oscar Wilde

A lot of people criticize supermodels and I think that's very unfair, because they can't answer back.
Jo Brand

The kilt is an unrivalled garment for fornication and diarrhoea.
John Masters

If the models get any younger they'll be throwing foetuses down the catwalk.
Patsy Stone, *Absolutely Fabulous*

Very few women can pull off anger in a tube top.
Samantha Jones, *Sex and the City*

Whenever I wear something expensive it looks stolen.
Billy Connolly

—There are times, Jeeves, when one asks oneself, 'Do trousers matter?'
—The mood will pass, sir.
P.G. Wodehouse

Where's the man could ease a heart like a satin gown?
Dorothy Parker

There is only one way to wear a beautiful dress – to forget you are wearing it.
Madame de Girardin

Her petticoat had stripes of broad red and blue and looked as though it had been made out of a stage curtain. I would have paid a lot for a front seat, but there was no performance.   **Georg Christoph Lichtenberg**

A dress has no meaning unless it makes a man want to take it off.

Françoise Sagan

Oh, Minnie Driver, whoever told you you could pull off a leather jumpsuit?   **Karen Walker, *Will and Grace***

The Pope. Great guy. But in a fashion sense, he's one hat away from being the Grand Wizard of the Ku Klux Klan.   **Jon Stewart**

What a lovely hat! But may I make on teensy suggestion? If it blows off, don't chase it.   **Miss Piggy**

Hats divide generally into three classes. Offensive hats, defensive hats and shrapnel.   **Katharine Whitehorn**

Her hat looked as if it had made a forced landing on her head.

Harriet Cobb

She had a passion for hats, none of which returned her affection.

Storm Jameson

A hat should be taken off when you greet a lady and left off for the rest of your life. Nothing looks more stupid than a hat.   **P.J. O'Rourke**

I think that a hat that has a cannon that comes out, fires and then goes back in is at least a decade away.   **Jack Handey**

They should put expiration dates on clothes so we would know when they go out of style.   **Garry Shandling**

Whoa! Where are you going in those pants? 1982?   **Monica Geller, *Friends***

Nobody ought to wear an American baseball cap who doesn't meet
two qualifications: 1. he is American, 2. he is playing baseball.

Chris Henderson

Old Mr Saxby looked like something stationed in a cornfield to
discourage crows.

P.G. Wodehouse

Some women hold up dresses that are so ugly and they always say
the same thing: 'This looks much better on.' On what? On fire?

Rita Rudner

I don't own a dress. I wear skirts but I look like a netball teacher.

Victoria Wood

I think the idea behind the tuxedo is the woman's point of view
that 'Men are all the same, we might as well dress them that way.'

Jerry Seinfeld

If women dressed for men, the stores wouldn't sell much – just an
occasional sun visor.

Groucho Marx

Jordan doesn't need a fashion designer. She needs a structural engineer.

Frank Skinner

What a lovely gown you're wearing! Such a shame they didn't have it
in your size.

Tania Plant

Those clothes they wore in the 1960s have to have some kind of
pharmaceutical explanation.

Darlene Conner, *Roseanne*

That blouse hurts like a hangover.

Karen Walker, *Will and Grace*

Do you know how many polyesters died to make that shirt?   Steve Martin

You have no idea how much it costs to look this cheap.

Dolly Parton

A sweater is a garment worn by a child when his mother feels chilly.

Nora Ephron

Designer clothes worn by children are like snowsuits worn by adults. Few can carry it off successfully.

Fran Lebowitz

How on earth did Gandhi manage to walk so far in flip-flops? I can't last ten minutes in mine.

Mrs Merton

Englishwomen's shoes look as if they had been made by someone who had often heard shoes described, but had never seen any.

Margaret Halsey

If high heels were so wonderful, men would still be wearing them.

Sue Grafton

That Prada shirt costs *how* much? Does it also somehow open into a small studio apartment?

Berger, *Sex and the City*

Husbands come and go, but Manolo Blahnik slingbacks are for life.

Liza Minnelli

If the shoe fits, get another just like it.

George Carlin

My daughter wanted some trainers. I said, 'You're 11. Make some!'

Jeremy Hardy

Clothes with pictures and writing on them are an unpleasant indication of the general state of things. I mean, be realistic. If people don't want to listen to *you* what makes you think they want to hear from your sweater?

Fran Lebowitz

He wore a shirt that looked like it had once belonged to Englebert Humperdinck.

Kinky Friedman

It is difficult to see why lace is so expensive; it is mostly holes.

Mary Wilson Little

Men who wear turtlenecks look like turtles.

Doris Lily

In England, if you are a duchess, you don't need to be well dressed.
It would be thought quite eccentric.   Nancy Mitford

I'd feel ugly if I wasn't decked out like a drag queen's Christmas tree.
                                                        Dolly Parton

When a heroine goes mad she always goes into white satin.
                                        Richard Brinsley Sheridan

Non-Jewish men are turtleneck kind of guys, while the Jewish man is a
crew-neck kind of guy.   Del Cassidy

I have to wear pants. I had both of my legs tattooed all over with designs of bougainvillea. Now, if I wear a skirt, I am constantly bothered by bees.

Ellen DeGeneres

She spotted an Armani suit in that shade of tan that comes from mixing
brown with a great deal of money.   Judith Kelman

One of Lobb's clients maintained that his hand-made shoes lasted a
lifetime only because they were so uncomfortable that he went
everywhere by taxi.   Harold Blair

Some women think bikinis are immodest. Others have beautiful figures.
                                                        Olin Miller

With an evening coat and a white tie, anybody, even a stockbroker,
can gain a reputation for being civilized.   Oscar Wilde

She wore a low but futile décolletage.   Dorothy Parker

The softer a man's head, the louder his socks.   Helen Rowland

Christian Dior's New Look consists of clothes by a man who doesn't know women, never had one, and dreams of being one.   Coco Chanel

I have never seen a pair of slacks that had very much slack in them.
                                                                Fred Allen

Anyone can rob a bank, but it takes a real man to do it in satin.
                                                                Brad Maine

If it was the fashion to go naked, the face would be hardly observed.
                                                                Mary Montagu

If God had meant us to walk around naked, he would never have invented the wicker chair.   Erma Bombeck

The thing that separates us from the animals is our ability to accessorize.
                                                                Lily Savage

Losing one glove is sorrow enough, but nothing compared with the pain of losing one glove, discarding the other, then finding the first one again.

Piet Hein

I just love finding new places to wear diamonds.   Marilyn Monroe

It's not what I do, but the way that I do it. It's not what I say, but the way I say it, and how I look when I do it and say it.   Mae West

Style is when they're running you out of town and you make it look like you're leading the parade.   William Battie

Enough cologne? You smell like Paco Rabanne crawled up your ass and died.   Chris Moltisanti, *The Sopranos*

Diana Vreeland rouged her cheeks to a colour otherwise seen only on specially ordered Pontiac Firebirds.
George V. Higgins

As Moslems, all the women in my family wear the burqa. It's brilliant. Five of us share a bus pass.
Shazia Mirza

All women dress like their mothers, that is a their tragedy. No man ever does. That is his.
Alan Bennett

HEALTH AND MEDICINE

Health is what my friends are always drinking to before they fall down.
Phyllis Diller

Health is merely the slowest possible rate at which one can die.
Martin Fischer

Health consists of having the same disease as one's neighbours.
Quentin Crisp

Come back next Thursday with a specimen of your money.
Henny Youngman

I hope all my blood tests come back as negative as my mother is.
Kate Mason

—Doctor, doctor, I can't pronounce my Fs, Ts and Hs.
—Well you can't say fairer than that then.
Tommy Cooper

They say we're 98 per cent water. That means if you drink one glass of water, you're in grave danger of drowning.
Steven Wright

The patient is not likely to recover who makes the doctor his heir.
Thomas Fuller

It's no longer a question of staying healthy. It's a question of finding a sickness that you like.

Jackie Mason

I told my doctor, 'It hurts when I do this.' He said, 'Don't do that.' Henny Youngman

I took a physical for some life insurance. All they would give me was fire and theft.

Milton Berle

My father invented a cure for which there was no known disease. My mother caught the cure and died of it.

Victor Borge

I tried to give blood the other day. But the blood bank wouldn't take it. They wanted to know where I got it from.

Wally Wang

All right, let's not panic. I'll make the money by selling one of my livers. I can get by with one.

Homer Simpson

I needed to get a strange mole checked out, but when I went to my doctor's surgery, the first available appointment with the specialist was in six months. I said, 'By that time I could be dead.' And the receptionist said, 'If that happens, be sure to cancel your appointment.' Stephanie Shiern

My doctor once said to me, 'Do you think I'm here for the good of your health?'

Bob Monkhouse

—What's the difference between God and a hospital consultant?
—God doesn't think he's a hospital consultant.

Anon

Never go to a doctor whose office plants have died.

Erma Bombeck

The doctors were very brave about my illness.

Dorothy Parker

Give a *pint* of blood? That's very nearly an armful.

Tony Hancock

TB or not TB, that is the congestion.

Woody Allen

First, the doctor gave me the good news: I was going to have a disease named after me.

Steve Martin

I asked my doctor what to do for a sprained ankle. He said, 'Limp.'

Henny Youngman

A man goes to the doctor with a strawberry growing out of his head. The doctor says, 'I'll give you some cream to put on that.'   Tommy Cooper

A woman goes to the doctor because her knees are all cut up. The doctor says, 'What have you been doing?' She says, 'Making love doggy-style.' The doctor says, 'Don't you know any other position but doggy-style?' She says, 'Yes, but my doggy doesn't.'   Jackie Martling

My uncle had diabetes before it became all the rage.   Rob Brydon

My nan told me her friend had collapsed outside Woolworths. She said, 'The ambulance men came and she wasn't breathing so they had to give her artificial insemination.'   Peter Kay

Everything that used to be a sin is now a disease.   Bill Maher

I had a cough so robust that I tapped into two new seams of phlegm.

Bill Bryson

Asthma doesn't seem to bother me much unless I'm around cigars or dogs. The thing that would bother me most would be a dog smoking a cigar.   Steve Allen

Colonic irrigation is not to be sniffed at.   Jennifer Saunders

I have a perfect cure for a sore throat – cut it.   Alfred Hitchcock

I have bad reflexes. I was once run over by a car being pushed by two guys.

Woody Allen

I'm one of the few males who suffers from penis envy. **Woody Allen**

A man goes to the doctor. The doctor tells him that he has three minutes to live. The man says, 'Doc, what can you give me?' The doctor says, 'A hard-boiled egg.' **Tommy Cooper**

Jewish Alzheimer's is when you forget everything except a grudge. **Jackie Mason**

I broke my arm trying to fold a bed. It wasn't the kind that folds. **Steven Wright**

I like having colonic irrigation because sometimes you find old jewellery. **Joan Rivers**

The doctor told me I should buy day-returns from now on instead of season tickets. **Hugh Leonard**

My Auntie Marge has been ill for so long now that we've changed her name to 'I Can't Believe She's Not Better'. **Jeff Green**

When I told jokes about cystitis, people would write in and say, 'I've got cystitis and it isn't funny,' so I would reply, 'Well, send it back and ask for one that is.' **Victoria Wood**

A mild heart attack is one you remember. **Jim Caffrey**

I'm on so many pills now, I'll need a childproof lid on my coffin. **Paul O'Grady**

My doctor gave me two weeks to live. I hope they're in August. **Ronnie Shakes**

The reason doctors' prescriptions are impossible to read is because they all have the same message to the pharmacist: 'I got my money, now you get yours.' **Jackie Mason**

It's chicken pox. He's running a high temperature and his chest looks like a bad Matisse.

Noël Coward

Fibroids – isn't that a breakfast cereal?

Victoria Wood

I think we can save your husband's arm. Where would you like it sent?

Nurse, *Naked Gun*

He had only two topics of conversation, his gout and his wife. I never could quite make out which of the two he was talking about.

Oscar Wilde

Oh! When I have gout, I feel as if I am walking on my eyeballs.

Sydney Smith

A doctor is the only man without a guaranteed cure for a cold.

Dominic Cleary

Be suspicious of any doctor who tries to take your temperature with his finger.

David Letterman

Please help me, I am suffering from attention deficit dis...

Anon

Why does a pharmacist have to be two and a half feet up above everybody else? Who the hell is he? He's a stockboy with pills. He's taking pills from a big bottle and putting them in a little bottle. Why can't he be down on the floor with you and me?

Jerry Seinfeld

When the doctor broke the news that I had cancer, I said, 'Tell me straight, doc, how long do I have?' He said, 'Ten...' I said, 'Ten what? Years, months, weeks?' He said, '9, 8, 7...'

Bob Monkhouse

He collected lists of fatal diseases and arranged them in alphabetical order so that he could put his finger without delay on any one he wanted to worry about.

Joseph Heller

The health insurance doctor has refused to renew my health policy.
The nefarious quack claims he found urine in my whisky.   **W.C. Fields**

Doctors, they're all crooks. Why do you think they wear gloves?
Not for sanitary reasons – fingerprints.   **Jackie Mason**

The only difference between doctors and lawyers is that lawyers merely
rob you, whereas doctors rob you and kill you, too.   **Anton Chekhov**

Her manner of enquiring after a trifling ailment gave one the
impression that she was more concerned with the fortunes of the
malady than with oneself, and when one got rid of a cold one felt that
she almost expected to be given its postal address.   **Saki**

The *New England Journal of Medicine* reports that nine out of ten
doctors agree that one out of ten doctors is an idiot.   **Jay Leno**

I was under the care of a couple of medical students who couldn't
diagnose a decapitation.   **Jeffrey Bernard**

As she lay there dozing next to me, one voice inside my head kept saying,
'Relax, you are not the first doctor to sleep with one of his patients,'
but another kept reminding me, 'Howard, you are a veterinarian.'
     Dick Wilson

My doctor is great. If I can't afford the operation, he touches up the X-rays.

Joey Bishop

My brain? It's my second favourite organ.   **Woody Allen**

If the brain was so simple we could understand it, we would be so
simple we couldn't.   **Lyall Watson**

A hospital is no place to be sick.   **Yogi Berra**

At times, my arm has shaken so violently from Parkinson's disease that I could mix a Margarita in five seconds.

Michael J. Fox

If it's wet, dry it. If it's dry, wet it. Congratulations, you are now a gynaecologist.

Patrick Murray

A male gynaecologist is like an auto mechanic who has never owned a car.

Carrie Snow

—Doctor, doctor, my arm is broken in three places.
—Well, stay out of those places.

Tommy Cooper

I'm not feeling too well. I need a doctor immediately. Quick, call the nearest golf course.

Groucho Marx

You show me something that doesn't cause cancer, and I'll show you something that isn't on the market yet.

George Carlin

Hypochondria is the one disease I haven't got.

David Renwick

I am not a hypochondriac, but my gynaecologist firmly believes I am.

Rodney Dangerfield

My doctor gave me six months to live, but when I couldn't pay the bill, he gave me six months more.

Walter Matthau

If your time hasn't come, not even a doctor can kill you.

M.A. Perlstein

He's on the mend, sitting up in bed blowing the froth off his medicine.

Flann O'Brien

The shin is a device for finding furniture in the dark. I myself find the little toe more effective.

Michael Hogin

The appendix resembles a four-inch worm, and like the Aldwych Tube leads nowhere.

Richard Gordon

A minor operation is one performed on somebody else.

Victoria Wood

One of the most difficult things to contend with in a hospital is the assumption on the part of the staff that because you have lost your gall bladder you have also lost your mind.

Jean Kerr

I have just learned about his illness; let us hope it is nothing trivial.

Irvin S. Cobb

Tell me your phobias and I will tell you what you are afraid of.

Robert Benchley

I have kleptomania, but when it gets bad, I take something for it.

Robert Benchley

Whenever I fill in an application, it says, 'In case of emergency, notify ...' I always put 'Doctor.' What the hell would my mother do in an emergency?

Steven Wright

Hospital is like a convent. You leave the world behind and take vows of poverty, chastity, obedience.

Carole Wheat

After two days in hospital, I took a turn for the nurse.

W.C. Fields

A private hospital bed is a parked taxi with the meter running.

Groucho Marx

I've just had an operation for piles. All my troubles are behind me.

Ken Brett

Before undergoing a surgical operation, arrange your temporal affairs. You may live.

Rémy de Gourmont

The morning after I had my heart bypass, the doctor called and said, 'Soon you'll be able to have sex.' I said, 'I've heard that for years.'

David Letterman

The stitches will be removed in a few days, so there is no reason why in about a fortnight you cannot begin denying your husband sex again.

Mark Bryant

If I'm ever stuck on a life support system, I definitely want to be unplugged, but not until I get down to size eight.   Henriette Mantel

—What's it like to be in a coma?
—How the fuck do I know? I was in a coma.   Evil Knievel

In the old days, it was called voodoo and you used to stick needles into a doll. Now it's called acupuncture and you just stick them straight into the person.   Cathy Hopkins

There must be something to acupuncture, I mean, you never see any sick porcupines.   Bob Goddard

I just got the bill for my operation. Now I know why those guys wear masks.
                    Jim Boren

The head of the studio needed a heart transplant but they couldn't find a suitable stone.   David Mamet

A heart transplant operation is as simple as changing the wheel on your car.   Richard Gordon

After my bypass surgery I knew I had to change my lifestyle, and then it occurred to me – I don't have a lifestyle.   David Letterman

God, my teeth itch.   Tommy Cooper

The worst thing about a lung transplant is coughing up someone else's phlegm.   Jackie Martling

A miracle drug is any drug that will do what the label says it will do.   Eric Hodgins

My friend, George, has false teeth – with braces on them.   Steven Wright

I put on my spectacles for the first time and the insults started –
'Four eyes! Goggle eyes! Joe 90!' To which I replied, 'Look, you're
not the only optician round here.'

Harry Hill

The art of medicine consists in amusing the patient while nature effects
the cure.

Voltaire

I said to my dentist, 'My teeth are going yellow.' He said, 'Wear a brown necktie.'

Rodney Dangerfield

When I get a lot of tension and headaches, I do what it says on the
aspirin bottle: take two and keep away from children.

Roseanne

Some tortures are physical and some are mental, but the one that's
both is dental.

Ogden Nash

So I went to the dentist. He said, 'Say Aaah.' I said, 'Why?' He said,
'My dog died.'

Tommy Cooper

She had so much bridgework, every time I kissed her I had to pay a toll.

Lou Costello

The thought of dentists gave him the same sick horror as the thought
of socialism.

H.G. Wells

When I go to the dentist, he's the one that has to have the anaesthetic.

Phyllis Diller

I have a crush on my dentist. He said, 'You have a cavity.' I said,
'I know, and I'd like you to fill it.'

Caroline Rhea

Aren't air fresheners very confusing for blind people? Pine forest?
I thought this was the loo! Bowl of oranges? Where's my mini-cab?

Harry Hill

The only reason I wear glasses is for little things, like driving my car – or finding it.
Woody Allen

I was walking down the street wearing my glasses when all of a sudden my prescription ran out.
Steven Wright

In second grade, the kids called me 'four eyes' even though I didn't wear glasses. In fifth grade, when I did start wearing glasses, they called me 'six eyes'.
Larry Sanders

I have poor eyesight. When I take an eye test, the doctor points to the letters and he calls them out and says, 'True or false?'
Woody Allen

I asked this woman why she had two Seeing Eye dogs, and she told me one was for reading.
Jonathan Katz

Laughter is the best medicine. Unless you've got VD, in which case penicillin's probably a better bet.
Bob Monkhouse

If you are cross-eyed and have dyslexia, can you see okay?
John Mendoza

DRUGS

I don't like people who take drugs – customs men for example.
Mick Miller

You should always say no to drugs. That will drive the prices down.
Geechy Guy

Reality is just a crutch for people who can't cope with drugs.
Lily Tomlin

I'll take a drugs test when George W. Bush takes an IQ test.
Dick Flanagan

Why is there such controversy about drug testing? I know plenty of guys who'd be willing to test any drug they can come up with. Especially if it's multiple choice.
George Carlin

Drugs have taught an entire generation of English kids the metric system.

P.J. O'Rourke

The problem with heroin is it's so moreish!

Harry Hill

After the match, an official asked for two players to take a dope test.
I offered him the referee.

Tommy Docherty

Medical marijuana. Can't we start slower? Medicinal chocolate?
Medicinal whiskey?

Patrick Keane

Kids today are no sooner off the pot than they are back on again.

Stuart Francis

Kids, don't buy drugs. Wait until you're a rock star and they give them
to you for free.

Billy Mack, *Love Actually*

A cap of good acid costs a few dollars and for that you can hear
the Universal Symphony with God singing solo and the Holy Ghost
on drums.

Hunter S. Thompson

I'll die young, but it's like kissing God.

Lenny Bruce

If God dropped acid, would he see people?

Steven Wright

We called him Mother Superior on account of the length of his habit.

Irvine Welsh

I would never advocate the use of dope – because I'm not a professional athlete, and I can't get my hands on the good stuff.

Greg Proops

My college had so many drugs, we didn't have class reunions, we
had flashbacks.

Charlie Viracola

I don't do drugs any more. I don't do them any less either.   **Bill Hicks**

We would have injected vitamin C if only they had made it illegal.

Irvine Welsh

They say cocaine intensifies your personality. Yeah, but what if you're an asshole?   Bill Cosby

Cocaine is God's way of saying you're making too much money.

Robin Williams

It's not called cocaine any more. It's now referred to as 'Crack Classic'.

Jay Leno

Cocaine habit-forming? Of course not. I should know. I've been using it for years.   **Tallulah Bankhead**

I have a three-hundred-quid-a-week sushi habit.   **Paul Kaye**

There's no happy ending to cocaine. You either die, go to jail, or else you run out.   **Sam Kinison**

I'm addicted to chocolate. I used to snort cocoa.   **Marilyn Francis**

Celebrity is as addictive and destructive as any drink and I am a recovering celebrity.   **Barry Manilow**

Ecstasy is a drug so strong it makes white people think they can dance.

Lenny Henry

I'm one of those guys who can't operate a screwdriver, but I could roll a joint in a twister.   **Scott Thompson**

I need a Valium the size of a hockey puck.   **Woody Allen**

I was high on life, but eventually I built up a tolerance.　　Arj Barker

The downside of coming off junk was I knew I would have to mix
with my friends again in a state of full consciousness.　　Irvine Welsh

You're never going to stop the human need for release through
altered consciousness. The government could take away all the drugs
in the world and people would spin around on their lawn until they
fell down and saw God.　　Dennis Miller

Two great European narcotics – alcohol and Christianity.
　　Friedrich Nietzsche

I began using the date rape drug Rohypnol. I took it twenty times. I
didn't know you were supposed to give it to the woman.　　Larry Sanders

ALCOHOL

—How would a beer feel, Mr Peterson?
—Pretty nervous if I was in the room.
　　Woody Boyd and Norm Peterson, *Cheers*

Beer is proof God loves us and wants us to be happy.　　Benjamin Franklin

To alcohol! The cause of, and solution to, all of life's problems.
　　Homer Simpson

In a study, scientists report that drinking beer can be good for the liver.
I'm sorry, did I say 'scientists?' I meant 'Irish people'.　　Tina Fey

I'd offer you a beer, but I've only got six cans.　　Terry Collier, *The Likely Lads*

—Could you be persuaded to have a drink, dear?
—Well, maybe just a tiny triple.　　Lucille Ball

I always wake up at the crack of ice.　　Joe E. Lewis

—Do you want a beer?
—It's seven o'clock in the morning.
—Scotch?

Jack Butler and Ron Richardson

Love makes the world go round? Not at all. Whisky makes it go round twice as fast.

Compton Mackenzie

Alcohol is like love: the first kiss is magic, the second is intimate, the third is routine. After that, you just take the girl's clothes off.

Raymond Chandler

The closest I have to a nutritionist is the Carlsberg Beer Company.

Colin Farrell

Is it bad when you refer to alcohol as 'Pain Go Bye Bye Juice'?

Patton Oswalt

These two Irishmen were passing a pub – well, it could happen.

Frank Carson

They drink with impunity, or anybody else who invites them.

Artemus Ward

Waiter! This ice is too cold.

Chico Marx

Alcohol is a misunderstood vitamin.

P.G. Wodehouse

—Will you join me in a glass of wine?
—You get in first, and if there's room enough, I'll join you.

W.C. Fields

It was my Uncle George who discovered that alcohol was a food well in advance of modern medical thought.

P.G. Wodehouse

Booze is the answer. I don't remember the question.   **Denis Leary**

I've known banks that gave loans to guys who wanted to open bars,
and their only collateral was that *I* was going to drink there.
                                                    Lou Grant, *Rhoda*

—What shall we drink to?
—About four in the morning.   **Sammy Davis Jr and Dean Martin**

Fix me a drink ... Champagne ... anything that will blur reality.
                                        Patsy Stone, *Absolutely Fabulous*

Would it be bad to have a Martini with my muscle relaxant or bad in
a good way?   **Samantha Jones, *Sex and the City***

Alcohol is necessary for a man so that he can have a good opinion of
himself, undisturbed by the facts.   **Finlay Peter Dunne**

—I'll have the usual – Bourbon and water.
—You were all out of Bourbon, so I made it straight water.   **Woody Allen**

She ordered the equivalent of a small safe to be dropped on her head.
                                                    Carrie Fisher

One tequila, two tequila, three tequila, floor.   **Buddy Shirt**

Let's get out of these wet clothes and into a dry Martini.   **Robert Benchley**

—Can I interest you in a nightcap?
—No, thanks, I don't wear them.
                            Jane Spencer and Lt Frank Drebin, *Naked Gun*

Whenever someone asks me if I want water with my Scotch, I say I'm thirsty, not dirty.
                                                    Joe E. Lewis

It is better to drink a little too much than much too little.

Herbert Beerbohm Tree

Don't blub, kid, and I'll let you smell my breath.

W.C. Fields

Beer. Helping Ugly People Have Sex Since 1863.

Slogan on T-shirt

My favourite drink is a cocktail of carrot juice and whiskey. I am always drunk but I can see for miles.

Roy Chubby Brown

I think this wine has been drunk before.

W.C. Fields

It's a naïve domestic Burgundy without any breeding, but I think you'll be amused by its presumption.

James Thurber

The wine tasted like a urine sample from someone gravely ill.

Frank Muir

The dandelion wine's all right but I lost the use of one side of my face for about half an hour after I drunk it.

Alan Ayckbourn

I wouldn't call myself a wine connoisseur. I'd suck the alcohol out of a deodorant stick.

Karen Walker, *Will and Grace*

My idea of a fine wine was one that merely stained my teeth without stripping the enamel.

Clive James

He's such a connoisseur. He not only knows what year the wine was made but he can tell you who stamped on the grapes.

Edith Gwynn

A good rule is to state that the bouquet is better than the taste, and vice versa.

Stephen Potter

Wine – very nice. I wonder how they got the cat to sit on the bottle?

Stephen Fry

I remember Billy Wilder opening a bottle of wine. As he strained at the cork, he said, '45 years of masturbation and I still don't have a muscle in my hand.'

Frederic Raphael

I'm an ABC now. Anything But Chardonnay.

John Major

In the summer, I drink Guinness, which requires no refrigeration and no cooking.

Quentin Crisp

A man who was fond of wine was offered some grapes at dessert after dinner. 'Much obliged,' said he, pushing the plate aside, 'but I am not accustomed to take my wine in pills.'

Jean-Antheme Brillat-Savarin

Vodka is for Russians what therapy is for Americans: habit-forming and it destroys your ability to live a normal life.

Yakov Smirnoff

Burgundy makes you think silly things; Bordeaux makes you talk about them; and champagne makes you do them.

Jean-Anthelme Brillat-Savarin

Champagne! I love it. It tastes like your foot's asleep.

Joan Davis

I drink champagne when I'm happy and when I'm sad. Sometimes, I drink it when I'm alone. When I have company, I consider it obligatory. I trifle with it when I'm not hungry and drink it when I am. Otherwise, I never touch it – unless I'm thirsty.

Lily Bollinger

Between the revolution and the firing squad, there is always time for a bottle of champagne.

Prince Boris Mizorzky

I drink only beer and a little wine. Champagne? Oh, no. Champagne I only bathe in.

Hedy Lamarr

I envy people who drink – at least they know what to blame everything on.

Oscar Levant

I hate champagne more than anything in the world next to Seven-Up.

Elaine Dundy

My favourite wine? Anything anyone else is buying.

Diogenes

There are better things in life than alcohol, but it makes up for not having them.

Terry Pratchett

Three highballs, and I think I'm St Francis of Assisi.

Dorothy Parker

I tried not drinking once. I heard myself talking all night and then, worse than that, next day I had total recall. It was terrifying.

Patsy Stone, *Absolutely Fabulous*

W.C. Fields has a profound respect for old age. Especially when it's bottled.

Gene Fowler

Gin was his tonic.

Al Drooz

Don't put any ice in my drink. Takes up too much room.

Groucho Marx

The drink in that pub is not fit for washing hearses.

Brendan Behan

Show me a nation whose national beverage is beer, and I'll show you an advanced toilet technology.

Paul Hawkins

Beer makes you smarter. It made Bud wiser.

Bill Mather

American beer is served cold so you can tell it from urine.

David Moulton

Nothing ever tasted any better than a cold beer on a beautiful afternoon with nothing to look forward to but more of the same.

Hugh Hood

The whole world is three drinks behind.

Humphrey Bogart

The hard thing about being a bartender is figuring out who is drunk
and who is just stupid.
Richard Braunstein

George Best, do you think, if you hadn't had to do all that running
around on a football field, you wouldn't have got so thirsty? Mrs Merton

—Winston, you're drunk!
—Bessie, you're ugly. But tomorrow I shall be sober.
Bessie Braddock and Winston Churchill

I'm not so think as you drunk I am.
John Collings Squire

I drink therefore I am.
W.C. Fields

I am a drinker with a writing problem.
Brendan Behan

I can't hold my liquor in the winter. I'm pretty sure it's the mittens.
Jonathan Katz

Drinking raw absinthe is like swallowing a Bengal tiger.
Sylvia Townsend Warner

After the first glass of absinthe, you see things as you wish they were.
After the second, you see them as they are not. Finally, you see things
as they really are, and that is the most horrible thing in the world.
Oscar Wilde

I have been advised, at my age, not to attempt to give up alcohol.
Bishop Haldane

The last mosquito that bit me had to book into the Betty Ford Clinic.
Patsy Stone, *Absolutely Fabulous*

We had gone there to pass the beautiful day of high summer like true
Irishmen – locked in the dark snug of the public house. Brendan Behan

When you look at the world through the bottom of a glass, may you
see someone ready to buy.
Irish proverb

I have taken more out of alcohol than alcohol has taken out of me.

Winston Churchill

Wouldn't it be terrible if I quoted some reliable statistics which prove that more people are driven insane through religious hysteria than by drinking alcohol.

W.C. Fields

May I suggest, sir, that if you want an impenetrable disguise for the fancy dress ball, that you go sober?

Samuel Foote

I never knew my husband was a drunk until one night he came home sober.

Gail LaBelle

Often Daddy sat up very late working on a case of Scotch.

Robert Benchley

Two guys walk into a bar. You'd think one of them would have seen it.

Daniel Lybra

I've only been drunk once before and that was from 1971 to 1990.

Jim Davidson

I don't have a drink problem except when I can't get one.

Tom Waits

In Hollywood, people think you're an alcoholic if you have a second drink.

Ben Chaplin

I eat Wheaties for breakfast. You can't beat a bowl of Wheaties with Bourbon.

Dizzy Dean

I saw a notice which said 'Drink Canada Dry' so I've started.

Brendan Behan

Hate your job? Join our support group! It's called EVERYBODY. We meet at the bar.

Drew Carey

One more drink and I'll be under the host.   **Dorothy Parker**

Drink is your enemy. Love your enemies.   **W.C. Fields**

You're not drunk if you can lie on the floor without holding on.
                    Dean Martin

The AAAA is a new organization for drunks who drive. Give them a
call and they'll tow you away from the bar.   **Martin Burden**

They say that drinking alcohol is slow poison. So who's in a hurry?
                    Robert Benchley

Some weasel took the cork out of my lunch.   **W.C. Fields**

I drink too much. Last time I gave a urine sample it had an olive in it.
                    Rodney Dangerfield

An alcoholic is a man who, when he buys his ties, has to ask if gin
makes them run.   **F. Scott Fitzgerald**

I was in love with a beautiful blonde once. She drove me to drink,
and I never even had the courtesy to thank her.   **W.C. Fields**

—That's your third brandy and it's only nine o'clock in the morning.
—It's Norma, she's left me.
—That was 35 years ago.
—I still miss her.   **Jack Benny and George Burns**

He puts down half a bottle of whisky a day and has two convictions
for drunken driving, but otherwise is a pillar of society.   **Alan Bennett**

I can't die until the government finds a safe place to bury my liver.
                    Phil Harris

I've stopped drinking.
But only while I'm asleep.
                    George Best

The alcohol warning should be more to the point. Warning: Alcohol turns you into the same asshole your father was.

George Carlin

What is on a drunken man's lips is on a sober man's mind.

Danish proverb

I always keep a supply of stimulants handy in case I see a snake, which I also keep handy.

W.C. Fields

Did you hear about the Irishman who joined Alcoholics Anonymous? He still drinks but under a different name.

Aubrey Dillon-Malone

Alcoholism is the only disease you can get yelled at for having.

Mitch Hedberg Martin

I exercise extreme self-control. I never drink anything stronger than gin before breakfast.

W.C. Fields

—Pay no attention to him. He's pissed.
—Has he?

Tim Brooke-Taylor and Graeme Garden

The difference between a drunk and an alcoholic is that a drunk doesn't have to attend all those meetings.

Arthur J. Lewis

If you drink, don't drive. Don't even putt.

Dean Martin

I was one drink away from a tattoo.

Lily Savage

I don't drink any more. But I don't drink any less.

Rod Fitzgerald

I only drink to make other people seem more interesting.

George Jean Nathan

A teetotaller is the very worst sort of drunkard.

E. F. Benson

I always say, if you've seen one gentleman of the press having delirium tremens, you've seen them all.

P.G. Wodehouse

Adrian Boult came to see me this morning – positively reeking of Horlicks.

Thomas Beecham

I made wine out of raisins so I wouldn't have to wait for it to age.

Steven Wright

I'm only a beer teetotaller, not a champagne teetotaller.   **George Bernard Shaw**

Real ale enthusiasts are the same as trainspotters, only drunk.

Christopher Howse

I had a horrible nightmare last night. I dreamt I drank the world's largest margarita, and when I woke up this morning, there was salt on the toilet lid. Thank God I didn't eat the worm in there.   **Larry the Cable Guy**

The Campaign For Real Ale is the last refuge of bearded Trotskyite Morris dancers.   **Alum Howkins**

I'd hate to be a teetotaller. Imagine getting up in the morning and knowing that's as good as you're going to feel all day.

Dean Martin

I only drink twice a day – when I'm thirsty and when I'm not.

Brendan Behan

Remember that time you drank three margaritas and thought you were the dancing broom from *Fantasia*?   **Dorothy Zbornak, *The Golden Girls***

You're not drunk as long as you can hold on to a blade of grass and not fall off the face of the earth.   **Irish saying**

The worst thing about some men is that when they are not drunk they are sober.

W. B. Yeats

An alcoholic is someone you don't like who drinks as much as you do.

Dylan Thomas

HANGOVER

Gaaad, what a night! I'll never mix radish juice and carrot juice ever again.

Bugs Bunny

He awoke with a severe hangover. His mouth felt as if it had been used as a latrine by some small animal.

Kingsley Amis

My mouth is so dry they could shoot *Lawrence of Arabia* in it.

Dyan Canon

My head feels like there's a Frenchman living in it.

Blackadder II

Someone put too many olives in my martini last night.

W.C. Fields

I woke up with the kind of headache you'd get if you'd been drinking cheap champagne from a size-14 Cinderella slipper.

Kinky Friedman

Have you ever felt so sick, you'd have to rally to die?

Lou Grant, *Rhoda*

He was in the sort of overwrought state when a fly treading a little too heavily on the carpet is enough to make a man think he's one of the extras in *All Quiet on the Western Front*.

P.G. Wodehouse

Try opening your eyes. It's like when you were young and you used to take the cellophane wrapper from a Quality Street toffee and hold it over your eyes.

Stephen Fry

He resolved, having done it once, never to move his eyeballs again.

Kingsley Amis

I've had hangovers before, but this time even my hair hurts.

Rock Hudson

If the headache would only precede the intoxication, alcoholism would be a virtue.

Samuel Butler

Hangover: the wrath of grapes.

Dorothy Parker

The more I behave like Whistler's Mother the night before, the more I look like her the morning after.

Tallulah Bankhead

To cure a hangover, take the juice of two quarts of whiskey.

Eddie Condon

The best way to cure a hangover is to avoid alcohol the night before.

Cathy Hopkins

The only cure for a real hangover is death.

Robert Benchley

SMOKING

Smoking is, as far as I'm concerned, the entire point of being an adult.

Fran Lebowitz

People are so rude to smokers. You'd think they'd try to be nicer to people who are dying.

Roseanne

Cigarettes are a much cheaper and more widely available alternative to nicotine patches.

Bob Davies

The nicotine patches work pretty well, but it's kind of hard to keep them lit.

George Carlin

It has always been my rule never to smoke when asleep, and never to refrain when awake.

Mark Twain

I'd give up smoking but I'm not a quitter.

Jo Brand

I'm not what you'd call a heavy smoker. I only get through two lighters a day.

Bill Hicks

If I'm told to stop smoking in a restaurant, I just say, 'Excuse me, do you mind not being bigoted around me. Bigotry killed six million Jews.'

Stephen Fry

I make it a rule never to smoke more than one cigar at a time.

Mark Twain

I've been smoking for 30 years now and there's nothing wrong with my lung.

Freddie Starr

I don't let men smoke in my apartment. But if I have a woman over, she can barbecue a goat.

Todd Barry

Having smoking and non-smoking sections in the same room is like having urinating and non-urinating sections in a swimming pool.

Ross Parker

There's no smoking in restaurants in Los Angeles. Which is a bit ironic, considering that you can't breathe the air outside a restaurant in Los Angeles.

Greg Proops

When I was a smoker, people were always coming up to me saying, 'Miss, your smoke is bothering me.' I'd say, 'Hey, it's killing me.'

Wendy Liebman

I never allow myself to be photographed if I'm not smoking. It's a strict policy I initiated when it became politically correct not to smoke.

Maggi Hambling

Why is it that whenever I step out for some fresh air, I run into some
guy smoking a cigarette?
Reno Goodale

Smoking will cure weight problems ... eventually.
Kit Hall

—How can you smoke so many cigars?
—I toil after it, sir, as some men toil after virtue.
Charles Lamb

If you're saying you don't know cigarettes are bad for you, you're
lying through that hole in your trachea.
Dennis Miller

It is now proved beyond doubt that smoking is one of the leading causes of statistics.
Fletcher Knebel

Giving up smoking is easy. I've done it thousands of times.
Mark Twain

I was so horrified when I read about the effects of smoking that I
gave up reading.
Henny Youngman

I've given up smoking before – worst eight hours of my life.
Lily Savage

Here's a tip to stop smoking: douse yourself in petrol every day.
Bill Bailey

I'd quit smoking if I didn't think I'd become one of those non-smokers.
Bill Hicks

Nobody can be so revoltingly smug as the man who has just given up
smoking.
Sydney J. Harris

If you saw the same warning label you see on cigarettes on any other
product, you wouldn't go near it. It's like looking at the warning label
on Domestos – 'Harmful or fatal if swallowed', and thinking, 'Well,
I'm down to three bottles a week. It relaxes me.'
Paul Provenza

I love all you ex-smokers because you leave more cigarettes for me.

Denis Leary

—Even passive smoking kills.
—Not often enough.   John Correli and Catherine Tramell, *Basic Instinct*

I have something to tell you non-smokers that I know for a fact,
and I feel it's my duty to pass on information at all times. Ready?
Non-smokers die every day. That's it. Enjoy your evening.   Bill Hicks

I think passive smoking is outrageous. They should buy their own.

Jenny Abrams

The room smelt of not having been smoked in.   Ronald Knox

Cigarette sales would drop to zero overnight if the warning said,
'Cigarettes Contain Fat.'   Dave Barry

They say if you stop smoking, you'll get your sense of smell back. I live
in New York City, why would I want my sense of smell back?   Bill Hicks

I've quit smoking. I feel better, I smell better, and it's safer to drink out
of old beer cans around the house.   Roseanne

The easiest way to give up smoking is to stop putting cigarettes in your
mouth and lighting them.   William Rushton

I have overcome my will-power and have taken up smoking again.

Mark Twain

—Happy 103rd Birthday, Mr Zukor. What is the secret of your long life?
—I gave up smoking two years ago.   Adolph Zukor

If smoking is not permitted in heaven, I won't go.

Mark Twain

FOOD AND DRINK

Peckish is not the word! I feel like a homeless tapeworm.   P.G. Wodehouse

I'm so hungry I could eat a nun's arse through the convent railings.
Lily Savage

I'm that hungry I could eat a baby's bum through a wicker chair.
Roy Chubby Brown

At bedtime in the school, the hungrier boys ate their toothpaste.
Arthur Marshall

If only it were as easy to banish hunger by rubbing the belly as it is
to masturbate.   Diogenes

Beulah, peel me a grape.   Mae West

Slice the pizza into four pieces not eight – I'm not hungry enough to
eat eight.   Yogi Berra

During one of our trips through Afghanistan, we lost our corkscrew.
We had to live on nothing but food and water for several days. W.C. Fields

Food is an important part of a balanced diet.   Fran Lebowitz

Americans regard food as something to sober up with.   James Agate

Water, taken in moderation, cannot hurt anybody.   Mark Twain

Ever wondered about those people who spend $2 a throw on those little
bottles of Evian water? Try spelling Evian backwards.   Jon Stewart

Never drink water. Fish fuck in it.   W.C. Fields

I mix my water myself. Two parts H, one part O. I don't trust anybody.
Steven Wright

I think Pringles' initial intention was to make tennis balls. But on the day the rubber was supposed to show up, a big truckload of potatoes arrived instead.

Mitch Hedberg

As life's pleasures go, food is second only to sex. Except for salami and eggs. Now that's better than sex, but only if the salami is thickly sliced.

Alan King

The worst thing that ever happened to me was that I offered a fellow a crisp from my bag and he took two.

Vic Reeves

Research tells us 14 out of any 10 individuals like chocolate.

Sandra Boynton

Who discovered we could get milk from cows, and what did he think he was doing at the time?

Billy Connolly

Cheese, milk's leap towards immortality.

Clifton Fadiman

Eating an anchovy is like eating an eyebrow.

Paul Merton

—Say Grace, Bart.
—Dear God, we paid for all this food ourselves, so thanks for nothing.

Marge and Bart Simpson

'Bee vomit,' my brother said once, 'that's all honey is,' so that I could not put my tongue to its jellied flame without tasting regurgitated blossoms.

Rita Dove

There are two things in life I like hard and one of them is eggs. Mae West

Custard is a detestable substance produced by a malevolent conspiracy of the hen, the cow and the cook.

Ambrose Bierce

I wouldn't give someone my last Rolo if they were in a diabetic coma.

Jo Brand

Chocolate is so delicious! What a pity it's not a sin!   Marquise de Sévigné

Just give me chocolate and nobody gets hurt.   Slogan on T-shirt

Fun-sized Snickers? Who's this fun for? Not me. I need six or seven of these babies in a row to start having fun.
Jeff Carlin

Ever hear the phrase, 'chocolatey goodness'? Know what that means? 'NO FUCKIN' CHOCOLATE.'
George Carlin

From the new Findus Dermatology convenience range – a boil in the bag.
Graeme Garden

I like vending machines, because snacks are better when they fall.
Mitch Hedberg

Training is everything – cauliflower is nothing but cabbage with a college education.
Mark Twain

According to my jar of pickles there's a 24-hour pickle hotline. I guess that's if you got brine problems that just can't wait until morning.
Tim Steeves

Jesus, look at the fridge. It looks like the laboratory of Sir Alexander Fleming.
William McIlvanney

Why is it all the things I like eating have been proven to cause tumours in white mice?
Robert Benchley

I'll have a double cappuccino, half-caf, non-fat milk, with enough foam to be aesthetically pleasing, but not so much that it would leave a moustache.
Niles Crane, *Frasier*

I think they should put a warning label on strawberries: Caution –
tastes nothing like a strawberry milkshake.   Ryan Kaplan

Melon is a good fruit: you eat, you drink, you wash your face.
                                                     Enrico Caruso

You can't get Dairylea cheese triangles in Bermuda.   Tim Vine

My favourite part of the body is the navel. I like to eat celery in bed
and it's an excellent place to keep the salt.   Gerard Hoffnung

Turkey is totally inedible. It's like eating a scrum half.   Willie Rushton

They just opened a Starbucks across the street from a Starbucks.
                                                     David Letterman

English coffee tastes like water that has been squeezed out of a wet
sleeve.   Fred Allen

I put instant coffee in the microwave and almost went back in time.
                                                     Steven Wright

There was an earthquake in Seattle, registering 6.8 on the Richter scale.
No one was hurt but buildings were damaged. On one block alone more
than four hundred Starbucks were destroyed.   Conan O'Brien

—I take my coffee like I take my women.
—Are you sure you want to spend 75 bucks on a cup of coffee?
                          Stuart Bondek and Stacey Paterno, *Spin City*

They just opened a Starbucks in my living room.   Janeane Garofalo

If this is coffee, please bring me tea; if this is tea, please bring me coffee.
                                                     Benjamin Franklin

They just opened a Starbucks in my pants.   George Carlin

Bernie made the kind of tea a mouse could stand on.   Liza Cody

If your eyes hurt after you drink coffee, you have to take the spoon out of the cup.

Norm Crosby

What would life be without coffee? But then, what is it even with coffee?

Louis XV

I like my coffee like I like my women – in a plastic cup.

Eddie Izzard

Whatever you tell them, people always make your tea or coffee the way *they* like it.

Russell Bell

Do illiterate people get the full effect of alphabet soup?

John Mendoza

I just heard I won a competition. The prize is a year's supply of Marmite – one jar.

Tim Vine

You can't trust water. Even a straight stick turns crooked in it.

W.C. Fields

Someone once threw me a small, brown, hairy kiwi fruit and I threw a waste basket over it until it was dead.

Erma Bombeck

Why do mums always buy crap pop?

Peter Kay

Diet Coke with lemon – didn't that used to be called Pledge?

Jay Leno

There are so many flavours of Coke now – Coke with lemon, Coke with vanilla, Coke with lime, Cherry Coke, and they've just brought out another new flavour – Coke with Pepsi.

David Letterman

Is this liver or am I changing a tyre?

W.C. Fields

I got food poisoning today. I don't know when I'll use it.

Steven Wright

Life is too short to stuff a mushroom.

Shirley Conran

I couldn't eat toast for years when I was drinking heavily, because it was too noisy.
Clarissa Dickson-Wright

He imported to the peeling of a banana the elegant nonchalance of a duke drawing a monogrammed cigarette from a platinum case.
Alexander Woollcott

Eternity is a ham and two people.
Sam Levenson

The herb crust on the cod could have been adapted, with minimal effort, for use in germ warfare.
Matthew Norman

Only Irish coffee provides in a single glass all four essential food groups: alcohol, caffeine, sugar, and fat.
Alex Levine

I don't drink water. Have you seen the way it rusts pipes?
W.C. Fields

Breakfast cereal is made of all those little curly wooden shavings you find in pencil sharpeners.
Roald Dahl

I tell kids they should throw away the cereal and eat the box. At least they'd get some fibre.
Dr Richard Holstein

The champagne's all right, but the blackcurrant jam tastes of fish.
Derek Randall about caviar

Fish and chips and, what's this? Avocado dip?
Peter Mandelson about mushy peas

'Escargot' is French for 'fat crawling bag of phlegm'.
Dave Barry

You never know where to look when eating a banana.
Peter Kay

I ordered a soda – caffeine-free, low sodium, no artificial flavours. They brought me a glass of water.
Robert Murray

The snails still had their horns and were curled up and wrinkled like frost-bitten snotty noses boiled to death in their beds. But the taste was miraculous.

A.A. Gill

I don't eat snails. I prefer fast food.

Roger Von Oech

Krispy Kreme Doughnuts: Konsult Kardiologist.

David Letterman

Critics say that Andy Warhol's famous portraits of Campbell's soup cans were a brilliant satire of culture, in much the same way that a Campbell's soup is a brilliant satire of food.

Craig Kilbourn

Campbell's soups – for those occasions when you have to cook, but hate the person you're cooking for.

Jon Stewart

The biggest marketing mistake in history was Campbell's Soup For One. They might as well have called it Cream of Loser Soup. 'Open can. Add tears.'

Traci Skene

An onion can make you cry, but there has never been a vegetable invented to make you laugh.

Will Rogers

Cured ham? No, thanks pal – cured of what?

Tommy Sledge

Tofu is actually enjoyed as a food in parts of Asia.

Vic Reeves

Tofu – have you ever had a yeast infection?

Ruby Wax

My friend, Lily, can recognize 157 different types of cheese just by looking at the labels.

Mrs Merton

I've decided to make Grammy Moon's Sheep's Head Soup. Don't worry, the name's a bit misleading. It's actually more of a stew.

Daphne Moon, *Frasier*

This stuff tastes awful. I could have made a fortune selling it in my health food store.

Woody Allen

A friend of mine drowned in a bowl of muesli. A strong currant pulled him in.

Tommy Cooper

Health food makes me sick.

Calvin Trillin

The process of making onion soup is somewhat like love – commitment, extraordinary effort, time, and will make you cry.

Ronni Lundy

Inhabitants of underdeveloped nations and victims of natural disasters are the only people who have ever been happy to see soybeans.

Fran Lebowitz

Cold soup is a very tricky thing and it is a rare hostess who can carry it off. More often than not, the dinner guest is left with the impression that had he only come a little earlier he could have gotten it while it was still hot.

Fran Lebowitz

I dislike soup. I don't believe in building a meal on a lake.

Elsie Mendl

A nectarine – Good God, how fine. It went down all pulpy, slushy, oozy – all its delicious *embonpoint* melted down my throat like a large, beatified strawberry.

John Keats

In Mexico we have a word for sushi – bait.

José Simon

I got kicked out of a movie theatre for bringing my own food in. I argued that the concession stand prices were outrageous. Besides, I hadn't had a barbecue in a long time.

Emo Philips

The German sausage looked like a cross-section through a dead dachshund.

Clive James

A bagel is an unsweetened doughnut with rigor mortis.   **Beatrice Freeman**

If lobsters looked like puppies, people could never drop them in boiling water while they're still alive.   **George Carlin**

When I make lobster, I just boil the water and play some Michael Bolton tapes. It commits suicide.   **Wendy Liebman**

I bought a box of animal crackers and it said on it, 'Do not eat if seal is broken.' So I opened up the box, and sure enough...   **Brian Kiley**

Carrots? Ugh! I don't know what company makes this stuff, but I hate it.
Dewey, *Malcolm in the Middle*

I personally stay away from natural foods. At my age, I need all the preservatives I can get.   George Burns

—Who is that man riding in the carriage with the portly Queen of Tonga?
—Her lunch.   **Noël Coward**

Two cannibals eating a clown. One says to the other, 'Does this taste funny to you?'   **Tommy Cooper**

If I ever had to practise cannibalism, I believe I might manage if there was enough tarragon around.   **James Beard**

Onion rings in the car cushions do not improve with time.
Erma Bombeck

—Would you like a prawn cocktail?
—No thanks, I don't drink.   **Jeff Stone**

The avocado is a lavatory-coloured fruit.   **Mike Barfield**

How to eat spinach like a child: divide into piles. Rearrange again
into piles. After five or six manoeuvres, sit back and say you're full.

Delia Ephron

This rock salt is over 200 million years old, formed through
ancient geological processes in the German mountain ranges.
Best before 01-04-2004.

Label on a container

Life expectancy would grow by leaps and bounds if green vegetables
smelled as good as bacon.

Doug Larson

I cook with wine. Sometimes I even add it to the food.

W.C. Fields

Eat up your greens! There are thousands of children in Hollywood
with eating disorders.

John Callaghan

A gourmet can tell from the flavour whether a woodcock's leg is the
one on which the bird is accustomed to roost.

Lucius Beebe

The hole in the doughnut is the most digestible part.

H.L. Mencken

Avoid beans as you would matricide.

Pythagoras

A fruit is a vegetable with looks and money.

P.J. O'Rourke

I didn't squawk about the steak, dear. I merely said I didn't see that
old horse that used to be tethered outside.

W.C. Fields

Mine eyes smell onions.

William Shakespeare

Chopsticks are one of the reasons the Chinese never invented custard.

Spike Milligan

The noblest of all dogs is the hot-dog. It feeds the hand that bites it.

Laurence J. Peter

If a lump of soot falls into the soup, and you cannot conveniently get it out, stir it well in, and it will give the soup a French taste.   **Jonathan Swift**

Everything you see I owe to spaghetti.   **Sophia Loren**

The trouble with eating Italian food is that five or six days later you're hungry again.   **George Miller**

If you're going to America, bring food.   **Fran Lebowitz**

I'm in favour of liberalized immigration laws in America because of the effect it would have on restaurants. I'd let just about everybody in except the English.   **Calvin Trillin**

Britain is the only country in the world where the food is more dangerous than the sex.   **Jackie Mason**

The great British contribution to world cuisine is the chip.   **John Cleese**

English vegetables taste as though they have been boiled in a strong soap.
                                                                     W.C. Fields

If the Germans can't stuff it into an animal casing they won't eat it.
                                                                      Tim Allen

You don't eat Mexican food – you just rent it.   **Alexei Sayle**

Mexican food is delicious and perfectly safe so long as you are careful never to get any of it in your digestive tract.   **Dave Barry**

Roumanian-Yiddish cooking has killed more Jews than Hitler.
                                                                    Zero Mostel

Tomatoes and oregano make it Italian; wine and tarragon make it French. Sour cream makes it Russian; lemon and cinnamon make it Greek. Soy sauce makes it Chinese; garlic makes it good.   **Alice May Brock**

He was a bold man that first ate an oyster.   **Jonathan Swift**

Never eat lettuce in Mexico unless it has been sterilized by a blowtorch.
Benjamin H. Kean

Dried fish is a staple food in Iceland. It varies in toughness. The tougher kind tastes like toenails, and the softer kind like the skin off the soles of one's feet.
W.H. Auden

I will not eat oysters. I want my food dead. Not sick, not wounded, dead.
Woody Allen

Oysters are supposed to enhance your sexual performance, but they don't work for me. Maybe I put them on too soon.
Garry Shandling

Even were a cook to cook a fly, he would keep the breast for himself.
Polish proverb

Cooking a crocodile is easy. You need two pots of boiling water, one for the crocodile and one for a rock. By the time the rock is tender, the crocodile will be cooked.
Paul Hogan

We were served boiled fish with that awful anchovy sauce that looks as if the cook had bled into it.
Raymond Chandler

Gem lettuce frisée looked a bit like the kind of forest you have to hack your way through to reach Sleeping Beauty.
Will Self

The omelette was so light we had to lay our knives across it and even then it struggled.
Margaret Halsey

Is there chicken in chickpeas?
Helen Adams, *Big Brother 2*

Outback breakfast: a piss and a look around.
Paul Hogan

—I got brown sandwiches and green sandwiches.
—What's the green?
—It's either very new cheese or very old meat.

Oscar Madison and Felix Ungar, *The Odd Couple*

The bread ate as if it had been made by a manic-depressive creative therapy class.

A.A. Gill

Men like to barbecue. Men like to cook only if danger is involved.

Rita Rudner

Barbecues are like overhead projectors – they never work the first time.

Digby Anderson

I'm at the age when food has taken the place of sex in my life. In fact, I've just had a mirror put over my kitchen table.

Rodney Dangerfield

When I ask for a watercress sandwich, I do not mean a loaf with a field in the middle of it.

Oscar Wilde

The most dangerous food is wedding cake.

James Thurber

There is no such thing as a little garlic.

Arthur Baer

Too many cooks, in baking rock cakes, get misled by the word 'rock'.

P.G. Wodehouse

A horseracing breakfast: a cough and a copy of the *Sporting Life*.

Simon Barnes

I hadn't the heart to touch my breakfast. I told Jeeves to drink it himself.

P.G. Wodehouse

The leek soup tasted like rusty water which had somehow leaked through the ceiling onto the plate.

Frank Muir

A nickel will get you on the subway, but garlic will get you a seat.

New York Jewish saying

I once took an after-dinner mint after breakfast and it threw me out for weeks.

Arthur Smith

Oats: a grain, which in England is generally given to horses, but in Scotland supports the people.

Samuel Johnson

A cucumber should be well sliced, and dressed with pepper and vinegar, and then thrown out, as good for nothing.

Samuel Johnson

The local groceries are all out of broccoli, loccoli.

Roy Blount

Broccoli is something that's difficult to say anything nice about except that it has no bones.

Johnny Martin

Hotel tea is when you have to mix together a plastic envelope containing too much sugar, a small plastic pot of something which is not milk but has curdled anyway, and a thin brown packet seemingly containing the ashes of a cremated mole.

Frank Muir

Why don't they just spell it ordervs?

Holly Thompson

I've learned to spell hors d'oeuvres which grates on many people's n'oevres.

Warren Knox

Artichoke: a vegetable of which one has more at the finish than at the start of a dinner.

Lord Chesterfield

You get about as much actual food out of eating artichoke as you would licking thirty postage stamps.

Miss Piggy

The scented flesh of the grouse tasted like an old courtesan's flesh marinated in a bidet.

Edmond de Goncourt

Americans can eat garbage provided you sprinkle it liberally with ketchup, mustard, chilli sauce or any other condiment which destroys the original flavour of the food.   Henry Miller

The piece of cod passeth all understanding.   Edwin Lutyens

Fish is the only food that is considered spoiled once it smells like what it is.

P.J. O'Rourke

The baked potatoes looked like they had been excreted by a buffalo.
Brian Sewell

Large, naked, raw carrots are acceptable food only to those who live in hutches eagerly awaiting Easter.   Fran Lebowitz

If it looks like a duck, walks like a duck, talks like a duck, it probably needs a little more time in the microwave.   Lori Dowdy

As everybody knows, there is only one infallible recipe for the perfect omelette: your own.   Elizabeth David

Mummy, must I eat this pie? It's such a particularly nasty bit of the shepherd.   *Punch*

My mother was the worst cook. Even I knew you didn't add fabric softener to meat loaf. She once made carrot cake but didn't grate the carrot.   Rita Rudner

My mother's menu consisted of two choices: take it or leave it.
Buddy Hackett

Mum only ever uses the cooker to light her fags off.
Saffy Monsoon, *Absolutely Fabulous*

The catch of the day was hepatitis.   Henny Youngman

For thirty years, my mother served the family nothing but leftovers.
The original meal has never been found.   Calvin Trillin

My husband said to me, 'Bette, if you would learn to cook, we could
fire the chef.' I said, 'Martin, if you would learn to fuck, we could fire
the chauffeur.'   Bette Midler

My mother is the only person in the world who cooks lumpy boiling
water.   David Brenner

Most turkeys taste better the day after. My mother's tasted better the day
before.   Rita Rudner

Leftovers make you feel good twice. The first time is when you save
them, 'Hey! I'm saving food.' The second time is when you throw
them away, 'Hey! I'm saving my life.'   George Carlin

It is odd how all men develop the notion, as they grow older, that their
mothers were wonderful cooks. I have yet to meet a man who will
admit that his mother was a kitchen assassin and nearly poisoned him.
                                                          Robertson Davis

A man is in general better pleased when he has a good dinner upon
his table, than when his wife talks Greek.   Samuel Johnson

I often put boiling water in the freezer. Then whenever I need boiling
water, all I have to do is defrost it.   Gracie Allen

I can't cook. I use a smoke alarm as a timer.   Carol Siskind

I was eating a lot of frozen TV dinners when I realized they would
probably taste better if they were warm.   Yakov Smirnoff

When compelled to cook, I produce a meal that would make a sword-
swallower gag.   Russell Baker

Everything my wife makes tastes like chicken. Even her coffee.
                                                             Woody Allen

My wife dresses to kill. She cooks the same way.   **Rodney Dangerfield**

Our toaster has two settings: too soon or too late.   **Sam Levenson**

The first time my husband asked me for an aspirin and a glass of water
I knew exactly what to do. I phoned my mother for the recipe.
Gracie Allen

Men are very strange. When they wake up in the morning, they want
things like toast. I don't have these recipes.   **Elayne Boosler**

A recipe is a series of step-by-step instructions for preparing ingredients
you forgot to buy in utensils you don't own to make a dish the dog
won't eat the rest of.   **Henry Beard**

My wife holds a black belt in karate and in cooking. She could kill you
either way.   **Curtis Sliwa**

My wife does wonderful things with leftovers. She throws them away.
Herb Shriner

If it wasn't for burnt toast, entire species of birds in Britain would
disappear.   **Jeremy Noakes**

When my girlfriend made French toast, she got her tongue caught in the
toaster.   **Rodney Dangerfield**

It is impossible to combine the heating of milk with any other pursuit
whatever.   **H.F. Ellis**

Anyone who eats three meals a day should understand why cookbooks outsell sex books three to one. L.M. Boyd

I was a vegetarian until I started leaning towards sunlight.   **Rita Rudner**

I no longer prepare food or drink with more than one ingredient.

Cyra McFadden

A refrigerator is a place where you store leftovers until they're old enough to throw out.

Al Boliska

When you see a vegetarian dinner you wonder – are they about to eat it or have they just finished?

Winston Churchill

A person of my spiritual intensities does not eat corpses.

George Bernard Shaw

I could be a vegetarian. There's no meat in beer, right?

Joey Tribbiani, *Friends*

I refuse to eat anything that has intelligence, so I would gladly eat a television executive or a politician.

Marty Feldman

Most vegetarians I ever see looked enough like their food to be classed as cannibals.

Finlay Peter Dunne

I am not a vegetarian because I love animals. I am a vegetarian because I hate plants.

A.W. Brown

I bought my girlfriend a book called *Cheap and Easy Vegetarian Cooking*, because she's a vegetarian and she's...

Jimmy Carr

What does a Jewish princess make for dinner? Reservations.

Maureen Lipman

No food with a face.

Dan Carson

RESTAURANT

Table for one in a draught, please.

Jeff Green

What the hell is this place? Must be one of those gay, Arab, biker, sushi bars.

Harvey Fierstein

Great restaurants are, of course, nothing but mouth brothels.

Frederic Raphael

If the sign on the restaurant uses the word *Cuisine*, it will be expensive. If they use the word *Food*, it will be moderately priced. However, if the sign says *Eats*, even though you'll save some money on food, your medical bills will be quite high.

George Carlin

The quality of food in a restaurant exists in inverse proportion to the quality of the view.

James Beard

Never eat in a restaurant that's over a hundred feet off the ground and won't stand still.

Calvin Trillin

The quality of food in a restaurant is in inverse proportion to the number of signed celebrity photographs on the wall.

Bryan Miller

The murals in restaurants are about on a par with the food in art galleries.

Peter de Vries

The disparity between a restaurant's price and the food quality rises in direct proportion to the size of the pepper mill.

Bryan Miller

Charles took me to dine at Boulestins. We ate oysters, and red mullet grilled with a slip of banana laid along it like a medieval wife on a tomb.

Sylvia Townsend Warner

Eating out is so expensive. I went to one restaurant and instead of having prices on the menu, they just had pictures of faces with different expressions of horror.

Rita Rudner

A gourmet restaurant in Cincinnati is one where you leave the tray on the table after you eat.
Tom Arnold

You can find your way across American using burger joints the way a navigator uses stars.
Charles Kuralt

I went into a McDonald's yesterday and said, 'I'd like some fries.' The girl at the counter said, 'Would you like fries with that?'
Jay Leno

The scent of McDonald's is almost as insistent and evocative as a late-night minicab or a Turkish campsite ablutions block in August.
A.A. Gill

McDonald's is closing a hundred and fifty locations. Clearasil immediately reduced their workforce by half.
Conan O'Brien

The wife said she's like to eat out for a change, so I moved the dining room table into the garden.
Les Dawson

Last night we went to a Chinese dinner at six and a French dinner at nine, and I can feel the sharks' fins navigating unhappily in the Burgundy.
Peter Fleming

Spud-U-Like: the DSS with potatoes.
Victoria Wood

Last night I ordered an entire meal in French, and even the waiter was surprised. It was a Chinese restaurant.
Tommy Cooper

I ate on the motorway. At the Grill 'n' Griddle. I had Ham 'n' Eggs. And now I've got 'ndigestion.
Alan Bennett

Thank you for taking this tour of Haworth, home of the Brontës. Snacks and light refreshments are now available in the Heathcliffe Nosher Bar, so please feel free to sample our very popular Brontëburgers, or for the fibre-conscious – our Branwell Brontëburgers.
Victoria Wood

I'd like to open a restaurant for single people. You walk in and it's all sinks. No tables, no chairs. Everyone just eats standing over the sink.

Elayne Boosler

The other night I ate at a real nice family restaurant. Every table had an argument going.

George Carlin

The golden rule when reading the menu is, if you can't pronounce it, you can't afford it.

Frank Muir

If there's a fancy tassel on the menu, you can add a couple of dollars per person.

Andy Rooney

The longer the description on the menu, the less you will get on your plate.

Shirley Lowe

Nouvelle cuisine is so beautifully arranged on the plate – you know someone's fingers have been all over it.

Julia Child

Nouvelle cuisine roughly translated means, 'I can't believe I paid two hundred dollars and I'm still hungry.'

Mike Kalina

In every restaurant, the hardness of the butter increases in direct proportion to the softness of the bread.

Harriet Markman

Can we just get rid of wine lists? Do we really need to be reminded every time we go out to a nice restaurant that we have no idea what we're doing? Why don't they just give us a trigonometry quiz with the menu?

Jerry Seinfeld

A Waldorf salad? I think we're out of Waldorfs.

Basil Fawlty

A good Greasy Spoon should resemble an Aegean holiday – swimming in grease.

Les Dawson

Some of the waiters discuss the menu with you as if they were sharing wisdom picked up in the Himalayas. **Seymour Britchky**

The food in this restaurant is terrible. And such small portions. **Woody Allen**

The Greasy Spoon restaurant was so bad that on the menu there were even flies in the pictures. **Richard Lewis**

I was polishing off the last mouthful of a dish in a restaurant when I overheard one waiter whisper to another, 'He's actually eating it.' **Gilbert Harding**

With regard to tomato ketchup, let me say this: the restaurant is like a theatre: we do two shows a day and when you are doing Shakespeare, you don't want to throw in something of Walt Disney. **Philip Britten**

I went to a restaurant that serves 'breakfast at any time', so I ordered French Toast during the Renaissance. **Steven Wright**

I eat at this German-Chinese restaurant and the food is delicious. The only problem is that an hour later, you're hungry for power. **Dick Cavett**

I once had dinner in a topless restaurant. I was really looking forward to it, but all the staff were men. **Emo Philips**

A hold-up man walks into a Chinese restaurant, and he says, 'Give me all your money.' The man says, 'To go?'

Slappy White

DIET

—Whatcha up to, Mr Peterson?
—My ideal weight if I was 11 feet tall.

Woody Boyd and Norm Peterson, Cheers

She looked as if she had been poured into her clothes and had forgotten
to say 'when'.

P.G. Wodehouse

I went to the 30th reunion of my preschool. I didn't want to go,
because I've put on like a hundred pounds.

Wendy Liebman

What's chips minus the 'c', girls?

Peter Kay

She fitted into my biggest armchair as if it had been built around her
by someone who knew they were wearing armchairs tight about the
hips that season.

P.G. Wodehouse

She had a gigantic rear end. It looked like she was shoplifting throw
pillows.

Frasier Crane, Frasier

I get stuck in the revolving doors of the hotel, and the porter, trying to
be helpful, says, 'Try backing out sideways. 'Honey,' I says, 'I ain't got
no sideways.'

Bernice Rubens

If her bum was a bungalow, she'd never get a mortgage on it.

Victoria Wood

Is she fat? Her favourite food is seconds.

Joan Rivers

She was so huge she had three skinny ladies orbiting her.

Bobby Collins

When my mother-in-law hangs out her bra on the line to dry, we lose
an hour of daylight.

Les Dawson

I saw a woman wearing a sweatshirt with 'Guess' on it. I said,
'Thyroid problems?'

Peter Kay

A 20-stone woman with buckling ankles smelt as if something had died in her creases.

A.A. Gill

On the charts of obese patients, doctors in hospitals write the code 'DTS' which stands for 'Danger to Shipping.'

Doctor Phil Hammond

But if you were in a hot-air balloon with Adolf Hitler and Winston Churchill and you were losing altitude, which one would you throw out?

Harry Hill

You know you're getting fat when you can pinch an inch on your forehead.

John Mendoza

Oh, loneliness and cheeseburgers are a deadly combination.

Phil Harrison

I'm anorexic really. Anorexic people look in the mirror and think they look fat. And so do I.

Jo Brand

I asked the sales assistant in the clothing store if she had anything to make me look thinner, and she said, 'How about a week in Ethiopia?'

Roseanne

Roseanne, is there anything you wish you hadn't eaten?

Dame Edna Everage

I'm fat and proud of it. If someone asks me how my diet is going, I say, 'Fine, how was your lobotomy?'

Roseanne

I'm not fat. I'm festively plump.

Eric Cartman

Fat people are brilliant in bed. If I'm sitting on top of you, are you going to argue?

Jo Brand

I wear a thong. You may not be able to see it, but I can wear it.

Jo Brand

He lived on a diet of fingernails and coffee.

May Livingstone

Pavarotti is very difficult to pass at the net in tennis with or without a racquet.

Peter Ustinov

—I know there's a thin person inside me trying to get out.
—Just the one, dear?

Edina Monsoon and Gran, *Absolutely Fabulous*

From the day on which she weighs 140 pounds, the chief excitement of a woman's life consists in spotting women who are fatter than she is.

Helen Rowland

I want to get as thin as my first husband's promises.

Texas Guinan

Those magazine dieting stories always have the testimonial of a woman who wears a dress that could slipcover New Jersey in one photo and thirty days later looks like a well-dressed thermometer.

Erma Bombeck

—If you want to lose weight, all you've got to do is eat less and take a bit of exercise.
—Sweetie, if it was *that* easy, everybody would be doing it.

Saffy and Edina Monsoon, *Absolutely Fabulous*

What would be easier? Losing 40 pounds by strict dieting and exercise or gaining 60 pounds to qualify for a gastric bypass?

Nancy Casurella

I don't know what all this fuss is about weight. My wife lost two stones swimming last year. I don't know how. I tied them round her neck tight enough.

Les Dawson

I want to lose ten pounds. I just don't know if I should start power-walking or smoking.

Lisa Goich

—Just look at that woman. She's practically a skeleton.
—Oh, Truman, that's Anorexia Nervosa.
—Oh, dahling, you know *everyone*.

Truman Capote and friend

I'm on a whisky diet. I've lost three days already.

Tommy Cooper

Backstage at the Fashion Awards, the models were so nervous they were keeping their food down.

Jack Dee

I've decided that perhaps I'm bulimic and just keep forgetting to purge.

Paula Poundstone

I went to a conference for bulimics and anorexics. It was a nightmare. The bulimics ate the anorexics. But it was okay, because they were back again in ten minutes.

Monica Piper

I don't diet. I just don't eat as much as I'd like to.

Linda Evangelista

Perfectly healthy people are working themselves into a passion over their weight. Anyone would think Saint Peter stands at the Pearly Gates with a tape measure.

Ann Widdecombe

Jimi Hendrix, deceased, drugs; Janis Joplin, deceased, alcohol; Mama Cass, deceased, ham sandwich.

Austin Powers

I'm a light eater. As soon as it's light, I start eating.

Henny Youngman

After *One Flew Over the Cuckoo's Nest*, people think the psychiatric ward is where an evil and sadistic person humiliates depressed people. This is actually a far more accurate description of Weight Watchers.

Jo Brand

Liquid diets: the powder is mixed with water and tastes exactly like powder mixed with water.

Art Buchwald

I've been on the Slim-Fast diet. For breakfast, you have a shake. For lunch, you have a shake. For dinner, you kill anyone with food on their plate.

Rosie O'Donnell

You know why fish are so thin? They eat fish.

Jerry Seinfeld

A great many people in Los Angeles are on strict diets that restrict their intake of synthetic foods. The reason for this is the belief that organically grown fruit and vegetables make the cocaine work faster.   **Fran Lebowitz**

I know you're on the Atkins Diet, but could you stop eating bacon during sex?   **David Letterman**

Food that contains no calories: frozen food; food you eat standing up; food licked off knives and spoons; late night snacks.   **Lewis Grizzard**

It is a scientific fact that your body will not absorb cholesterol if you take it from another person's plate.   **Dave Barry**

I've been on this vegetarian diet for three weeks now, and never have my houseplants looked so good to me.   **Daniel Lybra**

I'm on this great diet. You're allowed to eat anything you want, but you must eat it with naked fat people.   **Ed Bluestone**

Since I don't have access to the White House pastry chef any more, it's done wonders for my figure.   **Bill Clinton**

Marlon Brando has lost 83 pounds. It was about time he lost weight – he was being followed by poachers.   **David Letterman**

She's very bitter. She lost all that weight and turns out, she doesn't have a pretty face after all.   **Mindy Kovac**

Nothing in the world arouses more false hopes than the first four hours of a diet.

Nora Ephron

I'm on this amazing new diet. You can eat whatever you want, whenever you want, and as much as you want. You don't lose any weight, but it's very easy to stick to.   **George Tricker**

I don't have a beer belly. It's a Burgundy belly and it cost me a lot of money.   Charles Clarke

I'm on a seafood diet. I see food and I eat it.   Les Dawson

I feel about diets the way I feel about airplanes. They're wonderful things for other people to go on.   Jean Kerr

You know you're on a diet when cat food commercials make you hungry.

Andy Bumatai

She used to diet on any kind of food she could lay her hands on. Arthur Baer

I've been on a constant diet for the last two decades. I've lost a total of 789 pounds. By all accounts, I should be hanging from a charm bracelet.
Erma Bombeck

He's lost six pounds. Mind you, that's like throwing a deckchair off the *Queen Mary*.   Bill Parcells

No matter what diet you are on, you can usually eat as much as you want of anything you don't like.   Walter Slezak

The lunches of 57 years had caused his chest to slip down to the mezzanine level.   P.G. Wodehouse

I'm on a new diet – Viagra and prune juice. I don't know if I'm coming or going.   Rodney Dangerfield

In California, they think fat is something you can catch.   Roseanne

There's only one way to look thin – hang out with fat people.   Roseanne

I am on two diets at the moment because you simply don't get enough to eat on one.   Jo Brand

I haven't lost my hourglass figure but it looks like someone poured about 90 minutes of extra sand into it. **Dorothy Zbornak, *The Golden Girls***

My doctor has advised me to give up those intimate little dinners for four. Unless there are three people eating with me. **Orson Welles**

Outside every thin woman is a fat man trying to get in. **Katherine Whitehorn**

Look! I'm using the original notches that came with my belt.
Homer Simpson

I'm on a great diet. You drink beer, you get drunk, you pass out, you don't eat for two days. **Drew Carey**

A gourmet who thinks of calories is like a tart who looks at her watch.
James Beard

Part of the secret of success in life is to eat what you like and let the food fight it out inside. **Mark Twain**

Remember, there were people on the *Titanic* who turned down the sweet trolley. **Jonathan Ross**

Nobody's last words have ever been, 'I wish I'd eaten more rice cakes.'
Amy Krouse Rosenthal

EXERCISE

I paid four hundred bucks to join a health club last year. Haven't lost a pound. Apparently, you have to show up. **Rich Ceisler**

My favourite health club is the International House of Pancakes, because no matter what you weigh, there will always be someone who weighs 150 pounds more than you. **Lewis Black**

Do I lift weights? Sure. Every time I stand up. **Dolly Parton**

As a nation, we are dedicated to keeping physically fit – and parking as close to the stadium as possible.
Bill Vaughan

I'm Jewish. I don't work out. If God wanted us to bend over he'd put diamonds on the floor.
Joan Rivers

My favourite exercise is walking a block and a half to buy fudge. Then I call a cab to get me home. There's never a need to overdo anything.
Ellen DeGeneres

I keep fit. Every morning, I do a hundred laps of an Olympic-sized swimming pool – in a small motor launch.
Peter Cook

Pump iron? Niles, you've never even pumped your own gas.
Frasier Crane, *Frasier*

If God wanted me to touch my toes, he would have put them on my knees.
Roseanne

Sure, I'll continue to work out – until I get married.
Tom Arnold

Married people don't need to exercise, because our attitude is, 'They've seen us naked already – and they like it.'
Carol Montgomery

My mother-in-law had to stop skipping for exercise. It registered seven on the Richter scale.
Les Dawson

I exercise every morning without fail. Up, down! Up, down! And then the other eyelid.
Anthony Hopkins

I often take exercise. Why only yesterday, I had breakfast in bed.
Oscar Wilde

My idea of exercise is a good brisk sit down.
Phyllis Diller

When purchasing exercise equipment, make sure it is of sturdy construction and that there is enough space to hang all your wet washing on it.

Jeff Green

I bought all those celebrity exercise videos. I love to sit and eat cookies and watch them.

Dolly Parton

My favourite machine at the gym is the vending machine.

Caroline Rhea

I get out of breath playing chess.

Billy Connolly

It takes six months to get in shape and two weeks to get out of shape. As soon as you know this, you can stop being angry about other things in life and only be angry about this.

Rita Rudner

I'm not into working out. My philosophy is no pain, no pain.

Carol Leifer

You can overdo the work-outs. If your neck is as wide as your head, take a day off.

Margaret Smith

I like long walks, especially when they are taken by people who annoy me.

Fred Allen

Exercise? I tremble and shake for hours every morning.

W.C. Fields

The doctor asked me if I ever got breathless after exercise. I said no, never, because I never exercise.

John Mortimer

My grandmother started walking five miles a day when she was 60. She's 97 today and we don't know where the hell she is.

Ellen DeGeneres

The only reason I would take up jogging is so I could hear heavy breathing again.

Erma Bombeck

The first time I see a jogger smiling, I'll consider it. **Joan Rivers**

Jogging is very beneficial. It makes the ground feel needed. **Charles M. Schulz**

Go jogging? What, and get hit by a meteor? **Robert Benchley**

I go running when I have to. When the ice cream van is doing 60.
Wendy Liebman

Fun Run – now there's an oxymoron. **Joe Bennett**

There are only two types of exercise in Hollywood – jogging and
helping a divorced friend move. **Robert Wagner**

I take my only exercise acting as pallbearer at the funerals of my
friends who exercise regularly. **Mark Twain**

The word 'aerobics' came about when the gym instructors all got
together and said, 'If we're going to charge ten dollars an hour, we
can't call it 'jumping up and down'. **Rita Rudner**

I am pushing 60. That is enough exercise for me. **Mark Twain**

No gentleman ever takes exercise. **Oscar Wilde**

Eat Right, Exercise, Die Anyway. **Slogan on T-shirt**

SLEEP

Sleep is death without the long-term commitment. **Lea Krinksky**

I love sleep because it is both pleasant and safe to use. **Fran Lebowitz**

I go to bed early. My favourite dream comes on at nine. **Eddie Izzard**

If I'm not in bed by 11 at night, I go home. **Henny Youngman**

Last night I fell asleep in a satellite dish. My dreams were showing up on televisions all over the world.   Steven Wright

If your husband has difficulty in getting to sleep, the words, 'We need to talk about our relationship' may help.

Rita Rudner

I had a dream I was trapped in an elevator with Peter André, Geri Halliwell, and Bryan McFadden. And I had a gun with only one bullet.

Mark Lamarr

Did anyone ever have a boring dream?   Ralph Hodgson

People who say they sleep like a baby usually don't have one. Leo J. Burke

I have a feeling there's a correlation between getting up in the morning and getting up in the world.   Milton Berle

The amount of sleep required by the average person is about five minutes more.   Max Kauffmann

Many are called but few get up.   Oliver Herford

I need eight hours' sleep a day. And ten hours at night.   Bill Hicks

Early to bed and early to rise probably indicates unskilled labour.

John Ciardi

No civilized person ever goes to bed the same day he gets up.

Richard Davis

If you want the world to beat a path to your door, just try to take a nap on a Saturday afternoon.   George Burns

If you've ever suffered from insomnia you'll know what a nightmare it is.

Yogi Berra

His insomnia was so bad, he couldn't sleep even during office hours.

Arthur Baer

Seven beers followed by two Scotches and a thimble of marijuana and it's funny how sleep comes all on its own.

David Sedaris

Laugh and the world laughs with you; snore and you sleep alone.

Anthony Burgess

Snore? I had to turn you away from the window so you wouldn't inhale the curtains.

Sophia Petrillo, *The Golden Girls*

I missed my nap today. Slept right through it.

Henny Youngman

Early to bed, early to rise, and you will meet very few prominent people.

George Ade

Sleep faster, we need the pillows.

Jewish proverb

A good cure for insomnia is to get plenty of sleep.

W.C. Fields

Last night I dreamed I ate a ten-pound marshmallow, and when I woke up the pillow was gone.

Tommy Cooper

No human being believes that any other human being has a right to be in bed when he himself is up.

Robert Lynd

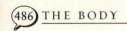

AGE

Every morning I get up, I read the obituary page. If my name's not
there, I shave.
George Burns

The older you get, the better you get – unless you're a banana.
Ross Noble

It's sad to grow old, but nice to ripen.
Brigitte Bardot

Thirty is a nice age for a woman. Especially if she happens to be forty.
Phyllis Diller

From birth to 18, a girl needs good parents. From 18 to 35, she needs
good looks. From 35 to 55, good personality. From 55 on, she needs
good cash.
Sophie Tucker

A woman telling her true age is like a buyer confiding his final price to
an Armenian rug dealer.
Mignon McLaughlin

Never trust a woman who tells you her real age. A woman who would
tell you that, would tell you anything.
Oscar Wilde

Life would be infinitely happier if we could only be born at the age
of 80 and gradually approach 18.
Mark Twain

One problem with growing older is that it gets increasingly tougher
to find a famous historical figure who didn't amount to much when
he was your age.
Bill Vaughan

—Age before beauty.
—Pearls before swine.
Clare Boothe Luce and Dorothy Parker

She said she was approaching 40 and I couldn't help wondering from
which direction.
Bob Hope

A woman is as old as she looks before breakfast.
Ed Howe

When a man has a birthday, he takes a day off. When a woman has a birthday, she takes at least three years off. **Joan Rivers**

There is still no cure for the common birthday. **John Glenn**

It is a sobering thought that when Mozart was my age he had been dead for two years. **Tom Lehrer**

American youth attributes much more importance to arriving at driver's licence age than at voting age. **Marshall McLuhan**

I'm 65 but if there were 15 months in every year, I'd only be 48. **James Thurber**

Big 3-0. It's the perfect age. You can date college girls *and* their mothers. **Stuart Bondek**

How old would you be if you didn't know how old you are? **Anon**

I'm so old, my blood type is discontinued. **Bill Dana**

I'm pleased to be here. Let's face it, at my age I'm very pleased to be anywhere. **George Burns**

I swear I'm ageing about as well as a beach-party movie. **Harvey Fierstein**

Here I sit, alone and 60, bald and fat and full of sin; cold the seat and loud the cistern, as I read the Harpic tin. **Alan Bennett**

You know you're getting old when you stoop to tie your shoes and wonder what else you can do while you're down there. **George Burns**

—I only hope I look as good as you do when I'm your age.
—You did. **Tallulah Bankhead and Bette Davis**

She may very well pass for 43 in the dusk with the light behind her. W.S. Gilbert

You know you're getting older when you have sex with someone half your age and it's legal.

Dan Savage

I don't feel 80. In fact I don't feel anything until noon, then it's time for my nap.

Bob Hope

I don't want to live to be 100. I don't think I could stand to see bell bottom trousers three times.

Jeff Foxworthy

In Los Angeles, people don't get older, they just get tighter.

Greg Proops

I can't believe I'm thirty. Do you know how much that is in gay years?

Jack McFarland, *Will and Grace*

I said to my husband, my boobs have gone, my stomach's gone, say something nice about my legs. He said, 'Blue goes with everything.'

Joan Rivers

I found my first grey hair today. On my chest.

Wendy Liebman

The secret of my youthful appearance is simple – mashed swede. As a face mask, as a night cap, and in an emergency, as a draught excluder.

Victoria Wood

—You know what the worst part about getting old is?
—Your face?

Blanche Deveraux and Dorothy Zbornak

I'm not really wrinkled. I just took a nap on a chenille bedspread.

Phyllis Diller

If you want to know how old a woman is, ask her sister-in-law.

Ed Howe

It's great to have grey hair. Ask anyone who's bald.

Rodney Dangerfield

Wrinkle cream doesn't work. I've been using it for two years and my balls still look like raisins.

Harland Williams

Men in their forties are like the *New York Times* Sunday crossword puzzle – tricky, complicated, and you're never really sure you got the right answer.
Samantha Jones, *Sex and the City*

When I looked at the wrinkled skin on W.H. Auden's face, I kept wondering, what must his balls look like?
David Hockney

Take my photograph? You might as well use a picture of a relief map of Ireland!
Nancy Astor

—How did your meeting with the movie producer go?
—Terrific. He said I have the eyes of a 12-year-old, the complexion of a 20-year-old, and the legs of a 25-year-old.
—What about your 60-year-old cunt?
—You were never mentioned.
Ernest Borgnine and Ethel Merman, husband and wife

How foolish to think that one can ever slam the door in the face of age. Much wiser to be polite and gracious and ask him to lunch in advance.
Noël Coward

Age is something that doesn't matter unless you are a cheese. **Billie Burke**

Is not old wine wholesomest, old pippins toothsomest, old wood burns brightest, old linen wash whitest, and old lovers soundest? **John Webster**

There are people who are beautiful in dilapidation, like houses that were hideous when new.
Logan Pearsall Smith

Like all good ruins, I look better by moonlight. **Phyllis Diller**

Mick Jagger told me the wrinkles on his face were laughter lines but nothing is that funny.
George Melly

—How old Cary Grant?
—Cary Grant fine. How you?
Cary Grant

A man is only as old as the women he feels. **Groucho Marx**

After forty, a woman has to choose between losing her figure or her face. My advice is to keep your face, and stay sitting down.   Barbara Cartland

I recently turned sixty. Practically a third of my life is over.   Woody Allen

It's official. I'm middle-aged. I don't need drugs any more. I can get the same effect just by standing up real fast.   Jonathan Katz

Middle age is when your age starts to show around your middle.   Bob Hope

I'm too old for a paper round, too young for social security and too tired for an affair.   Erma Bombeck

First, you forget names, then you forget faces. Next, you forget to pull your zipper up and finally you forget to pull it down.   George Burns

You know you're old when your family talk about you in front of you. What are we going to do with Pop? We have company tonight.
Rodney Dangerfield

I knew I was getting older when I was in Marks and Spencer's, saw a pair of Doctor Scholl's and thought, hmm, they look comfy.   Victoria Wood

My grandmother's 85 and starting to get forgetful. The family's upset about it but I don't mind because I get eight cheques on my birthday from her. That's forty bucks.   Tom Arnold

We've all seen them, on the street corners, many of them smoking, many of them on drugs; they've got no jobs to go to, and once a week we see them queuing for the state hand-outs – or pensions, as we call them.
Harry Hill

If you are allowed to smack children you should be allowed to smack old people as well, because they are just as much of a nuisance as children, if not more.   Jack Dee

If you live to be 90 in England and can still eat a boiled egg, they think you deserve the Nobel Prize.

Alan Bennett

I was introduced to a beautiful young lady as a man in his nineties. *Early* nineties, I insisted.

George Burns

When I turn my hearing aid up to ten, I can hear a canary break wind six miles away.

Sophia Petrillo, *The Golden Girls*

You can live to be 100 if you give up all the things that make you want to live to be 100.

Woody Allen

There's one more terrifying thing about old people: I'm going to be one soon.

P.J. O'Rourke

—To what do you attribute your long life?
—To the fact that I haven't died yet.

Sir Malcolm Sargent

There's one advantage to being 102. No peer pressure.

Dennis Wolfberg

—Who wants to be 95?
—94-year-olds.

George Burns

If I marry again at my age, I'll go on honeymoon to Viagra Falls.

George Burns

To what do I attribute my longevity? Bad luck mostly.

Billy Wilder

There are three stages of man: he believes in Santa Claus; he does not believe in Santa Claus; he is Santa Claus.

Bob Phillips

As a lady of a certain age, I am willing to let the photographers and their zoom lenses stay, but only if they use their Joan Collins lens on me for close-ups.

Kay Ullrich

I've never known a person who lives to 110 who is remarkable for anything else.
Josh Billings

If I'd known I was going to live this long, I'd have taken better care of myself.
Adolph Zukor

As a young man, I used to have four supple members and one stiff one. Now I have four stiff and one supple.
Henri Duc D'Aumale

Old age isn't so bad when you consider the alternative.   **Maurice Chevalier**

My grandmother is over 80 and still doesn't need glasses. Drinks right out of the bottle.
Henny Youngman

Anyone can get old. All you have to do is to live long enough.
Groucho Marx

Middle age is when you are sitting at home on a Saturday night and the telephone rings and you hope it isn't for you.
Ogden Nash

Whatever a man's age may be, he can reduce it by several years by putting a bright-coloured flower in his buttonhole.
Mark Twain

Whenever your friends compliment you about looking young, you may be sure that they think you are growing old.
Washington Irving

Growing old is like being increasingly penalized for a crime you haven't committed.
Anthony Powell

To me, old age is always 15 years older than I am.
Bernard Baruch

Maturity is a high price to pay for growing up.
Maurice Chevalier

Exactly how old is Joan Collins? We need an expert. Someone who reads the rings on trees.

Ruby Wax

My sister, Jackie, is younger than me. We don't know quite by how much.

Joan Collins

As a graduate of the Zsa Zsa Gabor School of Creative Mathematics, I honestly do not know how old I am.

Erma Bombeck

I refuse to admit that I'm more than 52, even if that does make my sons illegitimate.

Nancy Astor

To be young, really young, takes a very long time.

Pablo Picasso

The old believe everything; the middle-aged suspect everything; the young know everything.

Oscar Wilde

There are three ages of man: youth, middle age, and 'you're looking well'.

Red Skelton

Like the pro said, it's not the work, it's the stairs.

Elaine Stritch

I'm at the age where my back goes out more than I do.

Phyllis Diller

One of the delights known to age and beyond the grasp of youth is that of Not Going.

J.B. Priestley

Old age is like waiting in the departure lounge of life. Fortunately, we are in England and the train is bound to be late.

Milton Shulman

I attribute my long and healthy life to the fact that I never touched a cigarette, a drink, or a girl until I was ten years old.

George Moore

An archaeologist is the best husband a woman can have; the older she gets, the more interested he is in her.

Agatha Christie

The Grateful Dead are like bad architecture or an old whore. Stick around long enough and you eventually get respectable.

Jerry Garcia

To get back my youth I would do anything in the world, except take exercise, get up early, or be respectable.

Oscar Wilde

The years that a woman subtracts from her age are not lost. They are added to the ages of other women.

Diane de Poitiers

At my age, flowers scare me.

George Burns

—What is the secret of your long life?
—Keep breathing.

Sophie Tucker

What would I appreciate getting for my 87th birthday? A paternity suit.

George Burns

I knew I was getting old when the Pope started looking young.

Billy Wilder

Growing old is compulsory. Growing up is optional.

Bob Monkhouse

The secret of staying young is to live honestly, eat slowly and lie about your age.

Lucille Ball

DEATH AND DYING

Either this man is dead or my watch has stopped.

Groucho Marx

What's death like? It's as bad as the chicken at Tresky's Restaurant.

Woody Allen

Death: to stop sinning suddenly.

Elbert Hubbard

Death is a low chemical trick played on everybody except sequoia trees.

J.J. Furnas

I bought a cemetery plot. The guy said, 'There goes the neighbourhood!'

Rodney Dangerfield

Death is like the rumble of distant thunder at a picnic.　　　**W.H. Auden**

What do I dislike about death? Probably the hours.　　　**Woody Allen**

In the past year, over 800,000 million people have died. Despite
millions of dollars of research, death continues to be our nation's
number one killer.　　　**Henry Gibson**

There are worse things in life than death. Think of death as cutting
down on your expenses.　　　**Woody Allen**

I went into the undertaker's, lay out across the counter and shouted,
'Shop!'　　　**Spike Milligan**

The French duke, while on the tumbrel, was seen to be reading a book.
Arriving at the steps of the guillotine, he turned down the corner of his
text, and took the steps to the Great Library in the Sky.　　　**George Steiner**

Death is very sophisticated. It's like a Noël Coward comedy. You light
a cigarette and wait for it in the library.　　　**Theadora Van Runkle**

I'm terrified of dying in a plane crash. I hate the thought that peanuts
would be my last meal.　　　**Tanya Luckerath**

If I die before my cat, I want some of my ashes put in his food so I can
live on inside him.　　　**Drew Barrymore**

Our gardener passed away. He had a heart attack when he was out
trimming the elaborate hedge maze. The paramedics never stood a
chance.　　　**Niles Crane,** *Frasier*

The inventor of Crest passed away. Four out of five dentists came to
the funeral.　　　**Jay Leno**

If you die in an elevator, be sure to push the Up button.　　　**Sam Levenson**

My brother-in-law died. He was a karate expert, then he joined the
army. The first time he saluted, he killed himself.　　　**Henny Youngman**

It was confusion of ideas between him and one of the lions he was hunting in Kenya that had caused A.B. Spottsworth to make the obituary column. He thought the lion was dead, and the lion thought it wasn't.

P.G. Wodehouse

Drug kingpin, Amado Carrillo Fuentes, has died from nine hours of liposuction and plastic surgery or, as it's known in Beverly Hills, natural causes.

Bill Maher

When I die, I want it to be on my 100th birthday, in my beach house on Maui, and I want my husband to be so upset he has to drop out of college.

Roz Doyle, *Frasier*

How did Captain Hook die? He wiped with the wrong hand.

Tommy Sledge

The man who invented the hokey-cokey has died. His funeral was a strange affair. First, they put his left leg in...

Al Ferrera

In case my life should end with cannibals, I hope they will write on my tombstone: 'We have eaten Dr Schweitzer. He was good to the end.'

Albert Schweitzer

My auntie used to say, 'What you can't see can't hurt you.' She died of radiation poisoning a few months back.

Harry Hill

My cousin died. He was stung by a wasp – the natural enemy of the tightrope walker.

Emo Philips

My uncle was a circus clown, and when he died, all his friends went to the funeral in one car.

Steven Wright

A natural death is where you die without the aid of a doctor.

Mark Twain

No man goes before his time. Unless the boss leaves early.

Bob Hope

When the Earl of Sandwich died they buried him in between two
other guys.
David Corrado

I want to die with a smile on my face.
Hopefully, it won't be mine.
Matt Vance

Suppose he hadn't been dressed as a peanut. Would his death still
be funny?
Mary Slaughter, *Rhoda*

I want to die peacefully in my sleep like my father, not screaming in
terror like his passengers.
Bob Monkhouse

—My uncle fell through a trap door and broke his neck.
—Was he building a house?
—No, they were hanging him.
Stan Laurel and Oliver Hardy

Reports of my death are greatly exaggerated.
Mark Twain

The first sign of his approaching end was when one of my old
aunts, when undressing him, removed a toe with one of his socks.
Graham Greene

It is impossible to experience one's death objectively and still carry a tune.
Woody Allen

Self-decapitation is an extremely difficult, not to say dangerous thing
to attempt.
W.S. Gilbert

I don't mind dying. Trouble is, you feel so bloody stiff the next day.
George Axelrod

I contemplated suicide again – this time by inhaling next to an
insurance salesman.
Woody Allen

Our ice cream man was found lying on the floor of his van covered in
hundreds and thousands. Police say he topped himself.
Tommy Cooper

—I predict that you will die either by hanging or of some vile disease.
—That all depends upon whether I embrace your principles or your
mistress.   **William Gladstone and Benjamin Disraeli**

On the plus side, death is one of the few things that can be done as easily lying down.

Woody Allen

Suicide is man's way of telling God, 'You can't fire me. I quit.'

Bill Maher

I tried to hang myself with a bungee cord. I kept almost dying.

Steven Wright

How would I kill myself? With kindness.   **George S. Kaufman**

Guns are always the best method for private suicide. Drugs are too
chancy. You might miscalculate the dosage and just wind up having a
good time.   **P.J. O'Rourke**

Death is nature's way of telling you to slow down.   **Anon**

Soap-on-a-rope – for those times you're in the shower, and want to
hang yourself.   **Jerry Seinfeld**

Razors pain you; rivers are damp; acids stain you; and drugs cause
cramp. Guns aren't lawful; nooses give; gas smells awful; you might
as well live.   **Dorothy Parker**

Life is a great surprise; I do not see why death should not be an even
greater one.   **Vladimir Nabokov**

I bequeath my entire estate to my wife on condition that she marries
again. That will ensure there will be at least one man who will regret
my death.   **Heinrich Heine**

I don't mind dying. I just don't want to be there when it happens.

Spike Milligan

—When we die, certain things keep growing – fingernails, toenails, the hair on your head, the hair on your chest...
—Not the hair on *my* chest!
—My dear, you give up hope too easily.   Lawrence Olivier and Edith Evans

For three days after death, hair and fingernails continue to grow but phone calls taper off.

Johnny Carson

In this world, nothing is certain, except death and taxes.

Benjamin Franklin

I owe much; I have nothing; the rest I leave to the poor.   François Rabelais

Elvis Presley has died. Good career move.   Music industry executive

When I die, I want to decompose in a barrel of porter and have it served in all the pubs in Dublin.

J.P. Donleavy

Drown in a vat of liquor? Death where is thy sting?   W.C. Fields

You will find my last words in the blue folder on my desk.

Max Beerbohm

Only the young die good.   Oliver Herford

You live and learn. Then you die and forget it all.   Noël Coward

Once you're dead, you're made for life.   Jimi Hendrix

Never say you know a person until you have divided an inheritance with them.

Johann Lavater

For Catholics, death is a promotion.   Bob Fosse

There are worse things in life than death. Have you ever spent an
evening with an insurance salesman?   Woody Allen

—What's it feel like to be dead for 200 years?
—Like spending a weekend in Beverly Hills.   Woody Allen

I'll always remember the last words of my grandfather, 'A truck!'
                                                                 Emo Philips

Do you wish to be remembered? Leave a lot of debts.   Elbert Hubbard

The trouble with quotes about death is that 99.99 percent of them are
made by people who are still alive.   Joshua Burns

FUNERAL

He was a great patriot, a humanitarian, a loyal friend – provided of
course he really is dead.   Voltaire

One of the crying needs of the time is for a suitable Burial Service for
the admittedly damned.   H.L. Mencken

The last funeral I went to had people in the front pew that I wouldn't
have to my funeral over my dead body.   Spike Milligan

If you don't go to other men's funerals, they won't go to yours.
                                                                 Clarence Day

I'm just not someone who cries. It's not in my nature. When my
wife's uncle died, I had to shut my hand in the car door just to make
a decent showing at the funeral.   Niles Crane, *Frasier*

Funferalls.   James Joyce

There's nothing like a morning funeral for sharpening the appetite
for lunch.
                                                              Arthur Marshall

Memorial services are the cocktail parties of the geriatric set.
                                                              John Gielgud

I used to hate weddings – all those old dears poking me in the
stomach and saying, 'You're next.' But they stopped all that when
I started doing the same to them at funerals.
                                                              Gail Flynn

They say such lovely things about people at their funerals, it's a shame
I'm going to miss mine by just a few days.
                                                              Bob Monkhouse

The reason so many people showed up at Louis B. Mayer's funeral was
because they wanted to make sure he was dead.
                                                              Samuel Goldwyn

Did you see the crowds at Harry Cohn's funeral? It proves what they
always say: give the public what they want to see, and they'll come
out for it.
                                                              Red Skelton

Where would I like my ashes scattered? I don't know. Surprise me.
                                                              Bob Hope

I told my wife I want to be cremated. She's planning a barbecue.
                                                              Rodney Dangerfield

I want to be buried in Kilbarrack. It's healthiest graveyard in Ireland
being near the sea.
                                                              Brendan Behan

I know a woman who had her husband cremated and then mixed
his ashes with grass and smoked him. She said it was the best
he'd made her feel in years.
                                                              Maureen Murphy

My husband, Norm, is no longer with us. I often go to the cemetery
and buff up his obelisk.
                                                              Dame Edna Everage

I hadn't been there since her poor husband's death. I never saw a
woman so altered; she looks quite 20 years younger.
                                                              Oscar Wilde

EPITAPH

If tombstones told the truth, everybody would wish to be buried at sea.

John W. Raper

May my husband rest in peace till I get there.   Dame Edna Everage

Once I wasn't
Then I was
Now I ain't again.   Cleveland, Ohio

Did you hear about my operation?   Jack Benny

I told you I was ill.   Spike Milligan

Epitaph for a boxer: You can stop counting, I'm not getting up.   Jim Watt

Epitaph for a character actor: At last I get top billing.   Wallace Ford

Here lies Ezekiel Aikle. Aged 102. The good die young.   Anon

Stiff at last.   Anon

Always under one sod or another.   Anon

Posterity will ne'er survey
A nobler grave than this:
Here lie the bones of Castlereagh:
Stop, traveller, and piss.   Lord Byron

An epitaph is a belated advertisement
for a line of goods that has been
permanently discontinued.   Irvin S. Cobb

A single sentence will suffice for modern man: he fornicated and read the papers.

Albert Camus

Here Lies Harry Secombe, until further notice.

Harry Secombe

I demand a second opinion.

Spike Milligan

What are you looking at?

Margaret Smith

Surrounded by fucking idiots.

Lindsay Anderson

Let's do lunch next week.

Raoul Lionel Felder

Over my dead body.

George S. Kaufman

All things considered, I'd rather be in Philadelphia.

W.C. Fields

Epitaph for a waiter: By and by, God caught his eye.

George S. Kaufman

Elvis – accept it.

Anon

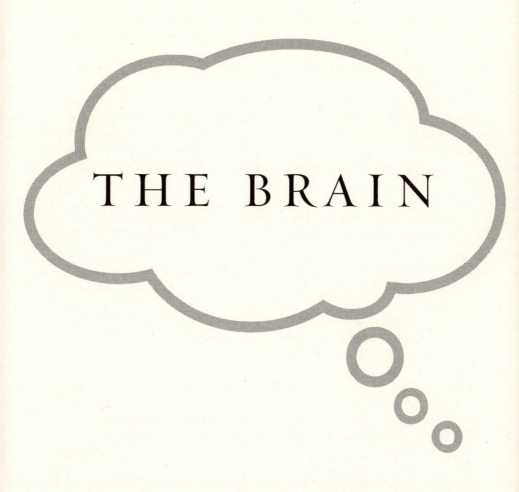

THE BRAIN

EDUCATION

I read Shakespeare and the Bible and I can shoot dice. That's what I
call a liberal education.   **Tallulah Bankhead**

Education is a method whereby one acquires a higher grade of prejudices.
                                                            Laurence J. Peter

With a thorough knowledge of the Bible, Shakespeare and Wisden you
cannot go far wrong.   **Arthur Waugh**

You can't expect a boy to be depraved until he has been to a good school.
                                                            Saki

Anyone who has been to an English public school will always feel
comparatively at home in prison.   **Evelyn Waugh**

Assistant masters came and went. Some liked little boys too little and
some too much.   **Evelyn Waugh**

You don't appreciate a lot of stuff in school until you get older. Little
things like being spanked every day by a middle-aged woman. You pay
good money for that in later life.   **Emo Philips**

Grammar schools are public schools without the sodomy.   **Tony Parsons**

I won't say ours was a tough school, but we had our own coroner.
We used to write essays like 'What I'm Going to be if I Grow up'.
                                                            Lenny Bruce

In our school, you were searched for guns and knives on the way in and
if you didn't have any, they gave you some.   **Emo Philips**

In high school, I was voted the person most likely to be a mental patient,
hillbilly or chimpanzee.   **Homer Simpson**

I trained at agricultural college. I got three BSEs.   **Jim Tavare**

My father wanted me to have all the educational opportunities he
never had, so he sent me to a girls' school.   Eric Morecambe

I had to go to Greek school, where I learned valuable lessons such as,
'If Nick has one goat and Nana has nine, how soon will they marry?'
                                                       Nia Vardalos

—So, what did you do in school today?
—I broke in my purple clogs.   Mel and Cher Horowitz, *Clueless*

If they ever come up with a swashbuckling school, I think one of the
courses should be Laughing, Then Jumping Off Something.   Jack Handey

If Thomas Edison went to business school, we would all be reading
by bigger candles.   Mark McCormack

Economists report that a college education adds many thousands of
dollars to a man's lifetime income – which he then spends sending his
son to college.   Bill Vaughan

I had the worst study habits in the history of college, until I found out
what I was doing wrong – highlighting with black magic marker.
                                                       Jeff Altman

I had a terrible education. I attended a school for emotionally disturbed
teachers.   Woody Allen

The schoolteacher is certainly underpaid as a childminder, but ludicrously
overpaid as an educator.   John Osborne

I owe a lot to my teachers and mean to pay them back some day.
                                                       Stephen Leacock

A teacher in a British school can be sacked for only two reasons: first,
gross immorality on the staff-room furniture and second and worse,
pinching the tea-things.   Isaac Asimov

Those who can, do. Those who cannot, teach.   George Bernard Shaw

When I was an inspector of schools I visited one classroom and looked at a boy's book. He'd written, 'Yesterday, Yesterday, Yesterday, Sorrow, Sorrow, Sorrow, Tomorrow, Tomorrow, Tomorrow, Love, Love, Love.' I said, 'That's a lovely poem.' He said, 'Those are my spelling corrections.'

Gervase Phinn

Those who can, do. Those who can't, teach. And those who can't teach, teach gym.

Sam Levenson

Those who can, do. Those who can't, teach. Those who can't teach, teach gym. And those who can't teach gym, become experts.

Roseanne

An expert is any lecturer from out of town, with slides.

Jim Baumgarten

An expert is a person who can take something you knew already and make it sound confusing.

Herbert Prochnow

Tony Blair puts two poems in a bus shelter and calls it a university.

Victoria Wood

At college, I majored in advanced fondling and minored in foreplay.

Woody Allen

Liberals have invented whole college majors – psychology, sociology, women's studies – to prove that nothing is anybody's fault.

P.J. O'Rourke

—I taught American Literature. Mostly contemporary. Last semester I taught Henry James.
—And was he a good student?

Peter de Vries

My lecturing method is simple: first I tell them what I am going to tell them; then I tell them; and then I tell them what I've told them.

Hilaire Belloc

A professor is someone who talks in someone else's sleep.

W.H. Auden

The average PhD thesis is nothing but the transference of bones from one graveyard to another.

Frank Dobie

Ooh, a graduate student huh? How come you guys can go to the moon but you can't make my shoes smell good?
                                                            Homer Simpson

We've all met people who are supposedly incredibly intelligent but don't know which way to sit on a lavatory.
                                                            Stephen Fry

I'd rather entrust the government of the United States to the first 400 people listed in the Boston telephone directory than to the faculty of Harvard University.
                                                            William F. Buckley

Common sense is not so common.
                                                            Voltaire

The advantage of a classical education is that it enables you to despise the wealth which it prevents you from achieving.
                                                            Russell Green

A plumber who has Latin is a better plumber than one who does not.
                                                            Enoch Powell

Lack of education is an extraordinary handicap when one is being offensive.
                                                            Josephine Tey

I performed badly in my Civil Service examinations because I evidently knew more about economics than my examiners.   John Maynard Keynes

I cheated in the final of my metaphysics examination. I looked into the soul of the boy sitting next to me.
                                                            Woody Allen

The only examination I ever passed was my cervical smear test.
                                                            Kathy Lette

I was thrown out of college for cheating – with the dean's wife.
                                                            Woody Allen

The world can never be considered educated until we spend as much on books as we do on chewing gum.
                                                            Josh Billings

What I have been taught, I have forgotten; what I know, I guessed.

Charles de Talleyrand

Everything I know I learned from Dostoevsky and the whores of New Orleans.

Matt Lincoln

I didn't have any education so I had to use my brains.

Bill Shankly

I owe my great learning to the fact that I have always kept an open book on my desk which I read whenever somebody on the phone says, 'One moment please.'

Helen Daley

The effects of youthful education are, like those of syphilis, never completely eradicated.

Robert Briffault

INTELLIGENCE

Got up. Shaved. Had breakfast. Did *The Times* crossword. Had another shave.

Arthur Smith

I wish I were a moron, he doesn't give a damn; I wish I were a moron: my God, perhaps I am.

Reginald Fairchild

An intelligence test sometimes shows a person how smart they would have been not to have taken it.

Laurence J. Peter

Why did I define 'pastern' as the 'knee' of a horse? Ignorance, madam, pure ignorance.

Samuel Johnson

You've got the brain of a four-year-old boy, and I bet he was glad to get rid of it.

Groucho Marx

He was so thick he couldn't tell which way a lift was going if he got two guesses.

Roy Chubby Brown

I'm not a complete idiot. Some parts are missing.

Emo Philips

His mother gives him a see-through lunchbox so he can tell whether he is on his way to work or on his way home.   Robert Klein

Until I met you, I didn't know that people actually talked back to their Rice Krispies.   Sophia Petrillo, *The Golden Girls*

Had his brain been constructed of silk, he would have been hard put to find sufficient material to make a canary a pair of cami-knickers.
                                    P.G. Wodehouse

How come dumb stuff seems so smart while you're doing it?
                                    Dennis the Menace

I was gratified to be able to answer promptly, and I did. I said I didn't know.   Mark Twain

What's the difference between an Essex girl and a supermarket trolley? A supermarket trolley has a mind of its own.   Ray Leigh

They say you only use ten per cent of your brain. What about the other ten per cent?   Lara Bliss

The average attention span is that of a ferret on a double espresso.
                                    Dennis Miller

The amount of noise that anyone can bear undisturbed stands in inverse proportion to his mental capacity.   Arthur Schopenhauer

He had one of those minds capable of accommodating but one thought at a time – if that.   P.G. Wodehouse

The bulk of mankind is as well qualified for flying as for thinking.
                                    Jonathan Swift

—How stupid can you get?
—How stupid do you want me?   Abbott and Costello

What luck for the rulers that men do not think.   Adolf Hitler

The dumber people think you are, the more surprised they are going
to be when you kill them.
William Clayton

—You know, Ollie, I was just thinking.
—About what?
—Nothing. I was just thinking.
Stan Laurel and Oliver Hardy

I've written a book. It's called, *How to Raise Your IQ by Eating Gifted
Children*.
Lewis B. Frumkes

A minute's thought would have shown him that it could not be true.
But a minute is a long time and thought is difficult.
A.E. Housman

No one has ever gone broke by underestimating the intelligence of the
great masses of the plain people.
H.L. Mencken

An intellectual is someone who has found something more interesting
to think about than sex.
W.H. Auden

A highbrow is anyone who can listen to the 'William Tell Overture'
and not think of The Lone Ranger.
Jack Perlis

Jonathan Miller is too clever by three-quarters.
Anon

Between me and Rudyard Kipling, we cover all knowledge; he knows
all that can be known, and I know the rest.
Mark Twain

What's all our knowledge worth? We don't even know what the weather
will be tomorrow.
Berthold Auerbach

I have come to the conclusion that a good reliable set of bowels is worth
more to a man than any quantity of brains.
Josh Billings

Few people think more than two or three times a year; I have made an
international reputation for myself by thinking once or twice a week.
George Bernard Shaw

GENIUS

—I'm a genius, but I'm a misunderstood genius.
—What's misunderstood about you?
—Nobody thinks I'm a genius. **Calvin and Hobbes**

Every family should have at least three children. Then, if one of them turns out to be a genius, the other two can support him. **George Coote**

In every work of genius, we recognize our own rejected thoughts. **Ralph Waldo Emerson**

A genius is a man who can rewrap a new shirt and not have any pins left over. **Dino Levi**

Some people come by the name of genius in the same way as an insect comes by the name of centipede – not because it has a hundred feet, but because most people can't count above fourteen. **Georg Christoph Lichtenberg**

The public is wonderfully tolerant. It forgives everything except genius. **Oscar Wilde**

I cannot tell if genius is hereditary because heaven has granted me no offspring. **James McNeill Whistler**

PHILOSOPHY

Boxing got me started on philosophy. You bash them, they bash you and you think, what's it all for? **Arthur Mullard**

What if everything is an illusion and nothing exists? In that case, I definitely overpaid on my carpet. **Woody Allen**

Philosophy is to the real world as masturbation is to sex. **Karl Marx**

I'm astounded by people who want to 'know' the universe when it's
hard enough to find your way around Chinatown.   Woody Allen

A philosopher is a blind man in a dark cellar at midnight looking for
a black cat that isn't there. He is distinguished from a theologian, in
that the theologian finds the cat.   Anon

Almost everyone who didn't know what to do at university did
philosophy. Well, that's logical.   Tom Stoppard

I'm a philosophy major, which means I can think deep thoughts about
being unemployed.   Bruce Lee

Hegel set out his philosophy with so much obscurity that people
thought it must be profound.   Bertrand Russell

'If you want the rainbow, you gotta put up with the rain.' Do you
know which philosopher said that? Dolly Parton. And people say
she's just a big pair of tits.   David Brent, *The Office*

Like so many contemporary philosophers, he especially enjoyed giving
helpful advice to people who were happier than he was.   Tom Lehrer

Existentialism means that no one else can take a bath for you.
                                                         Delmore Shwartz

Frisbeetarianism is the philosophy that when you die, your soul goes
up on a roof and gets stuck there.   George Carlin

There is no opinion so absurd that some philosopher will not express it.

Cicero

When he who hears doesn't know what he who speaks means, and when
he who speaks doesn't know what he himself means – that is philosophy.

Voltaire

Is it weird in here, or is it just me?   Steven Wright

I was once walking through the forest alone, and a tree fell right in front of me, and I didn't hear it.   Steven Wright

Nothing worth knowing can be understood with the mind.   Woody Allen

Philosophers before Kant had a tremendous advantage over philosophers after Kant in that they didn't have to waste time studying Kant.
                    Bertrand Russell

I have a simple philosophy: fill what's empty. Empty what's full. And scratch where it itches.   Alice Roosevelt

Change is inevitable, except from a vending machine.   Anon

'I think, therefore I am' is the statement of an intellectual who underrates toothaches.   Milan Kundera

I am an old man and have known a great many troubles, but most of them never happened.   Mark Twain

Everything happens to everybody sooner or later if there is time enough.
                    George Bernard Shaw

I have a new philosophy. I'm going to dread one day at a time.
                    Charles M. Schulz

I have come to the conclusion, after many years of sometimes sad experience, that you cannot come to any conclusion at all.
                    Vita Sackville-West

You know how it is when you're walking up the stairs, and you get to the top, and you think there's one more step? I'm like that all the time.
                    Steven Wright

One lives and learns, doesn't one? That is certainly one of the more prevalent delusions.   George Bernard Shaw

We are all in the gutter, but some of us are looking at the stars.

Oscar Wilde

To do is to be – Rousseau
To be is to do – Sartre
Dobedobedo – Sinatra

Anon

Reality may not be the best of all possible worlds but it's still the only place where you can get a decent steak.

Woody Allen

Reality is a collective hunch.

Lily Tomlin

Reality is something you rise above.

Liza Minnelli

I get into bed, turn out the light, say, 'Bugger the lot of them,' and go to sleep.

Winston Churchill

TRUTH AND LIES

The young man turned to him with a disarming candour, which instantly put him on this guard.

Saki

Something unpleasant is coming when men are anxious to tell the truth.

Benjamin Disraeli

I'm frank, brutally frank. And even when I'm not frank, I look frank.

Lord Thomson of Fleet

The truth hurts – maybe not as much as jumping on a bike with the seat missing.

Lt Frank Drebin, *Naked Gun 2½*

'Hello,' he lied.

Miles Rhodes

He lies like a cheap carpet.

Anon

Truth is the most valuable commodity – let us economize.

Mark Twain

A lie is a very poor substitute for the truth, but the only one known to date.   **Ambrose Bierce**

A man had rather have a hundred lies told of him, than one truth which he does not wish should be told.   **Samuel Johnson**

The broad mass of a nation will more easily fall victim to a big lie than to a small one.   **Adolf Hitler**

I took a lie detector test the other day. No I didn't.   **Steven Wright**

Never lie when the truth is more profitable.   **Stanislaw J. Lec**

There are two kinds of truth – the real truth and the made-up truth.
                                         Marion Barry, Mayor of Washington

When there are two versions of a story, the wisest course is to believe the one in which people appear at their worst.   **H. Allen Smith**

Everybody has a little bit of Watergate in him.   **Billy Grahame**

The things one feels absolutely certain about are never true.   **Oscar Wilde**

There is one way to find out if a man is honest – ask him. If he says 'yes', you know he is crooked.   **Groucho Marx**

The word liberty in the mouth of Mr Webster sounds like the word love in the mouth of a courtesan.   **Ralph Waldo Emerson**

I never know how much of what I say is true.   **Bette Midler**

There are three kinds of lies: lies, damned lies, and statistics.
                                                          Benjamin Disraeli

There are three kinds of liars: liars, damned liars, and politicians.
                                                               Will Rogers

You can always tell when he's lying. His lips move.   **Anon**

People never lie so much as after a hunt, during a war, or before an election.
Otto von Bismarck

This is a Washington, D.C., kind of lie. It's when the other person knows you're lying and also knows you know he knows.
John Sergeant

I was brought up in a clergyman's household, so I am a first-class liar.
Sybil Thorndyke

All those ladies who stuck their eggs on with chewing gum at the church picnic are asked to consult the bulletin for confessional times.
Church notice

Honesty is the best policy, but insanity is a better defence.
Steve Landesberg

A lie can be halfway round the world before the truth has got its boots on.
Winston Churchill

It is always the best policy to speak the truth, unless of course you are an exceptionally good liar. Jerome K. Jerome

We are inclined to believe those whom we do not know because they have never deceived us.
Samuel Johnson

Once in a while you will stumble upon the truth but most of us manage to pick ourselves up and hurry along as if nothing had happened.
Winston Churchill

A little inaccuracy sometimes saves a world of explanation.
Saki

There is nothing about which men lie so much as about their sexual powers. In this at least every man is, what in his heart he would like to be, a Casanova.
Somerset Maugham

It's not a lie if you believe it.   George Costanza, *Seinfeld*

The only form of lying that is absolutely beyond reproach is lying for its own sake.   Oscar Wilde

Several excuses are always less convincing than one.   Aldous Huxley

If you want to be thought a liar, always tell the truth.   Logan Pearsall Smith

I have too much respect for the truth to drag it out on every trifling occasion.   Mark Twain

If one tells the truth, one is sure, sooner or later, to be found out.
                                                        Oscar Wilde

There's a perfectly good explanation for this, which I'll make up later.
                                                        Mel Brooks

If you tell the truth, you don't have to remember what you said.
                                                        Mark Twain

A lie is an abomination unto the Lord and a very present help in time of trouble.   Adlai Stevenson

I told you a million times, don't exaggerate.   Rik Mayall

It is hard to believe that a man is telling the truth when you know that you would lie if you were in his place.   H.L. Mencken

I always wanted to be the last guy on earth, just to see if any of those women were lying to me.   Ronnie Shakes

THE MIND

MADNESS AND THERAPY

We are all born mad. Some remain so.   **Samuel Beckett**

Madness takes its toll. Please have exact change.   **Anon**

He has turned his life around. He used to be depressed and miserable.
Now he's miserable and depressed.   **John McClenahan**

I didn't have a nervous breakdown. I was clinically fed up for two years.
                    Alan Partridge

Normal is just a cycle on the washing machine.   **Whoopi Goldberg**

Insanity is just a state of mind.   **Alan Alda**

Wee Willie Winkie ran through the town, upstairs and downstairs, in his
nightgown. And you think *I'm* nuts?   **Tommy Cooper**

Nobody realizes that some people expend enormous energy merely to be
normal.   **Albert Camus**

One out of four people is mentally unbalanced. Think of your three best
friends. If they seem all right then you're the one.   **Slappy White**

Roses are red, violets are blue, I'm schizophrenic, and so am I.
                    Frank Crow

The neurotic builds castles in the air, the psychotic thinks he lives in
them, and the psychoanalyst collects the rent from both.   **Jerome Lawrence**

I'm in therapy now. I used to be in denial. Which is a lot cheaper.
                    Robin Greenspan

Denial is a river in Egypt.   **Mark Twain**

I've been married seven times – all to women named Brenda. It's just
a coincidence. The psychiatrists can make anything they like of that,
but as my mom, Brenda, used to say...   Otis Lee Crenshaw

What do we need a psychiatrist for? We know our kid is nuts.
                                                         Homer Simpson

In Los Angeles, there's a hotline for people in denial. So far no one
has called.   George Carlin

I said to my psychiatrist, 'I keep thinking I'm a dog.' He told me to
get off his couch.   Rodney Dangerfield

I have low self-esteem. During sex, I fantasize I'm someone else.
                                                         Richard Lewis

Most people with low self-esteem have earned it.   George Carlin

I don't understand people with low self-esteem. Why hate yourself
when you could hate others?   Amy Ashton

I went to my doctor's and he told me I had acute paranoia. I said,
excuse me, but I'm here to be examined not admired.   Gracie Allen

I went to the doctor the other day and he said I was a paranoid
schizophrenic – well, he didn't actually say it, but we know what he
was thinking.   Lily Savage

How to tell if you're paranoid: if you cannot think of anything that's
your fault, you've got it.   Robert Hutchins

I'm not a paranoid, deranged millionaire. Goddamit, I'm a billionaire.
                                                        Howard Hughes

I am a kind of paranoiac in reverse. I suspect people are plotting to
make me happy.   J.D. Salinger

Of all the things I've ever lost, I miss my mind the most.   Mark Twain

Right now, I'm having amnesia and déjà vu at the same time. I think I've forgotten this before.

Steven Wright

A wonderful discovery, psychoanalysis. Makes quite simple people feel they're complex.

S.N. Behrman

Being in therapy is great. I spend an hour just talking about myself. It's kinda like being the guy on a date.

Caroline Rhea

I told my psychiatrist I had suicidal tendencies. From now on I have to pay in advance.

Richard Lewis

Does 'anal retentive' have a hyphen?

Monica Geller, *Friends*

She was so anally retentive she couldn't sit down for fear of sucking up the furniture.

Patsy Stone, *Absolutely Fabulous*

I told my psychiatrist that everyone hates me. He said I was being ridiculous. Everyone hasn't met me yet.

Rodney Dangerfield

I'm paranoid. On my exercise bike I have a rear-view mirror.

Richard Lewis

Just because you're paranoid doesn't mean they're not out to get you.

Anon

My army medical consisted of two questions: 1) Have you got piles? 2) Any insanity in the family? I answered yes to both and was accepted A1.

Spike Milligan

In Hollywood, if you don't have a shrink, people think you're crazy.

Johnny Carson

In Hollywood, everyone goes to a therapist, is a therapist, or is a therapist going to a therapist.

Truman Capote

I once asked Woody Allen how his psychoanalysis was going after twenty-five years. 'Slowly,' he said.

John Cleese

Woody Allen is so dependent on his therapist, he won't even buy
sheets without consulting him. I know that several sessions went into
his switch from polyester-satin to cotton.   **Mia Farrow**

At the last count I had four therapists. Therapist Number 4 I go to solely
to discuss how angry I am paying $200 an hour to Therapist Number 3.
                                                     Paula Poundstone

I went to a psychiatrist. He said, 'Tell me everything.' I did, and now he's doing my act. **Henny Youngman**

After twelve years in therapy my psychiatrist said something that
brought tears to my eyes – he said, 'No hablo ingles.'   **Ronnie Shakes**

I'm in therapy at the moment. I don't need it, obviously, but I got all
these psychiatric gift vouchers for Christmas which my family clubbed
together for. What I really wanted was a crossbow.   **Bill Bailey**

He thinks he's a poached egg and spends his days seeking a suitable
piece of toast upon which to sit.   **Hermione Gingold**

There must be something very strange in a man who, if left alone in a
room with a tea cosy, doesn't try it on.   **Billy Connolly**

Therapy is like a really easy game show where the answer to every
question is, 'My mom.'   **Robin Greenspan**

Black people don't really have therapy. We just accept some people are
crazy and leave them alone in a corner somewhere.   **Will Smith**

Show me a sane man and I will cure him for you.   **Carl Jung**

The difference between the psychiatrists and the patients in a mental
hospital is that the patients eventually get better and go home. **Alex Tan**

A man walks into the psychiatrist's wearing only clingfilm for shorts. The psychiatrist says, 'Well, I can clearly see you're nuts.'   Anon

The only antidote to mental suffering is physical pain.   Karl Marx

I refuse to endure months of expensive humiliation only to be told that at the age of four I was in love with my rocking horse.   Noël Coward

A psychiatrist is a man who asks you a lot of expensive questions your wife asks you for nothing.   Joey Adams

One psychiatrist I know uses shock treatment. He gives you the bill in advance.   Harry Hershfield

I bought a self-help tape called *How to Handle Disappointment*. I got it home and the box was empty.   Jonathan Droll

—How many psychoanalysts does it take to change a light bulb?
—How many do you think?   Anon

A psychiatrist is a Jewish doctor who can't stand the sight of blood.
                    Henny Youngman

A Freudian slip is when you say one thing when you're actually thinking about a mother.   Carrie Anderson

The trouble with Freud is that he never played the Glasgow Empire on a wet Saturday night after Rangers and Celtic had both lost.   Ken Dodd

Psychoanalysis is the disease it purports to cure.   Karl Kraus

My psychiatrist once said to me, 'Maybe life isn't for everyone.'
                    Oscar Levant

Sometimes a cigar is just a cigar.   Sigmund Freud

Anyone who goes to a psychiatrist needs his head examined. Sam Goldwyn

Let the credulous and the vulgar continue to believe that all mental woes can be cured by a daily application of old Greek myths to their private parts.

Vladimir Nabokov

A couch is good for one thing only.

John Wayne

TIME

—This deep-fat fryer can flash-fry a buffalo in under 40 seconds.
—40 seconds? But I want it now!

Homer Simpson

Time is an illusion, lunchtime doubly so.

Douglas Adams

The dawn is a term for the early morning used by poets and other people who don't have to get up.

Oliver Herford

It's too early in the morning for it to be too early in the morning.

Terry Pratchett

If you wait in for a repairman, you will wait all day. If you pop out for five minutes, he will arrive and leave while you are gone.

Henny Youngman

Three o'clock is always too late or too early for anything you want to do.

Jean-Paul Sartre

A French five minutes is ten minutes shorter than a Spanish five minutes, but slightly longer than an English five minutes which is usually ten minutes.

Guy Bellamy

Heavens, 11 o'clock and not a whore in the house painted and the street full of sailors!

Anon

Some people are always late, like the late King George V.

Spike Milligan

This is the earliest I've ever arrived late.

Yogi Berra

The early bird may catch the worm, but it's the second mouse that
gets the cheese.   Jon Hammond

The early bird would never catch the worm if the dumb worm slept late.
                                                              Milton Berle

The early bird need not pursue the worm when he can order pizza at
midnight.   Charles M. Schulz

An appointment at 9.00 am? You mean to say, there are *two* nine
o'clocks?   Tallulah Bankhead

—You continually arrive late for work.
—Yes, but see how early I leave.   Charles Lamb

—If you can't get to work on time, I'll have to get another secretary.
—Do you think there'll be enough work for both of us?
                                             George Burns and Gracie Allen

We spend our lives on the run. We get up by the clock, eat and sleep
by the clock, get up again, go to work, and then we retire. And what
do they give us? A bloody clock.   Dave Allen

If you're there before it's over, you're on time.   James Walker

It's dishonour if Japanese man is late. It means he has cheap watch.
                                                            Tamayo Otsuki

I'm very proud of my gold pocket watch. My grandfather, on his deathbed, sold me this watch. Woody Allen

People who point at their wrist when asking for the time really annoy
me. I know where my watch is, pal, where the hell is yours? Do I point
at my crotch when I ask where the toilet is?   Denis Leary

Whenever I start to think the world is moving too fast, I go to the Post Office.

Billy Connolly

It is ironic that the only people unwilling to push the envelope are postal employees.

Dennis Miller

Today is the tomorrow you worried about yesterday.

Mark Twain

I pick the loser every time. If you ever see me in a queue at the railway booking office, join the other one; because there'll be a chap at the front of mine who is trying to send a rhinoceros to Tokyo.

Basil Boothroyd

Time flies like an arrow. Fruit flies like a banana.

Groucho Marx

I took a course in speed-waiting. Now I can wait an hour in only ten minutes.

Steven Wright

A man with a watch knows what time it is. A man with two watches is never sure.

Segal's Law

It gets late early out there.

Yogi Berra

A year is a period of 365 disappointments.

Ambrose Bierce

In the real dark night of the soul it is always three o'clock in the morning.

F. Scott Fitzgerald

Everywhere is within walking distance if you have the time.

Steven Wright

There was a pause – just long enough for an angel to pass, flying slowly.

Ronald Firbank

Eternity's a terrible thought. I mean, where's it all going to end?

Tom Stoppard

OPTIMISM AND PESSIMISM

Cheer up! The worst is yet to come!   **Chase Johnson**

He not only expects the worst, but makes the worst of it when it
happens.   **Michael Arlen**

Blessed is the man who expects nothing, for he shall never be
disappointed.   **Alexander Pope**

—Well, honey, look on the bright side.
—What bright side?
—Jeez, honey, it's just an expression.
                    Karen Walker and Grace Adler, *Will and Grace*

He was the sort of man who would have tried to cheer Napoleon up
by talking about the Winter Sports at Moscow.   **P.G. Wodehouse**

Matt Busby was the eternal optimist. In 1968 he still hoped Glenn
Miller was just missing.   **Nick Hancock**

Carl Llewellyn is so optimistic he would give himself a fifty-fifty chance
after a decapitation.   **Richard Edmondson**

An optimist is someone on death row who is also a member of
Weight Watchers.   **Jonathan Katz**

Optimist: a proponent of the doctrine that black is white.   **Ambrose Bierce**

An optimist is one who fills in his crossword puzzle in ink.
                                                      Clement Shorter

I like to think of myself as an optimist with a reality chaser. I know the
glass is half full. I just want to know who the hell's been drinking out
of it, and do I have to pay full price?   **Bob Zany**

Both optimists and pessimists contribute to society. The optimist invents the aeroplane, the pessimist the parachute. **George Bernard Shaw**

The light at the end of the tunnel is just the light of an oncoming train. **Robert Lowell**

An optimist is a fellow who believes a housefly is looking for a way to get out. **George Jean Nathan**

A pessimist is one who has been intimately acquainted with an optimist. **Elbert Hubbard**

Since I gave up hope, I feel so much better. **John Osborne**

I guess I just prefer to see the dark side of things. The glass is half empty. And cracked. And I just cut my lip on it. And chipped a tooth. **Janeane Garofalo**

If you say the glass if half full, you're an optimist. If you say the glass is half empty, you're Ted Kennedy. **David Letterman**

A pessimist is a man who thinks everybody is as nasty as himself, and hates them for it. **George Bernard Shaw**

—Tomorrow is another day, McKendrick.
—Tomorrow, in my experience, is usually the same day. **Tom Stoppard**

Between the optimist and the pessimist, the difference is droll:
The optimist sees the doughnut; the pessimist the hole. **Anon**

Due to budgetary constraints, the light at the end of the tunnel will be turned off until further notice. **Anon**

MORALITY

Sometimes I lie awake at night, and I ask, 'Where have I gone wrong?'
Then a voice says to me, 'This is going to take more than one night.'

Charlie Brown

My father was a man of great principle, though what those principles
were I cannot say.

Eugene O'Neill

He had the morals of a Baptist Sunday School minister in Paris for the
first time.

H.L. Mencken

Moral indignation is in most cases two per cent moral, 48 per cent
indignation and 50 per cent envy.

Vittorio de Sica

Be not too hasty to trust or admire the teachers of morality: they
discourse like angels but they live like men.

Samuel Johnson

There is always a right way and a wrong way, and the wrong way always
seems the more reasonable.

George Moore

An Englishman thinks he is moral when he is only uncomfortable.

George Bernard Shaw

Moral code? I have enough trouble with the Highway Code.

Mark Turner

Duty is what one expects from others, it is not what one does oneself.

Oscar Wilde

What's right is what's left if you do everything wrong.

Robin Williams

When you say you agree to a thing in principle, you mean that you have
not the slightest intention of carrying it out in practice.

Otto von Bismarck

These are my principles. If you don't like them, I have others.

Groucho Marx

LUCK

Everything went right for him until the day he was born.   **Victor Borge**

If it was raining soup, he'd be out with forks.   **Brendan Behan**

Just my luck. I was at the airport when my ship came in.
Henny Youngman

Abe Lincoln had a brighter future when he picked up his tickets at the box office.   **Frasier Crane,** *Frasier*

As one door closes another falls on top of you.   **Angus Deayton**

I got this letter, and when I opened it, it said, 'You may already be a loser.'   **Rodney Dangerfield**

Luck is not something you can mention in the presence of a self-made man.   **E.B. White**

Nothing is as obnoxious as other people's luck.   **Mark Twain**

It always looks darkest just before it gets totally black.   **Charlie Brown**

A man's gotta make at least one bet every day otherwise he could be walking around lucky and never know it.   **Jimmy Jones**

Just before I was about to have an operation, I heard the words you really don't want to hear: 'Now, where's my lucky scalpel?'   **Jonathan Katz**

My uncle had a rabbit's foot for 30 years. His other foot was quite normal.   **Tom Griffin**

Age does not diminish the extreme disappointment of having a scoop of ice cream fall from the cone.   **Jim Freiberg**

If it weren't for bad luck, I wouldn't have any luck at all.   **Dick Gregory**

What I'm looking for is a blessing that's not in disguise.

Kitty O'Neill Collins

Unseen in the background, Fate was quietly slipping the lead into the boxing-glove.

P.G. Wodehouse

Fate is what you call it when you don't know the name of the person screwing you over.

Bill Hart

My prospects were bleaker than a gerbil's in a bathhouse.

Lt Frank Drebin, *Naked Gun*

I'm so unlucky that if I was to fall into a barrel of nipples, I'd come out sucking my thumb.

Freddie Starr

I'm not a fatalist, but even if I were, what could I do about it?

Emo Philips

There is nothing worse than being stuck up the Andes Mountains in a plane crash with your anorexic buddy.

Denis Leary

Now and then, there is a person born who is so unlucky that he runs into accidents which started to happen to somebody else.

Don Marquis

—My mother died when I was six. My father raped me when I was twelve.
—So, you had six relatively good years.

Gloria and Arthur Bach, *Arthur*

LOST: black and white dog, blind in left eye, half of right ear missing, no tail, limps. Answers to the name of Lucky.

Newspaper advertisement

We must believe in luck. For how else can we explain the success of those we don't like?

Jean Cocteau

We all have enough strength to bear the misfortunes of others.

La Rochefoucauld

If your boat doesn't come in, swim out to it.

Jonathan Winters

Moses dragged the Jews through the desert for forty years to bring us to the one place in the Middle East where there was no oil.   **Golda Meir**

EQUALITY

All men are equal – all men, that is to say, who possess umbrellas.
                                                                E.M. Forster

After the game, the king and the pawn go in the same box.
                                                              Italian proverb

You don't know who to believe. Like Abraham Lincoln. He said all men were created equal. He never went to a nude beach.   **Rodney Dangerfield**

PREJUDICE

One good prejudice is worth twenty principles.   **Samuel Johnson**

Prejudice is a great time saver. You can form opinions without having to get the facts.   **E.B. White**

I am free of all prejudice. I hate everyone equally.   **W.C. Fields**

I hope I stand for anti-bigotry, anti-racism and anti-Semitism.
                                                            George Bush Sr

Now there sits a man with an open mind. You can feel the draught from here.   **Groucho Marx**

They added up all the people in the country who consider themselves a minority and it added up to more than the population of the country.
                                                              Bill Maher

I'm very secure with the fact that I'm not black.   **Bono**

If you'd like to find out what it's like to be a member of a minority group, try putting in an honest day's work occasionally.   **Kelly Fordyce**

This is the worst kind of discrimination. The kind against me.
   Bender, *Futurama*

Niles, owning the CD of 'Ella Sings Gershwin' does not qualify you as a soul brother.   **Frasier Crane, *Frasier***

The whites in our town were so prejudiced that a Negro couldn't buy vanilla ice cream. He had to be satisfied with chocolate.   **Maya Angelou**

I don't think Lee Bowyer is racist at all. I think he'd stamp on anybody's head.   **Phil Neal**

I was a Negro for 23 years. I gave it up. No room for advancement.
   Richard Pryor

Anyone in Nelson Mandela's position needs to be whiter than white.
   Jill Knight, MP

People always want to judge you according to your ethnic background. Like, if a white guy likes rap, he's trying to be black. If a black guy gets a job, he's trying to be white.   **Aisha Tyler**

I think racism is a terrible thing. I think we should all learn to hate each other on an individual basis.   **Cathy Ladman**

Why doesn't everybody leave everybody else the hell alone?
   Jimmy Durante

It is wrong to discriminate based on skin colour, when there are so many other reasons to dislike someone.

   Dennis Miller

VICE AND VIRTUE

I hate to advocate drugs, alcohol, violence or insanity to anyone, but they've always worked for me.   **Hunter S. Thompson**

Lead me not into temptation. I can find the way myself.   **Rita Mae Brown**

Good people sleep better than bad people, but bad people enjoy the waking hours much more.   **Woody Allen**

She smoked 120 gaspers per day, swore like a fisherman, drank like a fish, and was promiscuous with men, women and Etonians.

Quentin Crisp

—For a long time I was ashamed of the way I lived.
—Did you reform?
—No, I'm not ashamed any more.   **Mae West**

Everyone should have a few bad habits so you'll have something you can give up if your health fails.   **Franklin P. James**

Lust, pride, sloth, and gluttony, or, as we call them these days, 'getting in touch with your sexuality', 'raising your self-esteem', 'relaxation therapy', and 'being a recovered bulimic'.   **P.J. O'Rourke**

The Commandments don't tell you what you ought to do – they only put ideas into your head.   **Elizabeth Bibesco**

If there was an eleventh Commandment, they would have broken that too.   **Tagline,** *The Postman Always Rings Twice*

In my family, the biggest sin was to buy retail.   **Woody Allen**

Lust is the craving for salt of a man who is dying of thirst.

Frederick Buechner

An improper mind is a perpetual feast.   **Oscar Wilde**

I don't say we all ought to misbehave, but we ought to look as if we could.

Orson Welles

The problem with people who have no vices is that you can be pretty sure they're going to have some pretty annoying virtues.   Elizabeth Taylor

I am against vice in every form, including the Vice-Presidency.

Morris Udall

I can resist everything except temptation.

Oscar Wilde

Don't worry about temptation. As you grow older, it starts avoiding you.

Farmer's Almanac

—You smoke ten cigars a day, drink five martinis a day, surround yourself with beautiful women. What does your doctor say about all this?
—My doctor is dead.

George Burns

He has not a single redeeming vice.

Oscar Wilde

Good taste is the worst vice ever invented.

Edith Sitwell

I'm no angel, but I've spread my wings a bit.

Mae West

She may be good for nothing, but she's never bad for nothing.

Mae West

To err is human, but it feels divine.

Mae West

What I feel really bad about is that I don't feel worse.

Michael Frayn

I'm as pure as the driven slush.

Tallulah Bankhead

I used to be Snow White, but I drifted.

Mae West

When women go wrong, men go right after them.

Mae West

I climbed the ladder of success, wrong by wrong.

Mae West

When I'm good, I'm very, very good, but when I'm bad, I'm better.

Mae West

—Goodness, what beautiful diamonds!
—Goodness had nothing to do with it.

Mae West

Too much of a good thing can be wonderful.

Mae West

I've been things and seen places.

Mae West

Between two evils, I always pick the one I never tried before.

Mae West

There are no good girls gone wrong. There are only bad girls found out.

Mae West

Moderation is a fatal thing. Nothing succeeds like excess.

Oscar Wilde

The English vice is not flagellation or homosexuality as continentals sometimes suppose. It is whimsy.

A.N. Wilson

A saint is a dead sinner revised and edited.

Ambrose Bierce

There is no memory with less satisfaction in it than the memory of some temptation we resisted.

James Cabell

I don't drink these days. I'm allergic to alcohol and narcotics. I break out in handcuffs.

Robert Downey Jnr

I know a man who gave up smoking, drinking, sex and rich food. He was healthy right up to the day he killed himself.

Johnny Carson

If you resolve to give up smoking, drinking and loving, you don't actually live longer – it just seems longer.

Clement Freud

If I need a buzz, I have a piccalilli sandwich with Worcester sauce. That takes your mind off your bunions, believe me.

Victoria Wood

I hold it to be the inalienable right of anybody to go to hell in his
own way.   Robert Frost

GAMBLING

The race is not always to the swift, nor the battle to the strong –
but that's the way to bet.   Damon Runyon

The urge to gamble is so universal and its practice so pleasurable that
I assume it must be evil.   Heywood Broun

—Do you gamble?
—Every time I order out.   Lt Frank Drebin, *Naked Gun 2½*

There were three things that Chico was always on – a phone, a horse,
or a broad.   Groucho Marx

When I get home from the racetrack my wife never asks any questions
if I tell her I just ate a $400 hot dog.   Tom Conway

I went to the racetrack today but it was shut, so I just pushed all my
money through the gate.   W.C. Fields

No horse can go as fast as the money you put on it.   Earl Wilson

Horse sense is something a horse has that prevents him betting on people.
                                                        W.C. Fields

I've been writing a book for years called *Horses That Owe me Money*.
                                                        Sophie Tucker

The only man who makes money following the horses is one who does
it with a broom and shovel.   Elbert Hubbard

—If I find out the money on that horse was yours, Basil, you know
what I'll do?
—You'll have to sew 'em back on first.   Sybil and Basil Fawlty

Women don't gamble as much as men because their total instinct for gambling is satisfied by marriage.

Germaine Greer

According to statistics, it's a lot easier to get hit by lightning than to win the lottery. The good side is you don't hear from your relatives.

Johnny Carson

I figure you have the same chance of winning the lottery whether you play or not.

Fran Lebowitz

Don't knock bingo. It's the only chance working-class people like me will ever have of owning a giant ceramic cheetah.

Johnny Vegas

A casino is a place where you lose a hundred dollars in a slot machine and shrug your shoulders, then lose one dollar in a Coke machine and swear like crazy.

Jeff Shaw

Look around the poker table. If you don't see a sucker, get up, because it must be you.

Amarillo Slim

I stayed up one night playing poker with Tarot cards. I got a full house and four people died.

Steven Wright

When my bridge partner excused himself to go to the bathroom, it was the only time I knew what he had in his hand.

George S. Kaufman

King Farouk of Egypt was once in a game of poker and an opponent had the effrontery to declare he had three queens. Farouk reported that he had three kings, and when he turned up his cards to reveal only two kings, Farouk snarled, 'I'm the third.'

Omar Sharif

I joined Gamblers Anonymous. They gave me two to one I don't make it.

Rodney Dangerfield

HAPPINESS AND SADNESS

Happiness: an agreeable sensation arising from contemplating the misery of another.
Ambrose Bierce

Happiness is finding two olives in your martini when you're hungry.
Johnny Carson

I'm as happy as the day is long. The day in question being January. Somewhere inside the Arctic Circle.
Victor Lewis-Smith

Homer, lighten up. You're making 'Happy Hour' bitterly ironic.
Marge Simpson

Happiness is nothing more than health and a poor memory.
Albert Schweitzer

I never knew what real happiness was until I got married. And by then it was too late.
Max Kauffmann

The occasional lacing of my husband's dinner with cat food has done wonders for my spirit.
Lana Tate

If you observe a really happy man you will find him building a boat, writing a symphony, growing dahlias, or looking for dinosaur eggs in the Gobi desert.
W. Beran Wolf

Happiness is seeing the muscular lifeguard all the girls were admiring leave the beach hand in hand with another muscular lifeguard.
Johnny Carson

What's the use of happiness? It can't buy you money.
Henny Youngman

When I was young, I used to think that wealth and power would bring me happiness. I was right.
Gahan Wilson

When I look back, my happiest memory is not of the Goons. It's a girl named Julia with enormous breasts. **Spike Milligan**

Happiness is having a large, loving, caring, close-knit family in another city. **George Burns**

If you want to be happy for a short time, get drunk; happy for a long time, fall in love; happy for ever, take up gardening. **Chinese saying**

In Hollywood, if you don't have happiness, you send out for it. Rex Reed

Happiness is your dentist telling you it won't hurt and then having him catch his hand on the drill. **Johnny Carson**

I can sympathize with people's pains, but not with their pleasure. There is something curiously boring about somebody else's happiness.
Aldous Huxley

My Zen teacher said the only way to true happiness is to live in the moment and not worry about the future. Of course, he died penniless and single. **Miranda Hobbes, *Sex and the City***

A lifetime of happiness! No man alive could bear it. It would be hell on earth. **George Bernard Shaw**

He stood there looking as sad as a dead bird's birdbath.
Georg Christoph Lichtenberg

There are two tragedies in life. One is not to get your heart's desire. The other is to get it. **George Bernard Shaw**

I was sad because I had no shoes, till I met a man who had no feet. So I said to him, 'Got any shoes you're not using?' **Denis Leary**

She's like a mourner peeling onions. **Alan Ayckbourn**

A melancholy-looking man, he had the appearance of one who has searched for the leak in life's gas-pipe with a lighted candle.

P.G. Wodehouse

Some cause happiness wherever they go; others whenever they go.

Oscar Wilde

MISCELLANEOUS

Everything can be filed under miscellaneous. George Bernard Shaw

INDEX